THE POETRY OF PLACE:
LYRIC, LANDSCAPE, AND IDEOLOGY
IN RENAISSANCE FRANCE

LOUISA MACKENZIE

The Poetry of Place: Lyric, Landscape, and Ideology in Renaissance France

UNIVERSITY OF TORONTO PRESS
Toronto Buffalo London

©University of Toronto Press Incorporated 2011
Toronto Buffalo London
www.utppublishing.com
Printed in Canada

ISBN 978-1-4426-4239-3

Printed on acid-free, 100% post-consumer recycled paper with vegetable-based inks.

Library and Archives Canada Cataloguing in Publication

Mackenzie, Louisa, 1970–
The poetry of place : lyric, landscape, and ideology in Renaissance France /
Louisa Mackenzie.

Includes bibliographical references and index.
ISBN 978-1-4426-4239-3

1. French poetry – 16th century – History and criticism. 2. Pastoral poetry,
French – History and criticism. 3. Landscapes in literature. 4. National
characteristics, French, in literature. 5. France – In literature. I. Title.

PQ456.M32 2011   841'.309321734   C2010-906220-5

University of Toronto Press acknowledges the financial assistance to its
publishing program of the Canada Council for the Arts and the Ontario Arts
Council.

 Canada Council Conseil des Arts 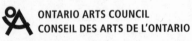 ONTARIO ARTS COUNCIL
for the Arts du Canada CONSEIL DES ARTS DE L'ONTARIO

University of Toronto Press acknowledges the financial support of the
Government of Canada through the Canada Book Fund for its publishing
activities.

pour Florence, *in memoriam*

Contents

Acknowledgments

I first discovered the French sixteenth century as an undergraduate in the 1990s thanks to Ian Maclean. If the Renaissance has stayed under my skin, it is thanks to him. Several years later, I had the extraordinary privilege of continuing my studies in the period with Timothy Hampton at University of California Berkeley. This particular project started to take shape during a graduate seminar he taught on Renaissance lyric. Indeed, *The Poetry of Place* is essentially a very protracted response to a question he then asked the class about landscapes. I owe Tim an incalculable debt of thanks, both specifically as a source of support and feedback on my research, and also more generally as an exemplary *seiziémiste* who will always, for me, model intellectual rigour, curiosity, and humility. No one asks better questions ... and as Rabelais knew, it's all about the questions.

I was fortunate to cross paths with Paul Alpers before he left UC, and to benefit from his generous and challenging readings of my dissertation. In particular, he encouraged me to think more seriously about past–present articulations: about my own work as an intervention in a particular intellectual moment, but in particular with respect to Renaissance (re)appropriations of antiquity. Thanks are also due to Nicholas Paige and Joseph Duggan, who provided encouragement from the inchoate mud of vague ideas to a completed dissertation. I'm particularly thankful that Nicholas Paige encouraged me to put more theoretical pressure on aspects of my work.

The transition from dissertation to book took longer than it should have; this was entirely my own fault. I admit to many moments of misgivings and inertia, which were only overcome by the support of many friends and colleagues. I am particularly grateful, at the University of

Washington, to Marshall Brown, who has given so generously of his precious time and skills as a reader. In this and many other ways he has modelled collegiality. The members of the Early Modern Research Group in the Puget Sound area have provided a vibrant early-modern-positive culture on the UW campus that has been a true boon. Benjamin Schmidt, Geoffrey Turnovsky, Susan Gaylard, and Rebecca Wilkin work tirelessly to sustain this community of readers and scholars, which has provided not only useful feedback on two chapters of this book (I'll never forget Rebecca's many pages of brilliant comments on the Belleau material, or Geoff's and Susan's crucial critiques of the cartography chapter), but an equally precious ongoing sense that what early modernists do matters. Donald Gilbert-Santamaría, Kevin Donnelly, Stuart Lingo, and Estelle Lingo, have also helped shape these chapters. Deep thanks to Vinay Swamy for being a constant friend, interlocutor, and colleague from whom I continue to learn. His sincere interest in my work, so far outside his own field, is the mark of a true intellectual, and the best kind of colleague. Thanks also to Nancy Rubino, Eugene Vance, Denyse Delcourt, Doug Collins, John Keeler, and Albert Sbragia, for unfailing advocacy, and material support especially during certain difficult periods.

I have been the lucky beneficiary of help and support from a wonderful community of early modernists beyond my institutional affiliations. Tom Conley's energy and enthusiasm for the period, his generosity towards those of us treading paths that he has blazed (and not just the ones on maps), have been inspirational; I can't thank him enough for his timely and heartening encouragement. I have long enjoyed many conversations with, and conference talks by, Elisabeth Hodges. She may never know the importance to me of one particularly wonderful conversation we had about literary landscapes the first time we met at an RSA conference. I regret that I had to finalize this manuscript before being fully able to incorporate the contributions of her recent book. Also, thanks to Elisabeth and to Claire Goldstein for an invitation to the Irvin Colloquium, during which I was privileged to share some of this work in progress with a very august group of interlocutors, including themselves, George Hoffman, and Jeffrey Peters, whose work, and ongoing kind interest in mine, have been a blessing; thank you. Conversations with Jeff, Tom Conley, Ricardo Padrón, Matthew Edney, and Frank Lestringant, have prompted me to think more widely and, I hope, more interestingly, about the literature–cartography encounter, among other things. Other generous and inspiring interlocutors –

whether they know it or not – have included JoAnn DellaNeva, Philip Ford, Mary McKinley, Michel Jeanneret, Jean-Claude Carron, the late Denis Cosgrove, Katherine Ibbett, Andrea Frisch, Nancy Frelick, Cécile Alduy, Marcus Keller, Richard Regosin, and Hope Glidden. I'd also like to thank François Rigolot, despite never having met him formally, for the prolific and seminal ways in which he continues to shape the field.

Many thanks to Suzanne Rancourt at the University of Toronto Press, who honoured me by selecting my book proposal, to Barbara Porter for steering the manuscript where it needed to go with wonderful efficiency and goodwill, and to Margaret Burgess for outstanding editing. Special thanks to the Press's two anonymous readers, both of whose comments were instrumental in revisions. The remaining weaknesses are entirely my own.

For support during my first few years at the University of Washington, I am grateful to the Simpson Center for the Humanities' Society of Scholars Program, and to the Royalty Research Fund for some course release. A particular thanks to the Office of the Dean of the College of Arts and Sciences at the UW, for very generous help with subventions. Thank you also to the Département des Cartes et Plans at the Bibliothèque nationale for allowing me access to the maps in their special reserve. A shorter version of chapter 3 has been published as 'Transplanting the Laurel: Mapping France in Du Bellay's Landscapes,' *e-France* 1 (2007): 69–107. A shorter version of the Ronsard material in chapter 5 has been published as '"Ce ne sont pas des bois": Poetry, Regionalism, and Loss in Ronsard's Gâtine Forest,' *Journal of Medieval and Early Modern Studies* 32 (2002): 343–74. I thank *e-France* and the *Journal of Medieval and Early Modern Studies* for permission to use the material.

For friendship and encouragement above and beyond, deepest thanks to Jennifer Monahan, Anne Eskridge, Leslie Robinson, Anne Graham, Gillie Murphy, Herdis Pelle, Fred Clarke, Frédéric Bougarel, Hetty Meyric-Hughes. Special thanks to Sonja Mackenzie, who makes me proud to share her name, and to Peter Mackenzie-Helnwein, who so supportively bore the brunt of this book's taking shape, and much more. Thanks to Florence Hunkel – truest of friends, spiritual mother, and the reason I chose French – for everything I should have thanked her for while she was alive. And all my love, thanks, and everything else, go to Virginia Rostad, who alone knows how she has changed my landscape.

THE POETRY OF PLACE:
LYRIC, LANDSCAPE, AND IDEOLOGY
IN RENAISSANCE FRANCE

Introduction

A traveller looking for a weekend getaway in the Vendômois region of France might come across this enticing description: 'En route pour une balade au pays de Ronsard. Mignonne, allons voir la rose du côté de Vendôme [...] on écoute le Loir murmurer dans le parc, on remonte le temps dans un lieu rempli de poésie, au milieu des marronniers roses centenaires' [Let's go for a walk in Ronsard's country. *Sweet one, let's go and see the rose* in Vendôme ... we can hear the Loir murmuring in the park as we turn back time in a place filled with poetry, among the ancient red horse chestnuts.] The detailed itinerary proposes a walk 'to the manor of la Possonnière, the birthplace of Ronsard,' then on to a botanical park in the 'valley of the Cendrine, dear to Ronsard.'[1] The poetry of the sixteenth-century French poet Pierre de Ronsard shapes the visitor's experience of the landscape, down to the paraphrase of the first line of the sonnet 'Mignonne, allons voir si la rose.' Whether or not we have read Ronsard's descriptions of the vineyards, the Loir river and valley, and the forest of the Gâtine, poetry not only captures and describes a certain affect towards this landscape but is also one of the filters we bring to our experience in the first place. We expect the landscape to be beautiful in a lyric way – and perhaps we experience it as poetic because Ronsard described it as such.

Ronsard is not the only Renaissance[2] poet cited today to express an affective relationship with French place. Joachim Du Bellay's descriptions of France, and in particular of his native Anjou, are widely cited today by French and non-French alike to describe place-based nationalist and regionalist sentiment. The work of preference is Du Bellay's *Les Regrets*, one of the most sustained poetic expressions of homesickness in French, written while the poet was unhappy in Italy and longing for his country and 'petite maison' in Anjou. A modern-day Angevin cardinal residing in Rome, for example, publically adopts Du Bellay's pose of homesickness in a published address.[3] In an otherwise scientific discussion of the mild climate of Anjou, an environmental historian cites Du Bellay's 'la douceur Angevine' to describe what makes the region particularly propitious for wine production.[4] And a recent candidate to the French presidency, François Bayrou, cited the lines known to most French schoolchildren, 'France mère des arts, des armes et des lois,' during a 2006 interview on *Le Franc-parler*.[5]

This book starts from the observation that Renaissance lyric landscapes constitute a foundational moment in the cultural history of the French *paysage*. Certain landscapes have perennially been invested with what the geographer Yi-Fu Tuan has called 'topophilia' or 'the affective bond between people and place.'[6] When seeking to express a topophilic relation to their country or a region therein, as the above examples show, the French often have recourse to Renaissance poetry. I believe that the third quarter of the sixteenth century in France marks a turning point after which poetry became an indelible mode of expressing and experiencing a local and national sense of place. Vernacular poetry written at this time produced a sustained series of descriptions of named French regions, mapping out the spaces of the kingdom in a way that has become an enduring part of national and regional sentiment. I do not take this for granted, but rather ask in this study why this distant and relatively brief moment of literary history should have provided such a durable sense of place. I also ask why this ideological work was taken up by poetry rather than any other cultural discourse.[7]

To answer these questions, I will situate lyric landscapes in the conditions of their production, analysing their relations to various historical and interrelated contexts: cartographic, political, social, environmental, and literary- and art-historical. Ronsard's Vendômois, Du Bellay's Anjou, and the places of other poets of their generation, will be shown to be freighted with some of the most pressing social, political, and cultural questions of the moment. During this brief but formative period, poetic landscapes *do* something, in the Aristotelean, dramatic, sense.[8] They describe and produce the emerging cultural, political, and environmental space of France, with all its complications, contestations, and ambiguities. They are, variously, aristocratic, royalist, anti-royalist, Catholic, traditionalist, nationalist, regionalist, literary, philosophical, cartographic, or gendered. All of these engagements intersect and compete with each other to create dynamic imagined geographies of France, 'spaces of hope'[9] in a time of turmoil.

Poetry and the Nightmare of History

Intellectually, socially, and environmentally, the Renaissance landscape was changing. Change was often unwelcome, often truly devastating. It is perhaps paradoxical that Renaissance lyric, produced during a time of increasing social and political upheavals which culminated in the horror of the Wars of Religion (1562–94), should have provided some of the most irenic and abiding descriptions of France ever written. In the 1550s, France seemed poised to put itself on the map culturally, politically, cartographically, and linguistically. But by the 1580s, all coherence was gone; the kingdom and its regions were sundered by civil war between Protestants and Catholics. With the horror of the 1572 St Bartholomew massacres fresh in the collective memory, attempts to describe France poetically were abandoned. It is precisely during the period of calm before the storm, roughly corresponding to the third quarter of the sixteenth century, that poets started to name the landscapes of their lyrics as specifically French, and to present them as refuges from which to hold the awfulness of history, however momentarily, at bay.

The history with which these spaces of hope engage is not limited to the wars of religion. Tumult and change were everywhere, if one was a nobleman, humanist, and poet. The feudal system was breaking down and the social status of aristocratic landowners changing.[10] Faced with an increasingly bureaucratized and centralized royal administration, the *noblesse d'épée* did not seem as relevant to the kingdom.[11] Unable to live from their rents, men of letters had to work for a living, a frustration wonderfully expressed by Du Bellay in *Les Regrets*: 'veoir Dubellay se mesler du mesnage' [to see Du Bellay getting involved in household affairs.][12] The crown had annexed region after region, but local identities and loyalties remained strong and challenged the hegemony of political nationhood.[13] Even a sense of native cultural coherence was complicated by the ongoing importance of Italian and classical exemplars. The literary landscape, despite the emergence of a self-conscious vernacular, was a palimpsest of foreign influence. The physical landscape was likewise transformed: population growth, water pollution, deforestation, and contention over use of forestry resources, the shift from feudal farming to sharecropping, all left visible effects on the real places of Renaissance France. These social, cultural, and physical changes will be revisited in detail in individual chapters.

Such changes in the lay of the land – literal and figurative – meant that representing France was a complex undertaking indeed. How to provide images of French landscape when the reality was so fractured and complex? But the power of these spaces of hope comes precisely from the bidirectional movement between first world (history) and second world (fiction; in this case, poetry), identified by Harry Berger as crucial to Renaissance fiction-making. Far from presenting poetic place as an expression of a timeless *genius loci*, they self-consciously engage with history and affirm their limits, opening up to 'forces that impinge from the outside.'[14] The referential richness of French Renaissance lyric landscapes lies in this central tension between ideal and real worlds, a tension which is also at the heart of the pastoral mode. Pastoral landscapes are not simply idealized representations of nature, as Paul Alpers and others have definitively shown: they are about the human and social dramas that play out therein.[15] The bower, then, is a social relation, above all a place of containment, where the 'nightmare' of history is held at bay for a while, but always looms on the horizon.[16] This is not to deny that pastoral thematizes evasion into or idealization of nature, but the evasion is complex, operated in full knowledge of its status as fiction. It is a poetics of suspension, characterized by Luigi Monga as 'constantly suspended between a bitter acceptance of reality and the need to create an ideal refuge.'[17]

I shall return in the first chapter to a more detailed and historicized discussion of pastoral. For the moment, I am simply underlining its dialectic relation to history. Indeed, all landscapes – physical and represented, pastoral or not – articulate with complex socio-cultural mediations. Chris Fitter has thus argued for a historical approach to literary landscapes, one that reconstructs the 'enabling cognitive world' of the text and uses the 'scrutiny of historical change as the condition for comprehension of human landscape perception.'[18] I agree with this principle. But to historicize lyric landscape should not be to ignore the signal importance of the poetic, or of inherited textual and intellectual traditions (nor does Fitter suggest this). Throughout this study, I will pay attention to questions of genre and form, to the abundant presence of classical and Italian poetic – especially pastoral – models, to the practice of imitation, and to humanist intellectual commonplaces. So important are these contexts to Renaissance literature that it is perfectly possible to read poetic landscapes as having very little to do with extra-textual realities. Danièle Duport's consummate studies of poetry and gardens (broadly understood as any landscape imprinted by human activity), for example, argue that landscapes in poetry are primarily about the poet's own craft.[19]

I take such genre-related questions seriously, but attempt to do so in a way that opens them up to socio-historical contexts. Mark Rasmussen, arguing that the recent critical 'flight from form' has impoverished both literary and cultural studies, posits a new formalism which takes as given that form is social, and that social history has form.[20] With respect to Renaissance France, Timothy Hampton makes a similar case for considering 'the ideological significance of the notion of literary form' at a time of 'discontinuity, violence, and fragmentation.'[21] Renaissance lyric landscapes, which intricately imbricate textual and social histories, are an ideal site in which to explore the connections between the poetic and its historical contexts. I propose that it was lyric poetry, more than any other cultural discourse, that mapped out a hopeful spatial and cultural identity for France during a time of increasing turmoil. Like Phillip Sidney's poet who grows a better nature but never affirms it as truth (and therefore 'never lieth'), French Renaissance poets insist on poetry's power and agency in the real world. While putting lyric landscapes in dialogue with various non-literary contexts, this analysis will therefore also take seriously specifically literary questions as I address the question of why it should have been lyric that took on this representational work.

Real and Imagined Place: The Problem of Metaphor

Landscape, of course, can signify either an exterior reality or its representation, and the notions of space and place have long been used metaphorically. Some geographers, in the tradition of Henri Lefebvre, see spatial metaphors as 'problematic in so far as they presume that space is not.'[22] I suggest throughout this study that Renaissance lyric landscapes offer us a way out of the impasse of metaphor, in that they dramatize an awareness of the interrelatedness of physical and mental landscapes. This is supported by recent critical thinking about landscape: as I shall further discuss in the following chapter, scholars now tend to understand *landscape*, and often *place*, as an inherently social and cultural relation to land, a meeting point between nature and human perception. It is a relationship itself, a 'way of seeing the world.'[23] This understanding of landscape as always already cultural blurs the distinction between the imagined and the real, and I believe that this blurring is entirely appropriate for Renaissance texts. Renaissance writers would not have been surprised by the idea that exterior, physical space and interior, mental place are necessarily and constantly producing each other. Ronsard himself defined poetry itself as a kind of landscape, writing in the address to the reader of the 1587 edition of his

Œuvres that 'poésie est un pré' while 'poème est une fleur' [poetry is a meadow, a poem is a flower].[24] Rhetorical theory since antiquity had taken as axiomatic the interpenetrabilty of mental and physical spaces: the etymologies of the words *topos* and *locus* themselves are both poetic and topographic.[25] The horticultural metaphors used in classical rhetoric (ornaments as flowers, the garden of letters), the dual meaning of *culture* as both biological and social, the idea of natural *varietas* reflected in the poet's creativity, as well as the spatial quality of the conception of rhetoric itself shown so decisively by Frances Yates,[26] all signal an awareness in the Renaissance not only that cultures have places, but that places are always cultural.[27] The implicit chiasmus of this book's title – the poetry of place, the place of poetry – might seem to elide the problem of metaphorical use of 'place' in the interests of a catchy turn of phrase. But perhaps one of the lessons of reading Renaissance texts is that, with respect to place at least, metaphor does not have to be a problem. It is part of how we understand the world around us.[28]

Some Traits of Renaissance Poetic Landscapes

The landscapes that are the particular focus of this book are those named as French in the lyric poetry of Joachim Du Bellay, Pierre de Ronsard, Jean-Antoine de Baïf, Jacques Peletier, Vauquelin de la Fresnaye, Pontus de Tyard, and Remy Belleau. These lyric places all share certain characteristics which I shall briefly review here, but which will all be discussed in detail in subsequent chapters. First, they are mostly rural. They are not wild: the idea of a wild 'beyond' of culture, 'call it nature or wilderness or environment, where deliverance from the constraints of culture [...] might be found'[29] is modern and post-Romantic. Renaissance literary rusticity has a lot to do with pastoral, and the related literary-philosophical tradition of debate on the merits of country versus court life. It also refracts the experience of landscape through the cultural and political lens of the petty aristocracy, the class from which the poets almost exclusively come. Second, they are very often regional before they are national, or they show the nation to be constituted by an aggregate of entrenched local identities. The sixteenth century has been identified as an important moment in the 'naissance de la nation France' [birth of the French nation],[30] during which the question of who defined, held power over, and used, the kingdom's territories is particularly fraught. Poetic places certainly perform important work in the elaboration of the idea of a French nation, but they also and perhaps more often challenge this idea.

They witness to what I shall show is a productive dialectic – rather than an opposition – between nation and region (or, to use more chronologically appropriate terminology, between kingdom and province). The production of 'la douce France' is only fully captured by fragmentation into constituent regions. The poets I consider come from a class of landowners identifying with their regional ancestral territories, but they are also royal subjects who must appear to support the national cultural project of the Valois monarchy if they are to enjoy royal patronage. These identities intersect, build on each other, destabilize each other, in a dialectic that reveals how the forming of nationhood is complicated from within.

The nation–region dialectic is also evident in cartography during this period, and a third shared trait of lyric landscapes of this period is that they are cartographic. I do not mean this metaphorically, or not only metaphorically: I show that Renaissance poets and cartographers are in explicit dialogue with each other as they present and circulate images of France. In particular, poets represent the nation–region question as a problem of scale, showing that local and regional descriptions (or chorographies, in cartographic terms) fit more comfortably into the space of lyric than descriptions of the whole kingdom. Poetic landscapes have a more active and productive relationship with cartography than with painting in this period; indeed I suggest that landscape painting of French subjects haunts this period and its poetry as a kind of absence. When poets do refer to painting or other plastic arts, I argue, the effect is to dissipate the possibility of representing France with any cohesion.

Fourthly, just as cartographic maps reinforce and justify royal power over the kingdom, lyric geographies of France reinforce a conservative, nostalgic, often feudal vision of land, a peaceful refuge from perceived change and threats to the social order. Their vision of a stable society is sometimes aligned with royalist ideologies, sometimes suspicious of them, sometimes overtly Catholic, sometimes willfully apolitical. But in each case they are concerned with presenting noble land ownership as a rightful, almost natural privilege and guarantee of social order, resistant to any historical change. Such conservatism (as in will-to-conserve) also extends to the land itself, and the threat of change is at times environmental. I give two examples of poets who directly confront actual – rather than imagined – depredation of rural places by human activities. In this respect one might say that poetry is a locus of proto-environmental protest, although the projection backwards of modern ecological sensibilities is to be done with great care.

It would be a mistake to read Renaissance lyric landscapes as if they were only about social, political, or environmental histories. They are also clearly about the place of poetry itself, about inherited traditions, about the dilemma of imitation. Even when identified as French, poetic landscapes are cluttered with references to classical and Italian *loci*, both textual and topographic. As Frenchmen writing in the vernacular, poets are acutely concerned with the problems and questions raised by writing in French while imitating *exempla* and *auctores* that are Roman, Greek, or Italian. In a sense, the poetic project of this period has to be a problem of place: poets must rewrite, or overwrite, inherited classical and Italian poetic traditions in order to present a native French landscape which is both topographic and cultural.

A significant consequence of this poetic referentiality is that it tends to eroticize and gender the landscape as female. Lyric tropes for expressing love of a woman – particularly admiration of her body which, as Nancy Vickers has shown, is fragmented into constituent parts by Petrarchan lyric and the French *blasons*[31] – are easily transformed into the constitutive parts of a landscape: the curve of a river, the rise of a hill. And as the woman is divided into parts by the process of lyric praise, so too is the kingdom, France, divided into smaller, local, parts by that same process. Inherited lyric tradition, then, lends itself above all to local scales of description. The fragile and threatened nature of these landscapes likewise facilitates their female gendering: the figure of the *nymphe éplorée*, begging male poets for help, becomes an allegory for trees or rivers as they are threatened by the brutality of human activity. And the trope of fertility, so often used in classical lyric to represent the poet's own creativity, is particularly apt for a generation of poets keen to present France as the soil from which a new illustrious vernacular will spring, with themselves as its figurative farmers.

Scope of Study

The tropes of fertility and cultivation are just as applicable to gardens as they are to the landscapes I consider here. Indeed, the garden has a rich allegorical tradition – bequeathed by antiquity – throughout the Middle Ages and Renaissance, its external order reflecting an internal quietude or self-knowledge. And representing France as a 'garden of letters' had become, by the sixteenth century, a common poetic trope, even a cliché.[32] However, I have chosen not to focus explicitly on poetic gardens, primarily because they are less likely to be freighted with the kinds of ideologies – so intimately responsive to political and environmental contexts – that I identify in pastoral poetic landscapes. When poets describe gardens, they are more likely to refer to philosophical and textual traditions, as Danièle Duport has shown.[33]

Equally intentional are the chronological parameters. I have limited their scope to about one quarter of a century, from 1549 (the publication date of Joachim Du Bellay's *La Deffence et illustration de la langue françoyse* and *L'Olive*) to 1584 (the publication of the last edition of Pierre de Ronsard's *Œuvres* to have been supervised by the poet himself). This generational moment represents the period during which the poetic coterie known as the Pléiade flourished and published most of its collections. I focus on the work of the Pléiade (or, in the case of Jean Vauquelin, a close acquaintance who never quite made it to Ronsard's exclusive list of members) because these poets were very much in dialogue with each other in their poetry in a way that is often spatialized and written into their landscapes. The late Rhétoriqueurs (especially Jean Lemaire), Clément Marot, and the poets of the Lyonnais school, are not considered here not because I consider their contribution to vernacular poetry to be any less, but because representing the landscapes of France is a particularly sustained and collaborative effort among the Pléiade. What is more, the principle period of the Pléiade's careers coincides with a complicated and crucial moment in the emergence of the image of France, the transition into the violence of the civil wars.

Another limitation, no doubt more arbitrary, is the exclusion of neo-Latin poetry. One might suppose that the vernacular played a particular and privileged role in the describing of native landscapes. But there are in fact descriptions of French landscapes in neo-Latin verse which could justify its inclusion.[34] French Renaissance intellectuals exhibited a fluid bi- or multi-lingualism to which our own zeal to identify one nation with one language have rendered us somewhat blind. The notion of a single French language is likewise simplistic, ignoring the significant dialectal variations of the period. The multi-lingual nature of Renaissance French culture is one of the most significant aspects of Renaissance literature, and while this study does not tackle such questions head-on, I hope to avoid using the concept of the vernacular as if it were a *fait accompli*.[35] Despite these crucial provisos, it is legitimate to talk of a nascent *ideal* if not practice of a 'langue françoyse' in the Renaissance, evidenced by the publication of grammars and treatises on the excellence of French (even if some were in Latin), most of which manifest a concern with identifying the language of certain social élites as correct usage.[36]

I am also keen to avoid suggesting that the period under consideration represents a radical break with the past, that the kingdom's landscapes are written for the very first time, or that the tensions and violence
of its history are unprecedented. Medievalists are rightly irritated when
early modernists – following the examples of many Renaissance intellectuals themselves – neglect the continuities that have been occluded
by our periodizations. The sixteenth century is of course not the first
time that France is described in poetry.[37] In the fifteenth century, Charles
d'Orléans gazes longingly towards France from exile in England. And
landscapes of the *chansons de geste* reference France specifically, both as
part of narrative 'itinéraires' and as a territorial cognitive map.[38] While
not common before the sixteenth century, then, topophilic descriptions
of a named France are not entirely absent from medieval poetry. Such
qualifications are important to bear in mind as a caution against taking
the sixteenth century (or any other) as the moment when national sentiment was 'born.' Without claiming radical novelty for the period, however, we can explore its specificity: the ways in which poetry – more than
other literary genres, royal iconography, or the plastic arts – comes to
perform important work in the imagining of the nation as a place.

Structural Overview

This book allies textual issues (imitation, the pastoral mode, formalism)
with external contexts (cartography, environment, social history, nationhood). Each chapter except the first treats a particular ideological or
thematic cluster (e.g., environmental change, the region–nation dialectic) through the work of one or two poets, while opening up the referential field of poetic landscapes to interdisciplinary contexts and discourses
(e.g., art history, cartographic practice). This structure allows for sustained consideration of the development and treatment of landscapes
throughout entire lyric collections, in a way that respects the collections'
integrity and complexity as well as the close way in which Renaissance
lyric demands to be read. This is not a transhistorical, universalizing
argument about what literary landscapes do in the abstract. Instead, I
propose a more situated and specific study: a generational moment during which poetry, consciously contrasted with other cultural discourses,
staged a particular national landscape in a particular way.

Chapter 1, conceived in order to avoid an overly long introduction,
contains more overview of Renaissance literary contexts, in particular
the status of lyric, and additional theoretical positionality (ecocriticism)

or discussion of key terms (e.g. nation, region, landscape, space, place). Chapter 2 expands the discussion of intersections between literary criticism and geography by considering the case of cartography. It acts as a bridge between introductory material and specific textual readings, establishing and justifying with historical specificity the privileged articulation between Renaissance poetry and cartography which will be evoked in subsequent chapters. Cartographically oriented readings of texts have become particularly fashionable, and are sometimes done in a rather tropist way. I show that with respect to sixteenth-century poetry, it is possible to historicize the encounter in ways that justify the use of terms like 'mapping' when talking about poetic place. I reveal some of the lived, historical relations between poets and cartographers – for example, the peculiarly Renaissance phenomenon of poems printed on maps – and argue that poetry and cartography directly espouse each other's representational vocabulary and practices, working together to create and circulate images of French place. The chapter concludes with reflections on the idea of interdisciplinarity as applied to Renaissance systems of knowledge.

Supported by the historical overview of the first two chapters, chapter 3 presents a viable articulation between cartography and poetry that furthers current critical discourse on, for example, the 'graphic unconscious' in literature.[39] The chapter, through readings of sonnet sequences by Joachim Du Bellay, suggests that the problem of Renaissance *imitatio* is as much spatial as it is historical. I show how, in *L'Olive*, Du Bellay not only imitates but – in the spatial, deep-etymological sense – *translates* Italian models, in particular Petrarchan love lyric, onto a singularly French landscape, transforming Petrarchan landmarks (the laurel tree, the Arno) into his native Anjou (the olive tree, the Loire). In *Les Regrets*, Du Bellay imagines French landscapes in contrast to those of Rome. But, in a very conscious engagement with cartographic scale, he reveals the landscapes of poetic affect to be the result of a perpetual motion between chorographic (local) and geographic (national) lyric maps. Regional identity is not the binary opposite of national sentiment but a necessary constituent part thereof.

Having shown how lyric poets espouse cartographic modes of representation in their landscapes, I turn in chapter 4 to the relation between poetry and painting. In the sixteenth century there are very few paintings of named French landscapes; it is lyric poetry that does most of the work of representing France. Through an analysis of references to the plastic arts in Remy Belleau's *La Bergerie* supported by a comparison with Ronsard's *La Bergerie*, and a reading of Pontus de Tyard's *Douze fables*, I argue that, unlike maps, painting haunts lyric landscapes as a sense of disillusion – and dissolution. In Tyard's *Douze fables*, the very possibility of representing French landscape is denied by an abundance of references to classical mythological scenes of metamorphosis, which suggest that France does not yet have the cultural descriptives to describe its places on its own terms: its landscapes are condemned to be endless repetitions of *loci classici*. In Belleau's *Bergerie*, the references to the plastic arts appeal to the sombre, critical, and fragmented aesthetic of Fontainebleau Mannerism in order to reveal the artificiality of idealized pastoral visions of landscape such as that seen in the more conventional *Bergerie* by Ronsard. Mannerist tension and formal self-awareness thus challenge and disrupt the 'spaces of hope' presented by other poets in their landscapes, making France unrepresentable as an ideal space.

Chapter 5 analyses poetic responses to deforestation (Ronsard's Odes and Elegies) and to water pollution (Baïf's poem 'La Ninfe Bievre'). In both, lyric poetry, brimming with classical references, configures landscape as a space of natural, social, and moral order threatened by the corrupting processes of modernity. The trees of the Gâtine in Ronsard's poetry represent a conservative, Catholic, and poeticized regionalism which is threatened by the Protestant monarch Henri IV, who instigated the partial clearing of the forest in 1572. And Baïf personifies the river Bièvre outside Paris, whose waters were contaminated by the dyers of the Gobelins, as a classical nymph begging poets – significantly, the poets of the Pléiade – to come to her rescue. In each case, poetry and its classical tradition are allied with a stable, unchanging landscape immune from exploitation. I avoid reading Ronsard's and Baïf's defences of their landscapes merely as antecedents of modern environmentalism, showing instead the extent to which the forest and river are overdetermined as poetic (pastoral) and aristocratic spaces. I also further engage my discussion of regionalism by showing how, in Ronsard, regional loyalty is not so much a bastion of liberal resistance against the exclusivity of royal power as it is an exclusive ideology in its own right.

Finally, chapter 6 discusses historical shifts in the role of the aristocracy (in particular of the poet-landowner) and the problem of France's internal coherence, in order to frame a discussion of two texts that present self-consciously poetic places of refuge. Vauquelin de la Fresnaye's *Les Foresteries* present the poet's ancestral Norman forest as a stable guarantor of his aristocratic name and identity, evidencing nostalgia for an imagined time when the nobleman was defined by his land and vice versa. The reality of his financial situation – debts, and the need to work as a lawyer – is willed away in the timeless, privileged space of his 'second world' woods, where he can be a true aristocrat-poet immune to historical reality. Jacques Peletier, in his long poem, *La Savoie*, seeks this place of refuge in the independent territory of Savoy. It is a fitting work with which to conclude, as it represents one of the last attempts to imagine landscape with hope and idealism – but it seems that this is already only possible on the perimeter of the French kingdom, not within France itself. Savoy's liminal historical position with respect to France suggests that the lyric space of hope has been chased to the frontiers. Peletier presents Savoy as a haven of peace away from the ravages of civil war, but, like Vauquelin's forest, his landscape contains within itself an awareness of its status as artifice, of the vulnerability of any 'second world' to the violence of history.

Which leads us to the vanishing point of this study: the dissolution, in the last quarter of the century, of the 'spaces of hope' previously represented by lyric landscapes. In such works as Agrippa d'Aubigné's *Les Tragiques*, landscapes are ravaged and chaotic, as a Baroque aesthetic of fragmentation comes to dominate court poetry. Poetic transcendence, if it is sought at all, is located no longer in France but in the cosmic spaces of scientific poetry. This turning away from landscape further accentuates the singularity of the poetic moment traced in *The Poetry of Place*, a moment when poetry produces French place in a particularly enduring way.

Landscape studies in general have become a productive point of contact between diverse disciplines, and my use of contexts such as cartographic or environmental histories might suggest the label *interdisciplinary*. While I embrace recent critical moves to interdisciplinarity, I put pressure on the concept itself by asking throughout what it might have meant for the sixteenth century. The word is not entirely appropriate to Renaissance forms of knowledge, of course, since the very concept of interdisciplinarity originates in a perceived compartmentalization to be overcome. Sixteenth-century humanists moved quite fluidly between knowledge spheres, a fact that gave rise to our concept of the 'Renaissance man.' If such perspectives are occluded to modern readers, it is because, as Anthony Grafton reminds us, 'we have allowed the divergent forms of scholarship that we now recognize and practice to delude us into reconstructing a past culture as fragmented as our own.'[40] But nor is it quite adequate to talk of Renaissance mentalities as *pre*-disciplinary; even if boundaries were somewhat permeable, each 'art libéral' was seen as occupying its own distinct place on the spectrum of knowledge.

Whatever their other skills may have been (I shall discuss poets who were also cartographers in the second chapter, for example), sixteenth-century French poets had a clear idea of the particularity of *poésie* itself, and it behoves us to take poetry seriously on its own terms, as well as inasmuch as it relates to other disciplines. To do so is already to try to render more specific the kinds of interdisciplinary encounters that have exercised literary scholars recently. In other words, interdisciplinarity – at least with regards to the early modern period – should not jettison historically appropriate considerations of the specificity of certain cultural discourses. Reading a poem primarily *as* a poem need not send us back into the world of New Criticism. Indeed, one of the best ways to honour and deepen the combined legacies of New Criticism and New Historicism is again to take the category of the literary seriously. Perhaps it is by retrenching ourselves somewhat in our various disciplinary strongholds that we can start to forge more meaningful connections between them.

1 Place and Poetry: An Overview

Lyric, Pastoral, Georgic

Something happens, in the third quarter of the French sixteenth century, to the ways in which poets describe landscapes. Poets start to identify their landscapes as specifically French, rather than as unnamed picturesque backdrops. They refer to multiple extra- and inter-textual contexts to produce an abiding sense of cultural, political, and topographic place, as dynamic and complex as Renaissance France itself. Poetic landscapes re-imagine national and regional places as 'spaces of hope' which are, variously, aristocratic, exclusive, gendered, regional, national, Catholic, or conservative. By the end of the century, however, the effort to describe France poetically is abandoned, as the violence of history becomes uncontainable. I make a sustained case throughout this study for the specificity of the *poetic* to the construction of these images of place. In other words, while I am interested in general articulations between literature and environment(s), there are also important formal and thematic reasons for poetry to have become the vehicle for a certain kind of imagining of French place. This chapter will discuss some of these.

One cannot, of course, discuss Renaissance poetry as if it were monolithic.[1] It was *lyric* poetry which became the vehicle, in sixteenth-century France, for irenic visions of landscape. Lyric was a somewhat fluid category, but as Du Bellay reminds us in the fourth chapter of his *Deffence et illustration de la langue françoyse*, it was intended to designate poetry that was sung 'au son de la lyre grecque et romaine' [to the sound of the Greek and Roman lyres].[2] More particularly, the types of lyric in which it seems possible to present France as a space of hope correspond to those listed by Du Bellay in the very same chapter of the *Deffence*, in which he sets forth 'quels genres de poèmes doit élire le poète françois' [which type of poem the French poet should choose].[3] The chapter starts with his well-known rejection of vernacular traditions, 'rondeux, ballades, virelais, chants royaux [...]' in favour of classical models: 'feuillette de main nocturne et journelle les exemplaires grecs et latins' [you should thumb through Latin and Greek examples night and day]. He then proceeds to describe the classical modes of choice: the epigram, the elegy, hendecasyllabic verse, the ode,[4] the sonnet, and the eclogue. When describing the last three, he uses musical language to describe the process of poetic creation:

> Chante-moy ces Odes, incogneues encore de la Muse françoise [...] Sonne-moy ces beaux sonnets, non moins docte que plaisante invention italienne [...] Chante moy d'une musette bien resonante et d'une fluste bien jointe ces plaisantes eglogues rustiques, à l'exemple de Sennazar.

> [Sing me those Odes as yet unknown to the French Muse ... Play me those beautiful sonnets, an Italian invention no less learned than pleasant ... Play me those charming eclogues, like Sannazzaro's, with a melodious pipe and a well-made flute.]

It is the genres associated with music – odes, sonnets, and pastoral *prosimetrum* – as well as certain of Ronsard's elegies, whose landscapes will become charged in the ways I shall suggest in the following chapters.[5]

Through the commonality of music, Du Bellay theorizes the already close association between lyric and pastoral: odes and sonnets, because they are sung, participate in a pastoral vision of poetry in which shepherds generate lyric. The themes and tropes of pastoral make it an obvious vehicle for the circulation of idyllic images of France as a beautiful and fertile land. Classical and Italian pastoral texts were some of the first texts published, translated, and imitated in Renaissance France: Virgil's *Eclogues* were published by the Sorbonne in the 1470s, the French bucolic *Temple d'honneur* by Jean Lemaire in 1503, and Virgil's First Eclogue translated by Marot around 1513.[6] Pastoral continues to hold appeal in the Renaissance because, as stated above, it is *not* just about idealization, yearning, and peaceful landscapes. I am here using the term in a more general, less taxonomic sense than Alice Hulubei, author of the authoritative study on French Renaissance eclogue. For Hulubei, pastoral is but one mode – along with the bucolic and the *bergerie* – of the eclogue, a 'poem with rustic settings and people.'[7] This is not to deny the Renaissance taxonomy of pastoral, nor its intensely complex (inter)textual traditions, which Hulubei so eruditely traces throughout her study. Rather, following Alpers and others working in the English tradition, I understand it as both a textual and a profoundly social mode, a self-conscious mediation between personal and public, between history and ideal.

To understand the pastoral impulse socio-historically is to understand that it almost always presents the point of view of those for whom country living means *otium*: the landed gentry. Since Raymond Williams's influential study of the tradition of the country–city opposition,[8] most readings of English literary rusticity have emphasized the way that social relations and tensions are embedded in landscape representation, or more specifically how idealizing country life 'provided the aristocracy with idealized images of the organic society on which their privileged status was supposedly founded.'[9] Scholarship on French traditions has not evidenced the same cultural orientation, although French ideals of rusticity in the Renaissance certainly lend themselves to analyses focusing on the ideologies of social class.[10] Renaissance poets themselves understood the mode as being a moral lesson to the nobility against a backdrop of social strife. Thomas Sebillet writes in his 1548 *Art poétique* that pastoral is 'un Dialogue, auquel sont introduïs Bergers et gardeurs de bestes, traittans sous propos et termes pastoraus, mortz de princes, calamitez du temps, mutations de Republiques, et telles choses [...] sous allegorie' [a Dialogue in which are presented Shepherds and keepers of beasts, dealing in pastoral terms with deaths of princes, disasters of the imes, political shifts, and other such things ... allegorically].[11] Renaissance France saw many publications discussing (and thus reifying) the opposition between court and country, particularly in the mid-century.[12] Agricultural treatises were also widely published, and while they were intended as practical advice, they were usually prefaced with moralizing chapters on the pleasure and virtue of farming. Charles Estienne's 1564 *L'Agriculture et maison rustique*, the translation of his 1554 *Praedium rusticum*, is a good example. This text was widely read in Europe: it was republished and expanded several times after his death by his nephew Jean Liébault, and appeared in England as *The Countrie Farm* in 1600. In its liminary material, the *Agriculture* puts rural life and labour morally ahead of the court. The notice to the reader exalts agriculture as a 'life of liberty and innocence' and identifies pastoral ('chansons bucoliques') as its descriptive mode.[13] The intended readers of such texts, of course, were the literate landowners, who could indeed experience the countryside as a life of liberty.[14] There was also a social critique behind the praise of rural life: as civil strife increased over the second half of the century, the order and plenty of georgic landscapes became symbols of desired political peace and reconciliation.[15]

French poets seeking to describe their native land had at their disposition a long tradition of literary rusticity, both pastoral and georgic, that promoted an aristocratic world view and could also be used for social critique. The question then arose of how to adapt the inherited tradition – Theocritus, Virgil, and Sannazaro are the exemplars cited by Du Bellay – to sixteenth-century France. Even Estienne's *Agriculture* wrestles with this question, as the author notes the limits of the exemplarity of ancient agriculture practised in different times and different places: French soil 'ne ressemble du tout à celuy des anciens,' [is in no way like that of the ancients], and so 'il faut apprendre les moeurs antiques, et faire comme de présent' [we must learn ancient ways, but do according to our own].[16] This is of course a version of the fraught question of imitation. In the second half of the century especially, imitation of exemplars became a guarantee of literary prestige, as the poets of the Pléiade downplayed the richness of existing French poetic traditions in favour of the erudite *imitatio* proposed by Du Bellay in his *Deffence et illustration de la langue françoyse*.[17]

Renaissance imitation is a creative and active process, and theorized as such at the time: Du Bellay urges poets not to imitate 'without reflection,' and Sébillet insists that French poets don't simply pillage 'all that we see, but only that which we judge to be useful to us.'[18] In order for the Pléiade to present themselves as the heralds of a new, illustrious native poetry, France has to be differentiated from classical territory even while imitating it. One sustained metaphor, paradoxically borrowed from classical literature, is that of fertile soil from which a new French literary culture will grow. There is an abundance of horticultural metaphors used to describe the art of poetry at this time. Du Bellay at the beginning of his *Deffence* describes the practice of imitation as a grafting process, and the vernacular as a plant that has as yet barely sprouted but that will one day, with the help of its farmer-poets, attain its full height. (In this sense, the georgic tradition, like pastoral, is about the production of poetry itself). Remy Belleau, too, is georgic about poetry, presenting his *Amours et nouveaux eschanges de pierres précieuses* to Henri III as 'ce que j'ay sogneusement receuilly de la fertile moisson des auteurs anciens qui en ont parsemé la memoire jusques à nostre temps' [that which I have carefully gathered from the fertile harvest of ancient authors who sowed the memory of it for our era.][19] Speech, or poetry, as gardening is not a notion peculiar to the sixteenth century; the metaphor goes back to Tacitus, Cicero, Quintilian, and arguably Pindar.[20] What is new is the rise in importance of the vernacular language in literature as distinct from Latin, and hence the need to imagine a new terrain on which such metaphorical planting and harvesting – textual fertility – would take place.

Given such a semantic and metaphorical cluster, it is not surprising that the conceptual space of such cultural gestation should be a reimagining of a female body. This is another reason why lyric in particular might lend itself to landscape description: its tradition of descriptives of the female body, easily transferable to landscape, is particularly appropriate for a feminized France. Thomas Greene has noted, in Ronsard, this 'tendency of a woman's body to become landscape and conversely, of a landscape to become her body.'[21] While Greene links this dynamic vitalism to the dominant perception of phenomena as constantly mobile and metamorphic,[22] there seems to be more at stake in this transformation of the lyric female body into features of landscape. Nature, of course, has usually been gendered female in the history of Western ideas.[23] This is not my concern here, since I am specifically not dealing with 'nature' as a philosophical concept. Rather, the process is analogous to what has been called 'national embodiment [...] a strategic process or program of natural-ization (sic) by which the nation is defined and redefined in critical historical moments,'[24] that is, the projection of human forms onto natural spaces. That is, rather than simply pointing out that almost all poetic landscapes were created by male poets, and thus likely to feminize a desiring relationship to French place, I am interested here in a more formal question: how Renaissance lyric offered a set of tropes which predetermined this gendered rendering.

Such considerations help us to better understand the specificity of lyric's contribution to French landscape history. The question of the pastoral mode in particular will be important to more than one subsequent chapter. I turn now to more theoretical questions, starting with the question of the applicability of ecocriticism – which has an intricate and sometimes problematic relation to pastoral and literary rusticity – to reading Renaissance French poetry.

Ecocriticism

Scholarly studies of landscape and nature in literature are not new, but not until recently was there a self-defined school of criticism devoted to them. The Association for the Study of Literature and Environment was founded in 1992, becoming an important laboratory for the newly self-styled ecocriticism, which 'takes as its subject the interconnections between nature and culture, specifically the cultural artefacts of language and literature.'[25] Ecocritics read literary landscapes as examples of a 'mutual constructionism: of physical environment (both natural and human-built) shaping the cultures that in some measure continually refashion it.'[26] Some early ecocritics rejected theory as part of the malady of modern thinking that has alienated humans from nature, promoting the idea that there is an unmediated, authentic relationship with nature recoverable by, ironically, rejecting the world of books entirely.[27] Many wrote exuberantly about the interdisciplinary possibilities of conversations about nature between scientists and literary scholars. For such reasons, ecocriticism has sometimes been characterized as lacking scholarly rigour, although it is considerably more sophisticated and self-aware than its detractors claim.[28]

While a study of literature and the environment surely must engage ecocriticism, application of current ecocritical theory to sixteenth-century French literature is nevertheless problematic. Reflecting the specializations of those who have developed it, the field is largely concerned with Anglo-American literature, and tends to focus on Romantic or post-Romantic literature, nature writing in particular.[29] The dominant ideas of nature and landscape in play are themselves the legacy of a post-Romantic mindset. The concepts of wilderness, of a restorative relationship between the human psyche and uninhabited spaces, of solitude in these spaces as desirable, are all anachronistic with respect to sixteenth-century mentalities. There are some points of contact. The poets I consider here certainly present their landscapes as sites of beauty and meaning, and also, like many nature writers today, as endangered by modernity. And like some contemporary environmentalists, their perspective is that of the privileged viewer or owner (or consumer) of landscapes rather than that of those who must labour in them. Yet one cannot see in them the harbingers of modern environmental sensibility. We must avoid the temptations of a teleology which would have these landscapes be of interest only inasmuch as they announce a relation to land that we decide to call modern, whether we are trying to locate the origin of a national imaginary, a post-Romantic environmentalist sense of connection to place, or will to protect it. For one thing, we do not have the same criteria for beauty. We privilege mountains, for example; solitude is salutary rather than suspect. But people did not always climb mountains for pleasure, solitude in a dehumanized landscape was not always desirable. Jacques Peletier, whom I consider in chapter 6, spent two years surrounded by the mountains of Savoy. In his book-length poem describing the landscape, he nowhere expresses anything resembling a recognizably modern affective relation to the mountains. Indeed, he is only echoing the dominant sentiment of his time when he wonders why anyone would want to climb a mountain.[30] A beautiful landscape, in sixteenth-century France, was above all pastoral, consciously reflecting rather than trying to ignore the dominant social order and the human processes that construct it.

But pastoral, as discussed above, has often been misread as a naïve and sentimental expression of a past golden age, its social complexity eschewed in favour of a reading that privileges the idea of happiness in unsullied nature.[31] Against the perceived depredations of commercial exploitation, construction, and pollution, we have adduced a lost ideal past when human and non-human nature coexisted in timeless and changeless harmony. Social élites seem to have a collective need through the ages to reinvent the function of the pastoral bower, 'a species of cultural equipment that western thought has for more than two millennia been unable to do without.'[32] Rather than reify a nature/culture binary, however, it behoves us to admit the degree to which the determining ideologies of pastoral are culturally contingent. Ecocriticism is useful in the intentionality it brings to the study of representations of nature, landscape, etc., and of the human historical processes that affect our perceptions and representations of landscape. The poetry I consider here, like Petrarch's ascent of the Mont Ventoux, foregrounds the inextricability of culture and human perceptions of nature; indeed, it would have been foreign to early modern mentalities to think otherwise.[33]

Space and Place, Land and Landscape

Just as ecocriticism encourages us to complicate our definition and experience of nature, the 'spatial turn'[34] in the humanities has revealed the extent to which our relation to space in general is inflected by ideology, or, to borrow Henri Lefebvre's terminology, how social space is 'produced.'[35] How is a topographic, environmental reality invested with cultural meaning? How is that meaning shared among a community, contested, politicized, defended, and how, in a bi-directional process, does this meaning itself come to transform physical space? How does power construct place, and vice-versa? How is power deployed in cartography? Such questions have been at the heart of work done by cultural geographers for a while, and are also informing literary studies, where we are starting to look at place as a theoretical category, and to use cartographic theory to nuance our definition and understanding of textual mapping.[36]

This spatial turn in the humanities has led to a necessary complicating of terms which once were considered innocent, but which have now, as Christian Jacob says of maps, 'entered the era of suspicion.'[37] The overlapping between these terms – landscape, space, place, nature – is significant, and too reductive or rigid a definition of any term would necessarily reduce their usefulness as mobile, flexible, and articulating terms. Nevertheless an overview of some recent theorizing will be useful. Place, as cultural geographers have worked hard to argue, is not just a backdrop for human activity but an activity, a produced relationship, a social experience, in its own right. Place is 'a meaningful location,' a space invested with affect, indistinguishable from – because constructed by – the 'subjective and emotional attachment' people feel for it.[38] Space, then, is a sort of *degré zéro* of place, its raw material before becoming place through various social and cultural lenses. Michel de Certeau, often cited by theorists of space, uses *espace* and *lieu* in the opposite way to most other theorists of space: *lieu* is immobile and unacted on, where *espace* is transversed by grids of human activity and movement ('l'espace est un lieu pratiqué'), but despite the reversed terms the basic distinction is very similar.[39]

Some influential work on space and place has manifested an almost essentialist Heideggerian *Dasein*, a conviction that it is possible to attain an absolute and timeless knowledge about a place if one inhabits it long enough, or sees it correctly. Such notions tend to be focused on rural and regional place, invested in the idea of authenticity, and occasionally belie, consciously or not, a nostalgia for conservative social orders.[40] From Rousseau's *Rêveries* to Thoreau's *Walden*, the image of a solitary privileged man – for it is usually a man, and he usually is not from the class that would have to labour on the land – accessing a deep connection with a place continues to hold great appeal in the West. I shall revisit this investment in authenticity in further chapters, as it informs, *mutatis mutandis*, many of the Renaissance landscapes of which I will offer readings. My analysis of poetic places, in other words, sees them, not as expressions of transcendent beauty, but – influenced by critical human geographers and historians such as Raymond Williams – as socially constructed by forces of capital, power, gender, and cultural memory.

Landscape, like place, is usually thought of as inherently social, differentiated from *land* or *pays*, which is its *degré zéro* as place is to space.[41] Landscape and place could almost be considered interchangeable, and while I won't use them entirely indiscriminately, my use of each term carries the weight of their articulation. *Landscape* includes, but is by no means limited to, areas of physical space selected for appreciation or description by human culture, or the resultant descriptions themselves. More than that, however, it is understood relationally, as a dynamic process, defined by Denis Cosgrove as a dialogue 'between changing social and economic structures on the one hand and human visions of a harmonious life within the natural order on the other.'[42] Simon Schama understands landscape as 'the work of the mind,' focusing on the role of the imagination in creating affective identification with landscapes, including national sentiment. He uses the image of strata to describe the ongoing cultural creation of landscapes, whose 'scenery is built up as much from strata of memory as from layers of rock.'[43] Understanding landscape as a social (and economic and cultural) relation to land enables us to go beyond the opposition, frequent in landscape theory since Raymond Williams, between a 'real' history of *land* on the one hand and an 'ideological' history of *landscape* on the other. The real and the ideological, land and landscape, are not mutually exclusive, but construct and inform each other, or, as Chris Fitter more eloquently puts it, there is a 'dialectical construction of environmental reality through the interplay of psychic and physical universe.'[44] One can thus consider textual and physical landscapes as articulating parts of a physico-cultural whole.

French scholarship on landscape similarly accepts the 'deep agency of the imaginary,'[45] and is equally insistent on the role of culture as a matrix for transforming *pays* into *paysage*. Alain Roger argues that land can only become landscape through the lens of culture: 'land can only become landscape under the conditions of art. Land is the *degré zéro* of landscape, that which precedes its aestheticization.'[46] Pierre Sansot's sociological study of French landscapes similarly argues that landscape is legitimated by cultural instances, defining it as 'a certain fragment of the world which has been legitimized, and, through this legitimation, is dignified with the word "landscape."'[47] The word *paysage* in Renaissance France seems to have had a primarily art-historical sense. Although it is not clearly defined in the Renaissance, often used as synonymous with *pays*, Pierre Nicot in his *Thresor de la langue française* writes that it is a 'mot commun entre les painctres.' It was also understood as being defined by human cognition, as an 'étendue de vue.'[48] The modern theorizations of *paysage* and landscape clearly broaden its meaning beyond its technical uses in the visual arts, but the continuity is in the acceptance of a cultural element in any landscape.

I should emphasize here that landscape, not nature, is the subject of this study. Nature in the sixteenth century was of course as multivalenced a concept then as it is now: it was invoked by writers both as a transcendent source of order and also as a source of variety and flux,[49] and I do not claim to make pronouncements on the rich taxonomy, epistemology, or categorization of nature in this period. Nor do I engage directly the Renaissance philosophy of nature, the natural, or natural philosophy. Such subjects have been admirably treated by historians of ideas or of science.[50] What is more, *natura*, in Renaissance Europe, is understood either as *natura naturata* or *natura naturans*, respectively, the creation of Nature or Nature as a creating force.[51] This distinction could perhaps be reformulated as one between ontological *nature* (land, or the subject of representation) and *landscape* (its cultural reproduction), and made to do some work here. However, I prefer to avoid any confusion with the precise philosophical Renaissance implications of the term *nature*, and will thus rather use *landscape* or *paysage*.

Preference for the term *landscape* over *nature* also avoids or preempts modern critical objections from those wary of an entirely socio-cultural definition of nature that would deny it its biological ontology. This has been a particularly important debate in the Anglophone academy, although many of the initial theoretical concepts that are now so hotly debated were framed by French theory. Barthes argued, for example, that all notions of nature (not just landscape) are socio-historical, even the apparently objectified scientific nature whose 'factual system' stands not alone but only as part of the semiology of scientific discourse itself.[52] But such theorizations of nature as inescapably cultural have provoked criticism from scholars concerned that non-human nature is being denied ontological value in itself, stuffed into the catch-all bag of social construction. There is a biological, scientific irreducibility to nature, they argue, which is too often ignored by culturally oriented scholarship.[53] Of course the biological reality of non-human nature cannot be calqued onto textual-cultural criticism, or vice versa. However, if we take land*scape* (rather than *land*) to mean land already transformed physically or conceptually by human culture, we can sidestep this problem. Landscape, as concept, material manifestation, or cultural representation, is by this definition necessarily ideological.

Nation and Region

One of the most ideologically invested kinds of place is, of course, the nation. Over a century after Ernest Renan addressed the Sorbonne with his lecture 'Qu'est-ce qu'une nation?' [what is a nation?][54] we are still asking the question. Renan's 'daily plebiscite,' the subjects' intentional consent to a shared ideal that constitutes the base for the soul of a nation, has become, *mutatis mutandis*, Benedict Anderson's 'imagined community.'[55] Even the physical space of a nation is in part imagined, although we tend to associate France with a well-defined space which has, according to Jacques Revel, become 'second nature.'[56] In other words, national geography – soil, frontiers, topology – is inextricably linked with (human) national history. This may seem obvious, but the two have been progressively separated since the Renaissance, when Ortelius wrote in 1570 that geography was the eye of history, *historiae oculus.*[57] More specifically with respect to landscape, John Agnew writes, 'Tying the nation to territory has often involved identifying a prototypical landscape as representative of the collective identity. In this way the natural environment can be recruited for the national cause not only to naturalize the connection between nation and territory but also visually to communicate and reinforce identity with the nation.'[58]

Textual images of place are crucial in the construction of nations as imagined communities. But in studies of literature and nation in the early modern period, the role of place description has been relatively neglected, with some notable exceptions for the case of Renaissance England.[59] This is accentuated by the problem of terminology. Many scholars and theorists insist that nation and especially nationalism are not appropriate terms before the eighteenth or nineteenth centuries.[60] Many choose a middle ground, rejecting *nationalism* for the early modern period but accepting related terms like national sentiment or national consciousness. The term 'nationhood' is used by some early modern scholars; Claire McEachern has also usefully blurred the modern/pre-modern divide in nationalism studies by proposing that all nations are proto-nations, constituted by the very process and the rhetoric of becoming.[61]

Many scholars identify the sixteenth century as a pivotal period in the becoming – or at least the prehistory – of the French nation and a French national culture. This is often tied in with an identification of the origins of absolutist monarchy (itself a contested notion).[62] But the becoming of France as a nation is less linear and unified than such histories suggest, fractured and complicated from within by the continuation of regional power, customs, cultures, languages, and loyalties. A significant thrust of this study is an emphasis of the role of the regional in constructing the imagined places of early modern French nationhood. I understand the region not primarily as political reality, but as an idea(l) of resistance and authenticity in the face of perceived change, what Marc Augé calls the 'clamor of particularism,' or Lucy Lippard the 'lure of the local.'[63] Eugen Weber's influential *Peasants into Frenchmen* encapsulated a common approach to the nation–region relationship, casting it simply as a question of opposition: according to this approach, the region, roughly synonymous with rural provincial France, had to disappear in order for citizens to identify with the urban, modern Republic. Recently, scholars are starting to question this binary and to understand regional specificity as a dynamic and integral part of national identity, the relationship not so much one of antithesis as of dialectic productivity.[64] Lyric landscapes also help us complicate the nation–region binary, showing the categories to be less oppositional than they are mutually constructive.

The region, as an ideological function, continues to have cultural and political power in France. Poeticized images of French regions, as idealized bastions of resistance to historical change and violence, still hold currency. Regionalism and other topophilic discourses today – praise of natural beauty and fertility, environmental conservation – are still very much inflected by the privileged and gendered vision of Renaissance lyric landscapes, even though they are sometimes assumed to appeal to an order that transcends culture. The ongoing appeal of Renaissance poetics of place surely belies a certain nostalgia for ideologies assumed to have disappeared; it certainly shows the extent to which any relationship to land is mediated through cultural discourse.

The Cartographic Turn

Notions like Anderson's imagined communities and Helgerson's forms of nationhood have acquired considerable currency in literary studies.[65] Texts imagine, represent, and circulate idea(l)s of place, community, belonging. And so, as many scholars now argue, do maps. Many literary critics, as Denis Cosgrove noted, are 'fashionably fascinated' by maps.[66] The fascination has been facilitated by recent theoretical moves in the study of cartography which bring the map – like the text – under the purview of post-structuralist suspicion: maps, like texts, are representational, ideological, allegorical; they have silences and blind spots; they have perhaps 'never been modern.'[67] Cartographic history is increasingly seen as not that of a progressive march towards absolute accuracy, but rather of a succession of different representative modes which evidence varying cultural, social, and technological relations[68] – in other words, more like literary history. The work of J. Brian Harley brought the Foucauldian power–knowledge paradigm to bear on the history of cartography, considering 'the intentional and unintentional suppression of knowledge in maps' which turns them into 'a form of political discourse concerned with the acquisition and maintenance of power.'[69] Harley's conception of power has been considerably reconsidered and refined, but the basic premises have underwritten most theorizing of cartography ever since, indeed the very acceptance of explicit theory within cartographic studies.

It seems intuitively convincing to develop articulations between maps, texts, and concepts and contexts such as absolutism, regionalism, empire, or nationhood. One can analyse the textuality of maps or the spatial play of texts. Indeed, cartographically oriented literary criticism ranging chronologically from the medieval to the modern, and geographically from England through Continental Europe to the Spanish colonies, North America, Japan, and beyond, has abounded since the 1980s.[70] And such moves allow us at least the impression of interdisciplinarity, and at best the new and unexpected objects of study that Barthes postulated in 'De l'œuvre au texte.'[71]

Nevertheless, our 'fashionable fascination' with maps is starting to produce some weary scepticism. A recent PhD thesis in English makes a substantial premise of the contrast between studies that look at 'synchronic textual and cartographic production and the cultural contexts these collectively reflect,' and those that use the vocabulary and concept of mapping more abstractly, as 'an explanatory metaphor for multiple forms of textual representation.' While the author sees the former type of study as productive, she argues that the latter's weakness – of which she unfortunately gives no examples – is in 'its failure to investigate how maps themselves operate.'[72] If the literary-cartography encounter is to be more than a passing fashion, it must be furthered and deepened by studies of the kind that Michael Schoenfeldt welcomes in a recent review of publications in early modern English literature, studies that tend towards the particular and the heterogeneous and '[warp] theoretical models by specific archival evidence.'[73] This is not to dismiss the importance of theoretical moves that enabled such refinement in the first place: without the 'spatial turn' in literary studies or the 'cultural turn' in geography,[74] specific studies of the relations between maps and texts would not be particularly meaningful, or perhaps even conceivable in the way they are practised today.

Scholars of early modern literature have produced a number of studies based on the perceived 'overlapping areas of cartography and literary analysis.'[75] The 'literature and maps' subsection of the third volume of David Woodward's *The History of Cartography* dedicated to the European Renaissance contains seven essays, as many as the entire section on technical production and consumption. The period lends itself well to such connections, since the boundaries between representational modes were more fluid than they are today, as we shall see with respect to poetry and cartography. Sixteenth-century culture evidences a pre-disciplinary, fluid relationship between forms of knowledge. Consider Christophe de Savigny's 1587 *Tableaux accomplis de tous les arts*, a chart of the 'partition' and 'liaison' [the separation and connection] of 'tous les arts et sciences' [all arts and sciences].[76] This curious work, subtitled as an *Encyclopédie*, shows the disciplines (the 'arts libéraux') – which are subsequently explained one by one – as intersecting links on an oval chain, in the middle of which is a knowledge tree branching off from the trunk of *philosophie*. Everything, from medicine to metaphysics to grammar, is linked. On this chain, *poésie* and *géographie* are almost exactly facing each other. On the tree of philosophy, poetry and *chorographie* (the mapping of particular regions – more on this term follows below) both come at the ends of their respective branches, occupying equivalent positions on the main branches of 'general' and 'special' philosophy respectively. There is a conceptual link between poetry and mapping, a link that goes beyond the encyclopedic ideal that all particular knowledge is unified in a greater whole.

Even more than in this paradigmatic conception of the 'liaison' of the disciplines, however, the relations between cartography and poetry in the French Renaissance are played out in specific, historical relationships. In the following chapter, I make the transition from positionality to more situated considerations, and argue that poets and cartographers were in explicit dialogue with each other as they represented the places of France. That is, to read French Renaissance lyric 'cartographically' is not only to trope on mapping metaphors (although metaphor can't entirely be avoided), but to situate both poems and maps in their contexts and conditions of their production. Maps and poems are historically related, both with respect to the image of France itself, and also with respect to each other. By establishing with more precision how poetic and cartographic landscapes were in articulation, we can start to better elucidate this relationship, and understand how – together and separately – they produced the 'knowledge space' of France.[77] This overview stands by itself as an expanded case study of the intersections between two discursive fields. It also provides some terminological support for the third chapter, in which I will shift to closer readings of poetic works, showing how Du Bellay constructs his landscapes with explicit reference, among other things, to cartographic practice. Subsequent chapters will consider other intertexts and contexts: painting and the plastic arts, environmental history, and socio-political history.

2 The Poet and the Mapmaker: Lyric and Cartographic Images of France

Let us start at the end: the end of the sixteenth century, and the vanishing point of this study. By the 1590s, France was reeling from the effects of the Wars of Religion (1562–98), which had pitted Catholics against Huguenots, the Guises and the Catholic League against the House of Bourbon, had involved Spain and England, and had sundered families and communities. The popular duc de Guise was assassinated in 1588 by direct order of the king, Henri III, who was himself killed a year later. Henri de Navarre, a Protestant, became Henri IV, and started his rule by winning some significant military victories in the mostly Catholic north in the hope of uniting the kingdom. However, Paris held out (with Spanish help) against the 'heretic' king, and Henri reconverted to Catholicism in 1593 to be crowned at Chartres in 1594. The Edict of Nantes, an uneasy truce, was issued in 1598.[1] After decades of violence, distrust, devastation of property and land, how could France be represented at all, let alone as a unified and beautiful kingdom?

It was in this troubled context that the Protestant Maurice Bouguereau published his 1594 *Le Théâtre françoys* in Tours, the first atlas of France published in French in the kingdom.[2] Its dedicatee was Henri IV, who was residing in Tours at the time due to tumult in the north. Text and image work together to present a picture of a unified kingdom under the new monarch, whose ascension had given hope to some of Huguenot France, and who seemed poised to take back the north. As Tom Conley points out, the *Théâtre* was intended to provide the king not only with an image of 'a common and collective land of French origin,' but also a 'decisive plan for statecraft,'[3] with strategic information to help in decisions about warfare and government. But this image of unity is composed of heterogeneous sources: the regional maps are of different scales and orientations, composed by a multitude of cartographers from different periods and with different skills. It was published with several regional maps missing: the region of Île-de-France, for example, is not shown, no doubt due to the difficulties in sending surveyors and cartographers to a region sundered by civil war.[4]

I use the *Théâtre* here as a departure point for a consideration of the particular relationship between poetry and cartography in the French sixteenth century. In a work whose goal is to provide an overview both graphic and textual of the *royaume de France*, poetry is an integral part of how the kingdom is presented, and poets themselves figure on the map 'as if they were famous sites.'[5] The subtitle of the edition of Bouguereau's *Théâtre* in the Bibliothèque Nationale, Paris, claims that it is 'Enrichy et aorné sur chacune Charte et Province d'excellents veres Heroïques, tirez de plusieurs Geographes & Poëtes, tant anciens que modernes' [enriched and decorated, on each map of each region, with excellent alexandrines by geographers and poets both ancient and modern]. On the verso of the title page, an acrostic sonnet spelling out 'Henry De Bourbon' is paired with a portrait of the king or a map of France, depending on the edition. The fourteen letters of the king's name fit perfectly into the form of the sonnet, while the sonnet itself plays with the king's name in a way that inscribes Henri into a genealogy of conquerors and naturalizes his claim to France by giving him half of Charlemagne's name:[6]

> Heroique Monarque, Allexandre puissant,
> Exercité en Mars: & second Charle-Maigne,
> Noble en faits & en dits, le premier Henri-Maigne [...]

> [Heroic monarch, powerful Alexander / Experienced in warfare, second Charlemagne, / Noble in actions and words, our first Henrimagne ...][7]

Poetry is more than mere ornamentation for the maps. From the beginning, it stakes out and even performs Henri's claim to the kingdom. Furthermore, in the text, the author lists the great poets of the Loire valley as if they were topographic landmarks:

> Aussi que ce climat abonde en bons esprits, entre lesquels de recente memoire, sont Arnoul & Simon les Grebans Poëtes. Les quatre freres du Bellay; Seigneurs de Langey d'incredible erudition. Lazare & Anthoine de Baïf. Guillaume Bigot Philosophe. Le grand Ronsard Prince des Poëtes

François. Jean et Jaques Pelletier freres [...] N. Denisot peintre et poëte.
J. Tahureau poëte. (fol. xiii r.)

[This climate also abounds in good minds, among the recent ones of which ·
are the poets Arnoul and Simon Gréban, the four Du Bellay brothers, the
most erudite gentlemen of Langey;[8] Lazare and Antoine de Baïf, the phil-
osopher Guillaume Bigot, Ronsard the great prince of French poets, the
brothers Jean and Jacques Pelletier ... the painter and poet N(icolas)
Denisot, the poet J(acques) Tahureau.]

In this case, 'literary geography' is more than a manner of speaking; the
poets of the Pléiade have been put on the map. The first composite atlas
of France to be printed in French and in France includes poets and poetry as an integral part of its vision of the kingdom.

This is not a unique instantiation; the poetry–cartography relationship throughout the second half of the sixteenth century is privileged
and intentional enough to warrant an expository chapter. More than
any other representational mode, cartography aligns and allies itself
with the poetic in order to (re)present France.[9] This alignment goes well
beyond mere chronological coincidence: that is, it is not sufficient simply to point out that both poems and maps represent French space in
meaningful ways during this period. The relations between cartography and poetry in the French Renaissance are played out in many specific, historical relationships like the ones indicated in Bouguereau's
Théâtre. The images of France produced by poets and cartographers in
the sixteenth century share a set of tropes about usefulness, pleasure,
glory, and imitation, and serve similar reading publics and patrons invested in seeing reflected images of their own land ownership and
power. They both have a sometimes fraught, sometimes complicit, but
always unavoidable relationship to royal and state power. They both
exhibit differences in the scale of their description, shifting between
particular locales to 'la France,' 'Francia,' or 'Gallia,' in ways that reveal
the national to be a process in dialectic tension with the regional (or, in
sixteenth-century terminology, the kingdom in tension with the provinces).[10] There are poems on maps and poems about mapmakers. Poets
and cartographers knew each other, worked together, and were sometimes one and the same person. I propose here an overview of some of
these heterogeneous relations, and suggest not only that they existed
more than has been discussed – which would be of limited interest in
itself, other than to justify further cartographically oriented readings of

poetry – but that together poetry and cartography created particularly enduring images of France as an ideal kingdom at a time when its internal cohesion was particularly problematic. Together they shape the social identities of a France whose notional coherence was still emergent, elaborating and circulating images that continue to construct the spatial and territorial aspects of the French national imaginary.[11]

From *Gallia* to *France*

Renaissance nationhood was not a monolithic, linear process, nor was it uncontested. The teleology of a nation-in-making, while useful and supported by historical tendencies such as the centralizing efforts of the Valois dynasty,[12] tends to overlook the ways in which the nation is fractured from within by 'a kind of mosaic of regional units.'[13] Both poetic and cartographic descriptions attest to this tension. On the one hand, there is an effort to imagine and represent a unified territorial France that would go beyond the confines of the Île-de-France and include the other regions of the kingdom. On the other hand, poets and mapmakers alike often attest to strong local loyalties and identities that continue to retain some of their specificity, and do not fit neatly into the ideas of nationhood that we might project onto the period. As suggested in the previous section, kingdom and region define and construct each other, rather than existing in binary opposition or rendering the other untenable. Whether regional or national, or some more complex position between the two, the relationship to landscape – affective, topographical, and political – elaborated by poets and cartographers has had a profound and lasting impact on the French sense of place.

This oscillation between region and nation can be seen in the cartographic practice of the period. Renaissance geographers such as Petrus Apianus had, in theory at least, assimilated the distinction made by Ptolemy in his *Geographia* between 'geography' and 'chorography,' although they modified and rendered them more fluid, adding topography and cosmography to the mix.[14] According to Ptolemy, geography is the mapping of the entire *oikoumene* – the inhabited world – using mathematical principles, while chorography is the technique of mapping distinct regions down to the smallest details using iconographic representation (that is, artistic skill). The relation between chorographic and literary (poetic) description is intuitively tempting, particularly as Ptolemy and his Renaissance commentators insist on the subjective and creative dimension of chorography which needs no mathematical knowledge, making it a possible cartographic analogue of poetic description. The poet Joachim Du Bellay, as we shall see in the following chapter, experiments with different scales of representation of his French landscapes, often defaulting to subjective preference for a local, chorographic description. However, such parallels, if further explored, would need to take into account the techniques of mapping themselves: the geographer Matthew Edney rejects the chorography–geography distinction in terms of Renaissance practice, since the techniques used were much the same.[15] The opposition between *quantum* and *quale* cannot be calqued directly onto *geography* and *chorography*, or *nation* and *region*, and maybe it should not be thought of in oppositional terms at all (why can one not have a qualitative rapport with the quantitative?)[16] Nor is the distinction only one of scale: Renaissance commentators and geographers complicated Ptolemy's scalar opposition. Oronce Fine called his map of France (which one might consider as geography, not chorography) a 'Galliarum chorographia nova.' Savigny's *Tableaux*, the encyclopedic exposition of the disciplines mentioned above, describes geography as the description of 'toute la terre' [the whole earth], chorography as 'ses contrées et régions' [its countries and regions], and topography as 'lieux particuliers' [specific places].

But despite their fluidity, the categories are nevertheless useful as ways to start thinking about the representation of space in the Renaissance. At least in some theoretical texts, like Pierre Apian's 1553 *Cosmographia*, one does find the quality/quantity binary applied to chorography and geography, and a comparison with portraiture which emphasizes scale: geography is, for Apian, like painting a head, whereas chorography is like painting an eye or an ear. For Frank Lestringant, chorography is primarily characterized by a qualitative epistemology: 'the chorographic map records, in a partial and detailed sort of mimesis, the quality of the earth's space. Cartography here is like a painted or literary landscape.'[17] Although it is not the exclusive purview of chorography or of regionalism (themselves fluid concepts in the sixteenth century), qualitative description is openly espoused by many Renaissance mapmakers, and it is this that justifies seeking further articulations between maps and poems.

In the practice of mapmaking, the very real regional diversity in terms of language, laws, and customs complicated the task of representing France. Local power structures persisted and produced chorographies and territorial knowledge that, explicitly or not, challenged the hegemony of the 'national' map.[18] Many mapmakers were primarily or only regional, and often had strong ties to the region they described: Lezin Guyet for Anjou, Jean Fayen for the Limousin, or Jean Chaumeau for Berry.[19] Local mapping was often initiated by diocesan authorities. The 1539 map of Le Mans attributed to Ogier Macé is such an example, and, like other regional maps produced earlier in the century, it ended up in Bouguereau's 1594 *Théâtre françois*. Bouguereau, like Mercator (1585) and Ortelius (1570) before him, was an adept collector of regional descriptions; the 'new' images of France are often composites of earlier regional maps which had continued to circulate. Far from being erased, these regional images produced at different times persisted as sedimented strata in the national map of France.

Although France as a unified geographic entity was more of an ideal than a reality, an ideal particularly perturbed by civil war, one can discern an effort on the part of cartographers to impose some kind of coherence on the idea and the image of the kingdom. Monarchs' commissioning of maps undoubtedly indicates an impulse to a unified state,[20] and the sixteenth century saw a proliferation of maps of France. The first map of France printed in the country was in 1525 by Oronce Fine, dedicated to François I, which was used by several foreign cartographers as a basis.[21] Jean Jolivet's *Vraie description des Gaules* (1560), a woodcut of which there were several reprints, served as a model for other cartographers, for example a certain 'Stefano Francese' who executed the Francia mural in the Terzia Loggia in the west wing of the Vatican.[22] Ortelius and Bouguereau also used Jolivet's woodcut in their atlases. The first royal commission to a geographer for a map of the kingdom – more specifically, and significantly, for a series of maps of each province – was given by Catherine de' Medici to Nicolas Nicolay around 1561, ratified by Charles IX in a *lettre patente* in 1570.[23] The idea was to put these territorial chorographies together to form a complete map of the kingdom. And by 1594, the year of publication of Bouguereau's *Le théâtre françois* in Tours, the consciously propagandistic image of France as a united kingdom is presented to its ruler, Henri IV, whose investment in a total vision of France goes beyond monarchic designs of statehood to address the more pressing issue of the religious wars.

Those who mapped sixteenth-century France were bound, then, to a kind of spatial dialectic between scales of description, between local and trans-local, the movement of which provided – rather than negated – a sense of nationhood.[24] But the dialectic was temporal as well as spatial. To map France in the sixteenth century was inevitably to refer to an ancient Greek text, Ptolemy's *Geographia* (also known as the *Cosmographia*), the rediscovery of which revolutionized cartographic practice in Europe and beyond.[25] Ptolemy's text did not bequeath a fixed set of maps to Renaissance Europe: the thirteenth- to fifteenth-century maps included in the extant manuscripts were quickly redrawn to reflect contemporary knowledge, as Anthony Grafton reminds us. But Ptolemy's general conception of geography as a discipline, the 'geographic concept of the Earth,'[26] and of course the projection, grid, and coordinate systems, became canonical.

Mapping France required reference to ancient Rome, too. The idea of a unified kingdom was predicated upon the simultaneous evocation and downplaying of the classical Roman categorizations of Gaul. The most sustained description of France which humanist-trained geographers had at their disposal (although verbal rather than cartographic) was Caesar's *Gallic War*. Not only was the text itself widely published in France, but Caesar's division between Transalpine and Cisalpine Gaul, and the further tripartite division of the former, seemed in the sixteenth century to provide a rather more stable picture of France than could be composed in the present, shaken as the kingdom was by civil war. Mercator's *Galliae tabulae geographicae* (Duisburg, 1585), provides an example of the persistence of the image of classical Gaul. It was the first atlas dedicated to France, comprised of thirteen regional maps and one of the whole 'Gallia.' Mireille Pastoureau has deftly shown that the appellation *Gallia* was used by mapmakers in the sixteenth century as an intermediary concept between classical Gaul and (early) modern France. Gallia is differentiated from Roman Gaul but still emerging into a notional unity that would subsume local differences: 'For Mercator, then, "Gallia" is no longer Roman Gaul, but nor is she yet the kingdom of France. It is a geographic frame ... a generic name hiding the chaos of its political boundaries.'[27] The Latin *Gallia* encapsulates the drama of France's emerging self-image, caught between a nativist impulse on the one hand and an overdetermination by its historical relationship with Rome on the other. Beholden to classical forebears, while striving to differentiate from these forebears in order to construct a notion of France and Frenchness in the present, French mapmakers struggled to imagine and define their *patrie* as a place distinct in both space and time. This complicated relation to the places, cultures, and languages of antiquity is the drama of *imitatio* or imitation, with which Renaissance artists, mapmakers, poets, historians, and philosophers alike were all familiar.[28] The rediscovery and the privileging of classical knowledge was not limited to what we now call literary texts. But it is in cartographic and poetic descriptions that the specifically spatial implications of *imitatio* for the concept of *le royaume de France* are played out.

For poet and mapmaker alike, there is no way to write France without it being also a palimpsestic overwriting of Greece or Italy. In the poet Joachim Du Bellay's 1549 treatise *La Deffence et illustration de la langue françoyse*, the classical past disrupts the idea of nationhood in the present. Of interest here is a striking instance of the translation (in both senses) of a classical landscape into France, and into French, the tropes of which are also found on several maps from the period. It is in the last chapter of the *Deffence*, where the poet explains why France is superior to Italy by evoking – as well as its readiness for war – some of France's topographical features:

> Je ne parleray icy de la temperie de l'air, fertilité de la terre [...] Je ne conteray tant de grosses rivieres, tant de belles forestz, tant de villes non moins opulentes que fortes, et pourveues de toutes munitions de guerre. Finablement je ne parleray de tant de metiers, arz, et sciences, qui florissent entre nous. [I will not speak here of the temperateness of the air, the fertility of the soil ... I will not recount the many great rivers, the many beautiful forests, the many cities, no less opulent than strong and provided with all the munitions of war. Finally, I will not speak of the many trades, arts, and learned disciplines ... that flourish among us].[29]

The aim of the *Deffence* is to urge the creation, through selective imitation of Greek, Latin, and Italian languages and poetic *topoi*, of an illustrious native poetic tradition that will finally rival and surpass those exemplars. This particular passage itself models such imitation: it is based on Virgil's praise of Italy in the *Georgics*.[30] Transforming the Latin source text into a French praise of a France specifically contrasted with Italy, Du Bellay represents the soil in which this poetry will germinate as fertile, georgic, the landscape in which it will grow and flourish as pastoral. Thus the poetic *translatio studii* is represented spatially, with the result being an abundance of images of native French landscape in poetry from the mid-sixteenth century.

We find a very similar comparison of France with Italy in a decorated cartouche on the above-mentioned Francia mural map,[31] copied from Jolivet's 1560 *Vraie description des Gaules*: 'She (France) produced men forever famous in glory and exploits, the abundance of their riches, and her territory is so fertile that she yields in nothing to opulent Italy.'[32] A Latin copy of Jolivet's map from 1570[33] contains a different Latin text in cartouche, addressed like many sixteenth-century maps to the 'lector,' evoking the relationship between France and Greece as a kind of reverse *translatio studii*:

> Studious reader, be greeted. All Gallia previously was famous not only for its riches and military prowess, in which it still shines, but also for their self-restraint and their learning, which attained renown among them. For Gallia also excelled in the illustrious arts, and also in the Greek language, I think because Marseilles, which lies at the sea coast, had a Greek city as its mother; once even students from Rome itself were sent here to obtain an education.[34]

Du Bellay reminds his readers in the conclusion to the *Deffence* of the same ancient prestige of Marseilles, which he calls a 'second Athens' (180); like the poet, the mapmaker reminds his own readers of their country's venerable military history and the fact that Gallia once was the source of learning for Rome, rather than the contrary. Both advance the same humanist commonplaces as they claim the excellence of France in terms that are nevertheless defined and framed by the classical world.

An integral part of any imagined community is, as Benedict Anderson reminds us, a shared language, which in European nations was facilitated by capitalist print culture giving greater fixity and privilege to certain dialects.[35] The push towards greater use of the vernacular(s) in France as opposed to Latin is well documented for literary culture. The same tendency is seen on maps. From 1525 to the 1570s, maps of France start to contain more French text and less Latin, presenting a gradually evolving image of a kingdom disassociating from classical definitions and languages. Oronce Fine's 1525 map, with its Latin title *Nova totius galliae descriptio*, is the work of a Latinate humanist. It draws on Caesar's distinction between Transalpine and Cisalpine Gaul and his names for Gaulish tribes, and gives most toponyms in Latin. Most subsequent maps of France produced in the country had French titles, including the above-mentioned *Nouvelle description des Gaules* by Jean Jolivet (1560), and Guillaume Postel's 1570 *La vraie et entiere description du royaume de France et ses confines*.[36] Jolivet's map, though it gives the names of countries and seas in Latin, gives regional names in the vernacular, even accounting for pronunciation differences. He also indicates the local governments, dioceses, etc., of contemporary France. By 1570, almost all town names on Postel's map are in French, as is his address to

Charles IX in the cartouche, in which he claims to have represented 'la France et Gaule universelle [...] la plus pres que [il] pourrai[t] de sa consumation et de sa nature plus parfaite' [universal France and Gaul ... as close as possible to completion and its most perfect nature].

To characterize the changes of any historical period as representing the *emergence* of a particular idea is to run the risk of anachronism, particularly with respect to an idea as contested as the nation, which many feel is not appropriate for early modern history. Perhaps we are too hasty to see periods before our own only inasmuch as they anticipate or prepare the way for our current theoretical or historical paradigms.[37] But it is hard not to read Postel's inscription, referring to the map of France as something to be perfected, as witnessing to a teleology of progress in cartography. He is by no means the only mapmaker to use the vocabulary of perfection and accuracy with respect to representation: even Oronce Fine in 1525 presents his map 'pour preparer la voye a chascun de lamplifier ou corriger a son plaisir' [to prepare the way for anyone to add to or correct it as they see fit]. What is more, the appellation 'France et Gaule' indicates the continuity of a kind of dual identity: France is not quite *France* by itself, but nor is it only classical Gaul. It is something in between. Likewise, the 'royaume de France' and the 'confines' of the title signify a vision of a kingdom emerging from the plurality of regional identities. As long as we give due voice to the complicating factors in the idea of nationhood – the persistence of the local and the classical, for example – and historically justify our use of such terms, it is justifiable to see, in both poetry and cartography from the sixteenth century, the beginnings of a 'national' image.

The Poet and the Mapmaker

The commonplaces, and common places, of Renaissance poetry and maps have had a significant impact on the socio-cultural relation to space that is now called France. But to say that two particular cultural practices respond to and help construct a sense of place in sixteenth-century France is to avoid the question: why poetry and cartography in particular? And to answer this, it is necessary to look more closely at the praxis of both, and how they intersect. Poets and mapmakers shared certain vocabularies, and often employed similar rhetorical strategies to argue for the interest of their work. What is more, poets and mapmakers knew each other, frequented the same social milieux, worked together, and were sometimes one and the same person in sixteenth-century

France. By uncovering some of the shared vocabularies and lived networks, we can start to historicize the literature–cartography encounter in a more rigorous way.

The boundary between (carto)graphic and written representation in the sixteenth century is far from clear. The etymology of the Greek suffix -*graphie*, the verb *graphein*, has both textual and graphic connotations. *Topos* and *locus*, of course, had long been used to designate both physical and textual place and characteristics, as is *lieu* today. And the word *description* (or the Latin *descriptio*) was commonly used both for pictorial and written texts. Svetlana Alpers argues that when Renaissance geographers use the word, they do so consciously to draw attention to the 'sense in which images are drawn or inscribed like something written.'[38] Then, of course, there was Horace's *ut pictura poesis*, commonly read in the Renaissance as suggesting parity between word and image. I shall treat painting in the next chapter, making a rather different kind of argument for its relation with poetry. Here, I explore a rather less well-known or less obvious historical relation, between poetry and cartography.

Mapmakers 'worked in a range of genres that had different conventions' and presented hybrid forms of information on their maps. Maps were published not so much with the goal of making knowledge more precise, but, in conjunction with verbal forms of representation, to make the world more 'readable.'[39] This hybridity and diversity within the business of making and reading maps rendered the boundaries between forms of knowledge particularly fluid. The idea of cartography as an autonomous professional discipline would have surprised sixteenth-century practitioners. Svetlana Alpers has shown that it was a 'common, even casually acquired skill' in the Dutch seventeenth century, and that many cartographers were also painters, poets, geometers, astronomers, and so on.[40] The same was true in Renaissance France. Like the ideal poet of Jacques Peletier's *Art poétique*, expert in all forms of knowledge,[41] Renaissance cartographers combined many skills and identified primarily as humanists, men of letters, and servants of the crown, not as 'cartographes.' In fact, the word *cartographie* was not consistently used in France until the nineteenth century. Mapmaking in the sixteenth century was part of the larger field of *géographie* or, more commonly, *cosmographie*. *Géographie* only started to gain currency in the early sixteenth century, and even as it did, *cosmographie* continued to be favoured. The Renaissance *Cosmographie* was a genre that drew as much on literary as cartographic modes of description, and, according to

Edmond Huguet, one of the first attested uses of the vernacular *géographie* was by a poet, Jean Lemaire.[42]

The appearance in the vernacular of the Greek-based *géographie* (with its various cognates) during this period was no coincidence. As mentioned above, Ptolemy's *Geographia* was frequently printed and translated from 1477 onwards. And despite chorography being the more subjective form of representation, with geography requiring mathematical skills, the latter was still not seen as entirely detached from poetic subjectivity. The first vernacular translation of the *Geographia* was in Italian, published in Florence in 1482 by the humanist scholar and poet Berlinghieri, containing many of the first extant maps of European countries including France. The Berlinghieri translation is notable for not being in prose but in verse, *terza rima*. The translator explains this choice, as well as the choice of Italian rather than Latin, at the beginning of the first book, comparing himself to Apollo and insisting – in an echo of Dante perhaps – that vernacular poetry is more likely to make readers 'marvel' at the wonders of the world: 'Aiming to tell things in the present time, with all the world in rhyme and verse, to make everyone marvel, so that my song be no different from you, shining Apollo, but conforming to you, showing the whole universe, ignorance of which is too serious.'[43] Poetry and maps become a joint epistemology, a way of accessing knowledge about the world. Geography, like Ptolemy's *Geographia*, was seen as both visual and textual – even poetic.

Maps themselves were often presented as a kind of text in the sixteenth century. Mapmakers are referred to as 'auteurs' and maps contain addresses to the reader, 'aux lecteurs,' in cartouches.[44] Published maps contain liminal and prefatory material, dedications, all of which strikingly resemble the prefatory material one finds to sixteenth-century texts. They share this, of course, with any text, but make particular use of poetic topoi. High-status maps – that is, maps whose goal is as much to be pleasing as useful – share with poetry the rhetoric of perfect imitation of nature, and sometimes describe the beauty of their topographic object as if it were a lyric love-object. The only (extant) sixteenth-century map of the Limousin is a good example. It is a diocesan map that found its way into Bouguereau's 1594 atlas, signed by one 'J. Fayanus' or Jean Fayen. Although it is dated 1594, its composition may date back to as early as the 1550s, the era of the first flourishing of the Pléiade's lyric poetry. The author writes to the dedicatee, the Duc de Ventadour, that he aims to reveal the 'laughing face' of Limousin *topographia* (in Greek characters), which has previously been hidden under a veil, neglected by cartographers: 'J'ai donc fait tous mes efforts pour découvrir son riant visage qu'un voile enveloppait' [I thus made every effort to uncover her laughing face, which was hidden by a veil].[45] Female beauty hidden under a veil is of course a Petrarchan lyric trope, popular among French lyric poets.[46] It is perhaps no surprise to learn that Fayen also considered himself a poet.

If cartographers borrow poetic tropes, sixteenth-century poets were fascinated by all aspects of geography. No less a poet than Ronsard himself saw great value in Nicolay's work. He seemed to know Nicolay personally and wrote an elegy for him which prefaced the *Navigations*. In this poem, the diversity of customs and landscapes encountered by the geographer is inscribed into a recognizably Ronsardian poetics of *varietas*, and presented as deserving of royal favour.[47] The library of the poet Remy Belleau included a book of 'cartes cosmographiques' by Antoine du Pinet, a French translation of Petrus Apianus's *Cosmographia*, Ptolemy's *Geographia*, and a Latin description of Rome.[48] Fellow poet and Pléiade member Jean-Antoine de Baïf was friends with the royal cosmographer, Nicolas de Nicolay, who as mentioned above was charged by Catherine de' Medici with producing maps of each region of the kingdom to be assembled into one larger project. Baïf wrote a poem, 'À Nicolas Nicolay,' which may have been intended as a liminary piece to Nicolay's account of his travels to the Middle East between 1542 and 1558, the *Navigations*, first published in 1567.[49] (The poem ended up in Baïf's 1573 *Œuvres en rime*, or *Poèmes*.) Nicolay himself sees poetry as an important part of the presentation of his geographic work. He even pens the occasional verse himself. In his own address to the king at the start of his 1576 *Navigations*, Nicolay has recourse to poetry at a point where knowledge, epistemology, and royal favour are all particularly at stake:

Connoissant en moy-mesme le peu de scavoir et suffisance (quant aux lettres) qui est en moy, pour n'y avoir faict tel exercice que le devoir de mon estat le requerroit, et par ce moyen l'eminent danger, qui se presentoit a mes yeux, de tomber aux filletz des malles bouches et ignorans, ausquelz à bon droit on peut dire que

La vertu leur sert de risée
Et la science mesprisée
S'escoule, et leur vient a mepris.
Rien ne leur plaict que l'ignorance

Dessoubz, le masque d'Arrogance
Qui faict rougir les mieux apris.[50]

[Knowing my own relative ignorance of and lack of skill in letters, which
comes from my having only done the duty required of me, and thus know-
ing the real danger I was in of falling into the traps of naysayers and fools,
of whom one can say that: They make fun of virtue / And knowledge,
which they disdain / Passes them by. / All they like is ignorance / Below
the mask of Arrogance / Which makes better-educated people blush.]

Nicolay's introduction modulates to the poetic at moments where
knowledge is at stake, as if geographic knowledge were not only com-
plemented but somehow completed by poetry. His son-in-law Antoine
de Laval, a man of letters and occasional poet, would seem to have
agreed. Laval wrote the liminary verse to Nicolay's 1573 'Description
du Lyonnais,'[51] in which he adds his lyric description of the Lyonnais to
his uncle's geographic description. In verse, he praises Catherine for
having 'invented' geography (a reference no doubt to her mandate to
Nicolay to map every region of France), despite the ravages of the wars
of religion.[52] The interest of this 'description Géographique' is in the
contrast between the landscape literally and figuratively ravaged by
war, and a Lyon idealized by both verse and map as a peaceful 'little
eye of France' (3), a bastion against the grim reality of history which, if
dwelt on, sunders the possibility of even the image of a peaceful nation
unified under one ruler.

Nicolay presents this map as 'delightful, useful, and profitable' for
the king. We see here another commonality between cartography and
poetry: this is of course the Horatian mandate for poetry, that it be both
pleasurable and useful. Cartographers often use this formula in describing how their work will benefit their patron.[53] It also indicates a
very tight relationship between royal power and mapping, which will
surprise no one except perhaps in its precociousness: we tend to think
of the seventeenth century as the period in which royal power first harnessed geography as a state-building project in France. But already by
the 1560s, maps were seen not only as a vehicle for glorifying the king's
name, but as essential to the state's interests.[54] And later, with civil war
openly raging, cartography provided precious information about the
kingdom which could help the monarch overcome civil strife. Much
liminary or prefatory material to Renaissance *descriptions* insists on
their joint laudatory and pedagogical functions.[55] The multi-talented

poet Pontus de Tyard, who instructed Henri III in astronomy, philosophy, maths, history, and geography, privileged the learning of geography above all, writing about the king's education in the preface to his 1578 *Premier Curieux*: 'je luy souhaite bien expressement l'usage de la Geographie, et description des mers et provinces diverses' [I particularly recommend to him the use of Geography, and descriptions of different oceans and regions].

The ideological work done by mapmakers, providing justification and reassuring images to the king of his power over the land as well as pedagogical lessons, is similar to that of some mid-century pastoral poetry, of which Ronsard's *Bergerie* (1565) is a prime example. The work was probably written in 1564 to be performed at a festival at Fontainebleau at which Catherine de' Medici and the young king Charles IX were the main guests, before setting out for their famous Royal Tour of the kingdom from 1564 to 1566. It is a dialogue between shepherds, thinly disguised analogues for royal personalities, who sing of the desired return of the golden age onto French soil which will be brought about by Valois rule. A detailed enumbration of each of France's provinces follows:

> Que dirons-nous icy de la haute montagne
> D'Auvergne, et des moissons de la grasse Champagne,
> L'une riche en troupeaux, et l'autre riche en blé,
> Au voeu des laboureurs d'usure redoublé?
> Que dirons nous d'Anjou et des champs de Touraine,
> De Languedoc, Provence, où l'abondance pleine
> De sillon en sillon fertile se conduit
> Portant sa riche Corne enceinte de beau fruit?   (161–2, lines 724–31)

[What shall we say of the high mountains of Auvergne, or the harvests of luscious Champagne, the one rich in livestock and the other in wheat, increased in worth by the faithful labourers? What shall we say of Anjou and the fields of Touraine, Languedoc, or Provence, where full abundance from furrow to fertile furrow offers its cornucopia of riches?]

Before the young king leaves to tour his kingdom, Ronsard offers an idealized verbal map of it, as Margaret McGowan writes, 'to suggest that France is a country ideally suited to a return of some golden age and to prepare Charles IX for an extended lesson in kingship.'[56] The moralizing, conservative lessons of pastoral are applied to a vision of a kingdom whose regions will be united under one ruler, in a poetic equivalent of Nicolay's cartographic project.

As well as sharing paratextual rhetoric, and a certain relationship to power and patronage and the growing kingdom, poems and maps sometimes literally share the same space: there are short poems on some sixteenth-century maps of French regions. Jean Fayen's Limousin map mentioned above is again a good example. It circulated widely in its time and beyond; one finds maps based on this block both separately and bound in seventeenth-century collections. The one constant in the many block cuts for this map, ornate or less so, is a short poem signed by Joachim Blanchon, in which Fayen, the mapmaker, is compared with Archimedes, and Limoges (his natal town) is described as a new French seat of Greek learning, inscribed in a very literary discourse of fame:

Homere Demosthene et Archimede ensemble
Lymoges a nourry ou la vertu s'assemble,
Muret Dorat Fayen, trois excellens esprits:
Muret son Demosthene et Dorat son Homere.
Fayen son Archimede ayant sa ville Mere
Sa Province et son Plan heureusement compris.

[Limoges, the seat of virtue, has raised a Homer, a Demosthenes, and an Archimedes: Murat, Dorat, and Fayen, three great minds: Muret is its Demosthenes and Dorat its Homer, Fayen is its Archimedes, having well understood his native town, his province and its map].

The author of these few lines, Blanchon, barely figures as a footnote in sixteenth-century intellectual history and is rarely read today.[57] However, all those involved in reproducing the map appear to have considered the poem an important enough component of the map to warrant its keeping. These six lines of verse were reprinted throughout the sixteenth century along with the elements of the map which we today would consider fundamental to our reading of the document: toponynms, coastlines, and symbols representing towns, bodies of water, rivers, or mountains.

Such direct collaborations between poets and mapmakers are not unusual. The second-oldest extant French regional map, from 1545, is of Berry, executed by Jean Jolivet (who was from Bourges).[58] The map bears an 'Au lecteur' in verse, written by Jolivet's friend Jacques Thiboust:

Tu vois Berry en perfection
Par ceste carte et pays et duché
Distances, lieux, Diocese, election,[59]
Qu'autre n'a point encore si bien touché.
Jehan Jolivet a ceci deffriché
En peu de jours, et n'y a artisant
Paintre ou sculpteur qui mieulx ait appenché
Rendre content l'œil d'un chascun lisant.

[You see Berry perfectly in this map, both region and duchy, distances, landmarks, diocese, jurisdiction, that no one else has yet so well described. Jean Jolivet has revealed all this in a few days, and there is no artisan, painter, or sculptor who has better succeeded in pleasing the eye of anyone who reads it.]

Thiboust, an occasional poet, was Marguerite de Navarre's secretary in Berry, and had taken up residence in the chateau de Quantilly in 1503.[60] On his insistence, Jolivet dedicated his regional map to Marguerite. Thiboust, who appears to have had a close friendship with Jolivet, was an active literary rassembleur in Berry, bringing together a large coterie of men of letters, legal figures, and clerics, all of whom enjoyed the support of Marguerite. We see here a regionally based collaboration between a poet and a mapmaker, a joint effort to present an image of Berry which is both cartographic and poetic.

There are no poems on maps from the seventeenth century, when cartographers more openly espouse an ideology of accuracy (actual accuracy, of course, being illusory) and cartography starts to autonomize. Renaissance maps witness to a transitional moment in the history of cartography, during which the more lyric and subjective aspects of mapmaking persist and are acknowledged, to be gradually disavowed by subsequent disciplinary boundaries that see maps and poetry as mutually impermeable.

Not only were poets and cartographers often friends, with poets inscribing cartouches on maps, but – confirming the relevance of Svetlana Alpers's observation about the ease with which cartographic skills were assumed – there were also men who did both. Nicolas Denisot, occasional poet, friend of the Pléiade, talented painter, tried his hand at mapmaking. He apparently collaborated with Ogier Macé on the map of Le Mans, and one small map of Peru has been found to be by him.[61] Aegidius Bulonius, or Gilles Boileau de Bouillon (1510–63), a Flemish writer, poet, and diplomat, tried his hand at various literary activities without much success. His 1550 translation of the *Amadis* was not well received, leading to Claude Colet's demanding that it be retranslated.[62] In what seems to have been an attempt to bolster his literary profile, he turned to geography. His *Sphere des deux mondes*, a popularized geography with pastoral tones, fell rapidly into obscurity after its publication in 1555 and has been little appreciated since, described by one of its few twentieth-century readers as exhibiting all the 'the typical pitfalls of the didactic genre: dryness, mundanity, obscurity, affectation.'[63] The text is in *prosimetrum*, an alternation of prose and verse seen in Renaissance pastoral, showing again the close rapport between geographic and poetic epistemologies. The title page makes the link explicit: the text is subtitled as 'enrichy de plusieurs Fables poeticques' [enriched with several poetic tales], and promises the reader (in verse) that 'l'achetant y trouuerez au net, / Bien figurez pays & territoires' [by buying (this book) you will find / Countries and lands well represented.] When his literary career seemed definitively washed up, he decided to try his hand at mapmaking, and in 1556 – only a year later – he drew what is the oldest extant map of Savoy.[64] The map does not evidence precise mathematical knowledge of geographic techniques, but ends up in Ortelius's 1570 atlas, showing again that geography was far from being considered an exact science. The unfortunate Boileau had no more success as a mapmaker than as a poet – he died in obscurity in 1563 – but the trajectory of his professional endeavours manifests the ease with which a poet could become a cartographer.

A poet could also, of course, be a painter (Nicolas Denisot), an astronomer (Pontus de Tyard), a mathematician (Jacques Peletier), a priest, physician, musician, or soldier. Many poets were lawyers, or attached to the court in some function, or ecclesiastics. There is no exclusivity to the poetry–cartography relationship. But the relationship did exist, concretely and historically, in ways that should encourage us to respond to Tom Conley's invitation to put 'French studies on the map' (or put the map in French studies) in order to perceive, with respect specifically to the Renaissance, 'how a sense of habitus was conceived, projected, and betrayed at a time of tumultuous change.'[65] Perhaps more importantly, historicizing these relationships allows us to do so in ways that go beyond the 'generalized or abstract sense of what mapping means'[66] that constitutes one of the most significant limits of cartographically oriented literary criticism to date.

The further interpretive step taken here is that consideration of the historical, lived articulations between poetry and cartography in the

French sixteenth century indicates that they work together in specific ways to imagine *place* in the French sixteenth century. At a time when the unity of the kingdom seemed threatened from within even more than from without, cartographers presented chorographic maps of the kingdom and its provinces that often drew on lyric modes. The use of poetry added to the maps' qualitative and idealized aspects. But, like the poetic places which will be the subject of the following chapters, maps witness to problems posed by the representation of the whole kingdom: the problem of how to reconcile local sentiments, authorities, loyalties, and powers with the authority and ambitions of the crown, and the problem of how to represent a present-day reality in the vernacular while working within the dictates of exemplarity which privileged Latin and the past.

In this chapter, I have discussed some instantiations of shared discursivity and practice between cartography and poetry, suggesting that Renaissance cartography can be poetic (as opposed to simply 'literary'). In the following chapter on Joachim Du Bellay's lyrics, I will reverse the terms, suggesting ways in which poetry is cartographic. However, having outlined some of the specificity of the poetry–cartography encounter in the Renaissance, I hope to do so in a way that avoids simple analogy, putting pressure on and refining the notion of cartographic writing by continuing to focus on the particularity of the poetic.

3 The Poet, the Nation, and the Region: Constructing Anjou and France

Joachim Du Bellay is, along with Pierre de Ronsard, one of the undisputed heavyweights of French Renaissance poetry. His 1549 *Deffence et illustration de la langue françoise*, in which he urges fellow men of letters to inaugurate a golden age of French language and literature, has secured him a place in the history of French vernacular culture as one of the first truly national poets. He was saluted in the liminary sonnet of the *Deffence* itself by Jean Dorat as a 'bon patriote' who 'plaid[e] pour la langue de la patrie' [good patriot ... who plead(s) on behalf of our country's language].[1] There are problems with this version of history, of course. First, Du Bellay's *œuvre* is far from monolingual: the *Deffence* itself borrows generously from a treatise on the Italian language, and Du Bellay published in Latin.[2] Second, the idea that there is one unified 'langue de la patrie' is more anticipatory than real.[3] Third, the *Deffence* itself can be seen as overstating the need to 'defend' French against its supposed detractors. (Du Bellay's first critic, Bartélémy Aneau, wondered as early as 1550: 'Qui accuse ou a accusé la langue Françoise?' [Who is accusing or has accused the French language?].)[4] The fourth blind spot of the narrative of Du Bellay as 'bon patriote' is my focus here: his conscious cultivation of a regional (provincial) identity. On the title page of the first edition of the *Deffence*, the publication of which Du Bellay followed closely, the poet aligns himself with a regional, not a national identity, giving his name in four initials: I.D.B.A. – Ioachim Du Bellay, Angevin. Du Bellay himself took care to identify himself with regional territory from the very beginning of his career. And his name is even today associated with Angevin identity, cited with pride by many a local history or travel guide.

If Du Bellay is hailed even today as an early representative of both French national and Angevin regional identity, it is, I argue here, in large part because of his presentation of both through lyric landscapes. Du Bellay's adherence to a regional identity has been largely neglected by literary scholarship, with the exception of an important recent intervention by Marc Bizer, who shows that both *Les Regrets* and the *Deffence* 'express considerable ambivalence about a French identity, even a resistance to it. Indeed, *Les Regrets* give strongest voice to a provincial, rather than a national identity.'[5] I show here, through a reading of Du Bellay's highly suggestive poetic landscapes, that the relation between provincial and national identity is not so much an either–or proposition as it is a necessary dialectic, or a productive tension that creates and sustains both as Angevin and French play off against and define each other. As Du Bellay instantiates the mutual dependence of France and Anjou in an almost structuralist way (there is no large-scale without small-scale, no province without kingdom), he reveals that place, at any scale, is a product of the imagination, 'connected to others in constantly evolving networks which are social, cultural [as well as] natural/environmental.'[6] Responding to Tom Conley's invitation to develop 'perspectives on the relations between literature and cartography,'[7] I shall further show that this dialectic draws significantly on the cartographic distinction between geography and chorography described in the previous chapter, representing the relation between nation and region as a qualitative scalar one.

A final aspect of my reading reveals the degree to which Du Bellay's landscapes spatialize and stage the paradoxes of poetic imitation. His lyric maps, like cartographic maps, are presented in conscious dialogue with the non-French and with the past even as they strive to describe France in the present. Landscape is a cacophonic 'intertextual space'[8] in which Latin, Greek, and Italian places and poets are confronted and overwritten. The core paradox of imitative practice – how to differentiate from exemplars – is, in ways not yet fully explored by scholars working either on imitation or literary nationhood, represented in poetry as a fundamentally spatial problem.[9] Du Bellay himself insists in his *Deffence* on the need to imitate Latin, Greek, and Italian models in order to write sonnets, epigrams, odes, elegies, and other approved forms of poetry in French. And to imitate classical and Italian models is to run up quite literally against the question of place; not only do foreign countries have a stronger poetic tradition, but their lyric verses name and describe foreign landscapes as the site of poetic creation itself. An increasingly self-conscious vernacular poetry must therefore not only adopt as its own traditions that are not native, it must also re-imagine their landscapes as French.

My focus here will be on Du Bellay's rewriting of Italy and Petrarch in *L'Olive* and *Les Regrets*, both of which operate a sustained series of transformations of Italian poetry through named French landscapes. Petrarch is by no means the only Italian lyric influence to be made French – an anthology of Italian poetry printed by Gabriel Giolito in Venice is another favoured source,[10] as is Ariosto – and the influence of Greek and Latin models is undisputed. However, Petrarch looms particularly large in the landscape of the *Olive*, and Italy is the place against which France and Anjou are differentiated in *Les Regrets*, and thus they will be my primary focus here.[11] A leading premise of William Kennedy's important book on the uses of the Petrarchan sonnet in France, Italy, and England, is that it becomes a 'site for early modern expressions of national sentiment' in those countries.[12] With respect to France, he shows how Du Bellay manipulates the form and content of Petrarchan lyric and resituates it in France, through a complex dialogue with other French poets.[13] I show here the particular role of landscape as the literalization of Kennedy's 'site,' and also suggest that more attention needs to be paid to the region, not simply as a category or affect that 'merges' with 'supraregional sentiments'[14] but as a necessary part of a creative dialectic that is constitutive of the nation. I conclude with some remarks on how these landscapes respond to the agenda of Du Bellay's poetic treatise, the *Deffence et illustration de la langue françoyse*, by mapping out the spaces of an imagined community distinct in time and space from Italy.

In *L'Olive*, published in 1549, with an expanded version a year later, Du Bellay makes Petrarchan poetry French, as JoAnn DellaNeva has shown, by transplanting it 'onto native French soil.'[15] It is French landscape itself that actively overwrites or transforms Petrarchan codes, and this landscape is primarily local. To imagine the space or place of a great national poetry is to imagine not France as a whole, but rather a region, in this case Du Bellay's native Anjou. Anjou, and the river Loire in particular, contain within themselves the material to challenge and rival Italy: they are ideal places of pure native poetry which guarantee fame to poet and country alike. *L'Olive* marks a first step in a poetics of nationhood, a preliminary and necessary setting of a stage which is not Italy, not Petrarchan, on which a French poet can proclaim, in French, love for a French woman.

In the later collection *Les Regrets* (1558), Du Bellay continues for a while to imagine Anjou as a place of poetic purity and inspiration in which his identity and reputation are grounded. However, this lyric provincial identity dissolves during the course of the *Regrets*, put in a productive but conflicted dialogue with an equally problematic French national identity. In the last few sonnets, it is the nation, incarnated in a lady, Marguerite de France, which eventually grounds the poet's search for an appropriate lyric space. This tension between region and nation is again played out through landscape, and use of cartographic distinctions in scale between the local and national. Du Bellay oscillates between national (geographic) and regional (chorographic) description in a movement that is ultimately productive of both: neither can be constructed without the other. Just as the nation needs the foreign outside its borders in order to constitute itself, so too does it need the region within. Rather than being antithetical to the nation, then, the region is essential to its production.

The *Regrets* finally reveal that both the region and the nation are idealizations. The 'lure of the local,'[16] so strong when Du Bellay is imagining Anjou from Rome, dissipates upon his return. Idealization, as Yvonne Bellenger has cogently shown, is only possible at a distance.[17] And the nationalist project of the praise of France undertaken at the end of the collection is revealed in part as self-conscious flattery. By revealing the insufficiencies or blind spots of ideal region and ideal nation, Du Bellay rewrites one of the perennial themes of pastoral since Virgil, which is the tension between ideal and reality, imagination and history, discussed in the introduction. If Du Bellay's descriptions of France or Anjou are still cited today, it is surely because they are presented as evanescent, fragile and threatened. As Philip Schwyzer has argued, a collective sense of national beauty is often predicated upon a sense of nostalgia: the nation is beautiful because threatened by loss.[18] The enduring beauty of Du Bellay's landscapes comes in part from this melancholic sense that they are fragile and threatened. Nevertheless, his France is a 'space of hope,' a landscape where poetic excellence, secure regional identities, and national greatness temporarily coexist.[19] And his praise of France at the end of *Les Regrets*, although it seems to be a disheartened return to conventional praise of a woman and an acknowledgment of his dependence on a patron, contains a powerful hope that poetry might just be able to make France great. At a time when transformed cartographic practice was mapping France and its regions for the first time, poetry too puts 'France on the map.'[20]

L'Olive

The first words of the first line of the first sonnet of Joachim Du Bellay's first published collection, *L'Olive*, are a negation: 'Je ne quiers pas la fameuse couronne / Sainct ornement du Dieu au chef doré' [I don't seek the famous crown, the sacred decoration of Apollo].[21] This *recusatio* has drawn the attention of many scholars: François Rigolot has identified negation as part of Du Bellay's strategic 'poésie du refus' [poetry of refusal] that navigates between the assumed poles of individuality and imitation, creating the enduring impression of an 'expression personnelle' in his poetry.[22] I show that in *L'Olive* Du Bellay's negations are constitutive not only of his individuated poetic identity, but also, by rejecting and rewriting Italy through an erotic cartography of Anjou, of an emerging French identity which is regional before it is national.

The object of negation, the crown of Apollo, is of course the laurel wreath, symbol of poetic fame since the ancient Greeks.[23] More particularly, the laurel wreath or *lauro* is the symbol and homonym of Petrarch's love-object, Laura, and of his poetic renown; Petrarch's *Canzoniere* are replete with the *Laura-lauro* homonym.[24] Du Bellay's refusal of this powerful symbol of classical and Italian poetic renown is surprising. In 1549 when *L'Olive* was published, sonnet sequences in French were unheard of, although the following decade would see them flourish. One might expect Du Bellay to make a more forceful case, and claim more powerful symbols, for his own poetic success, particularly as *L'Olive* was published in the same year as his polemical *Deffence et illustration*. Both texts 'share a common concern: the development of the French vernacular as an excellent medium of poetic expression.'[25] The *Deffence* promotes the notion that French has little native poetic tradition to speak of, and that the remedy for this is judicious imitation of classical and Italian models by poets such as him. More specifically, Du Bellay tells us in his preface to the expanded version of *L'Olive* that he wrote the *Deffence* partly as an explanation to his readers of his poetry; he clearly felt that the 'nouveauté' of a sonnet sequence in French emulating Italians, Romans, and Greeks needed some justification.[26] Like Ronsard and the other poets of the Pléiade, Du Bellay was self-consciously presenting his vernacular poetry as a kind of workshop in which the excellence of French would be forged and defended, one day to equal Latin, Greek, and Italian in its richness and variety. In the *Deffence*, he explicitly minimizes the importance of his immediate vernacular predecessors in the forging of this French poetic tradition, and is particularly disdainful of the native French medieval and late medieval forms such as the rondeau and ballade. If French poetry is to be considered great by posterity, he implies, it will be because of the immediate and urgent intercession of a small élite self-nominated coterie which will render it illustrious.

If Du Bellay is rejecting (among other vegetal symbols) the laurel wreath, Laura, and Petrarch, what is he to claim for himself? The answer lies in the landscape, and starts with an olive tree, which any reader initiated in the Petrarchan tree-for-woman substitution will recognize is also a woman: the homonymous Olive, the purported object of his desire.[27] The continuation of the first sonnet describes, elliptically, the substitution of the laurel by the olive:

> Celuy qui est d'Athenes honoré,
> Seul je le veulx, et le Ciel me l'ordonne.
> [...]
> Orne mon chef, donne moy hardiesse
> De te chanter, qui espere te rendre
> Egal un jour au Laurier immortel.   (*L'Olive* 1)

> [That (tree) which is honoured by Athens is all that I want, and the heavens require this of me ... Decorate my head, give me the courage to praise you, I who hope one day to make you equal to the immortal laurel tree.]

Nevertheless, this first sonnet leaves the poet with a geographical problem: he may have challenged Petrarch, dethroning the laurel in favour of the olive tree, but he is still firmly in classical Greece and Italy. The olive, gift of Athene, is of course the symbol of Athens. And the poet crowned with olive branches is found in Horace's ode 'Laudabunt alii,' itself a passing over of the beauty of Greek landscapes in favour of Roman.[28] Du Bellay may have transformed the laurel wreath into an olive branch, but he has yet to plant it in French soil.

He achieves this in the third sonnet, which he starts with an address to the 'Loire fameux.' Du Bellay's patriation of Petrarch will take place in and through local topography.

> Loyre fameux, qui ta petite source
> Enfles de maintz gros fleuves et ruysseaux,
> Et qui de loing coules tes cleres eux
> En l'Ocean d'une assez vive course.   (*L'Olive* 3)

[Famous Loire, who make your little source swell with many large rivers and streams, and who run your clear waters over a long, rapid course to the Ocean.]

The address to 'Loyre fameux' is surprising in a collection of love sonnets, where one might expect an address to a tree in this tradition of the metonymic substitution of the tree for the lady, but hardly to a river.[29] The poetic project of praise of a woman is transformed into the praise of his local river. By turning lyric convention on its head he is executing a sort of performative: that is, by saying that the Loire is well known, he makes it so.[30] The landscape of lyric love and praise is now unmistakably French, a large river running its entire course from spring to sea through France. Given the importance of the image of the source as generative poetic inspiration, it seems significant that the Loire has its source in France itself.[31]

Du Bellay loses no time, in the following quatrain, in claiming the Loire as a more beautiful river than the Italian Po, which flows through the Veneto where Petrarch lived the last part of his life.

Ton chef royal hardiment bien hault pousse
Et apparoy entre tous les plus beaux
Comme un thaureau sur les menuz troupeaux
Quoy que le Pau envieux s'en courrousse.   (*L'Olive* 3)

[Your royal head stands out high and bold among all of the most beautiful rivers, like a bull among the mere herds, although the jealous Po becomes angry.]

The Loire is a competitor in an international competition of fame in which the Angevin landscape trumps the Venetian, and Du Bellay trumps Petrarch. The renown of place and poetry are tied up together in a close-knit poetic metonymy that almost eclipses the original subject of praise: the woman, Olive. (Olive is only named twice in the whole collection, in sonnets 24 and 76, while the Loire is named specifically eight times, and evoked on many more occasions in formulae such as 'mon fleuve.') The fame of Petrarch's Laura will not be answered by Du Bellay's Olive so much as by his river. As we have noted, an olive tree – symbol of Athens – is not necessarily French. But the Loire is entirely French, from source to end. What is more, Du Bellay eclipses the historical Petrarch's significant presence in France by situating him firmly in

Italy rather than in Avignon, where Petrarch had spent part of his life and, more importantly, where he claimed to have met Laura in 1327. France, rather than Italy, is in fact the site of Petrarch's lyric love story, but for Du Bellay to admit this would lessen a lot of the work performed by his dialogue between Italian and French landscapes. Laura or the laurel tree is replanted in Italy, while a French river will assume the tropes of her fame and beauty.

The question of beauty is, as Philip Schwyzer has argued, an important category for understanding the self-definition and enduring appeal of nations: 'it is questionable whether [the nation] would have survived so long as an ideology, were it not for the fact that nations – all of them – are enduringly, achingly beautiful.' Schwyzer also gives due attention to the tension between regional and national, which is appropriate for France although he is discussing early modern England: 'to recognize the possibility of topographical beauty would be to locate beauty in a part rather than in the whole, and thus to invite the confusion of national and regional loyalties.'[32] In *L'Olive*, Du Bellay locates beauty in the 'part' of his regional Anjou, praising and sublimating local landmarks which take on the attributes and descriptives previously applied to a lady. Much of this transformation is effected through the body: Petrarchan descriptives of the female body are easily transferable to landscape and lend themselves particularly well to a (re)imagining of place.[33] The genre of the poetic *blason*, representing the woman 'by a series of part objects whose variety imposes an anatomically fragmented representation' renders her body parts, like topological landmarks, as 'privileged *loci* of physical celebration.'[34] Of course, the metamorphosis of landscape into woman or vice versa goes back to Ovid. In Petrarch's descriptions of Laura, too, there is an Ovidian permeability between Laura's body and the landscape, for example: 'I have many times (now who will believe me?) seen her alive in the clear water and on the green grass and in the trunk of a tree.'[35] Also at work is the Renaissance concept of nature as *perpetuum mobile*, constantly shifting matter into new forms, and seen as the source of potentially boundless *varietas* both exhilarating and troubling.[36] Du Bellay transposes this philosophical and Ovidian-Petrarchan fluidity onto French landscapes whose local topographies share descriptive conventions with the tradition of praise of the loved lady's beautiful body.

Poetry, then, allows for a particular kind of landscape to be described, and Petrarchan love lyric contains descriptive and thematic conventions which lend themselves well to the writing of an idealized landscape:

following the metamorphoses of exemplar poets, Du Bellay adapts the gendered topological praise of lyric, to a specific topography of Anjou. But his landscape is not only particular and local. There is also a sustained mythic dimension to Du Bellay's geography, already signalled in the sonnet discussed above by the capitalization of 'Ocean' in the fourth line of the first quatrain.[37] It is the landscape of myth that dominates the rest of the sonnet. The poet commands the river to command a troop of Naiads to praise his lady, who is still not named:

> Commande doncq' aux gentiles Naïades
> Sortir dehors leurs beaux palais humides
> Avecques toy, leur fleuve paternel,
> Pour saluer de joyeuses aubades
> Celle qui t'a, et tes filles liquides
> Déifié de ce bruyt eternel.   (*L'Olive* 3)

> [Command, therefore, that the sweet Naiads come out from their lovely humid palaces with you, their paternal river, to praise with joyful aubades she who has deified you and your watery daughters with this everlasting fame.]

Du Bellay is populating the Angevin landscape with the water nymphs of Greek and Ovidian tradition, claiming France as a legitimate site for such poetry. This is only the third sonnet of the collection, and by its conclusion, Du Bellay has claimed that his Angevin river is famous, that it is more deserving of praise than Petrarch's river, that it is inhabited by the denizens of classical poetry come to live in France, and that both river and Naiads praise his lady who has made them, in turn, famous. In the rest of the collection, the river becomes such an important poetic vehicle that it is scarcely necessary to name it (after a certain point, Du Bellay starts to write 'fleuve heureux' or 'mon fleuve').

L'Olive 60 highlights particularly well the equivalency between river and fame, and the kind of poetic nation-building, through landscape, I am identifying. In this sonnet, Du Bellay is asking his French peer Ronsard to leave his river, the Loir, to come and increase the fame of the Loire.

> Divin Ronsard, qui de l'arc à sept cordes
> Tiras premier au but de la *memoire*
> Les traictz aelez de la Françoise *gloire*,

Que sur ton luc haultement tu accordes.
Fameux harpeur et prince de noz odes,
Laisse ton Loir haultain de ta victoire
Et vien sonner au rivage de Loire
De tes chansons les plus nouvelles modes.
Enfonce l'arc du vieil Thebain archer,
Où nul que toy ne sceut onq' encocher
Des doctes Soeurs les sajettes divines.
Porte pour moy parmy le ciel des Gaulles
Le sainct honneur des nymphes Angevines,
Trop pesant faix pour mes foibles epaules.   (L'Olive 60, my emphasis)

We find the obvious rhyme of *Loire* with *gloire*, and also with *memoire* and *victoire*; in the tercets, the word *Angevines* rhymes with *divines*.[38] And so although Du Bellay is adopting a posture of humility towards Ronsardian greatness, he writes into his end-rhymes a direct equivalence between Angevin geography and the vocabulary of poetic renown that – formally at least – excludes Ronsard. It is true that Ronsard's river 'Loir haultain' is indistinguishable, in the spoken word, from Du Bellay's river; however, it is excluded from the privileged end-rhyme position and replaced in the tercets by the word 'Angevines,' which cannot be mistaken for any part of Ronsard's Touraine. This sonnet illustrates succinctly the simultaneous collaboration and rivalry between Ronsard and Du Bellay, and how it plays out in landscape as a productive tension between regionalism and national sentiment. The praise of Anjou is part of Du Bellay's particular bid for poetic renown, but it is also harnessed as part of the *collective* construction of a national poetry, as seen in line 12, where Ronsard is asked to trumpet Angevin greatness in the 'ciel des Gaulles' – to a pan-regional, national readership. The invocation of Ronsard thus has a double function: simultaneously to act as a foil for Du Bellay's regional and poetic specificity, and to serve as an ally in a collectively imagined construction of a lyric France. And behind this pose of humility lurks a third interlocutor, Petrarch, whose *Canzoniere XX* expresses his poetic incapacity faced with the greatness of his subject matter.[39] While Petrarch concludes with the familiar inexpressibility topos, Du Bellay trumps Petrarch by making an appeal to another French poet, to a poetic collectivity that Petrarch did – or could – not imagine.

Gradually, Petrarchan desire is deflected from a female love-object onto Du Bellay's Angevin landscape, particularly the Loire, which is thus eroticized. In the last sonnet of the first edition of *L'Olive*, which had only fifty sonnets,[40] we see that the lady's body has disappeared entirely and has become the river. Du Bellay uses the adjective 'fameux' to refer to a confluence of two rivers, and not to his lady, who is again only evoked vaguely. After the first quatrain in which he compares himself to Leander, he continues:

> Dessoubz mes chants voudront (possible) apprendre
> Maint bois sacré et maint antre sauvage,
> Non gueres loing de ce fameux rivage
> Ou Meine va dedans Loyre se rendre.
> Puis descendant en la saincte forest
> Ou maint amant à l'umbrage encor'est
> Iray chanter au bord oblivieux.   (*L'Olive* 59)

[Many a sacred wood and wild cave / Will perhaps hear of my singing, / Not far from that famous river bank / Where the Meine flows into the Loire. / Then, descending into the sacred forest / Where many a lover is still hiding, / I will sing to the forgetful bank.]

Du Bellay presents a mythological poetic landscape which is out of time and place, then telescopes by a sort of zoom-lens effect into a precise chorographic reference to the place where the Maine river joins the Loire,[41] and then zooms out again to the land of nymphs and lover-poets. The confluence of Maine and Loire is Lavoir, at Ruseboucq (now Bouchemaine), where Du Bellay visited his cousin Olive de Sévigné. It is not even the name of the place that he gives to stand in for the lady, but rather a verbal picture of a local chorographical feature, the joining of two rivers.

The expanded edition of *L'Olive* continues to substitute the Petrarchan lady with French landscape. In the median sonnet of the 1550 edition of *L'Olive*, number 71, we find in the conventional *blason* of the fragmented woman a gradual metamorphosis of her body into the Loire valley, with the rhyming of *Loire* and *ivoire* adding a new turn to this overused descriptive:

> Ce cler vermeil, ce vermeil unissant
> Œillez et lyz freschement enfantez,
> Ces deux beaux rancz de perles, bien plantez,
> Et tout ce rond en deux pars finissant,

Ce val d'albastre, et ces couteaux d'ivoire
Qui vont ainsi comme les flotz de Loire
Au lent soupir d'un zephire adoulci.   (*L'Olive* 71)

[This bright scarlet, which resembles both / The carnation and the lily just budding, / These two lovely rows of pearls, perfectly in order, / And the whole rounded off on either side, / This vale of alabaster, and these ivory hillsides, / Whose movements are like those of the Loire / Waving to the slow sigh of a sweet Zephyr.]

The median position is a privileged one in a sonnet sequence, particularly if one thinks in terms of Conley's 'graphic unconscious' ordering the space of the text;[42] the middle of the book, translated into visual terms, would be the area on which the gaze would first fall. What is going on in this sonnet is, then, particularly significant: another overwriting of Italy and Petrarchan conceits by French place. The direct intertext is Ariosto's portrait of Alcina in the *Orlando furioso*, itself derivative of Petrarchism, and much used by Pléiade poets to describe female beauty.[43] What may appear on first reading to be a derivative imitation of Italian models is in fact subtly transformed and claimed as French by Du Bellay's Angevin landscape. The lengthy list of similes – teeth as pearls, alabaster curves – culminates in a comparison between the lady's ivory breasts (couteaux d'ivoire) and the waves of the Loire, with the key words *ivoire* and *Loire* in the rhyme position.

Petrarch's *canzone* 'Di pensier in pensier,' *Canzoniere* 129, is a primary model for the movement between female body and landscape in this sonnet, and Du Bellay modifies the Petrarchan model in important ways. Petrarch describes the hallucinatory power of the lover-poet's imagination to create and recreate images of Laura's body within the landscape through which he wanders. Yet there is a strange fluidity of selfhood, an exchangeability of lover and lady, and an indeterminacy of landscape, in Petrarch's poem, which is replaced in Du Bellay by a unidirectional movement from lady out to landscape. From the first line of Petrarch's poem, landscape is described primarily as a mental state, thoughts as mountains, mountains as thoughts: 'From thought to thought, from mountain to mountain, Love guides me.'[44] With every step, he tells his readers, a new thought of Laura is born. He sees Laura in stones, in the water, on the grass, in a beech tree, in a cloud; the landscape he traverses functions as metaphor for the pain of burning Love. The last two stanzas resolve the movement between interior and exterior landscape as a problem of distance, the distance separating the poet in Italy from

Laura in France. Space is described in physical terms, and the mental landscape of suffering is projected outwards to become the Alps, the barrier separating the poet from his love. The space beyond the Alps, Vaucluse in France, is described as the place of poetic and amorous fulfilment, an Arcadia of contentment, a place where the poet can assume again a physical existence rather than remaining the disembodied intelligence roaming across a wild terrain of mental images:

> Song, beyond those Alps, where the sky is more clear and happy, you shall see me again beside a running stream, where the breeze from a fresh and fragrant laurel can be felt: there is my heart, and she who steals it from me: here you can see only my image.[45]

France is figured as a bucolic landscape from which Petrarch's poet is excluded. Du Bellay recaptures and redirects Petrarch's desire for France, grounding it firmly in Anjou: he, Du Bellay, is the Petrarch that Petrarch himself was not. He trumps his Italian rival by being a lover-poet *in* France. And whereas Petrarch's landscape is evoked to describe a sense of alienation from the self and distance from the lover, Du Bellay's is evoked to ground and resolve this lyric longing.[46]

This transformation of local chorography into an Arcadian landscape in which conventional love-lyric *topoi* can be included affords Du Bellay a means of placing – that is, territorializing – his poetic identity and enterprise in a way that Petrarch did not. Du Bellay resolves Petrarchan longing and not-belonging by mapping out an amorous landscape peculiar to him. In a direct imitation of Petrarch's famous invitation to his readers to come and admire Laura – 'Whoever wishes to see all that Nature and Heaven can do among us / let him come gaze on her'[47] – Du Bellay again redirects the readers' gaze towards Anjou. Petrarch's sonnet invites the readers, should they wish to, to contemplate the apogee of Nature's creation, Laura, before her beauty fades. The poem becomes a complex meditation on time, death, beauty, writing, and reading. Du Bellay, however, in *Olive* 62, invites his readers to admire a tree, an invitation that quickly becomes an invitation to look at his river, effecting another transformation of Petrarchan lyric through and into French landscape.

> Qui voudra voir le plus precieux arbre,
> Que l'orient ou le midy avoüe,
> Vienne, où mon fleuve en ses ondes se joüe:
> Il y verra l'or, l'ivoire, et le marbre. (*L'Olive* 62)

[Whoever wishes to see the most precious tree / Known to the east or the west, / Let him come to where my river's waves play: / There he shall see the gold, the ivory, and the marble.]

Du Bellay transforms the Italian lyric similes of gold (Laura's hair), ivory (teeth), and marble (skin) into features not of a French woman but of French landscape. This is a similar transformation of lyric convention to the one we saw in the median sonnet, where the alabaster bosom of a woman metamorphosizes into smooth river banks.

This sonnet then moves from Petrarch to a panoply of poets, classical and French, with whom he claims at least equality, if not superiority. The establishing of poetic reputation is again given in geographic terms, and in particular through rivers, which function antonomastically to represent other lyric poets.

Il y verra les perles, le cinabre
Et le crystal: et dira que je loüe
Un digne object de Florence et Mantoue,
De Smyrne encor', de Thebes et Calabre
Encor' dira que la Touvre et la Seine[48]
Avec' la Saone arriveroient a peine
A la moitié d'un si divin ouvrage:
Ni cetuy là qui naguere a faict lire
En letters d'or gravé sur son rivage
Le vieil honneur de l'une et l'autre lire.[49]   (*L'Olive* 62)

[There he shall see the pearls, the scarlet / And the crystal, and he shall say that I praise / An object worthy of Florence and Mantua, / Worthy too of Smyrna, Thebes and Calabra. / (The reader) will even say that the Touvre, the Seine / And the Saone will barely achieve / The half of such a divine project: / Not even the one who recently has celebrated, / By engraving it on his banks in letters of gold, / The ancient honour of Pindar and Horace.]

Poetic rivalry is not described in fluvial terms until Du Bellay arrives at the French poets. Petrarch, Virgil, Homer, Pindar, and Horace are invoked by naming their regions of origin. Saint-Gelais, Héroët, Scève, and Ronsard are named by their rivers. France's poetry is here described in cartographic terms, a map in which the Angevin river is drawn large, and other major rivers drawn in peripherally in order to illustrate the position of the Loire relative to them. He has dismissed

Laura and the laurel tree, replacing them with Angevin landmarks, and the negation of the opening sonnet (I do not desire the laurel) has become affirmation and invitation (let the reader come to my river bank and gaze on my tree).

Despite the presence, in this cartographic jostling for position, of Du Bellay's French peers and of classical forebears alike, Petrarch remains the primary interlocutor. Specifically, Du Bellay refers to Petrarch's *Canzoniere* 247, which directly precedes 'Whoever wishes to see.'

> It will perhaps seem to someone that, in my praise of her whom I adore on earth, my style errs in making her noble beyond all others, holy, wise, charming, chaste and beautiful. I believe the opposite, and I am afraid she is offended by my too humble words, since she is worthy [*degna*] of much higher and finer ones: and who does not believe me, let him come to see her. Then he will say: 'What this man aspires to would exhaust Athens, Arpinum, *Mantua, and Smyrna,* and *the one and the other lyre.*[50] Mortal tongue cannot reach her divine state; Love drives and draws his tongue, not by choice but by destiny.'[51]

Du Bellay's sonnet is in fact a conflation of *Canzoniere* 247 and 248. Du Bellay grounds in Anjou this quest for a worthy object of lyric praise, and rewrites Petrarch's comparison of himself with classical poets as a competition in which he himself triumphs. Petrarchan geography, in this case, is a spatialization of what poetry *cannot* do: no one could adequately describe Laura. Geography in Du Bellay's sonnet is an affirmation of what Du Bellay *can* do since he has found his 'worthy object,'[52] and it is expanded to include a poetic map of France itself in which Du Bellay and the Loire river triumph over other French rivers and their poets.

In 1552, three years after the publication of the first *Olive*, Charles Estienne published *La guide des chemins de France*, a written itinerary of routes (often based on information about pilgrimage routes), distances between and within regional agglomerations, and local information destined to be of use to the foot-traveller. Each region is shown as a discrete subject under its own heading, in relation to others, and implicitly to the Île de France, taken as the 'poinct milieu' [the mid-point].[53] The *Guide* does, as Cynthia Skenazi suggests, provide 'the elements from which a national identity can start to be imagined.' It starts with the words 'le royaume de France' [the kingdom of France] and a description of its natural confines; the hypothetical reader, walking from one place to another, is a truly national citizen. But the kingdom is mapped out through a series of verbal connected networks which, as Skenazi also points out, give rise to a 'reflection on the effects of the relationships between places.'[54] It is this relational dynamic which interests me, an almost infinite number of potential networks with which active readers, equipped with the index and the relative distances, can create a sense of place. Anjou is described almost entirely by how it relates to other regions: 'adher d'un costé a la conté de Touraine, le long de Loire: & de l'autre au Breton Gallo, & au Normand' [on one side it is contiguous with the county of Touraine, along the Loire: and on the other side with Gallo Brittany and Normandy]. This dialectic description is found everywhere in the *Guide*: the roads of Champagne, for example, are only described inasmuch as they lead to other places, 'adressans aux pays limitrophes de France, & conduisans aux autres regions' [directed to the countries bordering on France, and leading to other regions].[55] It is easy to lose sight of the overarching category of the 'pays de France' within the details of regional descriptions and the horizontal relations between regions. Estienne's text illustrates well the need to think of early modern France as a series of relations between places, rather than as a monolithic nation supplanting regional difference.

The *Guide* was very successful, and in 1553 Estienne published a revised version with an annex consisting of a list of 'les fleuves du Royaume' [the rivers of the kingdom]. This was included in the many subsequent editions, and, as Tom Conley has shown, contributed to a growing sense of national pride in France's great rivers among the country's geographers.[56] Symphorien Champier, in his 1556 *Petit traicté des fleuves*, explicitly ties the country's greatness to its rivers: 'La chose que plus anoblist une Province, sont les fleuves [...] la Gaule ha des fleuves aussi nobles et en aussi grand nombre que Provinces ou nation qui soit en Europe' [the things that most ennoble a country are the rivers ... Gaul has rivers as noble and numerous as any nation in Europe].[57]

Fluvial competition is a matter of pride in the emerging image of the nation. It is also co-opted by poets seeking to establish the poetic reputation of their region, their country, and of course themselves.[58] The Loire, described by Champier as the river which has 'un merveilleux cours, et passe par les meilleurs païs et citez de Gaule' [a beautiful course, and which flows by the best regions and towns of Gaul], is claimed by Du Bellay as a 'digne objet' [worthy object] of his lyric, and as a landmark in his poetic map that individuates and distinguishes him. In sonnet 105, addressed to Scève, the Loire takes its place in a competition of poetic achievement with the Saône (Scève) and the Arno (Petrarch). To the image of Scève's poetic glory taking flight, 'le hault voler de ta plume dorée' [the high flight of your gilded pen], he opposes a humble, modest image of his own fame:

> L'Arne superbe adore sur sa rive
> Du sainct Laurier la branche toujours vive,
> Et ta Delie enfle ta Saone lente.
> Mon Loire aussi, demydieu pas mes vers,
> Bruslé d'amour etent les braz ouvers
> Au tige heureux, qu'à ses rives je plante.   (*L'Olive* 105)

[The proud Arno adores on its banks / The evergreen branch of the blessed Laurel, / And your Délie makes your Saône swell. / My Loire, too, made a demi-God through my verse, / Burning with love, stretches out its open arms / To the happy stem which I plant on its banks.]

A sonnet that starts off as an encomium to Scève, describing him and his poetry in mythic-classical terms, turns back in the tercets to Angevin specificity, and to an entirely different image of creation.[59] While Scève is the Horatian swan flying across the known world, Du Bellay is an Angevin gardener, planting the olive branch on the banks of his river.[60] The Loire is the new Arno, Anjou the new Italy, Du Bellay the new Petrarch. Despite Du Bellay's assumed pose of modesty, he has presented a local lyric chorography as a site of poetic production to rival that of the most famous of all lyric poets.

Anjou in *Les Regrets* (1558)

It is clear that Du Bellay's poetic place in *L'Olive* is local and regional more than it is national. To 'map' France poetically in *L'Olive* is to do so regionally; it seems harder to include France as a whole within the thematic and formal constraints of lyric – the sonnet in particular – which lend themselves more to local and qualitative descriptions. Du Bellay himself, in the *Deffence et illustration*, notes the limits of the sonnet and contrasts the form with the expansiveness of the ode: 'le sonnet a certains vers réglés et limités et l'ode peut courir par toutes manières de vers librement' [the sonnet has a certain number of lines of a fixed length, while the ode can run through all sorts of lines freely].[61] The sonnet is an obvious site for the elaboration of chorographic, local description. The differentiation, and the relationship, between the national and the regional becomes a significant theme in Du Bellay's later collection of sonnets, *Les Regrets*, published nine years after the first edition of *L'Olive*. I will show that in this collection, Du Bellay shows how the respective ideas of region and the nation depend on and construct each other in a way that goes beyond metaphoric 'mapping' to a conscious play with cartographic scales.

The previous chapter overviewed the many semantic and practical links between cartography and poetry, and I refer the reader back to it for historical justification of the articulation, as well as for discussion of the often fluid terms *géographie*, *chorographie*, and *cosmographie*. While there is, as discussed, significant overlap between the terms, and no absolute distinction based on mapmaking practice, chorography is usually understood as the mapping of small, distinct regions, framed by natural boundaries such as the curve of a river or a hill. I would like to briefly revisit here my discussion of Frank Lestringant to suggest that implicit in his presentation of the chorography/geography distinction is also a distinction between analogous literary genres. Lestringant, we recall, argues that chorography is allied more closely with literary descriptiveness than is geography: the former measures the 'the quality of the space,' sharing a qualitative dimension with a 'literary or pictorial genre,' and the latter the quantity.[62] Additionally, he defines chorography as that which the human eye can take in at one glance. He adduces, to support this latter point, Pierre Apian's discussion of geography and chorography in his 1553 *Cosmographie*. Apian writes that chorography 'considère seulement aucuns lieux ou places particulières en soy-mesmes, comme si le peintre vouloit contrefaire un seul oeil, ou une oreille' [only takes into account locations and places particular to themselves, as if a painter wanted to represent just an eye or an ear].[63] Chorography is thus understood as the mapping of fragments, the cartographical equivalent of the painting of an eye or an ear, detached from their setting, the head. Recalling Nancy Vickers's analysis of the fragmentation of the female body in Petrarchan lyric, we can posit lyric as the literary analogue of chorography. Just as it is easier to isolate en eye or ear from the face than a cheek, for example, so certain features in the physiognomy of the land lend themselves more to circumscription than others.

The distinction between geography and chorography turns out not to be so much a distinction between *quantum* and *quale* as a difference of scale and perspective between two qualitative practices. Like chorography, geographical representation is subjective and selective, and can also be likened to literary discourse, to 'something written.'[64] Or to something painted: Apian writes that geography is 'constituée au regard de toute la rondeur de la terre, à l'exemple de ceulx qui veulent entierement paindre la teste d'une personne avec ses proportions' [constituted by the view of the whole earth, like those who want to paint a person's entire head with due proportion]. If the genre of localized chorographic description is lyric, then the genre which espouses the larger geographical perspective is epic. Apian observes that geography is a science 'prouffitable à ceulx qui desirent scavoir les histoires et gestes des Princes' [profitable to those who want to know the histories and heroic actions of princes]. The alliance of geography with *gestes* – the territorial expansion and conquests of the nobility – suggests a generic parallel between geography and epic.

L'Olive showed that the space of lyric tends to the local. National space in *L'Olive* is too large to be circumscribed comfortably by his lyrics; it is more through his identification with Anjou and his transformation of certain features of that region into poetic place that the poet can construct an identity and imagine his own poetic success. But the local is always constructed in dialogue with other scales, and this is clearly illustrated in *Les Regrets*. Indeed, Du Bellay's poetic journey from *L'Olive* to *Les Regrets*, and the journey to and from Rome within *Les Regrets*, can be seen as a search for appropriate boundaries and descriptive scales for poetry.

In *Les Regrets*, the image Du Bellay creates of the miserable exile (itself an appropriation of a Latin tradition), and the poetic identity this allows him to inhabit,[65] is achieved largely through his images of Anjou while he is in Rome. But – and this is a crucial move – this idealized Anjou, which is also that of *L'Olive*, breaks up upon his return, when he finds it is not the 'plaisant séjour' it seemed while he was away, and the poet is forced to turn elsewhere for a fitting subject of lyric idealization. Whereas *L'Olive* participates in a kind of lyric dialogue with the established norms of the Petrarchan love sonnet, *Les Regrets* announce a new subject matter and departure for the lyric project – an uneasy, messy, and miserable day-to-day life in Rome, a poetics which 'exploits the day-to-day and the trivial.'[66] While still using only sonnets, Du Bellay experiments with lyric content in ways that radically redefine it – sonnets that express boredom, disgust – and that are more epigrammatic or epistolary than lyric.[67]

Du Bellay tries to keep Anjou separate from the economic and mundane Roman world he depicts, but can only sustain this separation for so long. The lyric, poetic Anjou eventually dissolves, and becomes instead the focus for the same kind of anxieties he found in Rome. Regionalism as poetic discourse is exposed for what it is, a pure construct, and Du Bellay turns back to the nationalist imperative, finally finding an adequate subject in the traditional object of lyric praise: a women, Marguerite de France, who also happens to incarnate the nation.

Les Regrets start with chorography. Du Bellay establishes the local, large-scale parameters in the first sonnet, where he telescopes from the 'architecture' of the sky, in the first quatrain, into the 'accidents divers' of 'ce lieu' in the second – a shift from universal to particular, or in cartographic terms, from cosmography to chorography: 'Je ne veulx point fouiller au seing de la nature / [...] / Mais suivant *de ce lieu* les accidents divers.'[68] Here, as in the opening sonnet of *L'Olive*, Du Bellay starts with a negation, this time specifically of small-scale, undifferentiated space. The cosmological and the geographical are evoked uneasily, in a context of displacement, as if they were too grand and too large for the lyric mode. He is also rejecting a specific metaphysical kind of poetry – that of Pontus de Tyard, for example – and drawing the boundaries of his own poetry, a poetry of localized perspective.[69] The 'lieu' (place) corresponds to the sense of place discussed in the introduction. Implicitly contrasted with 'espace' (space), place is inhabited and defined by human perception: 'when humans invest meaning in a portion of space and then become attached to it in some way [...] it becomes a place.'[70]

Like *L'Olive*, *Les Regrets* start with a rejection – a rejection of space in favour, one would presume, of place. But the kind of redemptive chorography we see in *L'Olive*, where Angevin topography enables Du Bellay to replant Petrarchan lyric in French soil and to escape from a sense of non-belonging, is not possible in Rome. Rome is a space that resists any kind of mapping. Renaissance France had a fraught relationship with Italy in general, seeing it as a source of linguistic and political corruption, effeminate mannerisms, and cultural colonialism. War between the two countries had led in France to an anti-Italianism that itself helped define the parameters of Frenchness.[71] And the disappointment of French humanists in Rome, witnessing what they identified as the moral and cultural decline of the cradle of civilization, became a Renaissance cliché ('Rome n'est plus Rome,' Du Bellay writes in *Regrets* 131).[72] Whereas Anjou could be represented topophilically, Rome is what Marc Augé would call a 'non-lieu,' one that denies the possibility of roots and affective identification.[73] The Roman landscape is a confusing clutter of ruins (an image already elaborated in the *Deffence*, as we shall see), emptied of natural landmarks and horizons, and even these ruins exist in a vague place between myth and history, past and present, reality and ghosts. The Roman landscape is unruly, uncontainable by any natural chorographic boundaries. The first spatial imagery used to describe Rome (and even then it is metaphorical) is that of the plain, a space which can only be delimited by surrounding landmarks – a plain is understood as a space between prominent natural boundaries, and there are none here. This is in the preliminary 'À M. D'Avanson': 'J'estois à Rome / [...] / Ainsi voit-on celuy qui sur la plaine / Pique le boeuf.' The plain reappears in the famous sonnet 9, 'France mère des arts,' where the poet represents himself in Italy as wandering 'parmy la plaine' – a vague, unmapped space.

However it seems that even France cannot be mapped. In this very sonnet, part of the French national imaginary for generations, the country as a whole is unrepresentable.

> France mère des arts, des armes et des lois,
> Tu m'as nourry long temps du laict de ta mamelle:
> Ores comme un aigneau qui sa nourrice appelle
> Je remplis de ton nom les antres et les bois.   (*Les Regrets* 9)

> [France, mother of arts, of arms, and of laws, you long nourished me with the milk of your breast. Now, like a lamb that calls for its nurse, I fill the caves and woods with the sound of your name.]

The name of France, a designation of a specific geographical area, falls nowhere when he cries it aloud, indeed it sent back to him by Echo. France is an empty appellation without grounding, and the poet who speaks it fails to find comfort. His attempt at mapping has failed; he cannot include even an imagined, conjured French space within the sonnet.[74]

It will only be in the evocation of Anjou that Du Bellay is able to imagine a defined, delimited space with certain landmarks, which fits into the forms of lyric poetry. In one of the better-known homesickness sonnets, *Regrets* 19, his initial longing for France, which found no rhetorical resolution in 'France mère des arts,' finds an outlet through focusing on a smaller space – Anjou.

Ce pendant que tu dis ta Cassandre divine,
Les louanges du Roy, et l'heritier d'Hector,
Et ce Montmorancy, nostre François Nestor,
Et que de sa faveur Henry t'estime digne:
Je me pourmene seul sur la rive Latine,
La France regretant, et regretant encor
Mes antiques amis, mon plus riche tresor,
Et le plaisant sejour de ma terre Angevine.
Je regrete les bois, et les champs blondissans,
Les vignes, les jardins, et les prez verdissans,
Que mon fleuve traverse: icy pour recompense
Ne voiant que l'orgueil de ces monceaux pierreux,
Où me tient attaché d'un espoir malheureux,
Ce que possede moins celuy qui plus y pense.   (*Les Regrets* 19)

[While you sing your divine Cassandre, the praises of the king and
Hector's heir, and Montmorency, our French Nestor, and while Henry
judges you worthy of his favor, I wander alone on the Latin shore, longing
for France, and longing, too, for my old friends, my richest treasure, and
for my pleasant Angevin home. I miss the woods and the ripening fields,
the vines, the gardens, and the meadows turning green through which my
river runs: here, instead of all that, Seeing only the pride of these piles of
stone, where I am held by a vain hope for that which he least attains who
desires it most.]

The sonnet can be read as a quest for an appropriate lyric subject. The
first tercet addresses Ronsard, and the subjects of Ronsard's lyric praise,
subjects and discourses from which Du Bellay represents himself as excluded. His malaise draws significantly on the Petrarchan language of
longing, as if to be in Italy were inevitably to become Petrarch exiled
from the love and even the presence of Laura. The rest of the sonnet is
created by, and about, the voice of the exile, wandering alone on the
'rive Latine,' and the wandering itself becomes the lyric subject, settling
– albeit briefly – in Anjou. He passes from an evocation of 'La France' to
that of 'le plaisant sejour de ma terre Angevine,' and it is this regional,
chorographic limit to space which allows him to present a poetic map
of the area, its woods, fields, vineyards, and meadows traversed by
'his' river. Anjou thus imagined is the ideal poetic contrast to Rome,
which as we have seen resists any kind of spatial ordering. Its landmarks are arranged into an orderly space of pastoral ideal, each feature

standing in an antonomastic relationship with the whole Anjou. Rome on the other hand presents no such boundaries, nor any landmarks which can be taken as a figure for the whole: all the poet sees is 'L'orgeuil de ces monceaux pierreux' – more rubble. Anjou becomes a world of ideal lyric convention, a neat well-ordered space set against a chaotic world of commerce and corruption. It seems to repatriate the poet *qua* lyric poet, conjuring away the dispersion and banality of the Roman experience.

However, this will not last for long. One irony of the posture of the lyric poet who is homesick for France, and for a particular region of France already identified with a lyric love-object, is that it turns Du Bellay back into Petrarch, at least the Petrarch of 'Di pensier in pensier' discussed above. To articulate such longing for France from Italy, Du Bellay must adopt the pose of the lover separated from his lady in France by the mountains. Du Bellay, as I have argued, rewrote this posture in *L'Olive* by a deliberate celebration of being in France, in the place Petrarch longed to be. Here Du Bellay is, like Petrarch, in Italy and longing for France. French lyric regionalism only works to trump Petrarch if it is expressed from within France. Articulated from Italy, it turns him into Petrarch.[75]

Anjou must therefore disperse as a lyric space. As the 'digne objet' of lyric that Du Bellay seeks through the whole sequence, it is untenable. Du Bellay turns away from idealization of a localized French space from Italy that turns him into Petrarch (and that necessitates borrowing from Petrarchan language of longing), and in order *not* to be Petrarch any more, he introduces a new kind of discourse about Anjou into the sequence. This dissipation of Anjou as lyrically ordered space, and its redefinition as a space ordered more by Du Bellay's own voice, can be seen in Du Bellay's use of the most basic linguistic mark of identification: the possessive.

Du Bellay applies two kinds of possessive to Anjou, or to its landmarks, in *Les Regrets*, which we could categorize as subjective and objective. The subjective possessive is that which expresses, not actual possession, but an emotional identification with a place. Such is the case in sonnet 25:

Malheureux l'an, le mois, le jour, l'heure, et le poinct,
Et malheureuse soit la flateuse esperance,
Quand pour venir icy j'abandonnay la France,
La France, et mon Anjou, dont le désir me poingt.   (*Les Regrets* 25)

[Cursed be the year, the month, the day, the hour, and the instant, and cursed be the flattering hope, when to come here I left France, France and my Anjou, for which longing torments me.]

The passage from *la* France to *mon* Anjou marks an increased subjective identification. The conceit of the possessive is the stuff of lyric. The close echo of Petrarch's sonnet 61, 'Benedetto sia'l giorno e'l mese et l'anno' [Blessed be the day and the month and the year], in which he remembers the first encounter with 'mia donna,' places Du Bellay's whole sonnet in the context of Petrarchan convention, replacing desire for the lady with desire for Anjou.

Objective possession signals a relationship between speaker and object which is more than poetic conceit. In sonnet 19, the sonnet discussed above, we see 'mon fleuve' (which is subjective – the river only 'belongs' to him in the land of lyric), and 'ma terre Angevine,' which points to an objective reality, that of economic and social fact. The Du Bellay family did own territory, the estate of La Turmelière in the Angevin province of Liré.[76] The actual fact of possession seems to do something to poetic discourse; it introduces a set of uncomfortable social and economic anxieties into lyric space. The two kinds of possession in this sonnet announce the rupture between ideal and corrupted Anjou.

Thus the limited, chorographic space of Anjou is not, in *Les Regrets*, a successful metonymy for ideal lyric. As soon as it is actualized by a reference to its status as real land, it can no longer be a lyric space. Instead, in sonnet 31, it seems to become epic space, the uncomfortable, too-large space of geography that cannot fit into lyric.

Heureux qui, comme Ulysse, a fait un beau voyage,
Ou comme cestuy là qui conquit la toison
Et puis est retourné, plein d'usage et raison
Vivre entre ses parents le reste de son aage!
Quand revoiray-je, hélas, de mon petit village
Fumer la cheminée, et en quelle saison
Revoiray-je le clos de ma pauvre maison
Qui m'est une province, et beaucoup d'avantage?
Plus me plaist le sejour qu'ont basty mes ayeux,
Que des palais Romains le front audacieux:
Plus que le marbre dur me plaist l'ardoise fine,
Plus mon Loyre Gaulois, que le Tybre Latin

Plus mon petit Lyré, que le mont Palatin,
Et plus que l'air marin la doulceur Angevine.   (*Les Regrets* 31)

[Happy the man who, like Ulysses, has traveled well, or like that man who
conquered the fleece, and has then returned, full of experience and wisdom, to live among his kinfolk the rest of his life! When, alas, will I see
again smoke rising from the chimney of my little village and in what sea-
son will I see the enclosed field of my poor house, which to me is a province and much more still? The home my ancestors built pleases me more
than the grandiose facades of Roman palaces, fine slate pleases me more
than hard marble, My Gallic Loire more than the Latin Tiber, my little Liré
more than the Palatine hill, and more than sea air, the sweetness of Anjou.]

The return to Anjou is imagined in epic-mythic terms, with the reference to Ulysses and to Jason. Such figurings of the epic return were
commonplace in sixteenth-century writings; it is not my intention to
explore the full implications of Du Bellay's self-styling as Ulysses or
Jason, but rather to consider how this pose works spatially, what is the
poetic persona's relationship to land.[77] However, the references to epic
personae carry a note of foreboding that has been unpacked only by G.
Hugo Tucker:[78] neither Ulysses nor Jason returned home 'heureux,' but
rather were engaged in struggles to assert their claim to kingship – an
epic parallel to the Du Bellay family's struggle against the Malestroict
family. Conflicts between important families are hardly lyric matter.
The smoking chimney in the following quatrain is of course a conventional epic image of exile and strife: Ulysses expresses the same desire
in the *Odyssey*, before setting off for years of wanderings,[79] and Aeneas
and company see smoking chimneys before they land on the island of
the Strophades, where they encounter the Harpies.[80] The sense that this
will be an unhappy return is accented by the possessives 'mon village'
and 'ma pauvre maison,' which, as suggested above, introduce an economic reality that will in fact make his return troublesome. The adjective 'pauvre' in this context brings into the sonnet's sense of place the
financial hardship brought upon the Du Bellays by the Oudon trials.
The synecdochal relationship between the 'pauvre maison' and the
'province' – his house *is* his province – suggests that his whole experience of Liré will be inflected by these troubles.

In the three tercets, Du Bellay sets up a series of polar oppositions between his land and Rome. On either side, equivalent landmarks are compared – buildings, stone, rivers, hills, and climate. He is simultaneously

mapping the chorography of Rome and of Anjou. The geographical space between the points under comparison, from France to Italy and back again, set up the distance from which it is possible to imagine Anjou as an ideal space,[81] and apply lyric, subjective possessives to its landmarks: 'mon Loyre,' 'mon petit Lyré.' In fact, subjective preference is the only thing which distinguishes Rome from Anjou: the whole comparison hinges on 'plus me plaict.' He makes no claim to an inherent superiority for Anjou. He is illustrating the very process by which the poet builds his land into a perfect lyric space: by creating distance from which the land can be sublimated. The concluding words of the sonnet, 'la doulceur Angevine,' have been much discussed.[82] In an excellent discussion of the taxonomy of 'doulceur' in Du Bellay, Louis Terreaux points out the many ways in which it is primarily a literary term, and above all *not* climatic.[83] In particular, 'douceur' points to the pastoral mode. Homesickness for Anjou is shown to be an entirely literary type of experience, a lyric longing in the Petrarchan tradition. Ironically, then, when Du Bellay is appearing to claim his individual and poetic identity through description of his region of origin, he is also arguably at his most derivative. It is this realization that his homesickness cannot make him into the anti-Petrarch that drives Du Bellay to a more unusual and personal representation of Anjou, a territorial representation which is also a staking out of his own poetic 'territory,' or voice. This voice comes from the articulation of actual presence in Anjou, and Anjou's status as real, not literary, space. As we will see in sonnet 130, this new kind of Anjou leads to 'milles soucys mordants,' a peculiarly novel kind of literary and lyric experience that Du Bellay will claim as his own.

From 'Heureux qui comme Ulysses' onwards, Anjou will cease to be a perfect pastoral space, and will become the focus of economic concerns that preclude lyric description. There are no more idyllic tableaux of Anjou, only references to the worry caused by land ownership. Sonnet 38 presents an autarchic fantasy in which he imagines an ideal aristocratic existence on his home territory, not bound up with investments ('le miserable soing d'aquerir d'avantage'), or desiring anything beyond 'son propre héritage.' But the subject of this sonnet is an imaginary someone, 'heureux qui,' further distanced by his borrowing (again) from the well-established tradition of *Beatus ille*. Du Bellay himself was, as we have seen, forced to become involved in 'affaires d'autruy.' We find another imagined 'heureux qui' in sonnet 94: he who does not have to 'vendre sa terre' – a reference perhaps to René Du Bellay's sale of two family territories in 1532 to finance the acquisition of Oudon.

As noted above, Anjou is not evoked directly after sonnet 31. The only indication that he has actually returned there is in sonnet 130, where he observes that he has not left behind the 'vice' of Rome; in fact, he is 'encor' Romain.'

> Et je pensois aussi ce que pensoit Ulysse,
> Qu'il n'estoit rien plus doulx que voir encor' un jour
> Fumer sa cheminée, et apres long sejour
> Se retrouver au sein de sa terre nourrice.
> [...]
> Las mais apres l'ennuy de si longue saison,
> Mille souciz mordants je trouve en ma maison,
> Qui me rongent le coeur sans espoir d'allegance.
> Adieu doncques (Dorat) je suis encor' Romain.   (*Les Regrets* 130)

[And I too thought what Ulysses thought: that there was nothing sweeter than for a man one day to see again smoke rising from his chimney and after a long absence to find himself once more in the bosom of the land that nursed him ... Alas, but after the weariness of such a long time away, I find in my house a thousand biting cares that gnaw at my heart without hope of relief. So adieu, Dorat, I am a Roman still.]

The figure of Ulysses reappears from sonnet 31, as well as the smoking chimney, and the reader is hardly surprised that the return to the 'terre nourrice' is disappointing: the poet finds the same kind of *ennui* there as he did in Rome: 'Mille soucys mordants je trouve en ma maison.'

Anjou then is left out of the rest of the collection. It can no longer be written about as the lyric counterpart to corrupt Rome, and the attempt at chorographic description is abandoned. Nor is there is anywhere in the whole of France, it seems, that can be described as lyric landscape. The return into France is through Lyon, described in sonnet 137, addressed to Scève (whose poetry is one of the most important 'sites' of Petrarchism in France).[84] The sonnet starts with a reference to Aeneas in the underworld, with whom the poet compares himself. But the classical reference is quickly overwritten by a detailed, circumstantial, and surprising description of Lyonnais territory.

Sceve, je me trouvay comme le filz d'Anchise
Entrant dans l'Elysee, et sortant des enfers,
Quand après tant de monts de neige tous couvers
Je vis ce beau Lyon, Lyon que tant je prise.
Son estroicte longueur, que la Sone divise,
Nourrit mil artisans, et peuples tous divers:
Et n'en desplaise à Londre, à Venise, et Anvers,
Car Lyon n'est pas moindre en fait de marchandise.
Je m'estonnay d'y voir passer tant de courriers,
D'y voir tant de banquiers, d'imprimeurs, d'armuriers,
Plus dru que l'on ne void les fleurs par les prairies.
Mais je m'estonnay plus de la force des pontz,
Desus lesquelz on passe, allant au dela les montz
Tant de belles maisons, et tant de metairies.   (*Les Regrets* 137)

[Scève, I found myself like the son of Anchises entering Elysium and leaving Hades when after so many snowcapped peaks I saw this beautiful Lyon, Lyon that I so much admire. Its narrow length, which the Saône divides, supports a thousand craftsmen and people of all sorts. And let London, Venice, and Antwerp take no offense, for Lyon is not inferior in commerce. I was astonished to see so many couriers passing by, to see so many bankers, printers, armorers more thickly crowded than flowers in the fields. But I was more astonished by the strength of the bridges on which they transport so many fine houses and so many estates (given over to sharecropping) on their way over the mountains].[85]

First, he attempts to map Lyon with a lyric chorographical description ('ce beau Lyon … que la Sone divise'). But chorography is soon replaced by commercial discourse; the rivalry between different places associated with certain poets is replaced here with a purely economic rivalry; Lyon turns just as much trade as London, Venice, and Anvers. Indeed, the place appears very much as he described Rome, the lyrically unmappable place, with 'mil artisans,' flourishing commercial activity, and in the background the 'ponts' and 'monts' which lead back to Italy. Attempts to describe the city as a space of natural lyric beauty are thwarted by references to human activity, in a strange conjunction of natural and man-made which pushes the boundaries of landscape traditionally represented by lyric. The only attempt to describe Lyon as lyric landscape is in a somewhat awkward metaphor, in the first tercet, in which entrepreneurs are strewn along the streets as thick as meadow flowers. The strange comparison of businessmen with flowers on a prairie is accented by the fact that the rhyme word for 'prairies,' and the last word of the sonnet, is 'metairies,' or shareholdings. This is a reference to contemporary farming practice; sharecropping or *métayage* was gradually substituted, in sixteenth-century France, for traditional methods of agriculture, increasing urban investment in the land.[86] Thus in the rhyme scheme itself we have a direct contrast between a landscape which seems taken straight from pastorally inspired lyric, a flower-strewn prairie, and an altogether different view of land – exploitable terrain divided into units of production and used for economic gain through a contemporary farming method. The reader of this sonnet is transported from the *Aeneid* to the present day, and the transformation from ancient to modern takes place through the description of landscape.

The collapse of the mythologized Anjou and France gives a new dimension to French lyric poetry, and allows Du Bellay finally to free himself, momentarily, from the voice of Petrarchan longing. To inherited conventional lyric landscapes, Du Bellay has added the language of economics and actual land ownership. The presence of classical and Italian authorities is overwritten by a landscape that is undeniably French and of its time. He started in *L'Olive* by applying the language of Petrarchan love lyric to landscape instead, to his local region of France. The Petrarchan woman becomes Du Bellay's land in visible metamorphoses. In *Les Regrets*, sublimated Anjou is initially turned into an imagined rival space to Rome and Italy: Du Bellay is challenging Latin exemplarity literally with Angevin landscapes, but abandons Angevin pastoralism for a particular kind of experience of land and space that allows him to escape from Petrarch's shadow. The dissolution of ideal Anjou on his return, when he realizes that home is no different to Rome, continues the challenge to inherited literary tradition by inflecting its landscapes with contemporary economic discourse (Aeneas journeying through a bustling commercial district in Lyon). Du Bellay's regional identity may have been problematized, but a national French poetry is still imaginable, and indeed France emerges from *Les Regrets* as the poetic victor in the rivalry.

In the final sonnets of *Les Regrets*, the poet turns back to lyric convention and to national poetics. He abandons chorographical local identification to refound his poetic project again in women, Henri II's consort Catherine de' Medici, and her sister-in-law Marguerite de France, daughter of François I, sister of Henri II.[87] He has come full circle from *L'Olive*, where he turned from a woman to a place (a river): here, he turns back from place to women, where the women are emblematic of France as a whole (Catherine was of course queen consort from 1547 to 1559). And the name Marguerite itself, the vernacular name for the common daisy, underlines the conventionality of the praise: the white colour of the flower, a metonymy for the lady's skin, is a popular *topos* of French lyric in the 1550s.[88] The encomiastic tone of the last sonnets has bothered some critics who see in it too radical a departure from the quotidian tone of the rest of the sequence.[89] I propose, on the contrary, that in the final sonnets Du Bellay finds a 'digne objet' of lyric praise that allows him to conclude the sequence in a way that establishes not only himself, but France as a whole, as a rival site of production of lyric poetry to Italy.

The change in perspective is made explicit in sonnet 171, where he tells his muse and his 'souci' to leave Anjou for a higher subject:

> Muse, qui autrefois chantas la verde olive,
> Empenne tes deux flancs d'une plume nouvelle,
> Et te guindant au ciel avecques plus haulte aelle,
> Vole où est d'Apollon la belle plante vive.
> Laisse (mon cher souci) la paternelle rive,
> Et portant desormais une charge plus belle,
> Adore ce hault nom, dont la gloire immortelle
> De nostre pole arctiq' à l'autre pole arrive.
> Loüe l'esprit divin, le courage indontable,
> La courtoise doulceur, la bonté charitable,
> Qui soustient la grandeur et la gloire de France.
> Et dy, Ceste princesse et si grande et si bonne
> Porte dessus son chef de France la couronne:
> Mais dy cela si hault, qu'on l'entende à Florence.[90]   (*Les Regrets* 171)

[Muse, you who once sang the green olive, feather your two wings with a new plume and, lifting to heaven with a higher flight, soar where the beautiful living plant of Apollo resides. Quit, my dear care, the paternal shore and, henceforth charged with a more illustrious task, adore that high name whose undying glory stretches from our arctic pole to the other pole. Praise the divine spirit, the unconquerable courage, the courtly sweetness, the charitable goodness, which upholds the greatness and glory of France. And say, 'This princess, so great and so good, wears on her head the crown of France.' But say it so loudly that they hear it in Florence.]

The winged flight to the skies, a cliché of lyric since Horace, permits a cosmographic perspective which is associated, in a related Stoic philosophical tradition,[91] with wisdom. The turning away from locality to the name of Catherine operates a shift in perspective from the chorographic to the cosmographic, then to the geographic. His name is now bound up with that of Catherine, and thus with that of France as a whole. Catherine, as subject of inspiration, allows for the reappearance of geography (that is, national sentiment) within the space of his poems: her name will travel from one pole to the other. The whole world can be condensed in his poetry through her. His praise of her, which he hopes will be heard in Florence, thus also allows him to reconcile the comparison between France and Italy, a comparison which failed, as we saw, when Anjou was the point of comparison: the space between the two countries is bridged by her name, and France comes out the victor. Among her many praiseworthy qualities we find 'doulceur,' transferred from Anjou in the formula 'doulceur Angevine' to a lady, the original lyric object, but who stands as synecdoche for France as a whole.

The failure of sonnet 9, 'France mère des arts,' to map France – the name of France coming back to him in a lonely echo – is resolved in sonnet 189 in a direct echo of a line from the former sonnet. 'Je remplis de ton nom les antres et les bois,' from sonnet 9, becomes 'Je remplis d'un beau nom ce grand espace vide' [I fill with a glorious name that vast empty space] in sonnet 189. The 'vide' – the undifferentiated 'espace' which was rejected at the start of the collection in search of a 'lieu' – is filled this time by the name of Marguerite; the poet is no longer a lost lamb on the plains, but a swan in the skies, 'un cygne nouveau [...] vers les cieux' [a new swan toward the heavens], embracing the whole world with this new, larger perspective. The local and the individual are absorbed by the greater space of France and the image of a community of poets. He addresses each of a sequence of twelve sonnets (178–189) to a different living poet in turn,[92] including some who were or who had been considered members of the Pléiade. The poets addressed also have in common that they enjoyed the favour of Marguerite, reinforcing the sense of a chosen, closed community. The only non-French poet to be addressed in one of these sonnets (187) is Buchanan, a Scottish intellectual who frequented the courts of Francis I and Henri II. He is however clearly described as an exception, almost a miracle; Du Bellay attributes awesome powers to the Muses for having bred such talent on savage Scottish soil. The implication is of course that France is a more natural breeding ground for poets than Scotland, so even the inclusion of a foreign land in this sonnet sequence adds ultimately to the credit of France.

The sequence of personalized sonnets creates a national community of poets which is then figured as a 'blessed flock' in the penultimate sonnet, a flock needing the guidance and the patronage of Marguerite if France is once again to be the mother of the arts, a pastoral land where native poetry flourishes. Du Bellay has returned to the agenda of the *Deffence*, the construction on French soil of a national poetics; the individual poet wandering lonely on the plain in the beginning of *Les Regrets* has joined up with the rest of the flock and is now part of a group of poets seeking protection together.[93] The last lines of the last sonnet might be read as a cynical avowal of the poet's dependence on patrons, which suggests that the praise is insincere or, at best, merely self-seeking, supported by sufficient royal patronage. Du Bellay asks for the king's protection 'à fin de faire voir / Que de rien un grand Roy peult faire quelque chose' [so as to show that of nothing a great king can make something]. Martin Screech has glossed this as a 'hearty guffaw.'[94] But in the context of what has preceeded, the call for patronage is neither entirely cynical nor a simple *clin d'oeil*. It takes on a particular urgency, as poets are urged to write a different France into existence.[95] The penultimate sonnet echoes indirectly the call to arms of the *Deffence*:

Helicon est tary, Parnasse est une plaine,
Les lauriers sont seichez, et France autrefois pleine
De l'esprit d'Apollon, ne l'est plus que de Mars.
Phoebus s'enfuit de nous, et l'antique ignorance
Sous la faveur de Mars retourne encore en France
Si Pallas[96] ne defend les lettres et les arts.   (*Les Regrets* 190)

[The Helicon has dried up. Parnassus is a plain. The laurels have withered. And France, once filled with the spirit of Apollo, is now filled only with that of Mars. Phoebus will flee us, and ancient ignorance under the patronage of Mars will once again return to France, if Pallas does not defend letters and arts.]

The homonymous 'pleine,' meaning both 'full' and 'plain, wasteland,' accentuates the essential contrast; images of plenty opposed to images of emptiness, hope opposed to fear.[97] Although the wars of religion do not officially start until 1562, tension between religious factions has already erupted into sectarian violence; Henri II himself – Marguerite's brother – overtly favoured the persecution of Huguenots. Du Bellay is urgently calling poets and patrons to fight under the emblem of Apollo rather than Mars, with pens rather than with swords. The landscape of lyric has become a battleground for the future of French poetry and, in a way, of France itself. If the nation is not to be ravaged by civil war, the lyric battleground must replace the real one. Soldiers must become poets, royal favour must be turned away from military endeavours to literary ones. By the end of *Les Regrets*, poetry is the saviour of the nation; the imagining of France as idealized poetic garden takes on a particular urgency. Lyric landscape becomes the remedy to a war-torn one, a place where not only the questions of poetry itself are addressed, but also the most pressing questions of his time. Du Bellay's 'refus' of Petrarch and Italy, his appropriation of them for France, has taken on particular pertinence.

Place in *La Deffence et illustration de la langue françoyse*

Hassan Melehy has noted the spatial dimension to Du Bellay's celebrated treatise, *La Deffence et illustration de la langue françoyse* (1549), whose goal is 'a question not only of ultimately transforming French into a literary language on a par with Greek and Latin, as he would have it, but even more so of inventing a space that the modern language would both frame and occupy.'[98] The imitation of foreign poetic models is presented throughout the *Deffence* as agricultural labour: the French poet must graft and transplant foreign poetry in French soil, where he must tend to and cultivate it with care. The agricultural metaphor is particularly developed in chapter 3 of book 1: just as the Romans carefully cultivated their borrowings from Greek with the result that they appeared no longer 'adoptifs, mais naturels' [adopted but natural], so too must the French poet-farmer ensure that his language 'sortira de terre, et s'eslevera' [will spring from the ground, and grow]. Melehy sees the fraught dialogue with antiquity in the *Deffence* as opening up the space of French poetry, culture, and modernity itself, a more spatially focused reading of what Margaret Ferguson had earlier termed 'a space in which all the poet's conflicting attitudes toward the ancients wage battle.'[99] It is not only the ancients who must be supplanted or replanted in order for native culture to grow: as we have seen, Italy's presence looms as much in the present as in the past, with the *Deffence* borrowing heavily from texts by Italian humanists.

So how are the modern and the French to be constructed, if so many of the building blocks available are classical or Italian? The answer lies in the spatial dimension inherent in the very image of construction. Du Bellay saw the poetic endeavour as a kind of building,[100] and describes, in the first chapter of book 2 of the *Deffence*, poets and orators as the pillars that support the edifice of every language: 'le poëte et l'orateur sont comme les deux piliers qui soutiennent l'edifice de chacune langue' [the poet and the orator are like the two pillars that support the edifice of each language].[101] The almost obsessive reoccurence in the *Deffence* of images of movement through space and of architectural and gardening metaphors gives a physicality to Du Bellay's poetic project. In the rhetorical climax of the work, entitled 'Exhortation aux François d'ecrire en leur langue: Avecques les louanges de la France,' France, Italy, and Greece are presented quite literally as physical territory. The classical literary landscape is described as just that; indeed, it is a space so cluttered with literary landmarks that there is little place left any more for new ones: 'les larges campaignes greques et latines sont déjà si pleines, que bien peu reste d'espace vide' [the broad fields of Greek and Latin are already so full that very little empty space remains] (2.12). France, on the other hand, is described as almost virginal soil, with vast stretches of fertile land propitious for the generation of native literature, with in addition a moral uprightness in its people which contrasts it to Italy. The contrast anticipates that made in *Les Regrets* between a cluttered, messy Roman landscape and a pastoral, ideal France. 'La France [...] est de long intervale à preferer à l'Italie [...] Je ne parleray icy de la temperie de l'air, fertilité de la terre [...] Je ne conteray tant de grosses rivieres, tant de belles forestz, tant de villes non moins opulentes que fortes, et pourveuës de toutes munitions de guerre' [France is by far to be preferred over Italy ... I will not speak here of the temperateness of the air, the fertility of the soil, the abundance of every kind of fruit ... I will not recount the many great rivers, the many beautiful forests, the many cities, no less opulent than strong and provided with all the munitions of war.][102] In this pastoral description of French soil, the strategic mention of France's ample supply of munitions should she need to go to war is noteworthy. And, famously, his conclusion to the work elaborates an extended metaphor of a French flotilla's movement through the seas of poetry, through foreign waves or 'flotz etrangers' [foreign seas] towards Rome, which Frenchmen are encouraged to pillage and plunder as in war: 'Là donq', Françoys, marchez couraigeusement vers cete superbe cité romaine: et des serves depouilles d'elle [...] ornez voz temples et autelz' [Up then, Frenchmen! March courageously on that proud Roman city and from her captured spoils ... adorn your temples and altars]. Then the French are exhorted to continue to Greece, where they are to sow their Gallic seed: 'Donnez en cete Grece menteresse, et y semez encor' un coup la fameuse nation des Gallogrecz' [Attack that lying Greece and sow there once again the famous nation of Gallo-Greeks].[103]

The metaphor of poetic conquest of foreign soil has an interesting twist which has not, to my knowledge, been picked up by critics: the French ships are not in fact imagined in Rome or Greece, but in simu-lacra of these places *on French soil*: 'Or sommes nous, la grace à Dieu, par beaucoup de perilz et de flotz etrangers, renduz au port à seureté. Nous avons echappé du milieu des Grecz, et par les scadrons romains penetré jusques *au seing de la tant desirée France*' (my emphasis). [Now, by the grace of God, through many perils and foreign seas, we have safely reached the port. We have escaped from the midst of the Greeks and through the Roman squadrons have penetrated to *the bosom of much-desired France*]. Despite the calling to arms, the military language of pillage and conquest, he reverses the image of a military expedition into foreign land by situating the conflict on French territory. This is a call to French writers to construct their monuments on French ground. The space of the French language's illustration is imagined *as* space – and, of course, as heavily gendered space (the penetration, the breasts, the fertile body ready for implantation).

Conclusion

Du Bellay's lyric descriptions of French place have become common-place. Perhaps even more than the ladies to whom so many Renaissance French poets promised fame, the literary public associates the names of Du Bellay and Anjou. Today one can visit the Musée J. Du Bellay in his 'petit Liré.' The 'champs blondissants' of the 'terre Angevine' are fre-quently cited with regionalist pride. French schoolchildren learn to recite or even sing 'Heureux qui comme Ulysses,' that canonical expres-sion of the comforts of returning to one's own 'petit village.' National sentiment, too, finds plenty of *lieux* in his poetry: I mentioned in the Introduction French politicians' penchant for 'France mère des arts.' Du Bellay's landscapes are strata of memory on which the landscape of France continues to be built, whose 'scenery is built up as much from strata of memory as from layers of rock.'[104]

Du Bellay's vernacular lyric can help us understand why Renaissance poetry should have lent itself so particularly well to these enduring images of landscape. The form and themes of lyric (pastoral, admiration of female beauty) are easily co-opted by an imagined community in the making. By staging in his landscapes the problems of imitation, particularly imitation of the conventions of Petrarch's *Rime* which must be overwritten in order to affirm a native tradition, Du Bellay represents France as fertile, generative territory. If the *Deffence* anticipates the space, or place, of French culture, then that space, as I have shown here, is mapped out in Du Bellay's poetic landscapes through a dialogue with – and negation of – Italy and Petrarch. Laura's body is transplanted and reimagined in the feminized landscape of *la France*. Finally, the particular dialectic between nation and region, between geography and chorography, which informs cartographic images of France, becomes, in Du Bellay, a dynamic play between scales of description which reveals how both region and nation are mutually constructed as imagined communities. Du Bellay's landscapes invent and affirm the space of French poetry and the emerging nation, rewriting the geography of lyric.

4 The Poet and the Painter: Problems of Representation

The two previous chapters have shown how articulations between lyric and cartography produced formative images of France and its regions. As the analysis of Du Bellay's poetic places showed, however, cartography is by no means the only facet of the problematics of place in Renaissance lyric. I argue throughout that poetic places have multiple discursive and social contexts; their power comes from the many interrelated intersections between them and lived or imagined environments. So, bearing in mind that no articulation can be entirely separated from any other, I turn here to the relation between poetry and painting. Painting, unlike poetry and geography, was traditionally considered a mechanical art.[1] Despite this distinction, poetry might intuitively seem to have more of a privileged relationship with painting than with cartography in the sixteenth century. There are numerous lived relationships between poets and painters: the court painter François Clouet frequented the poets of the Pléiade, as did the poet and painter Nicolas Denisot.[2] Portraiture, the visual representation of powerful patrons, was the pictorial analogue and rival of praise poetry.[3] The *paragone* debate compared the relative merits of different art forms: the Horatian *ut pictura poesis* was often evoked in the comparison of poetry and painting. While the Horatian axiom originally did not suggest parity between word and image, some Renaissance theorists read it this way.[4] Jacques Peletier evokes only their similarities in his 1555 *Art poétique*, and Thomas Sébillet calls the poet and the painter 'cousins germains' in his 1548 *Art poétique françoys*.[5] Pierre de Ronsard describes the poem in painterly terms in his 1566 treatise. When advising the would-be poet about landscape description – 'les descriptions des lieux, fleuves, forests, montaignes' [descriptions of places, rivers, forests, mountains] –

he recommends 'l'imitation d'Homere, que tu observeras comme un divin example, sur lequel tu tireras au vif les plus parfaicts lineamens de ton *tableau*' [the imitation of Homer, whom you will hold up as a divine example and from whom you will take the most perfect outline for your *painting*].[6]

There was certainly a shared vocabulary between poetry and painting, but the implications for landscape description are somewhat different. Landscape in French Renaissance painting is usually decorative or backgrounded, and even when it does constitute a principal subject, it is a classical mythological setting rather than a named part of France. The same is true of book illustrations. The 1557 *Métamorphose d'Ovide figurée*, which features 148 Ovidian myths in *huitains*, each accompanied by a woodcut illustration, is one of the best and richest examples of landscape illustration in Renaissance print.[7] Nevertheless, its landscapes are not intended to describe France, but the places of Ovidian mythology. Since my focus here is on descriptions of places named as French, I will not compare lyric and painted (or illustrated) landscapes. Rather, I propose to analyse the thematic treatment of the visual arts in lyrics by Remy Belleau and Pontus de Tyard, to show that when these poets evoke the visual arts in their landscapes, much of the hope disappears from poetry's 'spaces of hope.' They reveal the inherent constructedness and limitations of any imagined landscape, manifesting a certain pessimism about their redemptive possibilities. When Belleau and Pontus describe visually represented landscapes, they self-consciously represent the *distance* between their poetry and 'a world in which riches and beauty abound, but whose ontological value is starting to be questioned.'[8] French place becomes fragile, incoherent, dependent on multiple and foreign mythologies, impossible to describe as anything more than a series of bounded, framed, fragmented images. In other words, the thematics of painting in poetry are that the first world of history is too grim to be at all changed by the second world of poetry. All a poet can do is retreat, Mannerist-like, into artifice.

Mannerism is the school most associated with the production of the Fontainebleau artists of the Renaissance. When poets refer to the plastic arts, particularly through *ekphrasis*,[9] it is not simply to an abstracted notion of the profession but to specific visual cultures and above all, I argue, to Fontainebleau Mannerism. The castle's Galerie François Premier, created by the first Mannerist school under the direction of the painter Rosso, remains one of the sixteenth century's outstanding decorative ensembles for the plastic arts in general.[10] Although the Fontainebleau school was constituted largely of Italians brought there by the monarch from as early as 1530 – Primatticio, Rosso, Cellini, dell'Abbate, and others – there were important French artists in residence there or at least heavily influenced by the school: the painters Jean Cousin, Antoine Caron, and Jean and François Clouet; the architects Philibert de l'Orme and Pierre Lescot; or the sculptors Jean Goujon and Germain .Pilon.[11] Mannerism is a very contested term among art historians,[12] often conflated with Baroque. But when used, it is usually associated with movement, metamorphosis, tension, fragmentation, distortion, reference to its own artifice, and retreat into form. Rather than debate the term's validity, I propose to use some of the concepts that have been associated with it to help understand the references to the plastic arts in written texts. Literary critics have adapted the word with varying degrees of success: James Mirollo distinguishes between visual and literary mannerism, seeing the latter as a more elastic term, 'a modal variety of Renaissance literary style rather than a separate, autonomous phenomenon [...] an art that comments upon art.'[13] I follow Mirollo's open-ended approach to Mannerism, seeing it as what John Shearman calls a shared 'community of ideas'[14] between poetry and painting which manifests particularly as a foregrounding of the processes and techniques of representation itself. This shared focus on artifice, even if presented as a retreat from history, does of course have historical determinants. Mannerism is thus, according to Wylie Sypher, a 'disintegration in style accompanying a crisis in faith.'[15] For Charles Sterling, Mannerism is 'an art that is, more than any other, turned towards the unreal' precisely because it is 'born in a period of anxiety and doubt,'[16] because it inhabits a historical moment of crisis. Mannerism is haunted by its own status as mere decoration, and points anxiously to the moment at which the High Renaissance illusion of unity breaks down: 'we seem to move away from the Classical principal of an interior unity of multiplicities to a kind of breaking-apart [...] the credibility of the work of art seems to weaken. The viewer has the impression of looking at an artistic invention rather than at a representation of nature.'[17] In other words, a Mannerist work represents representation itself, and it questions whether art has any power within the world it represents (although form and technique can themselves be sources of transcendence, not simply an avowal of superficiality).

We can apply to literary texts the troubled retreat into form – and away from history and *vraisemblance* – that is said to characterize the Mannerist aesthetic. Most interdisciplinary analyses of so-called Mannerist literature in France have focused on portraiture, in particular Ronsard's 'Elégie à Janet,' in which the poet gives instructions to the court painter François Clouet on how to paint his lady.[18] My focus here of course is not on portraiture but on landscape, as a point of contact between poetry and the plastic arts. Sixteenth-century landscape painting itself deserves more attention than it has received. Dismissed as a 'non-subject' by one of today's leading Renaissance art historians, Henri Zerner,[19] it nevertheless occupies a predominant place in some of the works of Mannerist painters such as Nicolò dell'Abbate and François Clouet. The word *paysage* already had a pictorial sense by the mid-sixteenth century. Robert Estienne notes in his 1549 French-Latin dictionary that *paisage* is a 'common word among painters,' while we have records of 'paysages' – referred to as such – hanging in the castles of Fontainebleau and Anet.[20] Nevertheless, it is true that landscape was less prominent in French painting than in Dutch or Italian, and represented more in the strictly ornamental arts – metalwork, enamelling, and engraving – than in painting. It was an important subject of prints (*gravures*) and *eaux-fortes* among such etchers as Fantuzzi and Jean Mignon, for example.[21] More importantly for our purposes here, Fontainebleau *paysages*, painted or printed, are constituted almost entirely of classical mythological settings, and do not represent France in the sustained and intentional way that lyric does.[22] Interestingly, while in many ways painting was a site of novelty and experimentation, less bound to the classical past than poetry, it is poetry that first replaces classical landscapes with French. References to painting in works by Remy Belleau and Pontus de Tyard, even to contemporary Fontainebleau styles, hold poetic landscapes more in the past, and dissipate the image of the French nation and of its literary landscape that other poets create. When poetic landscapes become Mannerist, it is no longer possible to imagine France with any kind of geopolitical or literary unity.

Pontus de Tyard, *Douze fables de fleuves ou fontaines*

Pontus de Tyard (1521–1605) was from a noble family of Bissy-sur-Fley. Like many noblemen of letters, he held ecclesiastical office (appointed *chanoine* of Mâcon in 1552, and bishop of Châlon in 1578). He was a polymath who studied mathematics, theology, astronomy, and philosophy, and an adviser and tutor to king Henri III. When the king's relative tolerance towards the Huguenots earned him the anger of the ultra-Catholic house of Guise, Tyard defended him staunchly. He is remembered today much more as a man of letters than as a political activist, though. A friend of Maurice Scève and admirer of Ronsard and Du Bellay, he was considered a member of the Pléiade's inner circle. He is credited with bringing the sestina into France, and Étienne Pasquier already esteemed him as 'worthy of the company of Sirs Ronsard and Du Bellay' in 1554.[23] His vast knowledge of philosophy, science, and mythology, can be seen in most of his poetic works.[24] I will focus here on a curious little work, *Douze fables de fleuves ou fontaines*, the only French poetic work from the period that provides not just one but a series of *ekphrases* of paintings. In this work, poetry and painting together create fluid, mysterious landscapes that suggest not only that landscape itself is constantly in flux, but also that the cultural descriptives necessary to describe France in particular do not yet exist.

The work contains twelve 'fables' or mythological stories about the virtues of certain springs or rivers, almost all of which are the result of a human metamorphosis. Each story is followed by a 'Description pour la peinture' (instructions to an unnamed painter on how to execute the story on canvas), and a moralizing 'Epigramme' in the form of a sonnet. The *Fables* were not published by the author, but in 1585 by his friend Étienne Tabourot, who explains in his preface that Tyard had composed them about thirty years previously – in the early to mid-1550s, when the poet was frequenting the court. Tabourot also tells the reader that the fables were written 'when the impressive castle of Anet was being decorated' (605).[25] The architect Philibert de l'Orme built Anet for Henri II's mistress Diane de Poitiers, completing it in 1552. Tabourot's reference has thus led most art historians and literary critics to assume that Tyard was providing instructions for a set of twelve paintings to be executed for the decoration of the castle. While the existence of the paintings, and Tyard's very intentions, remain something of an art-historical mystery, Valérie Auclair has convincingly argued that not only is there no reason to doubt that the *Fables* were intended as actual instructions (whether or not the paintings were executed), but that they were probably intended to decorate the 'grande salle' which either contained or led directly to the baths, hence the paintings' aqueous theme. The architectural plans do in fact include a great hall and a *baignerie*.[26]

Given the doubts about the paintings, the *Fables* have been read by some literary critics primarily 'for their internal coherence,'[27] dealing in a textual way with themes such as metamorphosis and imitation, or – in a cogent recent reading by Roberto Campo – as an example of 'semiosic drift.'[28] I see no reason to doubt that Tyard's work was intended as a part of the *inventio* of an artistic commission. Tyard was very much a part of the court culture of the time, and collaborations between poets and plastic artists were common in large-scale royal projects.[29] Moreover, Tyard's descriptions for paintings reference decorative details in the castle;[30] he amply describes colours and textures to be used; and he uses a technical vocabulary of some precision. In the fourth description, he stipulates that a forest must be painted 'en Perspective de lointaine veue' [backgrounded in perspective] (616), and in the twelfth description he recommends 'un temple d'Isis qui se pourroit faire par une perspective a ligne visuale de front, et basses diagonales de la maison d'Anet' [a temple of Isis which could be done in perspective, looking from the front, and elevated from (the viewer's position in) the château d'Anet] (631).[31] My intent here is not, however, to engage in an art-historical reading of the *Fables*, but to read them as a text that displays a Mannerist sensibility broadly understood, and that disrupts the stability and coherence of its landscapes.[32] I propose that Tyard's text, in its consciously copious references to classical mythological scenes, in its constantly metamorphosing universe, and in its treatment of the origin of toponyms, specifically dramatizes the impossibility of naming and describing France.

Landscapes in the *Fables* are barely distinguishable from the human drama unfolding in them – bodies becoming water, plants and rocks, and vice versa. But they are landscapes nevertheless: Tyard explicitly calls, in some descriptions, for a 'paysage,' which was, as noted above, a painterly term by the mid-sixteenth century. The fifth description calls for a 'paisage hyvernal' [a wintery landscape], the eighth, the *locus amoenus* of the Narcissus story, 'un paisage solitaire et escarté' [a solitary and far-flung place]. The painter of the scene of the second fable, a joyous Bacchanalia in which Silenus falls into a spring, is instructed thus: 'Il faudroit peindre l'Isle d'Andros en l'Archipelago d'assés large estendue' [the island of Andros, in the archipelago, should be painted fairly broadly] (611), while the fourth fable requires a 'forest de chesnes' [oak forest] to be painted in the background.

Roberto Campo has shown that the word 'fable,' for Tyard, is associated in his philosophical discourse on time with the 'metaphysical angst [...] of a universe in flux.'[33] Water, too, is a perennial symbol of transience and change: Ovid's *Metamorphoses*, in a key interpretive passage for the *Fables*, specifically reminds its readers that water 'gives and takes strange forms.'[34] Tyard's landscapes are constituted almost entirely by rivers or fountains (natural sources, not man-made structures), all situated in Greece or Asia, and many described in a strange state of half-completed metamorphosis. Importantly, these metamorphoses are for the most part Tyard's own inventions. Not only are the landscapes and characters therein represented in flux and movement, but Tyard draws on multiple textual sources, furthering the confusion.[35] The first fable is of the 'Fleuve Clytorie, qui a force de desenyvrer' [the river Clitorium which has the power to make sober] (609). The story is that of Semele in Ovid's *Metamorphoses* (3.259–315), in which Juno, suspecting that Semele is pregnant by Jupiter, beguiles Semele into asking the god to lie with her in the same way that he would lie with Juno. Bound by his promise, Jupiter does so, and the mortal Semele cannot withstand his force. The child inside her (the future Bacchus) is sewn up in Jupiter's thigh. In Tyard's version, Semele gives birth to Bacchus upon dying, and the nymph Clytorie – an avatar for the fountain of that name – puts out the surrounding fire with her tears, becoming a river, 'transformee et fondue en fleuve de son nom, qui depuis estaint la force du vin' [transformed and flowed into a river bearing her name, which ever since has countered the effects of wine] (609). The transformation of the fountain-nymph Clytorie into a river seems to be Tyard's invention. What is gained by this addition is seen in the instructions for the painting, where he describes a scene and a strange landscape in flux, surely difficult to render visually, and certainly Mannerist: 'Seroit peinte une Semelé foudroyée, et mourante dedans un feu tombant du Ciel [...] Aupres de Semelé seroit Clytorie à demy transformee en fleuve: et entre ses bras seroit le petit Bacchus, partie encores envelopé de feu, et en partie le feu estaint, selon que les larmes de Clytorie seroient versees sur luy' [a stricken Semele would be painted, dying in a fire falling from the sky ... beside Semele would be Clytorie, half-transformed into a river, and in her arms would be the little Bacchus, half-enveloped in flames, but where Clytorie's tears have fallen, the fire has been put out] (610). The nymph, who we learn in Tyard's text is fully transformed into the river, is in the painting represented in the *process* of melting; landscape is a perpetual moment of transformation. We see the same in the third fable, where the lovelorn shepherd Selemne is, in the story, 'transformé en un fleuve' [transformed into a river], but is described in the hypothetical painting as '*presque* transformé en fleuve' [*almost* transformed into a river] (613–14, my emphasis); Araxis in the sixth fable is to be painted 'en partie transformé en herbe' [*partially* transformed into a plant] after jumping into the homonymous river; and Hermaphrodite in the ninth painting is 'comme un commencement de transformation' [like the *start* of a transformation] (620, 625, my emphasis). Textual description allows for a past, present, and future, whereas the image captures just one moment, and this moment, in Tyard, evades classical stasis for a Mannerist shifting and lack of resolution. People and gods are half-transformed, blood and water flow into each other, bodies entangle, in reiterated instantiations of the *perpetuum mobile*. This is not because metamorphosis is mentioned in his classical sources; in most of the fables, Tyard adds it himself.

Not only do the scenes speak to the 'potential or actual ontological mutability of existence,'[36] they also show that toponyms are entirely accidental, having no essentialist relation with place. Tyard shared with many Renaissance humanists a philological and philosophical fascination with the origin of names, and made his own contribution to debates about Cratylism, a treatise entitled *De recta nominum impositione*, not published until 1603.[37] In this text, Tyard argues against the Adamic attribution of names, saying that names are arbitrary, carry no relation to place, and that universal language is an illusion. The treatise, like the *Fables*, is concerned almost entirely with Greek place-names; indeed one might see the *Fables* as an imaginative illustration of the principles of the later philosophical text. The toponyms of the *Fables* are literally accidental, in the sense that they almost always derive from someone's accident. The Armenian river Alma, we are told, was renamed Araxes after a king of that name 's'alla noyer dedans un fleuve nommé Alme, qui depuis fut, pour ce fait, appelé Araxe' [went and drowned himself in a river named Alma, which because of this fact was afterwards called Araxes] (619), and was turned into a plant, which also bears his name. Even the great river Indus has an accidental name, from a young man, Indus, who drowned in it while fleeing the wrath of a father defending his daughter's honour, and was turned into a stone (621).

If the places of antiquity are metamorphic and mercurial, France itself is almost invisible in the *Fables*. Tyard's rivers and sources are all Greek or Asian; French place appears only twice, and even then as a fleeting comparison. The fourth fable tells the story of the virgin Callirhoe, almost sacrificed by the priest Coresus, who has long loved her, to rid the people of Calydon of illness. At the last moment, Coresus kills himself instead, and Callirhoe, finally cognizant of his love for her, 'se tua aupres d'une fontaine, qui depuis fut appellee de son nom' [killed herself beside a fountain, which was afterwards called by her name] (616). The etymology of the Greek name Callirhoe is given by the modern editors as 'having a beautiful course or waters,'[38] and as such it recalls an alternate version of the etymology of Fontainebleau, 'fontaine belle eau' [fountain (of) beautiful water]. And Tyard, who studied Greek in Paris with Dorat and other Pléiade members, tells us at the end of the fable that 'Le nom Callirhoe a grande affinité à Fontainebleau' [the name Callirhoe has a great affinity with that of Fontainebleau] (616). He does not take the parallel any further, though: France appears in this *ekphrasis* as a fleeting suggestion, a flicker on the overwhelmingly classical landscape, associated with the Greek name and the scene of the painting by mere coincidence. Indeed, the mention of Fontainebleau even serves to further the spatial confusion, as the paintings were intended for Anet.[39]

The château d'Anet itself is mentioned, also ephemerally, in the last fable concerning the 'lavatoire d'Isis, qui sert d'asseurance contre les larves, malins esprits et chiens aboyans' [the fable of the baths of Isis, which protect against wicked spectres, evil spirits, and barking dogs]. The goddess Isis made the queen Garmathon wash in her baths to protect her from fear of the underworld (with its ghosts and the monster-dog Cerberus), where she was seeking her son. Tyard also informs us, in the initial story, of an alternative version of the fable (in Plutarch) which features the Nile, but he prefers the baths of Isis as 'plus propre à ce lieu' [more fitting for this place] since Isis 'n'est autre chose que la Lune, comme la peinture monstrera' [is actually the moon, as the painting will show] (630). He is reminding the reader, and the painter, of Isis's association – through the moon – with Diana the huntress, and thus with Diane de Poitiers. This is important enough for Tyard to request that the painter make the Isis-Diana association explicit, 'comme la peinture monstrera.' This is also the only fable in which Tyard considers the aptness of the paintings to the deictic 'this place,' the château d'Anet. In the instructions for the painting, he recommends, beside the temple of Isis, 'un Lavatoire, tel que celuy mesme d'Anet, dedans lequel Garmathon Royne Egyptienne descendroit' [baths, like those of Anet itself, into which Garmathon the queen of Egypt would descend] (631). A seventeenth-century visitor to the castle even mentioned a staircase descending to a large pool, a descent possibly mirrored by the position of Garmathon in the painting. The twelfth fable, then, would be a 'représentation en abîme'[40] of the castle's baths, which, like those of Isis-Diana, were reputed to have curative powers. Diane de Poitiers herself even had her own fountain in one of the courtyards at Anet, which represented the goddess Diana in full hunting apparel.[41]

The paintings participate in the referential echo chamber of the castle's decoration: water, Isis-Diana-Diane, forests, dogs, and stags. By themselves, they may only have attested to the royal taste for the representation of classical themes in the plastic arts. But Tyard, in his written descriptions, adds something more, an emphasis on the instability of the world, and a *mise en abîme* of landscape itself.[42] The omnipresent mythology of Diana may also recall the fate of Actaeon, the dismemberment of the viewer who cannot name what he sees, further destabilizing the gaze over landscape. Like the human drama unfolding in them, these landscapes ultimately illustrate their own cultural construction: how nature is appropriated and described by human stories, and how landscapes shift and drift through time, constantly redefined and reappropriated. Whereas the cultural underpinnings of landscapes are embraced and often celebrated by other poets as ways to affirm the power of French culture, they show, in Tyard, the still-overwhelming dominance of the classical world. The only way that France can be present is through allusion, comparison, or accidental affinity. The kingdom is not yet ready for its own landscape.

Royalist Landscape in Ronsard's *La Bergerie*

If Tyard's landscapes suggest the difficulty of making classical landscapes French, those of Remy Belleau suggest – via the self-conscious artifice of *ekphrasis* – the fundamental incoherence of any notion of French place as an ideal community. The landscape in Belleau's *La Bergerie* reveals the fictionalizing processes of pastoral, the exclusions and distancing that have to happen in order for the world to be rewritten as ideal. This meta-reflection on the creation of pastoral worlds is operated largely through Belleau's references to the plastic arts, which compete against and often supplant the traditional kinds of landscape description one expects from a pastoral work. Belleau's *Bergerie* is a remarkably reflexive and complex work, and in order to better understand its originality, it can usefully be compared with another work entitled *La Bergerie*, published in the same year (1565) by Pierre de Ronsard, and whose lyric map of the kingdom I mentioned in chapter 2. I therefore propose a brief analysis of the latter, before turning to an in-depth consideration of Belleau.

The *Bergerie* of Ronsard, a pastoral *mascarade*, was probably performed at Fontainebleau and has all the characteristics of a circumstantial piece.[43] The shepherds represent – and might have been played by – royal personalities, and they sing about the Valois dynasty heralding the return of the golden age onto French soil. Two generic tendencies of

pastoral clearly coincide here: nostalgia for an idealized past, and political allegory. Henri II's death in 1559 inspires an elegiac 'tombeau'
like Androgeo's in Sannazaro's *Arcadia*; Charles IX is the pastor 'bon
Carlin,' the protector of the flock of France; and Catherine de' Medici –
who will later be d'Aubigné's 'pestifere' – is a nymph, her name engraved on the trees of the kingdom. It is an uncomplicated tale of loss
followed by Arcadian redemption, and it describes France's landscape
correspondingly. The wars of religion have left the landscape deserted,
the absence of pastoral and poets signifying the absence, for Ronsard,
of pre-Reformation values:

> La France estoit perdue, et sa terre couverte
> De tant de gras troupeaux fust maintenant deserte,
> Et banis de nos champs eussions esté contraints
> Aller en autre part implorer autres Saints.   (153: 374–7)[44]

[France was lost, her land which once was covered / By fat herds of livestock, was now deserted, / And, banished from our fields, we would have
been forced / To go and pray elsewhere to other saints.]

But Catherine de' Medici, the royal nymph, restitutes France to the pastor-
poets, instructing them to recreate their nation's places as spaces of pastoral whence all cares are banished:

> La première [elle] nous dit: Pasteurs, comme devant
> Entonnez voz chansons et les jouez au vent,
> Et aux grandes forests si longuement muettes
> R'apprenez les accords de vos vieilles musettes
> [...]
> Elle nous rebailla nos champs et nos bocages,
> Elle nous fist rentrer en nos premiers herbages,
> En nos premiers courtils, et d'un front adoucy
> Chassa loin de nos parcs la peur et le souci.   (153: 384–93)

[She first said to us: Shepherds, like before / Ring out your songs and play
them in the wind, / And in the long-silent forests / Learn again the chords
of your old pipes / ... / She gave back to us our fields and pastures, / She
sent us back to our original grazing grounds, / Our first little yards, and
with a sweet look, / She chased fear and worry far away from our
grounds.]

This is a moment of supreme Arcadian containment. The image presented is that of an enclosed space ('parc') whence all cares have been banished – by an immediately performative royal decree. Catherine simply gives the order to the shepherds to play 'comme devant,' and the whole landscape enters back into a prelapsarian order that is also feudal-aristocratic. The poets are figured as poor tenant farmers grazing livestock on the commons and in the small yards adjacent to their farmhouses ('courtils,' or 'courtilles' in modern French). The terms of feudal land use are harnessed by an idealizing poetic discourse – the georgic model taken to the extreme, with the queen protecting her flock of poet-pastors from any possible inclemency.[45]

By the 1560s, Ronsard had elected himself master of the pastoral mode despite having previously handed it over to others to develop.[46] Pastoral convention is intimately related, in his *Bergerie*, to a kind of political and social nostalgia that sees in the tropes of bucolic poetry a correlative to social order. This order is mapped onto the landscape and onto the uses made of it. In his enumbration of French regions discussed in chapter 2 with respect to cartography, Ronsard transforms place into pastoral cliché and vice versa: 'Que dirons nous d'Anjou et des champs de Touraine, / De Languedoc, Provence, où l'abondance pleine / De sillon en sillon fertile se conduit / Portant sa riche Corne enceinte de beau fruit?' [What shall we say of Anjou and the fields of Touraine / Of Languedoc or Provence, where full abundance / From furrow to fertile furrow / Offers its cornucopia of riches?] (162: 728–41). The ordering of pastoral poetry is projected onto contemporary French landscape in a way that distorts both. That is, Ronsard is not only pushing the limits of what can possibly be believed about France, but he is also stretching the descriptive mode of pastoral itself. His question 'que dirons-nous?' [what shall we say?] is perhaps not purely rhetorical. He is searching for appropriate descriptive terms and modes with which to write about France. How to push the pastoral containment or evasion of history to its limits, how to brush aside the social criticism implicit or explicit in his poetic models and present an idealized, uncomplicated landscape that corresponds to the current royalist imaginary? The pastoral mode, as Ronsard inherits it, is by no means a catchall for 'sentimental' landscape description;[47] however, it contains within itself the possibility of being pushed to precisely that. It is this possibility that Ronsard represents through his alliance of encomiastic political rhetoric with pastoral landscape cliché.

The *des-Guysé* [dis-Guised] Landscapes of Joinville:
Remy Belleau's *La Bergerie*

Ronsard's world of singing royal shepherds and fertile peaceful land exemplifies Harry Berger's 'second world' of Renaissance fiction, which, by 'separating itself from the casual and confused region of everyday existence [...] promises a clarified image of the world it represents.' But it lacks the wry admission of its escapism that constitutes the sophistication, for Berger, of many Renaissance second worlds: 'fantasy becomes true creativity only when the limits of imagination are affirmed.'[48] These limits are not only affirmed but foregrounded in Belleau's *Bergerie*, a description of pastoral activities taking place at the castle of the Guise family at Joinville, a real, named, place. There are also abundant *ekphrases*, and these, I argue, ultimately reflect on the falseness of pastoral escapism (such as that found in Ronsard's *Bergerie*) by foregrounding the process of selection and distantiation upon which an idealized sense of place depends.[49] What must be distanced from Belleau's second world is the reality of the Guise's role in the religious tensions of the day. He also underlines the difference between the actual lives of the *peuple* who teem around the edges of Joinville, and their idealization in pastoral. If Ronsard's allegorical royal family are shepherds as well as landowners, joining in with the pastors' singing competitions, Belleau's Guise do not interact with the lower classes so much as decorate their walls with sentimental representations of them. The careful portrayal of the exclusivity of life at Joinville subtly undermines the kind of description found in Ronsard's *Bergerie*, which founds the hope of the nation itself in Valois patronage. But there is more to Belleau's rejection of encomiastic pastoral than mere cynicism: towards the end of the *Bergerie*, Belleau also suggests new directions for lyric, detached from particular places and people. In a sustained negotiation with the plastic arts, Belleau rethinks the parameters and subject matter of pastoral and lyric, suggesting that if poetry is to provide any meaning beyond its own performance, it must give up any attachment to politically and historically charged localities, and seek transcendence in nature and science.

Remy Belleau, a consumate Hellenist, translator of Anacreon and Sappho, and member of the Pléiade, was engaged by the Guise family in 1563 as the preceptor of the young Charles de Lorraine. Belleau divided his time between Paris, the court, and the castle of Joinville, in the

Haute-Marne, where the widow of the first duke of Guise, Antoinette de Bourbon, resided. It was at Joinville that he composed his pastoral work *La Bergerie* (1565; expanded edition with two *Journées* in 1572), a work which, along with his later collection *Amours et nouveaux eschanges des pierres précieuses* (1576), earned him the reputation of being something of a gentle, even apolitical, poet of nature. His patrons, however, were anything but apolitical: not only were they the unquestioned leaders of anti-Protestant sentiment and activities in the kingdom, there was also significant tension between them and the royal family (the Royal Tour of Charles IX and Catherine de' Medici skirted around Joinville in 1564).[50] Belleau had shown reformist sympathies in his youth in Paris from 1557 to 1562, and had written a pamphlet in support of the Protestant leader the Duc de Condé.[51] He was apparently converted by Ronsard, and his subsequent protection by, and friendship with, the strongly Catholic Guise family, has led to the assumption that he entirely renounced the Reformation and embraced conservative Catholicism. But, as this reading will suggest, there are reasons to believe that Belleau felt some discomfort with the political role of the Guise and its effects on mounting religious tensions in France. The years around the publication dates of the two *Bergeries* were particularly turbulent. It is surely not accidental that Belleau uses the word *déguysé* (disguised), a pun on the name *de Guise*, in his dedication to the 1565 *Bergerie*, when observing that there has never been a period or country in which 'le faux se soit mieux désguysé en aparance de vraye' [falsehood has been better disguised as truth].[52] If it is ultimately unprovable that Belleau harboured some misgivings about his patrons, he certainly had some about the kind of fictionalizing that has to take place in order for Joinville and its family, the leading Catholic faction in France, to appear as the seat of all virtue.

The historical context is increasingly troubled: civil war had broken out in 1562 (officially – acts of violence had been perpetrated much earlier against the Huguenots), the Guise were directly involved in this and the wars in Italy,[53] and 1572 was the date of the infamous massacre of St Bartholomew during which Parisian Catholics murdered thousands of Protestants. Belleau himself had been through a period of bad health in the early 1560s.[54] The text describes a day of pleasant, bucolic activities in the castle and grounds of the Guise château at Joinville. It alternates between prose and verse, a form known as *prosimetrum* and seen in Sannazaro's *Arcadia* as well as in a few French texts before 1565.[55] The descriptions of the place, its many works of art, and the

Guise family, are often taken as unproblematically encomiastic.[56] But the castle at Joinville and its territory appear in *La Bergerie* as a strange, Mannerist, disjointed landscape, far from the confident space of hope one might expect from a pastoral work whose landscapes are based on a real French aristocratic territory, written by a Guise protégé and friend of the court.

Much of the interpretive puzzle of *La Bergerie* comes from Belleau's descriptions of works of art. The poet shifts at key moments from more traditional pastoral landscape description to *ekphrases* of works of art, which he describes in minute ornamental detail. At moments in the *Bergerie* where *ekphrasis* takes precedence over a more straightforward narrative description of surroundings, there emerges a more troubled, even cynical relation to praise poetry and to the idealization of France.

The question here is not so much whether the works referred to existed: many of them seem to have been real, as Doris Delacourcelle has shown.[57] Moreover, Belleau was not only surrounded but also profoundly influenced by leading painters of his time, including many from the school of Fontainebleau.[58] Rather, in Belleau's strange universe, the puzzle centres around the relations between the poetic, the plastic, and the real. Belleau filters much of the landscape of *La Bergerie* through visual representation, whether real or fictional. Of course, Belleau practises textual imitation – of Theocritus, Virgil, Longus, Sannazaro, among others – but his textual imitation is often disguised as imitation of a work of art that itself imitates a text. *La Bergerie* exemplifies the Mannerist focus on artifice, on individual objects as opposed to a unifying ensemble, and this tendency manifests a certain pessimism about current discourses on the transformative role of poetry. The appropriation of Mannerist style is ideologically motivated, a signal to Belleau's readers that he is turning away from the kinds of images that poetry – pastoral poetry in particular – had been presenting of French landscape. Whereas other poets of his generation attempted, albeit in full awareness of the limits of their medium, to imagine and represent a French landscape shaped by the values of poetry, Belleau clearly indicates that such a space is only ever the domain of art.

Not surprisingly, Belleau anticipates and distances himself from suppositions that he might be engaging in ideological critique. He starts the 1565 *Bergerie* with a dedication to the Marquis d'Elbeuf, the son of Claude de Lorraine (the Duke of Guise) and Antoinette de Bourbon, usually taken as proof of Belleau's absolute devotion to the Guise family, and of his intentions to present Joinville as a peaceful pastoral refuge far removed from the calamities of the times. In this dedication, he describes his *Bergerie* as 'ce petit ouvrage, fait et recousu de telles pieces, et de telle estoffe, qu'il ne peut offencer que celuy qui forge en son cerveau nouvelle occasion de s'alterer soymesme' [this little work, made and put together with such pieces and such material that it could only offend a person susceptible to self-delusion]. The *Bergerie* is not political, he promises, deflecting any suspicion that this work might contain any pro-Reform bias; in fact it is utterly non-committal on the subject of religion, since 'rien ne peut plaire à l'un, qu'il ne déplaise à l'autre' [nothing can please one person without displeasing another] (4).[59] It is true that both days of the *Bergerie* are more a collection of individual poems loosely tied together by the string of prose.[60] But I believe there is more to this espousal of disorder than a *captatio benevolentiae*. Belleau is also diffusing any suspicion that his work might have an ideological agenda. In the preface to the 1572 edition, he further insists on its incoherence in a way that evokes Mannerist aesthetic disorder: '[T]antost un sonnet, tantost une Complainte, tantost une églogue [...] voulant recoudre ces inventions mal cousues, mal polies, et mal agencees, sans l'esperer je trouve un livre ramassé des pieces rapportees, chose veritablement qui n'ha membre, ny figure qui puisse former un corps entier et parfaict' [now a sonnet, now a Complaint, now an eclogue ... wanting to patch together these scrappy, badly wrought inventions, without intending to I find it to be a grab-bag book of miscellaneous material, really a thing without the limbs or the shape to form a whole and perfect body] (147). The almost Montaignian imagery of the book as an imperfect body corresponds to the Mannerist favouring of the human body as subject over nature, and to the contortions or dismemberments often imposed on the body in works such as Jean Cousin's *Jugement dernier* (1585) or Antoine Caron's *Massacres du Triumvirat* (1566).[61] Some modern critics have taken the lack of thematic unity in the *Bergerie* as an aesthetic fault, and have preferred the first edition to the second *journée* because it seems to offer slightly more cohesion.[62] I focus here on both editions (1565 and 1572) of the first *journée*, not for aesthetic reasons but simply because the two days together constitute too large a body of work for this chapter. The first day is, I believe, not as coherent as modern editors would have it, and at any rate the charge of thematic confusion misses the point: Belleau turns to a style of representation that bypasses the primacy of narrative logic in favour of discrete descriptions of individual objects, essaying a kind of textual Mannerism.

The beginning of the *Bergerie* – the same in both 1565 and 1572 versions – is worth reading in detail, since it operates a subtle shift in perspective, taking the reader along with the narrator as he slides almost imperceptibly from a pastoral to a Mannerist landscape. The narrator sets the stage with a conventionally bucolic sunrise:

> Le soleil ayant chassé la brune espaisseur de la nuict, acompagné de la troupe doree des heures, desja commançoit à poindre, estendant ses tresses blondes sur la cime des montagnes, faisant la ronde par les plaines blanchissantes de l'air, visitant les terres dures, et réchauffant les flots escumeux de la mer [...] (5)

> [The sun, along with the gilden troop of hours, having banished the brown thickness of night, was already starting to appear, spreading its blond tresses over the mountaintops, making its rounds on the brightening plains, touching the hard ground and warming the frothy waves of the sea ...]

This recalls the sunrises and sunsets of Sannazaro's *Arcadia*, for example, or Ovid's *Metamorphoses*, which typically evoke notions of mutability, shifting perspective, figures in motion – all characteristics of Mannerist painting and poetry.[63]

There then follows a strange moment in which the narrator loses all the senses on which he (and by extension the reader) would normally rely to interpret his surroundings. This is an original moment – that is, not imitated from another text – which he portrays as a *gift* from Fortune and destiny. Belleau describes the almost proto-surrealist state of sensory inebriation that follows, and the place that induces this state, as a respite from the world:

> lors que la Fortune, et le destin [...] lassez et recreus de me tourmenter, me presterent tant de *faveur*, qu'ils me conduirent en un *lieu*, où je croy que l'honneur, et la vertu, les amours, et les graces avoient deliberé de suborner mes sens, enyvrer ma raison, et peu à peu me dérober l'ame, me faisant perdre le sentiment, fust de l'oeil, de l'ouye, du sentir, du gouter et du toucher. Et quant à l'oeil. (5–6, my emphasis)

> [when Fortune and destiny ... tired of tormenting me, bestowed a favor on me such that they led me to a *place* where, I think, honor, virtue, love, and the graces, had planned to overcome my senses, make drunk my reason,

and little by little take away my soul, making me lose all feeling whether it be sight, hearing, feeling, tasting or touching. And as for sight.]

We are now in a 'lieu' where normative sensory data, reason, and even the narrator's soul, are altered or taken from him.[64] The description that follows must therefore rely on *altered* perception, on the absence of normative evaluative criteria. He thus puts Joinville in a category outside reality, beyond the realm of normal perception: despite having lost his sight, Belleau's narrator continues nevertheless to describe what he sees. In fact, visual perceptions compose the entire *Bergerie*. Clearly, the 'oeil' that sees what is described differs from the 'oeil' that was lost. This change becomes apparent as the narrator's gaze shifts from the landscape to small ornamental objects. From pastoral to Mannerist, from landscape through sculpture and architecture, his eyes come to rest finally on painting.

C'estoit une croupe de montagne moyennement haute, toutesfois d'assez difficile acces: du costé où le soleil raporte le beau jour, se découvroit une longue terrasse pratiquee sur les flancs d'un rocher, portant largeur de deux toises et demie, enrichie d'apuis et d'amortissemens de pierre [...] L'un des bouts de cette terrasse estoit une galerie vitree, lambrisee sur un plancher de carreaux émaillez de couleur. Le frontispice, à grandes colonnes, canellees et rudentees, garnies de leurs bases, chapiteaux, architrave, frise, cornice, et mouleures de bonnes grace, et de juste proportion. La veuë belle, et limitee de douze coupeaux de montagnettes, ruisselets, rivieres, fontaines, prez, combes, chasteaux, villages, et bois, bref de tout cela que l'oeil sauroit souhaitter pour son contentement. Or dedans ceste galerie couverte se monstroit une infinité de tableaux. (6–7)

[It was the flank of a mountain, not too high but still quite hard to get to: on the side of the rising sun there was a long terrace hewed into the flanks of a rock, two and a half measures wide, decorated with stone ledges and barriers ... One of the edges of this terrace was a windowed panelled gallery with a floor of enamelled colored tiles. The frontispiece had large fluted and cabled columns, decorated at the base, with capitals, architraves, borders, cornices, and moldings all in proportion. The beautiful and confined view was of twelve mountain knolls, streams, rivers, fountains, meadows, valleys, castles, villages, and woods: in short, everything that the eye could desire for its pleasure. But in this covered gallery there was an infinite number of paintings].

This *entrée en matière* echoes Ovid's *Metamorphoses* via Sannazaro's *Arcadia*. The *Arcadia* starts with a plateau 'on the summit of Parthenius, a not inconsiderable mountain of pastoral Arcadia, a pleasant plateau.' Sannazaro's description of the plateau closely imitates the *Metamorphoses*, 10.86–108, and both focus on the trees, in particular on the cypress. Ovid tells the story of the transformation of Cyparissus, and Sannazaro introduces the shepherds who sing and play under the trees. Belleau's narrator, in contrast, focuses immediately on the man-made terrace, relating its width and its architectural and sculptural embellishments. His gaze then wanders over to the gallery with its stained glass, enamelled tiles,[65] cornices, and mouldings, all of 'juste proportion' [appropriate proportions]. He then grants the reader one last – highly circumscribed – glance at the surrounding landscape before entering the gallery of paintings, and the vista he offers merely pleases the eye rather than surveying a named territory.

Belleau's framing moment is imitated from Longus's *Daphnis et Chloé*,[66] in which the narrator also turns away from the landscape of Lesbos in order to contemplate a stunningly beautiful painting, which takes all his attention and motivates the entire text.[67] Belleau repeats this gesture on several occasions in his *Bergerie*, preferring to contemplate a sentimental representation of a love story in a painting rather than the surroundings in which the painting is located. His text shares with its source a rejection of the fiction of the immediacy of place in favour of representations that expose place as already distanced by the work of art. The containment of landscape within the frames of paintings not only repeats Longus's initial containment, but evokes the strong visual culture associated with *Daphnis et Chloé* in France. The Flemish painter Ambroise Dubois (1542–1614) decorated the Cabinet du Roi at Fontainebleau with a pictorial history of Longus's pastoral. Four extant sketches of scenes from *Daphnis et Chloé* show that the story inspired an independent culture in the plastic arts very soon after Amyot translated it into French.[68] Belleau indeed seems more concerned with the visual transmission of the story than with intertextual detail, as in most of his textual borrowings.

Belleau's technical description of the gallery at Joinville recalls another important source that had given rise to an independent visual culture in France: the *Songe de Polyphile* [Dream of Polyphilus], translated in 1546 into French from the *Hypnerotomachia Poliphili* attributed to Francesco Colonna, with significantly expanded engravings and a contracted text. In the very lengthy first book, the lover Polyphilus wanders through an allegorical landscape of intricately described ruins, tombs, monuments, and statues. The architectural accuracy makes this a curious text for modern readers, but it enjoyed a huge success in the sixteenth century, tapping into similar aesthetic sensibilities that gave rise to Mannerist painting and sculpture (Jean Cousin's *Jeux d'enfants*, for example, in which tiny children play in a landscape of ruins that overwhelm them).[69] Belleau shares the author's taste for the technical details of architecture and masonry, and he too presents the reader with a landscape that serves merely as a backdrop to the many works of art that the narrator contemplates.

To return to the text: Belleau's narrator, who would surely have evoked Polyphilus to a contemporary reader, enters the gallery where three paintings in particular seize his attention. This is where he will linger, and where his description begins. The first is a pastoral scene, with two shepherds caught in an attitude of despondency, their songs conveniently engraved on the trunks of the trees against which they lean:

Le premier estoit un paysage si bien et si naïvement raporté au naturel, que la nature mesme se tromperoit s'elle osoit entreprandre de faire mieux,[70] au milieu se découvroient deux bergers assis et apuiez du dos contre le tronc de deux ormes, ils estoient si pensifs et de si triste contenance qu'on jugeoit facilement quils se lamentoient sur les miseres de nostre tems, et à la verité ils portoient l'œil baissé, le visage palle et chagrin, et si jay bonne memoire, je vous diray leurs complaintes que je vis si mignonnement traçees et contrefaictes au pinceau sur le tronc de ces arbres, qu'il sembloit qu'elles fussent de relief, creües et engrossies avec leur escorce.[71] (7)

[The first was a landscape so well done and so simple and natural that nature herself would be wrong to dare to do better; in the middle were two shepherds sitting and leaning their backs against the trunks of two elms. They were so sad and contemplative that it was easy to tell they were complaining about the current hard times, and in truth their gaze was downcast, their faces pale and sad, and if I can remember correctly I will recount their laments which I saw so well traced onto the trunks of these trees that they seemed to be embossed, growing and thickening with the bark.]

A poetic dialogue between shepherds, lamenting the misery of the times, follows. These verses were originally published in 1559 as the *Chant pastoral de la paix*, with three interlocutors, Bellin, Thoinet, and

Perot (the poets Belleau, Baïf, and Ronsard). In the 1565 *Bergerie*, Belleau repartitioned the same verses between two interlocutors, Charlot and Francin, whom Delacourcelle supposes might represent the cardinal and the duke of Guise. In the 1572 edition of the *Première journée*, however, the shepherds are once again the three poets. This gesture back towards a poetic dialogue on the state of the nation seems significant, reinforcing the solidarity originally envisioned by Du Bellay, and the idea of poetry itself as a communal effort to construct a place of social protest. The difference however is that Belleau's poet-shepherds are (in the fiction of the poetry) paintings, fixed in time and space and inanimate. Their words, too, are part of the painting, carved in the tree rather than pronounced out loud. The palpable conceit of hundreds of lines of poetry being painted onto a painting of a tree further underscores the impossibility of the ideal: mere disembodied words.

These words paint a landscape inhabited by the knowledge of war and of its own collapse: 'Il n'y a dans ces bois lieu tant soit solitaire, / Qui ne sente de Mars la fureur ordinaire, / Vous le savez taillis, et vous coustaux bossus' [In these woods there is no place, however solitary / That does not feel the fury of Mars / You know it, coppices, and so do you, rounded hillsides] (8). It is a collapse that has already taken place, since the landscape described exists only in the words engraved on the tree, not even in the painting itself. Images of sterility, of silence, abound: France, 'la perle du monde / Est maintenant sterile, au lieu d'estre feconde' [the pearl of the world / Is now sterile rather than fertile] (8), the rocks are deaf, the rivers are dry. The imagined landscape of the Golden Age is turned upside down, all has become its opposite. Belleau is taking the pastoral tension between willed and actual truth to an extreme that breaks all forms of containment. The return of the regretted Golden Age is now not sufficient to counter what has happened; the seasons may resume their natural cycle, says Belleau's shepherd, but there will be no more flowers, no more fruit: 'Le beau tems reviendra, mais les branches rompues / Ne seront ny de fruits, ny de feuilles vestues' [good times will come again, but the broken branches will carry neither fruit nor flowers] (10).

Belleau links the death of civility, of the greatness of France, with the now inevitable constatation of poetry's failure. As the shepherds give their litany of woes, a strange sense of futility increases: more and more, they speak only to say that their words are in vain, that they can no longer produce poetry. The shepherd Bellot's fingers are stiff, he has forgotten how to play the pipes, and Tenot complains that the wind simply carries away their woes: 'Que servent nos plaintes? Tousjours avec les vents elles s'en vont esteintes' [What good are our complaints? They always go off silenced by the wind] (12). At this point, there is a significant difference between the two editions of the *Bergerie*. The 1565 edition here contains a narratorial interjection that bizarrely actualizes Tenot's complaint that their words are carried away by the wind. The narrator informs the reader that the shepherds had more to say, but 'on avoit laissé une fenestre ouverte, qui regardoit droit sur ce tableau, et le vent avoit donné à l'endroit où estoit ces vers, de façon qu'il ne me fut possible d'en retirer d'avantage' [a window, which directly faced this painting, had been left open, and the wind had blown right where these lines were, such that I couldn't read any more of them]. The narrator, in a playful, almost Rabelaisian moment, taking a cue from his interlocutor at the second level of fiction, transposes the metaphor down to the first level; the wind quite literally takes away Tenot's words. In addition to the initial suspension of disbelief required to imagine hundreds of lines of poetry on the painted tree, we are further required to momentarily forget that these words are part of a painting, and as such that they cannot blow away: for a moment, the words become disembedded, disembodied, floating somehow on top of the painting rather than painted into it, and susceptible to a gust of wind.

The longer 1572 edition defers the moment at which the shepherd's poetry is blown away. In response to Tenot's complaint that his words are always blown away, Bellot urges him instead to rejoice in the beautiful spring day and the gifts of nature, and to follow the example of Perot (Ronsard), who still manages to make the landscape speak in response to his song. The fictional Ronsard arrives, in fact, and urges the other two to make merry and celebrate peace, which they do, in the 'Chant de la Paix,' [the Song of Peace], a celebration of the peace of Cateau-Cambrésis in 1559, concluded between the Valois and Habsburg dynasties. This cycle ends on a Ronsardian note of optimism; Charles IX is invested with all the symbolism of the Golden Age, the French landscape is once again imagined as fertile and forever green.[72] However, it is at this point in the 1572 text that we find the narratorial interjection of the 1565 edition, the wind blowing away the poetry, and its effect is more powerful than in the earlier edition, coming as it does after the optimistic alliance of pastoral tropes with political fact. It is not merely the complaints that are carried away by the wind, but also a certain type of affirmative, propagandistic poetry. Belleau has given the reader the full cycle of pastoral modes, from the mourning of the irretrievable loss of the Golden Age to the celebration of its return through a political figure, and has quite literally (fictionally at least) thrown it all – including Ronsard himself, perhaps – out of the window with a gust of wind, a gesture heretofore unknown in pastoral poetry.[73]

Here, Belleau picks up the order of the 1565 edition: an *Ode à la paix*, then an ode to the Duke of Guise, with seven extra stanzas omitted from the 1565 edition. The *Ode à la paix* is, again, spoken by a shepherd in a painting. The 'pauvres bergers' are praying to Astraea, imploring her to return to 'la France enyvree' [crazed France] to restore peace. Although we cannot directly claim a source painting for this, the representation of France suffering under the civil war was undertaken by the painter Bombas, whom Belleau almost certainly knew, in a now-lost *Tableau de la France désolée*. Belleau describes the afflictions of the country in the words of the shepherd, rather than by direct images:

> Assez les flammes civiles
> Ont couru dedans nos villes,
> Sous le fer, et la fureur,
> Assez la palle famine,
> Et la peste et la ruïne,
> Ont ébranlé ton bonheur.   (13–14)

[Enough have the flames of civil war / Raced through our cities / With iron and fury, / Enough have pale famine / And plague and ruin / Shaken your (France's) happiness.]

The images are standard descriptives for the sacks and sieges of towns, and hark back to that archetype of great sieges, the description of the fall of Troy in the *Aeneid*. In order to restore peace to France, the shepherds ask specifically that Astraea 'fay un cœur de tous nos Princes / Et rasseure nos Provinces' [unite all our Princes / And reassure our Provinces] (14). The shepherds locate the cause of civil strife in the divided intentions of the peers of the realm, who – like the Guise – pull their provinces down with them as they fight each other.

The shepherds' prayer for peace is interesting in light of the following *ekphrasis*, a description of the third painting, which is 'tout guerrier' [all about war]. This painting illustrates precisely the kind of war-torn landscape lamented by the shepherds in the previous painting. On one side of the painting, we are told, 'c'estoient sieges et prises de villes' [there were seiges and sackings of towns]. Belleau describes them in detail, echoing the imagery of the shepherd's complaints. On the other side 'se voyoit le voyage d'une jeunesse Françoise en Italie, sous la conduitte de ce vaillant Chevalier' [one could see the youth of France traveling to Italy under the leadership of that valiant knight] (16). This alludes to the Naples expedition led by the Duke of Guise in 1556, in which Belleau participated. The stated goal of the expedition was to come to the aid of Pope Paul IV, whose estate was threatened by the Spanish. However, the real goal was nothing more than the princely and factional ambition denounced by the peaceful shepherds in this painting: to claim the rights of the house of Lorraine in Naples, and to ensure the Papal succession in favour of the Duke's brother Charles, the Cardinal of Lorraine.

The Duke of Guise did in fact display his military trophies, along with paintings and sculptures of his exploits, in the gallery Belleau describes.[74] However, Belleau turns pictorial representation against itself: he undermines the celebration of conquest more than he reinforces it. Belleau had been to Naples with the Duke; had he wanted to write a eulogy of the campaign, he could have done so more convincingly by writing a poem in his own voice of what he saw. As it is, he uses the medium of the painting to mediate his own historical witnessing, to the point of obscuring it entirely. The narratorial Belleau's viewing of the painting eclipses the historical Belleau's witnessing of the campaign. This distance is further reinforced by the disembodied poem that is associated with the painting. The poetry of the first painting was engraved on the tree trunk, and the prayer to Astraea in the second painting came from the shepherds. But we have no idea from where, or whom, the poem about the third painting comes. It is presented without framing or introduction right after the description of the military exploits the narrator sees on the canvas. Whether the poem is in the narrator's voice, the voice of the Duke or another person represented in the painting, or simply unattributed verses found somewhere on the painting, we never know. Thus, the most laudatory verses towards the Duke of Guise in the *Bergerie* are attached to no voice, no source. What is more, Belleau places the painting in the narrative beside the painting of the shepherds' complaints, a detail that serves, if not explicitly to criticize the territorial ambitions of the Guise, at least to confront the reader with questions about their effects on the country.

The poem ends as abruptly as it began, with no transition or narratorial comment, and the narrator starts to describe 'ceste terrasse,' the physical location of the gallery of paintings, which the reader has most likely forgotten. Briefly, Belleau grants the reader a glimpse of the vine-yards of Joinville, where 'la vigne commençoit à ébourrer le coton deli-cat de son bourgeon' [the vine was starting to open the delicate cotton of its bud] (20). Decontextualized and unannounced, the effect of this panorama is disconcerting. The reader is left wondering where exactly this terrace and these vineyards are located, supposing perhaps that they constitute part of a new painting. When the narrator shifts again abruptly from contemplating the vines to reporting yet another poem that he found carved into the terrace by a shepherd, the effect is even more dislocating. Michel Jeanneret has aptly observed that the bounda-ries between plastic and narrative worlds in the *Bergerie* are indistinct, arguing that this blurring confers to the castle 'the dimensions of the marvelous.'[75] If it does so, though, I think it is in order to problematize the project of praise rather than to enhance it. Belleau presents a real place that is not quite real, that is not so much a geographical entity as a kind of museum for painted flights of fancy about what it should be.

These works of art themselves are inspired by the Mannerist school whose tendency is itself disillusioned, dissociative, and fragmented. Landscape is no longer imagined as a French space reinvented, unified, and reinvigorated by poetry, but as already littered with the remains of memorials and monuments to what it was trying to be. Landscape in the *Bergerie*, if it is described at all, exists as an epitaph to a moment of hope that is no longer, or is only in fiction. The glimpse of the castle's territory is fleeting and, it seems, unsustainable; the narrator returns rapidly to his comfort zone, the world of art. On the terrace, he finds several poems, and a tapestry. The poems vary between editions;[76] they are followed by the frequently anthologized *L'Esté*,[77] which is not a de-scription of Belleau's halcyon summer days in Joinville as one might expect, but some verses that the narrator found embroidered along the edges of a tapestry representing a harvest scene.[78] The 1572 version is very long, and shows the allegorized Belleau, Bellot, suffering from un-requited love that burns like the heat of the sun. What makes this not just another Petrarchan lover lamenting his torment is the strange posi-tioning, or distancing, of the scene that pushes the bounds of the read-ers' credibility. We follow the narrator into a hall where he sees a tapestry, the edges of which have literally hundreds of lines of poetry woven into them, lines that describe the amatory anguish of the allego-rization of the narrator himself. We are in a referential hall of mirrors such that we are no longer able to situate where the action is taking place, or even what the action is. Geography seems suspended; we are not able to locate just where or what pastoral landscape is any more. It is constantly referred back to another level of representation.

The ruling family in this landscape is similarly hard to locate. Rather than being allegorized as shepherds and participating in the processes of an ideally ordered society, as are Ronsard's Valois in his *Bergerie*, the Guise are strangely invisible. The Duke, of course, is dead, as is his older son. Antoinette de Bourbon, the Duke's widow, is not so much described as glimpsed floating from one appointment to another. After the relation of the poem *L'Esté* on the tapestry, the narrator meets a troop of *bergères* on their way to 'donner le bon jour à leur maistresse, pour luy faire compaignie à visiter une chapelle et là faire leurs prieres' [to greet their mistress and to accompany her on a visit to a chapel where they would pray] (23).[79] These shepherdesses have stepped right out of one of the castle's paintings or poems, it seems, further blurring the boundaries between the pictorial and the narrative. They accompany an aging Antoinette to her ablutions at the tomb of her late husband. Doris Delacourcelle tells us that Primaticcio was commissioned to draw the plans for this tomb and that it was sculpted by Domenico Barbiere.[80] Belleau's description appears to be faithful, and Antoinette's ritual visits did apparently take place almost every day at Joinville;[81] Belleau turns historical fact into a poignant moment signifying the absence, more than the presence, of this family. Antoinette is an elderly and infirm widow; her husband is present only in his pictures and in his sepulchre. We are far from the productive and healthy shepherd-royals of Ronsard. Here, a whole notion of aristocratic activity and patronage seems to be threatened.

A small but pertinent detail elegantly signals the decline of the persuasive power of aristocratic pastoral. The marking of the various activities at Joinville is characterized by a strange and novel insistence on the punctual keeping of time. At nine o'clock, Antoinette washes her hands and leads her ladies to table, where meals are taken at nine and five o'clock 'sans jamais y faire faute' [without fail] (32). The mechanical marking of time is at odds with the conventional pastoral cycles of day and night, where the passing of time and the ordering of activities is based on the rising and setting of the sun. As far as I know, Belleau's is the first pastoral to keep mechanical time.[82] Towards the end of the day, leisurely pastoral activity, including masquerades and singing competitions, actually closes with the chiming of a clock. This new punctuality directly opposes lyric poetry itself, by interrupting the poetry of Ronsard – the very voice of French lyric – because it is eight o'clock. In the 1565 edition, Ronsard has himself appeared to participate in the festivities and is singing verses from his own *Bergerie*. His audience disperses suddenly however: 'pendant ce discours qui n'ennuya gueres à ces bergeres huit heures sonnent, et soudain toute la compaignie sort de la terrasse' [during this performance which greatly entertained the shepherdesses, eight o'clock rang out, and suddenly the whole group left the terrace] (106).[83] The leisure to linger, so characteristic of pastoral poetry, is here curtailed by a strange new imperative – the need to be somewhere else at a specific time. Quite contrary to an idealized haven where French lyric can flourish untainted by the cares of the world outside, Joinville is a place where French lyric comes to die, to be superseded by the exigencies of modern times (signalled by the clock), or written into the edges of paintings that preserve the pastoral vision as pure ornament, pure artifice.

The most complete and eulogistic description of Joinville as a pastoral haven is, again, part of a painting rather than a direct observation. When the shepherdesses sit down to dine, they can talk of nothing but a painting: 'ces filles n'eurent autres propos que d'un tableau qui pendoit dessus la cheminee' [these girls could talk of nothing but a painting which hung above the mantlepiece] (32–3). It is not only Belleau's narrator, it seems, who can talk of nothing but paintings. This is a painting of a distraught nymph, 'un chasseur apres qui la poursuivoit; en fin elle se sauvoit en un lieu beau et frais, où ce chasteau estoit fort bien raporté en perspective' [who was being pursued by a hunter, and finally got away to a fresh, beautiful place where this castle was well drawn in perspective].[84] A wise old man explains to the shepherdesses that the hunter is Desire, and the nymph, Chastity, who is running to the safe haven of Joinville. It is here that we have one of the most complete descriptions of the territory of 'ce chasteau de Joinville, et de fait il monstroit avec une petite verge blance, les terrasses, les galleries, les salles, les chambres, antichambres, les cours, les offices, le jeu de paume, l'Eglise, les vignes, les bois, les routes, les montagnes, les vallons, les rivieres, les prez, la ville basse' [this castle of Joinville, and in fact he was indicating with a little white stick the terraces, galleries, rooms, chambers, anterooms, butleries, courtyards, tennis courts, church, vineyards, woods, roads, mountains, valleys, rivers, meadows, and the town] (33). But the point of view is not that of the narrator looking directly upon Joinville; it is refracted through the painting. What Belleau's narrator is describing for us is a landscape painting.[85] Why does textual narrative give way to visual? The narrator seems unable to describe the topography of Joinville as a whole without the containment offered by the painting. He gives us partial descriptions, mere glimpses in certain directions. Even when he does try to describe an aspect of landscape, his attention, as we have seen, is quickly diverted by a poem he finds engraved on a rock, or by a painting or tapestry. Landscape for Belleau is no longer the business of poetry; the *Bergerie* negotiates the poet's handing over of landscape to the visual arts, leaving us wondering what might be the new subject matter of lyric. At the moment when lyric poetry would engage landscape, the narrator cedes the work of the description to a plastic art.

What, indeed, is the new subject of lyric explored in the *Bergerie*? If Belleau excludes or relegates landscape description to other art forms, these art forms in their turn give poetry a new kind of inspiration. An interesting moment of negotiation between painting and lyric comes towards the end of the first *journée*. A lovelorn shepherd describes the beauties of his mistress; his description evokes an image of what can only be a Mannerist portrait, the antithesis to Leonardo's or Michelangelo's anatomically precise representation of human muscular structure.[86] 'Sa gorge, elle est longuette, grassette, et marquée de deux petits plis sous le menton [...] Ceste gorge finist en un sein large, blanchissant, sans monstrer ny muscle, ny jointure, ny aparance d'os' [Her neck is prettily long, roundish, and marked by two little folds under the chin ... this neck ends in a wide, white bosom showing neither muscle, joint, or any bone structure]. And the breasts, usually static in lyric descriptions, here start to move, 'tirant et repoussant ses soupirs d'une juste cadance, ainsi qu'on voit les petits flots sur la greve de la mer' [breathing in and out with a regular cadence, like little waves on the sea shore] (67). Marcel Raymond, in his characterization of both Mannerist painting and poetry, insists on the primacy of movement which 'can reach extreme agitation,' and on the frequency of erotic subjects. This odd moment of animation of the female subject evokes a school of portraiture more than the literary tradition of the *blason* (in which female body parts tend to stay still as the male poet describes them).

Indeed, the lovelorn shepherd reinforces the conflation between textual and visual by giving the narrator a 'portrait' of his lady that he pulls out of his pocket. There is initially a willed confusion as to whether this is a written or a pictorial portrait. The shepherd presents it as 'le pourtrait de ma maistresse que j'ay fait et traçé au pinceau' [the portrait of my mistress which I had made and drawn with a brush]; the reader assumes it is a picture, as does the narrator: 'C'estoit veritablement le

pourtrait de sa maistresse.' But the portrait turns out to be a set of instructions to a painter, like Ronsard's *Elégie à Janet*. Imitated both from
Ronsard and from Anacreaon,[87] the poem itself is derivative and unre-
markable. Details that might at first seem to refer to the portraits produced by the school of Fontainebleau turn out to be close calques of
Anacreaon, for example the insistence on the space between the eye-
brows. The narrator himself apologizes for this poem to the reader, justifying its inclusion as a matter of narratorial integrity: 'Je ne fay doute
que ceste trop longue chanson vous aura ennuyez, mais si je l'eusse
oubliee possible vous en eussiez esté malcontens' [I have no doubt that
this overly long song has bored you, but you might have been upset if
I had left it out] (75). In the quest for lyric subjects, this bid has failed.
Poetry has negotiated with painting for the subject of portraiture and
has been found wanting. The message seems to be that when painting
takes over from poetry, the result is successful; when poetry tries to do
the work of painting, the result is tedious.

If poetry can't even describe female beauty without tedium, what is
left for it to describe? Belleau gives his answer after the failed lyric portrait. The shepherdesses interrupt the boring song, as it seems that the
shepherd reciting it wants to continue. And so the shepherd changes
subject, and recounts for the women his 'voyage d'Italie,' offering each
of them a small pen as a token of his esteem. Each pen is offered with a
short poem whose function is to present the gift and render it agreeable.
The poem is precious in style, addressing the anthropomorphized pens
as if they were lovers, instructing them to find a place in the hearts of
the young women to whom they are offered, and to fan the fires of their
love 'par le doux vent de vostre plume' [by the sweet inspiration of
your feather]. Belleau puts the pen, the instrument of writing, in the
service of a gallant Amour; indeed the pen has been fashioned by
'Amour de ses plus legeres (plumes)' [Love, with his lightest (feathers)]
(77). Not only are pens given instructions to serve love, but the poem
itself that accompanies this gift of writing participates in the same spirit
of courtly gallant exchange. This is, it would seem, an acceptable direction for lyric to take: to renounce any attempt to be about anything else
but the lyric subject *par excellence*, love. This bid for a subject is apparently acceptable, because the shepherdesses are 'fort contentes de ces
petites nouveautez' [delighted with these little novelties] (78), and
when the shepherd-poet proceeds to recite a prayer to Pan, they judge
it to be 'pastoralle' and 'a propos' [pastoral and appropriate] (80). The
conversation continues for a while in this vein, and every poem of this

genre is judged favourably; in fact, the more precious the poem, the more positive the reaction.

Belleau does propose one other direction for lyric that does not condemn it to the limited and repetitive economy of love poetry. This is the detailed and minute description of ornamental objects, which he fully develops in the 1576 *Amours et nouveaux eschanges des pierres precieuses*. The shepherdesses judging the precious poetry also spend much time admiring a sumptuously decorated mirror, the description of which is easily the longest *ekphrasis* of the work.[88] As the day goes on, the presence of ornamental artisanship increases. After the recital of love poetry has ended at eight o'clock, the narrator wanders down into the village of Joinville, where he admires various works produced by the artisans of the village on display in the marketplace. This is the first time that the narrator has left the confines of the castle and its immediate grounds; he is now in a different space entirely. Here, the producers of works of art are neither unnamed painters nor generic shepherds, they are village craftspeople; the audience for their work is not the restricted population of the castle but the crowds in the marketplace. A democratic vision, perhaps, of art's producers and its consumers, all the more so since among the many goods, 'ceintures, rubans, bracelets [...] toutes sortes de vaisseaux propres à la bergerie,' as well as the intriguing 'petites prisons de joncs mollets pour enfermer des sauterelles,' [belts, ribbons, bracelets ... all kinds of utensils for keeping livestock, and little grasshopper cages of soft rushes] (107), the narrator finds some objects that he deems worthy of the label 'chef d'œuvre.' He describes, in alexandrine verse, a wooden cup sculpted by a local shepherd. The entire poem is descriptive-ornamental, and as such may seem to be no more than a curiosity. However, the attention to detail is more than an aesthetics, or poetics, of minutiae. Belleau brings together different spheres of knowledge and production of culture into a new, inclusive kind of lyric. He is reconciling court poet and marketplace artisan, including within lyric a relationship between the aristocrats in the castle and the vendors in the marketplace. This redefines the relationship between the upper and the working classes typical of pastoral. To present a relationship of consumption between the castle and the products of the marketplace is to extend the social domain of lyric far beyond the pastoral.

Belleau not only shows us the possibility of a more inclusive or democratic lyric that acknowledges other sources of cultural production; he imagines a poetry that will engage with different disciplines. He describes an encounter with a 'gentil artizan venu de la rive d'Uvigne' [a pleasant artisan from the banks of the Huisne] (109),[89] who is accomplished in almost every possible science. The artisan gives Belleau a cane that shows the hours of the day and the days of the week, in relation to the positions of the signs of the Zodiac and the planets. A small needle indicates the time and the day within this solar and astrological calendar. The cane also functions as a compass and barometer, and 'il pouvoit servir à arpenter, à prendre largeurs, longueurs et hauteurs; à cognoistre quel chemin fait la Lune en une heure artificielle, les distances des estoiles fixes de l'une à l'autre' [it could be used to survey, to measure width, length, and height; to find out what trajectory the moon is following at a given time, the distances between the fixed stars] (118). The cane's usefulness as a surveying tool is perhaps indicative of the new relationship to landscape in the *Bergerie*, one that is both ornamental and scientific, as opposed to pastoral.[90] However the cane is also a tool for the production of art, since the handle is adapted to hold paints and dyes, and the stem to hold paintbrushes and paper 'pour designer paisages, villes, chasteaux, et bastimens rustiques' [to draw landscapes, towns, castles, and rustic buildings] (119) – another example of the designation of landscape description to painters. The stem is composed of four flutes, which four *bergers* start to play, accompanying themselves as they sing love songs. This remarkable instrument is thus the source of love poetry as well as being a scientifically accurate tool. Belleau is making poetry scientific, and science poetic.

Belleau here anticipates a significant new direction for lyric poetry, one he will take up in earnest, with many other poets, in the last quarter of the century, when he turns away entirely from any attempt at landscape description to a type of scientific poetry that seeks to explain the mystical connections between the created world and divine intention.[91] I shall return to scientific poetry in the conclusion, as its turn to cosmic order (and away from landscape description) is in some ways the vanishing point of the poetic moment I describe throughout this study. As Dudley Wilson points out, 'scientific poetry' is a definition very much after the effect.[92] However, at least by the seventeenth century Colletet had given a definition of 'poésie naturelle' as 'celle qui traitte à fond des choses de Nature' [that which treats natural themes exhaustively].[93] Belleau's contribution to the genre, his *Amours ou nouveaux eschanges des pierres precieuses* (1576), is a kind of mystical lapidary in which fundamental truths about the mechanics of the universe are sought in the properties of various stones.[94] Belleau makes much more use of classical and Neoplatonic sources than of direct observation, and the 'secrets de nature' that he claims to uncover are more occult than scientific.[95] He seeks correspondences between the smallest scale and the largest, between stones and universal principles. The principle of perpetual movement in nature, the constant shifting of one form to another, is illustrated by stories of metamorphoses of people into stones or vice versa,[96] as is the principle of love by the phenomenon of magnetic attraction in the poem 'La pierre d'aymant' [the magnetic stone]. The *Pierres précieuses* have been taken to correspond to the taste of a rising bourgeoisie who could afford luxury objects and were particularly interested in gems, a phenomenon fuelled by the influx of precious stones from the New World.[97] It seems however to correspond more directly to the tastes of the court and of the nascent literary salons, where valuable trinkets and jewels changed hands. Belleau addresses individual poems about gems to individual ladies at court, the circulation of his poems mimicking that of gems themselves in the courtly milieu. This is precious or galant, not bourgeois, literature, aimed very consciously at a select section of society. Gone are the moments of contact with the marketplace and the artisan producers of culture. Gone too is any interest in the geographical location of his poems. Belleau's focus is on the minute and ornamental, or on what the minute might reveal about universal principles. Place, it seems, is now irrelevant. He moves away from the nostalgic description of an idealized society on an idealized French landscape, and towards a more asocial, and transnational, understanding of the physical universe. Remy Belleau's *Bergerie* anticipates this new direction. The narrator's wanderings through Joinville represent an exploration into new poetic territory, a rejection of written images of the land, a Mannerist shattering of the possibility of imagining a unified poetic – and real – space, with eventually the suggestion in the marketplace that even this fragmented reality might, through scientific knowledge of discrete small objects, yield its own, transcendent truth.

The question of the 'real' in the *Bergerie* has exercised a number of critics. Françoise Joukovsky has argued that the prose sections of the *Bergerie* in which the castle and its surrounding grounds are described situate the works of art 'in a topography that makes them participate in reality.'[98] But as I have shown, the space into which the works of art are inserted is just as unreal as they are. Michel Jeanneret is, I think, closer to the mark when he argues that 'there are no longer two levels of reality, but only one homogenous level where the real and the fictional are conflated.'[99] The very categories of real and fictional no longer obtain, due to Belleau's willed confusion between the plastic and the narrative worlds. However, this confusion does not garner unadulterated praise for the Guise family. Rather, it critically exposes the self-conscious acts of exclusion and containment operated by a certain type of pastoral construction of French landscape, such as that of Ronsard's *Bergerie*. Belleau's Mannerist aesthetic fragments the unity of any ideal vision of France which pastoral might offer, and seeks new directions for the mode. His *Bergerie*, then, is a 'a tiring of the most fashionable literary genre.'[100] But it is more that this: it is also a political critique, and an engagement with the very question of poetry's power and subject. France will never become the kind of pastoral space imagined by Ronsard. French aristocrats and monarchs cannot enable the return of the Golden Age; all they can do is what Belleau describes – shut themselves off physically and mentally from the rest of the country, contemplate works of art, and imagine what might be.

Conclusion

I argue in the other chapters that sixteenth-century French poets strive collectively to write images of French landscape as 'spaces of hope' in the face of historical catastrophe, albeit in full awareness of the limitations of their representations. Cartography, exemplar texts, and environmental and social reality sustain these landscapes. But when they engage the plastic arts, something else happens. The 'domain of irreparable falsehood' identified by Roberto Campo as subtending Tyard's *Fables* can no longer be kept at bay.[101] The disintegration of classical style and unity operated by the school of Fontainebleau impacts the representation of landscape. As Josiane Rieu observes, Mannerist paintings of landscape 'urgently pose the problem of the representation of space in the sixteenth century – the condition of landscape's existence. Spatial coherence is both proposed and refused by the multiplying of spaces which coexist in the same painting. By studying this ambiguity we can better understand the very idea of space in sixteenth-century mentalities.'[102]

In different ways, Remy Belleau and Pontus de Tyard illustrate the moment perceived, but deferred, by their fellow poets: the moment at which the space of hope imagined by poetry closes in on itself and ceases to refer to anything outside the self-consciously fictional, when poetry gives up any attempt to engage with and define real landscape. By replacing the relative coherence of poetic descriptions of French landscapes with fragmented descriptions of paintings and with the foreign metamorphic world of classical myth, they abandon the attempt to put France on the map and self-consciously resort to convention and artifice. Having considered here the distancing of French place in poetry through reference to the plastic arts, which renders it as a self-conscious cultural echo chamber, I will turn in the following chapter to poetry that attempts to make native landscapes more present by engaging the historical experience of environmental degradation.

5 The Poet and the Environment: Naturalizing Conservative Nostalgia

Thus far, we have discussed ways in which landscapes of lyric are in dialogue with the drama of their historical moments, and with other representational modes (cartography and painting). What happens, though, when the named landscape is itself undergoing dramatic change at the hands of humans? In other words, how does poetry engage with environmental history; how does it represent a stable space of hope when the land itself is in flux? I propose here that poets evoke human contamination of natural spaces the better to present the 'second world' of poetry not only as a 'green world,' but as an alternative and superior moral order. Its plea for a return to an uncontaminated landscape is a plea for a return to a notional morality perceived as lost. Jean-Antoine de Baïf laments the pollution of the river Bièvre in the Parisian suburb of Arcueil, and calls upon poets to rewrite the landscape as one of pure poetry. Through myth and poetry, Baïf reinvents the Arcueil of his youth, a place that had held significance as a gathering place for the poets of the Pléiade in the 1550s, as a pristine retreat far from the depredations of modernity. Ronsard, who pleads against the felling of the trees of the Gâtine forest, evidences nostalgia not only for a primaeval forest but also – and primarily – for an aristocratic, Catholic social order. In both cases, the conservationist impulse shows its conservatism; to defend the environment is to defend the privileged world of the aristocratic poet. And both poets present the second world of poetry as one that has, potentially at least, agency in the real world: a true space of hope.

Baïf and the Bièvre: Polluted Poetry

The parish of Arcueil outside Paris boasted a fourth-century Roman aqueduct, a fountain, vineyards, and chalk dunes with caves. The Bièvre, a small river, flowed through Arcueil and into the Seine at Asnières.[1] Many manufacturers – tanneries, starchers, dyers, laundries – were located on its banks. Charles Estienne mentions the dyers in the 1553 *Guide des chemins de France*, where he describes, in the addendum 'Les fleuves du Royaume,' the Bièvre flowing through 'Arcueil, Gentilly [...] and Paris, where it is used to make excellent scarlet dyes.'[2] The scarlet dye is a reference to the Gobelin family, who had settled on the Bièvre in the Faubourg Saint Michel in the mid-fifteenth century, and who had become particularly renowned for that colour. Estienne does not mention it, but by the 1550s it was well known that the dyers were polluting the river by expelling into the water chemicals and urine used in the dying process. There is a record of an *arrêt* from 1538 which contains an injunction against dumping noxious dyestuffs into the river: one branch of the family had apparently taken the other to court over their dumping of chemicals in the river upstream from their house.[3]

Arcueil was a favourite rural retreat of Parisian intellectuals in the mid-sixteenth century (Rabelais's Ponocrates famously took his pupil there to relax). The poets of the Pléiade, who were in Paris in the late 1540s and early 1550s, often went there to picnic, and in their writings made the place into an idyllic pastoral retreat conducive to the production of poetry. Jean Dorat wrote a Latin ode to the fountain; Ronsard, Du Bellay, and Baïf all evoked halcyon youthful days at Arcueil in various poems; and non-Pléiade poets such as Nicholas Ellain and Jean Passerat also celebrated it.[4] In particular, Arcueil was the site of some infamous poetic baccanalia. In 1549, Ronsard and Baïf (who were sharing a room in Paris) made a trip to Arcueil with some other poets, which was celebrated in Ronsard's 'Les bacchanales ou le folastrissime voyage d'Herceuil,' published in 1552.[5] 1553 saw an even more infamous poetic picnic: as part of the celebration in Paris of François de Guise's return from Metz, and Henri II's daughter's marriage, the poet Étienne Jodelle's play *Cléopâtre captive* had played in front of the queen (Remy Belleau had acted). The play was a resounding success, and Jodelle's friends organized a *Pompe du bouc* at Arcueil in his honour. There were over twenty poets attending, and their Bacchic celebrations – which included imbibing much wine, dressing up and singing, leading an ivy-bedecked goat in procession to Jodelle and cutting its beard – left quite an impression on the residents. The poets were denounced as impious by the local *curé*, and Protestant humanists like Jacques Grévin accused them of pagan acts and actually sacrificing the goat.[6] Ronsard and Baïf, both principal organizers of the fête, commemorated the event in respective 'Dithyrambes.'[7]

The mid-sixteenth century was a time of intense interest in Hellenism, during which such Bacchic texts (and, apparently, practices) flourished.[8] I mention it here because Arcueil, as a retreat for poets in general and as the site of the infamous *pompe* in particular, became an indelible part of the poetic landscape, a place of exuberant poetic production where past tradition and present creativity met (imitation is foregrounded by the fact that the toponym was often written as *Hercueil* in the sixteenth century, recalling the tradition of the *Hercule gaulois*).[9] By the 1570s, the poetic landscape seemed a lot less hopeful, as poets were forced to confront – and often take a public position on – the wars of religion. Whereas Ronsard, as we shall see, responded by entrenching his belief that Catholicism was in the best interest of the state, Jean-Antoine de Baïf shifted his belief somewhat to a more *politique* centrism and willingness to accept Henri IV as monarch.[10] I argue that Baïf encodes the changes in the political landscape in his description of the topographic landscape of Arcueil, using water pollution as a symbol of the greater social ills facing France, and invoking the place's association with poetry to call for a return to a more peaceful order.

Baïf's poem 'La ninfe Bievre' [the nymph Bièvre] appeared in the ninth of his books of *Poèmes* in 1573.[11] The poet's Muse visits a nymph, the Bièvre itself, and prompts her to lament on the river bank. Poems addressed to rivers were quite common among the Pléiade and neo-Latin poets, but Baïf does something rather unusual. Rather than associating the river with poetic fame, he deplores, through the *prosopopoeia* of the nymph, the pollution of the water as it flows into the Seine. The poem becomes an elegy for lost purity, and a call to poets to restore not only a notional, poetic purity (a space of hope), but also to effect real environmental change. Pollution is an environmental reality, but also a symbol of contaminated poetry and a perverted moral order. Throughout the poem, Baïf allies myth and history to create what Elizabeth Vinestock calls a 'new myth,' which seeks to persuade its readers of the necessity of action in the real world. The enemy is the Gobelin family, guilty of sullying the waters of the Bièvre. There were other dyers polluting the river, of course, but Baïf picks the Gobelins because of their notoriety, and the mythic possibilities of the name itself: 'the villains are represented both as evil goblins in the mythological world of river nymphs and gods, and at the same time as the avaricious Gobelin family in the real world of sixteenth-century France.'[12] Vinestock admirably analyses the effect of Baïf's *enargeia* and other rhetorical devices which seek to move his readers, showing how this effect is amplified by the real-world referent of a polluted river well-known to Baïf's inner circle of readers. My interest is more in the *confluence* of poetry and place, and the specificity of Arcueil's significance as a synecdoche for a fertile, native poetic terrain.

The poem is addressed to Pierre Brulart, secretary of state from 1569 to 1588, with whom Baïf seems to have enjoyed respectful relations, and who 'does not disdain the Muses.'[13] The power of the addressee, both political and through patronage, is no coincidence: one of Baïf's points is that poetry and poets can *do* things in the real world, and that they thus must be supported. In fact, despite the many literary anteced-ents for the 'ninfe eploree,' it is the historical particularity of this nymph, the river Bièvre, that takes precedence over any exemplars. The poem begins with a remarkable degree of cartographic specificity, as the nymph describes her course:

> Gardant dés ma source mon nom,
> Jusqu'à tant que mon ruisseau treuve
> Contre Paris le large fleuve
> De vostre Séne au grand renom.[14]   [15–18]

[Keeping the same name from my source / All the way to where my stream joins / The wide river in Paris, / Your widely-renowned Seine.]

She mentions the aqueduct, again very specifically: 'une rigole cons-truite / De ciment, œuvre des Romains' (21–2) [a canal built / Of ce-ment, the work of the Romans]. And the generic cliché of pure unsullied water, 'l'eau nete, et saine' (14), is fairly quickly overwritten by indi-viduating particulars, until it becomes impossible to identify the river as anything but a historical, French place, the symbolism of its pollu-tion giving way to the material reality of toxic dyestuffs:

> Aujourdhuy je me traine vile
> Pour des teinturiers inhumains.
> Qui font de l'eau de mon rivage
> Dans leurs chaudieres un lavage
> De guesde et pastel meslangé:
> Qu'apres dans mon sein revomissent.   (24–9)

[Today, I flow dirtily, / Because of the inhuman dyers / Who make in their tubs / A wash from my banks' waters, / A mixture of woads, / Which they vomit afterwards into my breast.]

The contamination is then inscribed into a more generalized narrative of lost purity, which recalls the pastoral idyll of 1550s Arcueil as a contrast to contemporary reality: 'Racueillant mainte source vive / Je m'egaioy dans mon canal' [Joining with many a fresh stream, / I used to laugh in my river bed] (39–40), before the 'poisons de vos Gobelins' [the poisons of your Gobelins] (46) infected her. Now, she fears to flow into the Seine, addressing its male-gendered river god and telling him that she now does her best to avoid him. The unnaturalness of her state is emphasized by this aversion of heteronormative union. Whereas she used to unite joyfully with him, she now fears their coupling: 'Je coule tant loin que je puis / Sans que mon onde soit confuse / Avec ton eau, qui me refuse' [I flow as far as I can, / So my water is not mixed / With yours, which refuses me] (70–2).

The nymph decries a whole world turned upside down, perverted by the 'avarice méchante' [cruel greed] (59) that motivates the dyers. The Gobelins were of course extremely wealthy, a *nouveau riche* wealth that did not depend on aristocratic status. Their exploitation of natural resources is the wrong kind of land use: unlike a gentleman-farmer, whose relation with the land is easily represented as georgic or pastoral, the dyers pollute and threaten irenic pastoral – they threaten the very basis of feudal-aristocratic land ownership. They also threaten the (re)productivity of nature, replacing the union of the Bièvre with the Seine by something seen as perverse and infertile. And since natural fertility is so often a trope for the production of poetry, this threat is also literary. The Gobelins thus represent the end of all order: environmental, social, moral, literary, and class-based all at once.

The defenders of the old world order are, for Baïf, poets. He genuinely believed in the 'ability of poetry to produce practical effects,'[15] and the poem ends with an extended exhortation to his friends to reverse the pollution by writing. He calls to arms the 'bande' of poets who had enjoyed the Bièvre in bygone days of innocence, 'Soit au valon de Gentilly / Soit d'Arcueil au peupleux rivage, / Ou des arcs est debout l'ouvrage' [Either in the dales of Gentilly, / Or of Arcueil with its poplared banks / And still-standing arches] (88–90). Dorat, the father figure of the Pléiade, is invoked first, then Ronsard, Desportes, and Passerat; Belleau is given special attention because his name comes from 'la belle eau' [the beautiful water], and in the second world of poetry one can conjure an occult connection between a name and a thing.[16] These men are urged to avenge the 'sacrilege erreur' [sacrilegious error] of greed by the 'juste fureur' [righteous furor] (112, 115) of their verse (furor, of course, connotes poetic inspiration as well as moral outrage). By re-presenting the Bièvre as part of the world of poetry, the poets will either move the dyers to repentance, or at least publically shame them into changing their ways. Nowhere is the power of poetic place, the power of writing France, more fervently espoused than in this poem by Baïf. Even more than Du Bellay, who at the end of *Les Regrets* implores Marguerite de France to support poets as they rewrite and reimagine a war-torn France, Baïf advances the idea that poetry, *pace* W.H. Auden, does indeed make something happen.[17] To imagine a better world is, in a sense, to start to bring that world into being.

Ronsard and the Gâtine: Conservat(ion)ism and the Forest

The 'sacrilege' that Baïf identifies in the Gobelin's thirst for profit is also at stake in a poem by Ronsard, which was very possibly composed around the same time. Ronsard in his twenty-fourth elegy, spuriously titled the 'Elégie contre les bûcherons de la forêt de Gâtine,' also uses the *prosopopoeia* of a nymph, this time a tree-nymph, who pleas for an end to greed-motivated environmental destruction in the name of a much broader value system perceived as threatened. Parts of the Gâtine forest were, as we shall see, sold and logged starting in 1572. In his elegy, Ronsard's sylvan nymph tells the woodcutters that they are murdering the goddesses who inhabit the trees. The Gâtine, with which Ronsard had a deep familial and personal connection, becomes the poetic analogue of an entire set of principles destroyed – conservative, conservationist, feudal, regional, Catholic, classical, and poetic – and the logging is an analogue to forms of progress to which Ronsard remained firmly opposed. The trees of the Gâtine, unavoidably threatened in the present of history, are reimagined as part of a classical past, a lost poetic and moral order. And like Baïf, although less overtly, Ronsard insists on the power and value (in both senses) of poetry in the (re)writing of place.

The notion of the ancestral forest has long held great cultural power. It is a repository for collective memory, a nostalgia for something primaeval, 'un avant-moi, un avant-nous' [a before-me, a before-us], a place of pure 'littérature.'[18] Ronsard presents the Gâtine forest as just such a place overloaded with cultural meaning. It is a prelapsarian world of poetry that excludes the tensions of contemporary France, a world of aristocratic virtue and value, immune from sectarian strife and historical disruptions. Although one might be tempted to read Ronsard's anti-logging protest as evidencing primarily a proto-environmental sensibility (and there is no reason to eliminate entirely the idea that Ronsard was affected by the sight of the clearcuts), I shall argue that the ideological stakes have more to do with the status of the region with respect to the kingdom, and the status in sixteenth-century France of the Catholic, the aristocratic landowner, and of poetry itself. Local landscape is defined by an agonistic relationship to history; the forest, more than a poetic convention, more even than a beloved local haunt menaced by human activity (although it is certainly that), allows the poet to contest some of the most powerful social changes of his time, in particular the erasing of local identities by monarchic ambition, the threat of religious upheaval, and an exploitative, money-driven relation to land.

The forest of the Gâtine is named directly ten times in Ronsard's *œuvre*,[19] and many more by implication. Before turning to the twenty-fourth elegy, I will trace Ronsard's early construction of the forest in his *Odes*, where the Gâtine is established as a place of poetic significance, a place that also produces poetry by inspiring Ronsard's creativity. The ode entitled 'À sa lyre,' the final ode of the *Premier livre des odes*, is the first ode to name the forest directly.[20] It is significant that the first instance of naming of the forest comes in a poem addressed to an object, the lyre, whose image is so directly associated with poetic inspiration, and with Ronsard's own reputation.[21] It is also the final ode of its book, a position, following Horace's *Exegi monumentum*, often reserved in lyric tradition for meditations on the poet's own fame and fortune. Ronsard's entire poem is heavily derivative of both Horace and Pindar,[22] whom he harnesses to further his reputation.

Ronsard begins his ode with a close transcription of Pindar's first Pythian Ode:[23]

Lyre dorée, où Phoebus seulement
Et les neuf soeurs ont part egalement
Le seul confort qui *mes* tristesses tue
Que la danse oit, et toute s'esvertue
De t'obeyr, et mesurer ses pas
Sous tes fredons accordez par compas
Lors qu'en sonnant tu marques la cadance
De l'avant-jeu, le guide de la danse.   (1–10, my emphasis)

[Golden lyre, to whom only / Phoebus and the nine Muses have a claim, / The only comfort of *my* sorrows, / Whom the dance hears, and entirely strives / To follow you, and to measure its steps / By your well-tuned strings, / When with your playing you mark the cadence / Of the overture, which leads the dance.]

This is, for the most part, a very close imitation of the source. However Ronsard does make one important innovation: while Pindar presents an encomium to lyres in general, with no particular poet associated with its creative power, Ronsard in the third line introduces himself, the 'moi.' Ronsard thus creates a much closer association between the lyre and his own poetry. And while the voice of the first person starts off relatively weakly – not as predicate but simply as the possessor of sadness acted upon by the lyre – there is a transition in the third verse, where in the same sentence Ronsard moves from past to present through precisely the grammatical mediation of the lyre, which allows him to use the 'je' self-referentially. The poem then moves closer to home, in all senses:

> Celuy ne vit le cher-mignon des Dieux
> A qui deplaist ton chant melodieux,
> *Heureuse Lyre*, honneur de *mon* enfance,
> Je te sonnay devant tous *en la France.*   (17–20, my emphasis)

[He who dislikes your melodious song / Never saw the beloved of the Gods, / Blessed Lyre, honour of my youth, / Above all others in France it was I who made you speak.]

At the mention of the 'blessed Lyre' Ronsard departs from his Pindaric source and speaks on his own terms. The lyre has a mediating function both syntactically, in the structure of the sentence, and poetically: it is Ronsard's lyre, or his creative capacity, which allows him thus to transform past into present, or exemplars into himself. Such an act of transformation and creation works on the level of geography also, as Greece and Italy are replaced by 'la France.'

Ronsard's Frenchness then becomes more specific, and he starts to name his particular region of origin, the Vendômois, as the source of new native poetry. Still addressing his lyre, he tells it how he imitated Pindar and Horace, who are named metonymically by their homelands: 'Je pillay Thebe, et saccageay La Pouille' [I pillaged Thebes and put

Apulia to sack]. Ronsard then situates himself specifically on the banks of the Loir river: 'Et lors en France avec toy je chantay, / Et jeune d'ans sur le Loir' [And then I sang with you in France / On the banks of the Loir when I was young] (21–34). It is at the point of assimilation of the classics that regional space – as opposed to that of France as a whole – is introduced into the poem. Thebes and Apulia are replaced, through Ronsard's efforts, not just by France, but by Ronsard's own home region in particular.[24]

There is an interesting variant maintained in editions up to 1578: in this section of the poem, Ronsard had proposed that both he and Du Bellay were due the credit of the renaissance of French lyric. Here, Ronsard also named Du Bellay metonymically by his homeland:

Je t'envoiai sous le pousse Angevin
Qui depuis moi t'a si bien fredonnée
Qu'a nous deux seuls la gloire en soit donnée.   (50–3)

[I entrusted you then to Angevin hands / Which strummed you so well, second to me, / That to only the two of us is glory due.]

However, after the 1578 edition, Ronsard dropped Du Bellay from the cursus. By the last edition of his lifetime, Ronsard presents himself alone as the vehicle by which the worthy ancients are brought into France. If he presents France as a whole benefiting from his pillaging of Pindar and Horace, it is also quite clear whence in France this munificence emanates: his own Vendômois, superior this time to Du Bellay's Anjou, rather than collaborating with it. Geography (the nation, or kingdom) is, as in Du Bellay, replaced by chorography (the region).[25] But in Ronsard chorography is affirmative; there is not the disillusionment that Du Bellay feels towards his homeland at the end of his *Regrets*. Rather, the Vendômois is presented as the capital of poetic France, a place of pure poetry thanks to its association with Ronsard himself.

It is at this point in the ode, in the context of redemptive chorography, that the Gâtine forest enters the picture. Like the Loir, which appears again beside it, the naming of the Gâtine forest is inspired by a Horatian intertext.[26] Ronsard writes:

Mais ma Gastine, et le haut crin des bois
Qui vont bornant mon fleuve Vandomois,
Le Dieu bouquin qui la Neufaune entourne,

Et le saint choeur qui en Braye sejourne,
Le feront tel, que par tout l'univers
Se cognoistra renommé par ses vers.   (45–50)

[But my Gâtine, and the high canopy of the trees / Which runs alongside
my Vendomois river, / The goatlike God who inhabits the Neufaune valley, / And the blessed choir that resides in the valley of Braye, / Will make
him so famous that throughout the whole universe / He will be recognized through his poetry.]

Here, the past and the present coexist in suspension, in a landscape of
pure poetry and of Ronsard's invention. The named forest brings the
poem into the space of the French sixteenth-century lyric, but the
Horatian intertext anchors it still in the domain of the ancient masters.
The winner obviously is Ronsard himself, as he transforms the tri-
umphant ending of Horace's ode into a triumph for himself. Horace
writes, 'I am pointed out by passers-by as the minstrel of the Roman
lyre; the fact I breathe the breath of music and give pleasure (if I do give
pleasure) is all of your doing.'[27] And Ronsard:

C'est toy qui fais que Ronsard soit esleu
Harpeur François, et quand on le rencontre
Qu'avec le doigt par la rue on le monstre.
Si je plais donc, si je sçay contenter
Si mon renom la France veut chanter,
Si de mon front les estoiles je passe,
Certes mon Luth cela vient de ta grace.   (62–8)

[It is thanks to you that Ronsard is elected / The lyricist of France, and that
when he is seen / In the street, people point him out. / If then I please, if I
give pleasure, / If France sings my praises, / 'If my head stands above the
stars, / Indeed, my Lute, this is by your grace.]

Note the expansion, or *dilatio*, of Horace by Ronsard. Ronsard is not
only pointed out in the street, but his whole country sings his praises
and he stands above the stars. The classical poets are there not to trouble his reputation but to bolster it.

This presentation, at the end of the first book of odes, of the Gâtine as
a place closely associated with Ronsard's own poetic reputation gives
rise to a cluster of odes about the forest in the second book. In the short

ode entitled *À la forest de Gastine*, another piece of early composition,[28] the forest is again presented as a refuge from strife and as a place where the poet may renew his connection with the Muses. There is nothing particularly unusual about this presentation of the forest *per se*. What makes it notable, for our purposes, is that it is framed by a contrast between present and past. The first stanza reads:

> Couché sous tes ombrages vers
> Gastine, je te chante
> Autant que les Grecs par leurs vers
> La forest d'Erymanthe.[29]   (1–4)

> [Lying in your leafy shadows, / Gastine, I sing of you / As much as the Greeks in their verse / Sang about the forest on Erymanthus.]

This first *strophe* is dissected in the middle by a time line, signalled by the very Ronsardian transition 'autant que': what is above it belongs to the present moment of composition, and what is below, to the past moment which inspired the present. So it is not clear what is being admired here: the forest itself, or the Greeks' admiration of theirs. The referent is obscured all the more by the fact that this is not simply an evocation of the Greeks, but of Horace's reference to this forest in his ode 'Dianam tenerae dicite virgines.'[30] It is a confusion with which Ronsard plays, simultaneously naming a contemporary French forest and turning his admiration of it into admiration of the Greeks' admiration as suggested to him by a Latin poet.

Ronsard at once privileges the local and actual, and overwrites it with the past and foreign. What is at stake in this double movement becomes apparent if one reads the Horatian source to the end. Horace's address to young men and women to pray respectively to Apollo and Diana concludes by saying that doing so will protect them from plague and famine, an evocation of the grain shortage of 23 B.C.[31] The lyric geography of the ode is thus not only contrasted with real troubles, but presented as a refuge and protection from such troubles. The movement of Ronsard's ode is very similar. He too is constructing the Gâtine forest as a place of refuge from the reality of the present moment, rebuilding the present as he would wish it to be, a world ordered by his poetry. Ronsard is the mediator between the moment and place he inhabits, and the lost, idealized world of classical poetry, and his mediation, unlike Du Bellay's, has the potential to redeem the present through the past. While Horace's ode praises Apollo's power to ward off suffering, the main body of Ronsard's ode deals, not surprisingly, with his own poetic process, which replaces the classical divinities of his source. He is, indirectly, making quite a claim for the transformative power of his verse, but the reader can only understand this by supplying what is suppressed from his intertext – the power of Apollo himself. Ronsard replaces this power with images of himself communing with the Muses in the woods of Gâtine. The woods are a refuge from day to day cares, and his poetry is an activity which will somehow guarantee the survival of such places of refuge, since it is only, as he makes clear, through his mediation that the woods are thus transformed:

Toy, qui fais qu'à toutes les fois
Me respondent les Muses.
Toy, par qui de ce mechant soin
Tout franc je me delivre,
Lors qu'en toy je me pers bien loin
Parlant avec un livre.
Tes bocages soient tousjours pleins
D'amoureuses brigades,
De Satyres et de Sylvains,
La crainte des Naiades.
En toy habite desormais
Des Muses le college,
Et ton bois ne sente jamais
La flame sacrilege.   (11–24, my emphasis)

[You, thanks to whom always / The Muses make reply to me: / You, through whom from this heavy care / I escape freely, / When I lose myself far in you, / Conversing with a book. / May your groves be forever full / Of amorous troops, / Of Satyres and of Silvans, / The dread of the Naiads. / Henceforth in you / May the College of the Muses live, / And may your woods never catch a hint / Of the flame of sacrilege.]

The forest is a shelter from the woes of present reality, including the sacrilege of Protestantism threatening the imagined cohesion of Christendom. But the forest is not just a shelter: Ronsard presents it as a utopian answer to the problems he has just evoked, a place where past can redeem present through poetry.

Ronsard has created a certain reader response in his early collections: the reader has the Vendômois Gâtine forest mapped out as the place that both creates and is created by Ronsard's particular genius. Ronsard's regionalism, in other words, is exclusive and privileged. His mapping of the Vendômois is not a discourse of a minority oppressed by the violent exclusivity of nationhood. Rather, his regionalism speaks 'the same language' as the nation, it instantiates the same desire 'of purity and authenticity,' of an originary and pristine culture. Ronsard's region is an ideological rather than a geographic place, what Roberto Dainotto calls the 'beautiful discourse of what we ought to be.'[32] Ronsard's Vendômois is a metaphor for yearning: yearning for the return, always deferred, of an idealized past, and for the self-conscious exclusion of all perceived threats to its possible return. The agent of this return is Ronsard himself: the association he creates between the region and his own poetry is truly exclusive. His lyrics abound with moments of prophesy in which he imagines future readers visiting the Vendômois region as an act of homage to him alone. As early as 1550, he figured later generations of 'readers' of his landscapes in this way, when, in a variation of the male poet's promise to make his lady famous through his poetry, he tells the 'petit païs' of his Vendômois: 'Je voi ton nom fameus par mes écrits.'[33] In another early sonnet, 'Cesse tes pleurs, mon livre,' the poet imagines a future reader visiting his Vendômois and admiring not so much the countryside per se, but the poet, Ronsard, who was born there.

> Quelqu'un après mille ans, de mes vers étonné,
> Voudra dedans mon Loir comme en Permesse boire
> Et, voyant mon pays, à peine voudra croire
> Que d'un si petit champ tel poète soit né.[34]   (5–8)

[In one thousand years, some admiring reader / Will want to drink from my Loir as from Permessus, / And, on seeing my homeland, he will scarcely believe / That such a great poet was born of such a small land.]

Such prophetic moments are typical of Ronsard's lyric Vendômois: in a closed logical loop, the poet constructs landscape to send the reader back, through landscape, to the poet himself.[35] Ronsard, in a kind of performative statement, says he is famous, and makes himself so. The efficacy of such a gesture can be seen in the tourist brochure mentioned in my introduction, which invites us into a landscape always already described by Ronsard. Literary critics have not been exempt from this mimetic appreciation. Edmond Rocher, author of the tellingly titled *Pierre de Ronsard, prince des poètes*, cites these very lines by Ronsard and obediently transforms himself into exactly the reader Ronsard is prefiguring. His book is an account of his ecstatic pilgrimage to the Vendômois, where he walks reverentially, stopping to admire various landmarks celebrated by the poet: 'It is while walking along the banks of the Loir that I evoke this powerful image of the first Prince of Poets. And I take delight in following his long shadow on his familiar walks, along the river, around his priories, his favourite spots, and as I reread his poetry and trace his steps, during the realization of this worshipful pilgrimage, I feel personal, fervent admiration and emotion rising within me. He loved this graceful river as I feel I do.'[36] Rocher's experience of landscape is directly – and exclusively – mediated through Ronsard; the objects of his admiration have been preselected for him by Ronsard's poetry. One wonders whether Rocher has a volume of Ronsard in hand while walking, or whether seeing the landmarks is itself a kind of 'rereading,' and in fact there is little difference. The acts of reading Ronsard and appreciating natural beauty are simultaneous.

Ronsard's Vendômois in his poetry, as he intends it to be read and as Rocher obligingly reads it, is a world symbolically ordered only by the processes of poetry and imagination, where the poet, Midas-like, turns everything he sees into pure poetry. This transformation presents a harsh critique of present values, notably greed for monetary gain,[37] and the challenges posed to a Catholic nation by Protestantism. Central to this critique is the invocation of ancient authorities, whom Ronsard presents as allies belonging to the world whose passing and values he mourns, and who stand in contrast to the threats from the actual world he inhabits. Ronsard's relationship to classical poets is affirmative; he builds them into his poetic landscape as refuges from assaults by present corruption. Poetry and the past, Ronsard suggests in his Vendômois landscapes, have the potential to redeem the present.[38]

The uncomfortable reality of Ronsard's France is never far, though, and threatens to erase entirely this fragile lyric utopia. And its integrity and potential is challenged in the elegy on the clear-cutting of the forest, where the trees – and by implication his own lyric world and the entire tradition – start falling down around him. In this poem, the *Élégie XXIIII*, the trees of the Gâtine forest are sites of ideological contention where the stability of the ideal lyric world is radically challenged by intrusions from the modern world. The only protection comes from the invocation of the past. The lyric traditions associated with trees, allied with the representation of a real forest, the Gâtine, allow Ronsard to foreground the struggle between past and present, a struggle which is ultimately a moral one, between a lost world of integrity and an actual world of strife and degradation. His poetry stands precisely for this lost order – a pre-Protestant, pre-monetary, aristocratic ethic that alone could turn the nation back from the brink of destruction.

The *Élégie XXIIII* is a combination of historical fact, reflection on the poetic process, and imitation of classical poets so bewildering that it merits consideration at length. The presentation of the forest is complicated from the outset by the fact that historical events of the 1570s, when the poem was published, render it impossible to continue idealizing the Gâtine forest. The forest belonged to the Bourbon-Vendôme family. For most of Ronsard's life, it had remained essentially untouched. However, this was to change after 1572, the year in which Henri de Bourbon became king of Navarre and the debts of his family were evaluated at one million *livres*. The council of the town of Vendôme recommended the sale of the Gâtine forest as the most propitious way to re-establish the family finances. Henri accepted the recommendation, hired a surveyor, and in 1573 the trees started to fall.[39] How does the poet react when the real-life emblem for his poetry is menaced? How is this threat transformed into poetry? Deforestation stands not only for the threatened end of Ronsard's poetry and the end of the entire lyric tradition with all its redemptive potential, it also represents all that is wrong with the society he inhabits.

The twenty-fourth Elegy is often published under the title 'Élégie contre les bûcherons de la forêt de Gâtine' (Elegy against the woodcutters of the Gâtine forest). But this title appears for the first time in a posthumous edition of 1624, added by the editors; Ronsard simply called it *Élégie XXIIII*. This spurious title has in turn determined most modern readings, which tend to read it primarily as a touching defence by Ronsard of the forest and trees he loved.[40] In volumes which do not give the whole poem, the extract typically starts with the line that is addressed directly to the woodcutters.[41] It is undeniable that Ronsard's poem is in part a reaction to the events of 1572. However, there is much more at stake; the poem both is, and is not, about the particular events in the Gâtine forest. The forest is not even named in the poem; the association with the Gâtine, while it would have been obvious to any contemporary reader, is not as direct as the title suggests. But it would be foolish to suggest the other extreme, that the poem has nothing to do with historical events in the Gâtine. The answer lies between the two: on the one hand, it is a meditation on poetry and what it could do, brimming with classical references to the point of not seeing the wood for the Ovids and Horaces. On the other, it is an obvious reaction to, and critique of, certain historical events and people. Ronsard takes as his point of departure a contemporary event, but transforms it into a literary event, without however completely overwriting the history that produced it. Throughout the poem, we see this tension between real and imagined space, past and present, literature and other discourse. And it is precisely in the coincidence of history and poetry that meaning is constructed, as we shall see.

The false title, and the starting line of anthologized extracts of the poem, precondition the reader to see the addressee of the poem as the woodcutter. This obscures another possible addressee, as Ute Margarete Saine has suggested: this is Henri de Bourbon, king of Navarre, owner of the forest, the man who agreed to its sale, a Protestant, and the future king of France.[42] He, not the woodcutter, is the initial target of Ronsard's ire:

> Quiconque aura premier la main embesongnée
> A te couper, forest, d'une dure congnée,
> Qu'il puisse s'enferrer de son propre baston,
> Et sente en l'estomac la faim d'Erysichthon,
> Qui coupa de Cerés le Chesne venerable,
> Et qui gourmand de tout, de tout insatiable,
> Les boeufs et les moutons de sa mere esgorgea,
> Puis pressé de la faim, soy-mesme se mangea:
> Ainsi puisse engloutir ses rentes et sa terre,
> Et se devore apres par les dents de la guerre.   (1–10)

[Whosoever first turns his hand / To cut you, forest, with a hard axe, / May he spike himself with his own stick, / And feel in his stomach the hunger of Erysichthon, / Who cut Ceres's sacred oak tree / And who, greedy and insatiable for everything / Ate his mother's sheep and cattle, / Then, spurred by hunger, ate himself: / Thus may he swallow up his money and land, / And then devour himself with the teeth of war.]

Saine argues that the giving of the hand, in the first line, is the royal mandate (*manu dato*) for the sale, and thus that Henri is implied from the beginning. Perhaps more indicative of Henri are the mentions of money, land, and war in lines 9–10. Land ownership and *rentes* are not applicable to a woodcutter, and focus the curse on the aristocratic agent of destruction. The criticism is made more direct by the fact that the apogée of the curse, lines 9–18, is the first part of the poem that is entirely original, that is, not imitated from classical sources.

The sacredness of forest sanctuaries is a fairly common *topos* in classical literature in general,[43] so Ronsard initially appears to be adding his voice to a well-established ancient chorus. In fact, the first eight lines are a conflation of Horace and Ovid that obscures the historical fact of deforestation in Ronsard's present, and only gradually makes it clear who is the object of Ronsard's fury. Even the initial direct address to the forest ('à te couper, forest') is mediated by Horace, who opens his Ode 2.13 thus: 'Whoever it was that planted you in the first place did so on an evil day, and with an unholy hand he raised you, Tree, to bring harm to his descendants and disgrace to the district.'[44] Horace's ode is a humorously exaggerated account of a tree of the Sabine farm falling and nearly crushing him. His mock fury is directed against the person who planted the tree in the first place. Ronsard's tone is anything but light, and rather than cursing the planter of the trees, he focuses on the agents of the wood's falling.

This mention of the person responsible for the destruction allows him to bring Ovid's Erysichthon into his poem, a figure who introduces the themes of sacrilege, punishment, violence, and, as Richard Seaford has recently suggested, a misguided economic valuation of nature's worth, 'the transformation of nature into product.'[45] In Ovid, Erysichthon is a powerful man who scorns the gods; the measure of his godlessness is shown when he 'violated the sacred grove of Ceres with the axe.'[46] Initially, his slaves are wielding the axe. However, they hesitate when they come to a venerable oak tree, surrounded by wreaths and votive tablets, at which point the king snatches an axe and starts to chop. Blood streams from the tree; a slave who tries to hold back the king's arm is beheaded for his 'pious thought.' The voice of a nymph from inside the tree assures the king that he will be punished. At the behest of her nymphs, Ceres curses him with insatiable Famine, who leads him to eat his entire inheritance ('patrias') and property ('census' – a word also encompassing high social standing), to attempt to sell his daughter, and ultimately to consume himself.

Much of Ovid's moral vocabulary, railing against greed, sacrilege, and consummation, is picked up by Ronsard. Central to Ovid's myth is the idea of appropriate and adequate punishment. Erysichthon is punished by Famine, the opposite ('contraria') to Ceres, the goddess of natural abundance. If he has sinned by not respecting the vitality and inspiritedness embodied by Ceres, he will be visited by dearth and famine, and will be unable to find any satisfaction from the world. Ronsard similarly wishes an appropriate punishment upon his king, whose sin is to attribute economic value to a sacred place. Pushing the sin to its extreme, he wishes an infinite accumulation of debts and interest, and ultimately financial ruination in a kind of bourgeois financial speculative hell:

> Qu'il puisse, pour vanger le sang de nos forests,
> Toujours nouveaux emprunts sur nouveaux interests
> Devoir a l'usurier, et qu'en fin il consomme
> Tout son bien à payer la principale somme.
> Que tousjours sans repos ne face en son cerveau
> Que tramer pour-neant quelque dessein nouveau,
> Porté d'impatience et de fureur diverse
> Et de mauvais conseil qui les hommes renverse.   (11–18)

[So that the blood of our forests may be avenged, / May the interest on his debts be forever accumulating, / And in order to pay back the principal, / May he end up spending his entire fortune. / May his mind always restlessly be hatching / Some useless new scheme or other, / Driven by impatience, by fits of anger, / And by bad advice which is the downfall of men.]

These lines are the first and only lines purely of Ronsard's invention, and as such they would stand out to a contemporary reader familiar with the sources. A new, threatening kind of vocabulary is introduced into the idealized space of lyric (the old forest) and into the domain of classical poetry, a vocabulary of mercantile accumulation, debt, compound interest (presumably), and restless speculation on new, ill-advised ventures.[47] This is the world antithetical to Ronsard's poetry, and the image of the falling trees allows him a powerful visual correlative to the idea of the destruction of a certain moral and poetic universe by an emerging new order. In ecocritical terms, this is the notion that our exploitive relationship with nature signifies a more general, philosophical crisis in modernity.[48] In Raymond Rogers's terms, modernity's 'emergent forms' include the process of capitalistic accumulation, and replace the 'residual forms' of pre-capitalist economies. These residual forms persist in spaces such as poetry as a residual 'cultural record.'[49] Ronsard's protest against the logging of the Gâtine is just such a residual cultural record, a strong sense of the loss of a vanishing way of life or of thought, a moment of protest against the new way.

In this scheme, the woodcutter cannot count for much. He is the mere agent of forces beyond his control. In both Ronsard and Ovid, it is clear on whose shoulders blame should fall: those of powerful men in the position of making such decisions. Erysichthon's slaves, the real wood-cutters, are the men who refuse to fell the sacred oak, and one man even loses his head for holding back the king's arm. Ronsard incorporates this moment of detention of the arm about to take a stroke into a direct address, in the best-known line of the poem, 'Escoute, buscheron, ar-reste un peu le bras.'

> Escoute, Bucheron, arreste un peu le bras,
> Ce ne sont pas des bois que tu jectes à bas,
> Ne vois-tu pas le sang lequel desgoute à force
> Des Nymphes qui vivoyent dessous la dure escorce?
> Sacrilege meurdrier [...]   (19–23)

> [Listen, woodcutter, hold your arm right there, / This is not a wood which you cut down, / Don't you see the fast flow of the blood / Of the Nymphs who used to live under the thick bark? / Sacrilegious murderer ...]

Line 20 is to be taken quite seriously: these are not woods, or not only woods, or even only nymphs, they are also poetry itself, the vanishing poetry of the literary golden age, and of Ronsard himself.[50] The place of the crime is as much Ovid's sacred grove as it is the Gâtine: lines 21 and 23 are direct echoes of the Latin source.[51] The concluding epithet, 'sacrilegious murderer,' brings together ancient myth and Ronsard's present – exploitative evaluation of nature, and religious impiety – which form the moral horizon against which Ronsard rails. The Gâtine of his poetry stands in contrast to the Gâtine of sixteenth-century France.

One might object that, since neither Henri nor the Gâtine are directly named, it is speculative to assume that they are among the intended referents. Were the events of 1572 – the sale and subsequent clear-cutting of the forest – the inspiration for the poem? The *terminus ad quem* of the poem is 1584, the date of publication, but Ian McFarlane has suggested that 'Ronsard composed at least part of his poem any time after 1553,'[52] the date of publication of a neo-Latin source by Gervais Sepin which McFarlane was the first to point out. The similarities be-tween Sepin and Ronsard are striking, but it does not follow that because a model poem was in circulation in the 1550s, Ronsard must have written the entire poem then. I believe that the finished poem was indeed intended as a response to the sale and clearing of the Gâtine. Ronsard wrote the bulk of his *Elégies* in the 1570s. Disabused of life at court, he returned to his native Vendômois in 1576, a date by which the forest had been surveyed, divided into parcels, and certain parts were being clear-cut. The resulting poem may draw on much more than biography or history, but there is no reason to doubt that elements of the poem were prompted by Henri's decision and its visible results.

However it is also true that the 'quiconque' in the first line, and the woodcutter, are symptomatic of greater social trends. The elegy is not only about Henri's particular financial situation, but rather criticizes what Ronsard perceived as a general and lamentable tendency to consider value in economic terms. Nor is it so much about one man's Protestantism, as it is about the effects of the religious schism on the nation. A writer whom Ronsard may have had in mind is Bernard Palissy, who unites the figure of the Protestant with that of the socially mobile bourgeois. Palissy enjoyed protection from some of the most powerful families in France, and he and Ronsard flourished at the same time; under the supervision of Catherine de' Medici, Palissy worked on the grotto in the Tuileries in the 1560s, years during which Ronsard was also often present at court.[53] Both men were fully engaged in opposing sides of religious polemic in the 1560s.[54] In 1563 Palissy published his *Recepte veritable*, whose expanded title is the more provocative *Moyens de devenir riche ou Recepte veritable par laquelle tous les hommes de la France pourront apprendre à multiplier et augmenter leurs trésors*.[55] From the title at least, there could hardly be a clearer representative of the 'avaricieux' mentality Ronsard so ironically lambastes in poems such as the 'Hymne de l'Or,' or the ode 'Contre les avaricieux.'[56] Palissy was Protestant and working-class. He prided himself on not reading Greek or Latin, and on his status as an artisan with practical knowledge who had pulled himself up through sheer hard work and skill. He represented all that Ronsard so mistrusted about his world: social fluidity and promotion of the bourgeois, rejection of learning, preference for agricultural labour over aristocratic *otium*, and Protestant, Reformed sympathies. In his *Recepte veritable*, Palissy discusses the cutting of trees, in a passage which makes for an interesting case study of the kinds of discourses around trees and wood to which Ronsard objects. Palissy talks of wood as the nation's most important economic resource, since every trade depends on it, and he insists on the need to manage carefully any clear-cutting so as to ensure a future supply of timber. Palissy has no quibble with the idea of felling trees but he insists on replanting, and on felling the right trees at the right time. This highly utilitarian discourse around the value of trees to the economic survival of the country is a direct contrast to Ronsard's notions of poetic value.

Ronsard's Gâtine is everything Palissy's trees are not; its loss is the loss of a whole world order to unwelcome forces of change. In the middle of his elegy, Ronsard starts to bid farewell to lyric convention in general, and then to his own work in particular. As we have seen, the reader is trained by the early poems to associate the Gâtine forest with Ronsard's inspiration and genius, so, when Ronsard addresses the forest as the place where he heard Apollo's arrows, tuned his lyre, and other clichés of lyric creation, we ourselves supply the name. However, Ronsard takes a while to get there. First he takes leave of a panoply of lyric *topoi*, evocations mostly of Virgil:

> Forest, haute maison des oiseaux bocagers,[57]
> Plus le Cerf solitaire et les Chevreuls legers
> Ne paistront sous ton ombre, et ta verte criniere
> Plus du Soleil d'este ne rompra la lumiere.
> Plus l'amoureux Pasteur sur un tronq adossé,
> Enflant son flageolet à quatre trous persé,[58]
> Son mastin à ses pieds, à son flanc la houlette,
> Ne dira plus l'ardeur de sa belle Janette:
> Tout deviendra muet, Echo sera sans voix:
> Tu deviendras campagne, et en lieu de tes bois,
> Dont l'ombrage incertain lentement se remue,[59]
> Tu sentiras le soc, le coutre et la charrue:[60]
> Tu perdras ton silence, et haletans d'effroy
> Ny Satyres, ny Pans ne viendront plus chez toy.   (27–40)

[Forest, high refuge of woodland birds, / No longer will the solitary hart and the lightfooted roes / Graze in your shadow, and your green canopy / Will no longer filter summer sunbeams. / The amorous shepherd, leaning against a tree trunk, / Playing his four-holed wooden pipe, / His hound at his feet, his crook by his side, / Will no longer speak of his passion for the lovely Janette: / All will become quiet, Echo will have no voice, / You will become farmland, and instead of your woods / Whose quivering shadow slowly changes, / You will feel the ploughshare, the coulter, and the plough: / Your silence will be lost, and, gasping with fear, / Satyrs and Pans will come to you no more.]

This is a sweeping adieu to the golden age, to the world of pastoral and lyric poetry whose integrity is destroyed by greed and 'sacrilège.' The 'amoureux pasteur' is, of course, Virgil's Tityrus, the emblem of lyric ease and contentment in the face of dispossession, who has an affective and creative relationship with his land. By silencing this shepherd, Ronsard is effectively silencing himself, erasing the possibility of tranquil enjoyment and refuge from the world's cares. However, there is a play on the concept of silence, which shows the conflict of two different discourses, one of which is silenced and the other not. Line 35 is about the vanishing of lyric poetry; its voices will no longer be heard in the forest, and 'all will become quiet.' In line 39 however, we read 'you will lose your silence.' The felled forest is simultaneously a place of silence and of cacophony, which is only possible if two different kinds of noise are at stake. The silence is the absence of the poetic order; the noise, the presence of exploitative activity.

This elegy is, in part, a gesture of capitulation of the former to the latter, the epitaph of a certain kind of poetry. While it is not 'the last poem of the last volume of poetry published in Ronsard's lifetime,'[61] it does still deserve to be read as a testament to lyric and the world it stands for in Ronsard. If it was in fact written on the occasion of Ronsard's return to the Vendômois in 1576, it is one of the last poems he wrote, even if it does not conveniently occupy the final pages of the 1584 edition. The accumulation of adieus in the second half of the poem gives it the air of a funereal oration. Ronsard starts the formal farewells with his own poetic voice, a trope which he has built up throughout his earlier work:

Adieu vieille forest, le jouet de Zephyre,
Où premier j'accorday les langues de ma lyre,
Où premier j'entendi les fleches resonner
D'Apollon.   (41–4)

[Goodbye, old forest, Zephyr's plaything, / Where first I tuned the languages of my lyre, / Where first I heard quiver the arrows / Of Apollo.]

Next to go is the commemorative and religious function of the trees, harking back to Erysichthon's sacrilege: 'Adieu vieille forest, adieu testes sacrées, / De tableaux et de fleurs autrefois honorées' [Goodbye, old forest, goodbye sacred heads, / once honoured with paintings and flowers] (49–50). And finally, a farewell to the kind of society and individual that the trees stand for, a lost world of upstanding heroes: 'Adieu Chesnes,

couronnes aux vaillans citoyens' [Farewell, oak trees, the crowns of valiant citizens] (55). The intertext here is Virgil – not the *Eclogues* or *Georgics*,
but the *Aeneid*, the epic of the founding of Rome. The line comes from the
dead Anchises' eulogistic prediction about the future Roman state.[62] The
civic oak was awarded to one who had saved a fellow citizen in battle.
This is one of the most optimistic and patriotic moments in the *Aeneid*,
and through his imitation, Ronsard is evoking a now-lost world of civic
virtue, of a nation of valiant soldiers and just wars, precisely the kind of
nation sixteenth-century France, to Ronsard, is not.

Thus far in the poem Ronsard has presented a complex web of references to historical fact, to real space, to poetic space, to his own poetic
project and his harnessing of his exemplars. It is in the interplay between them that meaning is constructed: for example, in the layering of
the example of Erysichthon onto the curse against the agents of destruction of the Gâtine, the 'woodcutter' becomes Henri de Navarre.
The image of the felled trees also evokes that of the truncated family
tree – the Navarre line will soon replace the Valois dynasty, the
Protestant Henri being the one who 'fells' the Catholic Valois tree. In
the figure of Erysichthon, two principal characteristics are crystallized,
avarice and sacrilege, that are transferred to Henri and become symptomatic of the corruption of the age. The forest, historically a space
whose use was already strongly contested,[63] becomes in Ronsard a
space caught between the poet and poetry on one side, and the king
and money on the other. Lyric poets are presented as the last bastion of
a righteous, Virgilian kind of society where all are god-fearing and
there is no economic demand made upon land. But as the trees fall, so
does the world of lyric, and Ronsard and his chosen allies – Virgil,
Horace, and Ovid – run from the scene of destruction like the woodland spirits of his poem.

The image of a lost ideal world is helpful for our understanding of
the curious ending of the elegy. Ian McFarlane is one of the only readers
to have tackled the issue of the apparent lack of unity of the poem; he
sees discontinuity between the Horatian and Ovidian beginning, almost half of the poem, and the rest, which is for him a 'rich treatment'
of 'the themes of Nature and Time.'[64] The last eight lines do seem to fit
uncomfortably with the rest of the poem:

Que l'homme est malheureux qui au monde se fie!
O Dieux, que veritable est la Philosophie,
Qui dit que toute chose à la fin perira,

Et qu'en changeant de forme une autre vestira:
De Tempé la vallée un jour sera montagne,
Et la cyme d'Athos une large campagne,
Neptune quelque fois de blé sera couvert,
La matière demeure, et la forme se perd.   (61–9)

[How miserable is the man who trusts in the world! / O gods, how true is
that philosophy / That says everything perishes in the end, / And as it
changes form, assumes a new one: / The valley of Tempe will one day be
a mountain, / And the summit of Athos a wide plain, / The ocean will at
some time be covered in wheat. / Matter remains, and form is lost].

Michel Jeanneret uses this last line as his epigraph in his study of metamorphosis in sixteenth-century art and literature.[65] Ronsard, for Jeanneret,
seeks a salutary power in the process of transformation, a recycling of
death into life.[66] Ronsard does indeed seem to be taking consolation from
the fact that all landscapes shift and change, a classical commonplace
since Ovid. But more is at stake, surely, than a *consolatio*. What Ronsard
has just presented is not the force of Nature acting on the shape of the
land, but the rapid and destructive effect of human activity. And there is
a complex intertextual game being played with his sources in these last
few lines that reveals a profound meditation on the transformative power not only of nature, but of poetry itself.

Ronsard's inspiration now is Lucretian and Ovidian. Again, it is
helpful to look beyond the immediate intertextual lines to the source
texts surrounding them. The Lucretian lines paraphrased by Ronsard
say 'the earth is diminished and grows again,'[67] and 'all things gradually decay and go to the reef of destruction, outworn by the ancient
lapse of years.'[68] These last lines, at the end of Lucretius's second book,
come in the context of a mildly ironic commentary on the human tendency to idealize bygone times, precisely what Ronsard has been doing. The farmer in Lucretius 'compares times present with times past
and often praises the fortunes of his father,' and 'grumbles how the old
world, full of piety, supported life with great ease on a narrow domain.'
It is this farmer who does not understand that 'all things gradually decay.' Ronsard seems to be taking a final jibe at himself, ironizing the
very process by which he built up the Gâtine forest, the Vendômois,
and his poetry as representative of a lost moral order.

However, he contrasts this with another intertext, Pythagoras's teach-
ings in the last book of Ovid's *Metamorphoses*. This is a long discourse
with several particular lines that Ronsard seems to have in mind: 'all

things change, but nothing dies [...] nothing is constant in the whole world [...] nothing lasts long under the same form.'[69] However Pythagoras starts his disquisition with a praise of the lost Golden Age which stands in distinction to the Lucretian irony. This juxtaposition of self-irony with apparently serious and wistful yearning for the lost age is, I think, Ronsard's message. While pointing out, through his reference to Lucretius, the very poetic process by which such an age is constructed by poets, he also maintains, with Ovid's Pythagoras, the validity of such visions, and the fact that poets will always construct such a 'space of hope' faced with the degradation of their times.

Conclusion

In *Spaces of Hope*, the book whose title gives this study one of its key terms, the geographer David Harvey takes Henri Lefebvre to task. Lefebvre objects to the closing-off, the authoritarian act of definition and exclusion inherent in the act of imagining an alternative space to the capitalist space we inhabit.[70] However, according to Harvey, Lefebvre provides us with no alternatives and leaves us hanging in 'an agonistic romanticism of perpetually unfulfilled longing and desire.'[71] Harvey addresses the question of how to fulfil this longing by insisting on the primacy of the imagination – 'we cannot ignore the question of the imagination' – in a retort to the Thatcherite defence of globalized capitalist culture.[72] The role of the imagination, and more specifically of a hopeful imagination, in constructing space, can help us understand Ronsard's and Baïf's poetic responses to threats to their world as they argue potently for the place of poetry.

The fluvial and sylvan nymphs of Baïf and Ronsard, respectively, also foreground the cultural and historical mediation of environmental reality. In sixteenth-century French poetry, such mediation is of course the privilege of a small social élite, and the history they face is not only the threat of their old way of life disappearing, but that of the sundering of any coherence due to the wars of religion. The France that they imagine and hope for is not only peaceful in the general sense; it corresponds to the specific desires of humanist, aristocratic, regionally based land-owners. In the following and final chapter, I will turn to poetic places that are mapped out as responses to social instability and that are exclusive in different ways: the first is an aristocratic ancestral domain, the second, an isolated region that is as far as possible from the strife of the kingdom.

6 The Poet and the Bower: Escaping History

The previous chapter showed that Baïf's polluted river and Ronsard's falling trees not only represent aspects of the poets' environmental reality, they also function as synecdoches for other historical processes of which the poets disapprove: religious wars, Protestantism (for Ronsard), monetary greed, the threatening of regional identities, and the disruption of social hierarchies. The poetic call to a return to pristine waters and forests is also a nostalgic call to a certain political and social order. While there is no reason to doubt that the poets' respective protests witness to a concern about degradation of a real environment which they considered beautiful and meaningful, the main extra-textual focus of their poetic vision of the world is a fundamentally *social* conservatism. In this chapter, I will show how poetry engages social and political history to construct landscapes that also function as spaces of conservative hope, poetic refuges that contrast with specific historical tendencies. The bulk of the chapter deals with shifts in the position of the aristocratic landowner, through a reading of Vauquelin de la Fresnaye's *Les Foresteries* (1555) and the *Satyres* (published in 1605 but containing works composed as early as the 1550s). I argue that Vauquelin presents his ancestral lands in Normandy, in particular his forest, as a stable guarantor of his aristocratic name and identity, evidencing nostalgia for an imagined time when the nobleman was defined by his land and vice versa. The reality of his financial situation – debts, and the need to work as a lawyer – is willed away in the timeless, privileged space of his sylvan 'second world' where he can be an aristocrat-poet immune to historical reality. His nobility is, as David Posner has argued about early modern nobility in general, a 'performance,' a navigation between the ideal of a timeless essential identity, and the reality of historical change.[1]

Second and last, I address directly the historical problem that has haunted most of my readings: the question of how to imagine France as a coherent space at all when it was torn apart at all levels by civil war. Jacques Peletier, in his long poem *La Savoye* (1572), describes Savoy as a place of refuge from the ravages of war; indeed it is one of the period's most sustained descriptions of a real place. I argue that this is only possible because of Savoy's liminal status – politically and geographically – with respect to the French kingdom. As the horror of religious violence spreads over the kingdom, it is increasingly difficult to describe any part of it irenically; Savoy is close enough to France, without actually being part of the kingdom, for it to be possible to imagine it as a redemptive place. But both Peletier and Vauquelin's landscapes are always aware of their status as artifice, of the vulnerability of any second world to the violence of history.

Les lois or les bois?
Vauquelin de la Fresnaye and the Social Dilemmas of the Humanist Aristocrat

Jean Vauquelin de la Fresnaye (1536–1608), a poet and lawyer from Normandy, was the first to publish, as far as we know, a volume of bucolic poetry in French: *Les Foresteries* (1555). He was the first to dedicate a substantial part of his output to theorizations of the pastoral mode, and one of the first (after Jean Lemaire) to write in *prosimetrum* after the example of Sannazaro. Despite these various foundational roles – and the fact that Ronsard and other poets imitated his pastoral – Vauquelin is the only poet in this book whom Ronsard did not include in his list of Pléiade members, and he has never attracted many readers or editors.[2] Although Guillaume Colletet in the seventeenth century did recognize him as an initiator of vernacular pastoral, critics have largely underestimated his influence on subsequent practitioners of the genre.[3] In Vauquelin's own time, although he was well acquainted with the Pléiade and the literary scene in Paris, and had friends in high positions in Caen, his books gathered dust on booksellers' shelves. He was only given one commission, from Henri III for the *Art poétique*, not published until 1605.[4] This marginality in the world of letters makes his poetry particularly interesting from a socio-historical point of view. Unlike Du Bellay or Ronsard, Vauquelin does not successfully negotiate his own position in the French literary landscape. The struggle to define and inhabit an appropriate public reputation, in the case of someone who is conscious of not having the status of his peers, can be more revealing about social and cultural anxieties than are voices that are very heavily mediated by literary identities. Vauquelin, throughout his career, is haunted by the problem of securing a poetic reputation in the shadow of the Pléiade and of foreign models. The landscape of his lyric 'second world' is as much a world of ideal poetry as it is a world of social stability, a vision of an untarnished aristocratic and literary territory.

But this vision is, like any pastoral second world, threatened from outside. Like many poets of his generation, Vauquelin is a petty aristocrat with family roots and property in a certain region, and haunted by the idea that traditional nobility is in decline. The idea of an actual crisis of nobility in Renaissance France has been seriously contested,[5] but it is clear that many French noblemen *thought* of their identity as threatened. In particular, land ownership was not the exclusive aristocratic privilege of an idealized *seigneurie*: by the mid-sixteenth century, wealthy bourgeois were investing in land as a passport to 'the most prized status of all, that of nobleman.'[6] And even among the nobility, land could be a source of financial tribulation as much as of status and pride. Vauquelin creates lyric landscape out of the biographical facts of land ownership, something that no other poet of this period does, except perhaps for Du Bellay's brief mention of the 'soucis' he found at home on returning from Rome. Vauquelin's landscape, while brimming with lyric conventions and borrowings from other poets, is nevertheless defined from the beginning as his family's territory at Fresnaye-au-Sauvage. This suspension between the poetic and the real witnesses to a social and professional dilemma particular to an aristocrat-poet. His bid for individual renown is made through and with his Norman forest, a place no other poet has yet glorified and with which his family name is strongly identified. Yet even as he describes an experience and a place that should individuate him, he runs up against the presence of precursor poets. And as he describes what should be an ideal place of pure poetry and stable aristocratic privilege, he encounters the uncomfortable facts of land ownership and money. Identity, for Vauquelin, is a constant negotiation between ideal and history, poetic tradition and innovation. His land, the very place that would seem to guarantee his status, both socially and poetically, is traversed by this 'torture of status anxiety.'[7]

In 1605, one year before his death, Vauquelin published his *Satyres*, in which he makes what he probably knows will be a final bid to be remembered as a poet: 'moy qui dans mes vers laisseray ma semblance' [I who will leave my likeness in my poetry] (246).[8] Looking back on his life, the poet reflects on his career, his reputation, and his family history and standing. Many of the *Satyres* have an autobiographical, almost confessional, tone, and have in fact been used by critics as a source of biographical information about Vauquelin.[9] The apparent autobiography, however, is better read as a negotiation of public identity through a series of *personae*, a reading suggested by the genre of satiric poetry itself.[10] The anxiety that punctuates the performance of the *Satyres* witnesses to the constructed nature of the ideal, timeless nobiliary public self in the face of historical change. The relation to land, we shall see, plays a particularly important role in aristocratic identity, and is co-opted by a poetic fantasy of noble privilege immune from shifting demographics.

In a *Satyre* addressed to a cousin, Vauquelin criticizes the human tendency to want to rise above one's class and birthright. Happiness, he says, echoing the common poetic trope of autarchic fantasy, is to content oneself with one's station, 'en la condition / Ou premier tu fus né, vivre en paix et liesse' [live peacefully and happily in the condition into which you were born], rather than 'courr[ir] miserable apres cette grandesse' [running wretchedly after grandeur] (327). This kind of rhetoric against social mobility, and supporting the maintenance of the strict divisions of the three estates, is hardly new. However, at the end of this poem, he gives a rather more original definition of what it is to know and accept one's social status: it is to acknowledge one's region of origin.

Et qui veut vivre bien, il ne doit meconnoitre
Son pere ni les siens, ni l'endroit de son Estre:
Ni taire le surnom qu'il a des le berceau:
Ni se dire Angevin quand il est né Manceau.   (328)

[And he who would live well must not be ignorant / Of his father or his people, nor of the place of his Being: / Nor hide the nickname he holds from the cradle: / Nor claim himself to be Angevin if he was born in Le Mans.]

Vauquelin, perhaps more than any of his peers, explores the question of the 'l'endroit de son Estre' in his poetry. At the start of the *Satyres*, in the address 'À son livre' [To His Book], he initially frames the question of place in a conventional way, adopting the pose of the honest country poet intimidated by court culture and warning his book not to go to Paris. Ovid's *Tristia* and Du Bellay's *Regrets* start with the same trope.[11]

However, the book seems set on going, so the poet tells it what to say if anyone in Paris should ask about its author. At this point, Vauquelin individuates himself from Du Bellay and Ovid by giving an extensive autobiography. Vauquelin is simultaneously evoking his unoriginality (overtly imitating a tired trope that goes back to Ovid), and his originality (the history that individuates him). In these verses, he defines and defends his family name by association with his land, insisting on his name's derivation from a fief granted in return for military service. Name and land, as with any European aristocratic family *de souche*, define each other: 'Les Fiefs, que du nom d'homme alors on surnommoit, / Firent que pour surnoms ces noms on retenoit' [Fiefs, which back then were named after men / Thus were retained as surnames] (186). Inherited land is a principal means of defining oneself as full-blooded nobility. The final proof of his own nobility, he says, is that his family name does not have the 'de' that indicates newly bestowed titles:

Le Dé, le Du, n'estoient point encor en usage
[…]
Ce Dé sans propos ne doit estre adiouté
Afin que nouueau noble on ne soit point noté.
Les Roturiers aussi nez de familles basses,
Le Dé, comme le Noble, usurpent en leurs races.   (186)

[The *De* and the *Du*, were not yet used. / … / This meaningless *De* should not be added / Lest one be considered of recent nobility. / The common people born into lowly families / Are usurping the *De*, and the nobility.]

The absence of the 'de' as a distinguishing trait of the *noblesse de race* suggests that the traditional nobility are not simply 'of' the place they are associated with, they somehow *are* that place. The true noble has an essential and transgenerational connection to land that the ennobled bourgeois lacks.[12] And when Vauquelin speculates on the origin of his own family name, he gives a precise etymology referring to the name of a particular valley in the fiefdom: 'Di, Que peut estre vint mon nom du Val-d'Eclin,[13] / Qu'au langage du temps on nommoit Vauc-Elin' (185) [Say that my name might come from Valley of Eclin / Which over time became Vauc-Elin].

However, despite insisting that he is not Jean *de* Vauc-Elin – and thus not a new noble – he prefaces the explanation with a *peut-estre* and destabilizes any claim to a naturalized identification of name with land. This foregrounds the contingent and constructed nature of his family's land-based identity, which is then furthered by a shift in the way his ancestral lands are described: from the specifics of local toponymy, he moves into the timeless, non-specific territory of lyric tradition, the domain of Ceres and Pomona, '... la belle contree / Que Cerés et Pomone entre toutes recree' [the beautiful region which, more than all the others, Ceres and Pomona make anew] (185). This not only recasts Vauquelin's land as a poetic domain, it also puts him directly in dialogue with Du Bellay, who, in the opening ode of his *Vers lyriques* (1549), had described his native Anjou as touched by the sacred footsteps of Ceres.[14] By making his land compete with Du Bellay's, Vauquelin is putting his family name on the honour roll of French poets, making a bid for poetic standing through the social standing implied by land ownership. The shift from Val d'Eclin to Ceres' country shows the multivalent status of land in Vauquelin's poetry. Land is the origin and guarantor of his family's name, a sign of authentic social status, his aristocratic identity card. But it is also co-opted by his poetic identity, inscribing him and identifying him as a lyric poet through the use of standard inherited lyric topoi, which, in turn, poses the classic dilemma of imitation: how to make his own mark on the literary landscape within the discursive confines of the genre. His land, written into poetry, becomes suspended between places ancient and modern, classical and French, caught between his social and poetic ambitions as he was himself.

It is a commonplace of sixteenth-century history that the *noblesse de robe* – state servants with a humanist education rewarded for service by a title, or successful bourgeois who simply bought their titles – was displacing the traditional role and privileges of the military *noblesse d'épée*.[15] As already stated, historians dispute the basis of claims about an actual 'crisis' of nobility, but the perception of crisis was very real. The centralizing of royal power in the sixteenth century was seen as a threat not only to the local autonomy and power of the landowners, but to the ideal nobiliary identity based on military service. According to political thinker Claude de Seyssel in his 1515 *Monarchie de France*, the aristocrat was supposed to live 'noblement,' which meant exemption from the *gabelle* tax, the right to bear arms 'partout et jusques dedans la chambre du Roi [car] à eux appartient la défense du Roi et du royaume' [everywhere, even in the king's chamber, because it is up to them to defend king and country], and not engage in commerce or the professions, 'sans exercer art mécanique ni questuaire qui leur est interdite' [without practising a manual or money-making trade which is forbidden to them].[16] However, petty nobles, the class to which most sixteenth-century poets belonged, found themselves forced to compete at court with a new humanistically educated civil service, who advanced through merit and connections, and not through name. Self-identified *nobles de race* perceived serving the court as a humanist as distinctly less prestigious than the profession of arms. Vauquelin insists at some length on the antiquity and military credentials of his lineage:

> Des ce temps mes majeurs desja nobles vivoient,
> Et nos Ducs genereux en nos guerres suivoient:
> Mais Vauquelin du Pont, Vauquelin de Ferieres,
> Capitaines portoient gouffanons et banieres,
> En passant l'Occean, quand leur grand duc Normant
> Alla contre l'Anglois tous ses suiets armant.   (186)

[From that time, my ancestors were already noblemen, / Following our grand Dukes into battle: / And the captains Vauquelin du Pont and Vauquelin de Ferieres / Carried gonfalons and banners / Across the sea when their great Duke of Normandy / Fought against the English with all his armed subjects.]

The reference to his ancestors fighting for the Norman conquest might have convinced some contemporary readers, given that this family was fairly well established in Normandy. Still, the truth seems to be that the family at Fresnaye-au-Sauvage was rather a recent arrival to the ranks of the nobility – since 1470, in fact.[17] And J.H.M. Salmon points out that the idea of a venerable dynasty of the warrior class was a fiction, since very few noble families could in fact maintain a direct male line for more than four generations.[18] The pose of belonging to an ancient line of warriors was part of the cultural practice of the French aristocracy of the time.[19] And, in literary terms, Vauquelin is ventriloquizing epic and chivalric heroes, warrior noblemen, who often pause before combat to detail their lineage. His performed nobility is a self-conscious exploration of the gap between the 'flawed present and a supposedly actualized ancestral ideal.'[20]

The reality of Vauquelin's professional activities diverged somewhat from the ideal. Poetry, a profession that carried an acceptable amount of cultural capital, was a way for nobles whose traditional identity was waning to distinguish themselves from run-of-the-mill careerists.[21] But as a poet, Vauquelin struggles with marginal success and recognition, with the problem of making a reputation for himself to rival those of his better known and more acclaimed models. As a result, his relationship with the *persona* of poet was openly vexed, and his public identity was vehicled more through his activities as a lawyer than through his writing. Many men of letters earned a living by practising law, but this autobiographical fact sits particularly uncomfortably in Vauquelin's poetry. Despite the success of his law career – which included the positions of *avocat du Roi*, then eventually *président du siège*, in Caen – Vauquelin is constantly apologizing, in his poetry, for the fact that he works for a living. There is an ongoing contrast between the profession of law, which he presents more as a disagreeable obligation, and that of poet, an ever-unattainable, almost prelapsarian state of existence. And his ancestral lands, in particular the forest at La-Fresnaye-au-Sauvage, are transformed in his lyrics into highly invested sites of meaning that dramatize much of this personal conflict between law and letters, *les lois* and *les bois*.

This tension between the personae of poet and lawyer is more than a phase; in the retrospective *Satyres*, Vauquelin presents it as a defining anxiety of his life. Vauquelin had been sent at a young age to Paris by his mother, to study Greek and Latin under such teachers as Turnèbe and Muret. Many *petits nobles* were sent to study letters rather than to pursue a military career. In Paris, Vauquelin became an ardent disciple of the Pléiade, and a conscript to the cause of vernacular poetry. However, in 1553, aged seventeen, he left his studies in Paris to study law in Poitiers. It was in Poitiers, two years later, that he published his first volume of poetry, *Les Foresteries*. The transition to Poitiers seems to have been as much a search for like-minded poets as it was for a law degree. Vauquelin was accompanied by two equally enthusiastic young would-be poets, Ravend Grimoult and Charles Toutain.[22] Scévole de Sainte-Marthe, born in the same year as Vauquelin, was already in Poitiers and had just published his first collection of poems; Jacques Tahureau was in Angers, where the young scholars stopped on the way to Poitiers.[23] Vauquelin's leaving Paris to complete his education is quite typical of sixteenth-century scholars: it was not unusual, in fact it was often desirable, to complete different stages of one's education at different institutions.[24] What makes Vauquelin's decision more than a forgettable piece of sixteenth-century humanist trivia is that the excursion into the provinces – Anjou and Poitou – seems to be a journey in search of a poetic voice that he could claim as his own. Despite claiming to adore Ronsard, the young poet only started to write once he left the

Pléiade in Paris (where he had gone to study letters) for Poitiers (where he went to study law). Differentiation from the overbearing reputations of Du Bellay and Ronsard, associated with Paris and the Île-de-France, is a necessary prerequisite to finding his own muse.[25]

One might reframe this differentiation in cartographic terms: in order to find and write his poetic territory, Vauquelin has to discover French regionalism, and the descriptive modes it offers. Here is how, in the *Satyres*, he describes his departure from Paris and journey to Angers and Poitiers (the verses are again from the autobiographical 'À son livre,' in which he is instructing his book on what to tell the court about his life):

> Nous quittames Paris et les rives de Seine,
> Vinmes dessus le Loir, sur la Sarte et sur Maine.[26]
> Lors Angers nous fist voir Tahureau, qui mignart
> Nous affrianda tous au sucre de cet art.
> De là nous vinmes voir les Nimphes Poitevines,
> Qui suivoient par les Prez, Françoises et Latines,
> Le jeune Saintemarthe, et ses vers enchanteurs
> Apres eux attiroient les filles et pasteurs.
> Et di, qu'ayant encor sans coton le visage,
> Je mis au jour les vers de mon apprentissage.
> Au lieu de desmesler les epineuses lois,
> Les Nimphes, les Sylvains nous suivions par les bois.   (188)

[We left Paris and the banks of the Seine, / Came upon the rivers Loire, Sarte, and Maine. / Then we were shown Angers by the refined Tahureau, / Who excited us with the sweet taste of this art (of poetry). / From there we went on to see the Poitevin nymphs, / Both French and Lain, who in the meadows followed / The young Sainte-Marthe, whose enchanting verses / Pulled after them maidens and shepherds. / And say that while I was still beardless / I had published my very first poems. / Rather than figuring out thorny legal problems, / We followed nymphs and woodland creatures through the woods.[27]

The fact that this is a retrospective description makes it all the more revealing: Vauquelin is recounting the events of his life as a journey into and through poetry, and the journey into the provinces is co-opted by this metanarrative. Paris and the provinces are described metonymically by the rivers that run through them, in a way reminiscent of Du Bellay's poetic fluvial map of France discussed in chapter 3. After this local topography, the poem shifts perspective, and the encounter with Scévole de Sainte-Marthe is given in mythico-poetic terms. Sainte-Marthe himself is Orpheus, enchanting maidens and shepherds, and followed through the Poitevin meadows by native 'Nymphes Poitevines.' These nymphs are, however, both French and Latin – a bilingual image of the province that starkly stages the intertwining of the two languages and cultures in Renaissance France. These bilingual, bicultural nymphs are also signs of the dual function of Vauquelin's landscape, written as both a *locus* of Latin poetry and as distinct provincial landmarks. Even the order in which the three Angevin rivers are given corresponds to a precise and actual geographical order (the Loir flows into the Sarthe, and the Sarthe becomes the Maine).

The journey from Paris to the provinces, through the particular and idealized description of a small, well-defined region, opens up for Vauquelin the type of poetic discourse necessary for him to articulate a private safe haven in poetry: the journey's endpoint is in fact the writing of the poet's first volume, the *Foresteries*. Note the rhyming, in the last two lines of the citation above, of *bois* (woods) with *lois* (laws). The *bois* – the place of idealized lyric production – are the place inhabited and written by the poet precisely because he is not studying *lois*. However, as we shall see, the opposition is not clear-cut. The *bois* are immanently threatened by the very world of *lois* they are conjured to exclude. Law and poetry are two separate worlds only in the fiction of poetry; the reality that Vauquelin dramatizes is the impossibility of finding an actual space of pure poetry that is not already contaminated. Any poetic and social integrity is always on the point of collapsing in on itself from outside pressures.

Vauquelin only assumes his legal persona because of such external pressures: failure as a poet, and the need to maintain the family's social standing. The law, at least in the poetic-autobiographic world of the *Satyres*, is what he does because he has to. After describing in idealized terms his coming-to-writing, Vauquelin continues by recounting the relative failure of the *Foresteries*. Vauquelin was by his own account deeply upset by the lukewarm reactions of his friends, his mother, and Charles de Bourgueville, the father of Anne, his intended bride.[28] Discouraged, he left Poitiers to complete his legal studies in Bourges. There is no attempt in the *Satyres* to describe the landscape of Bourges. The contrast is striking, between the halcyon days spent conversing with nymphs in a timeless bucolic landscape, and a severe calling-back to duty described in almost repentant terms, the prodigal son returning to the father: 'ayant souffert une dure reprise [...] Nos loix plus que devant et plus soigneux j'aimé' [having suffered a harsh setback ... I diligently loved our laws more than before] (188). The law here could be read as a Lacanian mirror-stage, enabling or demanding Vauquelin's initiation into the world of the symbolic, into society and its patriarchal laws.[29] Vauquelin undertook his juridical career partly in order to make himself into a more attractive suitor, that is, in order to marry and perpetuate the family name. His father-in-law played an important role in Vauquelin's conversion to lawyer, much more so than his biological father, who died at war when he was nine.[30] In the *Satyre* 'A Monsieur du Perron,' concerned with the question of paternal authority, there is a close tie between the function of the law and that of the father-figure requiring the study of the law:

> Enfin guidé d'une chaude *espérance*
> De parvenir à la belle *asseurance*
> De mon autre oncle, or' *grave* en *jugement*,
> Chef du parquet de nostre Parlement,
> Et que d'ailleurs j'estoy né pour apprendre
> Au long habit j'allay du tout me rendre.
> Lors de Poitiers quitant le mont Joubert
> Mon but je mis aux Forenses d'Imbert[31]
> Et dudepuis du libre fait *esclave*.   (220, my emphasis)

[Finally, guided by the strong hope / Of attaining the reassuring approval / Of my other uncle, whose judgment was of such consequence / And who was head prosecutor of our parliament, / And also because I was born to learn, / I gave myself over entirely to the long robe (the legal profession). / When I left Mont Joubert in Poitiers / I set myself to Imbert's *Forenses* / And, after freedom, became a slave.]

Vauquelin's vocabulary here belies anxiety and obligation – he is a *slave* to legal books, and *hopes* to win the *approval* of a man whose *judgment* is *of consequence*. The presence of this father-figure pushing him to study law, and the anxiety about gaining this patriarchal approval, is writ large in Vauquelin's poetry. In 'À son livre,' he inscribes the study of law into a filial narrative of becoming his father-in-law:

> Di, que le court habit j'eusse pris de Nature,
> Mais que le long me vint par ma bonne aventure,

Ains par la main de Dieu, qui m'y voulut guider,
Me faisant d'un beau père à l'estat succéder.   (189)

[Tell them that I would have put on the short coat (of the poet) following
my natural inclination, / But good fortune brought me the long one (of the
lawyer), / Thus by the hand of God, who guided me there, / I acceded to
the status and estate of my father-in-law.]

Vauquelin's career here is a progression from the state of Nature to that
of culture, the authority of God and father-in-law: from poet to lawyer.
The trouble is that Vauquelin rather prefers the former. The practice of
law is consistently presented as a sacrifice, as conformism to social
norms and obligations that he would rather ignore had he the choice.
He writes in an epistle addressed to Sainte-Marthe in the *Satyres* that he
would willingly burn all his law books and be known as a pastoral
poet, if he could only do so without public opprobrium:

Et si je ne croyay qu'on me tint pour volage
[...]
Je ferois un beau coup! tous mes livres de lois,
D'Ordonnances, d'Edits, tant Latin que François,
Je mettroy dans le feu: je prendray pour devise
Le bonnet et la vigne[32] en signe de franchise.   (174)

[And if I didn't think that I'd be thought a fool / ... / I'd surprise them! All
my law books, / The Ordonnances and Edicts, both Latin and French, / I
would burn: I would take as my emblem / The bonnet and the vine, as a
sign of honesty.]

Vauquelin makes a sustained poetic contrast between law as conform-
ity to a paternally figured authority, and poetry as a personal choice not
sanctioned by society. The period spent writing poetry in Angers and
Poitiers represents a kind of prolonged infancy before his initiation to
the law, to which he yearns to return.[33]

We shall come shortly to the question of Vauquelin's mother, but before doing so it is worth asking what Vauquelin's blood father represents in his son's poetry. The father-in-law is clearly the *father* and the
law, but what of his dead biological father, who died in battle, an honourable death for a nobleman? This ghost allows Vauquelin to assert
the identity of the true aristocrat, to imagine, perhaps, that if his father

had lived, he would be leading the leisured life of a landowner as opposed to that of an ambitious lawyer. His father's being dead opens up
a realm of imagined possibilities that reveal, through the stark contrast
with his relationship with his in-law, the classic social anxiety of the
sixteenth-century nobility. In the *Satyre* 'À Monsieur du Perron,' the
same one in which the father-in-law prompts Vauquelin to study law,
Vauquelin paints a rather pathetic Arcadian picture of himself imitating
his dead father that is strikingly opposed to his imitation of his living
father-in-law. He becomes his father-in-law by practising law; he becomes his biological father by practising traditional aristocratic behav-
iours such as hunting in his forest:

> Tantost voulant mon feu père imiter,
> Et comme luy les forests habiter,
> Entre les miens, mes vassaux et mes hommes,
> Vivant joyeux plus qu'au temps ou nous sommes,
> Aimant les chiens, la chasse et les chevaux.   (219)

> [Sometimes I wanted to imitate my dead father, / And, like him, spend my
> time in the forest / With my people, my servants, and my men, / Living
> more happily than we do nowadays, / Loving dogs, hunting, and horses.]

Through his dead father, the son imagines bygone days as a halcyon
period of social order when vassals and the lower classes knew their
places and dog-loving aristocrats could spend their days hunting.[34] The
place of such noble pleasure is the forest; in fact, the immediate identification made is between his father and this space. To be the father is to
live in the forest. And the woods of Fresnaye are, of course, the father's
actual – not merely fictional – legacy to the son, transferred at his death.
The forest and the father who gave it to him thus represent a familial
and a poetic identity, or prestige, that Vauquelin attempts to protect
from the threat of collapse from outside, from history.

But the facts of history are never completely excluded from the pastoral bower. The forest his father left him was a financial liability and
the son found himself in debt:

> heritier d'une terre endettee,
> Que chacun estimoit bien tost voir decrettee
> Par tant de Creanciers à qui, pour suivre Mars,
> Il s'esoit engagé quasi de toutes pars.   (187)

[heir to a mortgaged territory / Which everyone thought would soon be repossessed / By all the creditors to whom he had become endebted / In every way, in order to go into battle.]

His father only got into debt, of course, in order to 'suivre Mars,' to be a soldier. The family name is still an honourable one, despite the family land being on the auction block. The threat of history – of debts and the worries of real land ownership – is countered in this instance by an appeal to another marker of nobility, the bearing of arms. The father becomes an avatar for the ideal aristocrat, all the more so because he died at war, but he can only be idealized because he is dead. The living must get on with the less-than-ideal business of reality, and the reality of managing an estate requires financial know-how.

It is Vauquelin's mother who must assume the distasteful implication in money, the law, and hard work, in order to save the forest. And she does, according to the son, ingeniously paying off the debts left by Vauquelin *père* and saving the land from sale. Vauquelin acknowledges his debt to her in the *Satyres*:[35]

Di, que contre l'espoir de plusieurs toutefois
Gardez premierement entiers furent nos bois,
Quand par un heureux soin ma mere gouvernante,
Ayant ma Garde-noble,[36] en fut la conservante,
Et maniant du mien l'annuel revenu,
Mes debtes aquitta depuis par le menu.   (187)

[Tell them that against the hopes of many (creditors) / We managed to keep our woods entirely, / Because my mother, who managed them with great care / And who was their beneficiary and trustee (until I came of age) / Managed my annual revenue / And paid off my debts most carefully.]

By attributing the economic turnaround to his mother, Vauquelin, intentionally or not, exempts himself from direct involvement with monetary affairs. Such financial hard-headedness was, however, critical to reestablishing the family's status. During the second half of the sixteenth century, the fortunes of the family increased, shown by the royal privilege for the *Diverses poésies*, published in 1605, which gives all of Vauquelin's accumulated titles: 'sieur de la Fresnaie au Sauvage, Sassi, Boessey, les Yveteaux, les Aulnez, et d'Arri, Conseiller du Roy, et president au Bailliage et Siege Presidial de Caen.'

Vauquelin's poetic forest is never free from the anxiety of the financial worries imposed on him by land ownership. The feared loss of his forest stands not just for family shame in Vauquelin's poetry, but also for the loss of a particular poetic identity. The cohesion of the family's social standing symbolized by the forest depends on a suspension in time, an impossible exclusion from the processes of history. Only in poetry can Vauquelin's family live in the forest and can the forest's pastoral integrity remain intact. The joyful hunter in the woods can only exist as a ghost haunting an Arcadian golden age. As soon as the woods are considered as real territory, they are vulnerable to the fluctuations and depredations of the world outside poetry.

The productive tension between first and second worlds is seen in Vauquelin's representation of his forest in his first volume of poetry, the eponymous *Les Foresteries* [The Forest Poems]. Published when the poet was about eighteen years old, it is a pastorally inspired collection set in the poet's ancestral woods, which a youthful Vauquelin introduces as the site of the regeneration of pastoral in France. Vauquelin imagines that the woods at Fresnaye-au-Sauvage will become a *lieu commun* of French pastoral. Most of the poems in the *Foresteries* are exuberant imitations of classical and Italian pastoral poems, and if read without the first poems and the preface, their sylvan setting would not appear to be particularly important. But the importance of this collection lies precisely in the initial setting of the scene, and in the last poem which reminds the reader that the geography of the poetic forest is coterminous with that of the woods of Fresnaye. The collection is both framed by, and situated in, the forest associated with Vauquelin's family name. Yet even in this apparently confident presentation of his own land as the site of French pastoral, and the landowner – Vauquelin himself – as its principle agent, the social and literary anxieties of a young, unknown aristocrat-poet still surface to destablize the forest's integrity as a poetic locale. These moments of uncertainty and contamination make the *Foresteries* significantly more complex and revealing than has previously been suggested.

Let us start with the title itself, *Les Foresteries*, or, more completely, *Les deus premiers livres des Foresteries de I. Vauquelin de la Fresnaye*. The word 'foresterie' to designate a poetic form appears to be a neologism. Hulubei posits that Vauquelin's use of the word is a conflation of *églogue* and *idylle* with the Latin *silvae* (woods), used as a title for Latin collections of improvised poems.[37] Marc Bensimon suggests that Vauquelin sought to 'attribute to himself the invention of a new genre';

Lemercier also attributes the title to a 'desire to appear original,' and locates the originality specifically in the poet's privileging of his family's land, 'an entirely literary acknowledgement of his hereditary domain.'[38] The generic novelty of the forest poems alone argues for a reconsideration of Vauquelin's role in the making of French pastoral. Vauquelin claims, not without reason, to be the first to write sylvan bucolic poetry in French. In the later *Idillies et Pastorales*,[39] whose title recalls Theocritus, he directly claims to be one of the first to have transported the 'sylvan muse' from Syracuse (Theocritus's probable birthplace) to France:

Si je t'ay des premiers, o Forestiere Muse,
Conduite aux champs François des champs de Syracuse,
Anime nos forests a bruire pour toujours,
De ces loyaux amants les loyales amours.   (449–50)

[O sylvan Muse, I was one of the first / To bring you from Syracuse to the fields of France, / Therefore make our forests ring out forever / With the sound of the loyal lovers' loyal loves.]

Vauquelin here claims to be the Virgil of sixteenth-century France: these lines are a direct imitation of the first two lines of Virgil's Sixth Eclogue, 'My muse first deigned to sport in Sicilian strains, and blushed not to dwell in the woods.'[40] The *musa agrestis* of Virgil's Sixth Eclogue does not, however, have a named dwelling; Vauquelin goes Virgil one better by replacing the landscape of classical lyric with his own local geography.

As significant as Vauquelin's generic innovation might be, it is the thematics of land ownership, and its relation to a notional aristocratic identity, that will be of principal interest here. Lemercier's speculation above, about the poet's 'literary acknowledgement of his hereditary domain,' suggests a relationship between poetry and land ownership that has not been studied in the French context.[41] But the eponymous forest of the *Foresteries* is nothing less than the vehicle through which the young poet attempts to define his particular contribution to vernacular poetry. In the liminary essay of the *Foresteries*, addressed to the bishop of Séez, Vauquelin stakes out his ground literally and figuratively. These few pages, too long to quote in full, are an invitation to the bishop to come and walk around his, Vauquelin's, forest, and to read the lines of poetry scratched into the tree trunks. The invitation is into a world of pure poetry, an inspirited world in which nature listens and responds sympathetically to lovers' complaints, where every tree bears an engraved poem. What is more, the Norman forest is presented as the site of classical pastoral's revival:

> Pour le long tens qu'il i a que les Forests sont muetes enmie la France, et dénuées de pasteurs qui les enseignent après eus à resonner le nom de ceus que plus ils estiment: je pense monsieur que vous ne dédaignerés de visiter les nôtres [...] vous amusant à lire les vers gravés à fine force aus écorces des tendres Freneteaux, qui croisants feront croitre votre nom en mes vers [... je vais] sainctement Forestiser, comme celui qui promet de reveiller en France les Forests par ci devant endormies, et donner des oreilles aus valées, aus montaignes, aus marests, et aus rochers assourdis: à fin que les pasteurs avenir counoissent que la musette à sept voix[42] peut accorder à d'autres genres d'écrire. Mais pour cet'heure il me suffira, monsieur, qu'à la façon antique je face retentir les antres et les valées profundes. (2–4)[43]

> [Since the forests of France have been mute for so long, and devoid of pastors who would teach them to echo back the names of their loved ones, I think, sir, that you will not be opposed to visiting ours ... entertaining yourself by reading the poems etched delicately into the bark of the young ashes which, as they grow, will make your name grow in my verse ... I will blessedly Forestify, as I am the one who promises to wake up the forests in France that have until now been sleeping, and to give ears to the deaf valleys, mountains, marshes, and rocks; and thus future shepherds will know that the seven-fluted pipe can accompany other kinds of writing. But for the moment I will be content, sir, to make the caves and valleys sing out again in the ancient way.]

There are too many individual landmarks associated with the poet's family name for these woods to be anything other than those of Fresnaye-au-Sauvage. The engraved trees are 'tendres Freneteaux,' the trees after which Vauquelin de la Fresnaye is named. These delicate ash trees are, metonymically, his youthful poetry, and as they grow, so will the bishop's renown through the poet's verse. The carving of names or poems on trees has a long literary history, going back as early as Aristophanes, but it is the use of the motif in Latin and Italian pastoral which provides the richest source of imitation for Renaissance poets.[44] In particular, Rensselaer Lee has shown the popularity in pictorial representations of Ariosto's nineteenth canto, in which Angela and Medoro carve their names on trees. This episode, as he points out, is a 'pastoral oasis [...] an interlude or passing experience of unforeseen happiness and repose in a life of demanding action or exhausting emotion.'[45] Vauquelin inscribes this Ariostan pastoral oasis into his woods, and it functions in contrast to the historical processes in which he is implicated, while he domesticates and makes his own a powerful image of poetic fame.

Vauquelin's forest – his poetry – is a response to the silence of French woods, that is, the demise of the pastoral mode in France. The key moment is when pastoral is perceived to be *absent*, the moment of the woods' silence, for if the forests of France are not diagnosed as silent in the first place, they do not need a poet to make them speak again. This moment, which allows the poet a generative role in the history of pastoral, is not as individuating as it might seem: Virgil and Sannazaro had both made the same claim for their own roles in pastoral. Jacopo Sannazaro's *Arcadia* had been translated into French by Jean Martin in 1544, and enjoyed quite a vogue,[46] along with Martin's other translation from Italian to French in 1546, that of the *Hypnerotomachia Poliphili* or 'Dream of Polyphilus' attributed to Francesco Colonna. Both helped bring into France the Italian sensibility towards landscape that was evidenced not only in literary imitations but also in landscaping fashions.[47] Sannazaro's epilogue to the *Arcadia*, addressed to his 'sampognia' (Vauquelin's *musette à sept voix*, the seven-fluted pipe or syrinx that stands for pastoral), praises the instrument for having been the first to 'reawaken the slumbering woods, and show the shepherds how to sing the songs that they had forgotten.'[48] This in turn is an echo of Virgil's First Eclogue, in which Tityrus teaches the woods to sound again the beauty of Amaryllis. By referencing Sannazaro imitating Virgil, Vauquelin is transplanting Latin and Italian poetry onto his native soil. But the lost world of pastoral – sylvan nymphs and talking pines – exists only as a kind of infinite regress, evoked as an ideal already disappeared.

The related theme of the disappearance of an old aristocratic order, seen already in our reading of the *Satyres*, is present from the very first page of the *Foresteries*, in which Vauquelin makes the explicit link between poetic and social nostalgia. 'Je ne doute point,' he writes, 'que quelques grossiers d'entendement [...] qui n'eurent jamais, di-je, nulle réponse des Pins parlants de Menale, ne jugent incontinent ces vers Foresters indignes' [I do not doubt that some uneducated types ... to whom Maenalus's talking pines never responded, will judge these forest-poems unworthy] (3). The talking pines are a reference to Virgil's Eighth Eclogue, in which Damon sings a 'song of Maenalus,' an Arcadian mountain sacred to Pan, on which grew talking pines.[49] The word *grossier* had several connotations in the sixteenth century, but coupled with 'entendement' it inevitably points to a lack of education, ignorance of Latin and Virgil, the lot of the third estate. Vauquelin codes the ideal reader of pastoral – to whom the pines of Maenalus have spoken – as aristocratic.

We will encounter later the further circumscription of the pastoral woods as noble space. For now, we will return to the question of imitation, the multiple foreign poetic voices with which the woods of Fresnaye are fairly brimming. Even though Vauquelin insists that these are his woods responding to his voice, almost all of the descriptives he uses to describe this landscape are taken from other poets. This creates a barely disguised uncertainty that lurks behind every tree, in every cave:

> il me suffira qu'à *la façon antique* je face retentir les antres et les valées profundes, *repoussantes* le son de *ma vois* à elles *peu acoutumé*: et que mollement étendu à la plus ombreuse islete, que *mon Orne* entoure de ses eaus caquetardes, j'accorde ma Sampogne. (3, my emphasis)

> [I will be content *in the ancient way* to make the caves and deep valleys sing out again, which *throw back* the *unfamiliar* sound of my voice, and it suffices me that, lying back on the shadiest little island, surrounded by the waters of *my Orne*, I tune my Sampogna.]

There is a tension here that is never quite resolved. Despite his best efforts to transform Normandy into Arcadia, Vauquelin cannot get around the fact that Arcadia is a creation of classical and Italian poets. The caves and valleys throw back to the poet the sound of his voice, which is unknown to them. There is something disjunctive about the presence of the river Orne, a river in Normandy, in a sentence describing the languid shepherd-poet tuning his *sampogna*, Sannazaro's word for the pastoral pan-pipes which are played on the banks of the Italian Sebeto. Vauquelin cannot imagine physical space without referencing *loci classici*.

The notion of *locus* is, as discussed in the introduction, both geographic and textual: it means both physical space and a place in a text. Vauquelin himself evokes the polysemantic 'lieu' in a passage that lays bare the contradictions of trying to conflate local geography with poetry:

[P]our orner les rives de mon Orne [...] j'ai cueilli des plus mignardes fleurettes desquelles la Nimphe Arethuse ait point illustré la Sicile: et de celles dont le Mince enflé borde ordinairement ses bords: et dont le petit Sebethe a le lieu empeinturé les prairies Neapolitaines [...] Et ce sont là les trois *lieus* desquels j'ai taché le plus à décorer ces Foresteries. (5)

[To make ornate the banks of my Orne ... I have picked some of the sweetest little flowers with which the nymph Arethusa ever decorated Sicily, and some with which the Mincio usually lines its banks, and with which the little Sebeto painted the Neapolitican prairies ... And those are the three *places* with which I have tried the most to decorate these Forest Poems.]

The homonym *orner/Orne* underlines the river's status as poetic cliché, or rather that it exists to be decorated with the clichés (the rhetorical 'flowers') of others. Du Bellay, we remember, makes frequent use of agricultural images of transplantation in his *Deffence et illustration de la langue françoyse*, published six years before the *Foresteries*. Vauquelin here responds to Du Bellay with images of planting, on his native river bank, flowers (that is, poetic figures) taken from Sicily (Theocritus), the Mincio in Mantua (Virgil), and Sannazaro's Neopolitan Sebeto. These three poets are the 'lieus' he has imported into his own. The Norman Orne is thus a conflation of three Italian rivers; the flowers on its banks are Italian transplants. In a liminary sonnet, the poet's friend Charles Toutain adds to this topographic confusion by addressing the Greek river-god Alpheus, who flowed under the sea from Greece to Sicily to mingle with the fountain Arethusa whom he loved. Alpheus is enjoined to hurry, its waters swelled by those of Virgil's Mincio and Sannazaro's Sebeto, 'pour voir en Occident naissante une Arcadie' [to see an Arcadia rising in the West] (7). The sources, both literary and fluvial, of France's new Arcadia are invoked from Greece and Italy.[50] Vauquelin's poetic space in the *Foresteries*, before he even starts, is thus cluttered with multiple claims that dissipate its cohesion as local, ancestral land, as native French poetry, and as his own individual production.

The first two poems of the collection contrast each other in ways that reveal the multiple and contradictory roles of Vauquelin's sylvan landscape, in particular the irreconcilable difference between pastoral ideal and historical fact. The first poem is addressed to Diana the virgin huntress. It begins thus:

Chaste Dictinne en *nos* forests princesse,
En *nos* forests où les brouans sangliers,
Les cerfs craintifs, les dains de peur legers,
Vivent sous toi [...]
D'un oeil arrêté ton Forestier regarde,
Ton Forestier sacré,
Qui dans *tes* bois librement à son gré
Folâtre sans mégarde,
Car au vent de sa voix
Il fait plier *tes* bois.   (9, my emphasis)

[Chaste Diana, princess of *our* woods, / *Our* woods where the rowdy boar, / The timid stag, the fearful deer, / Live under you ... / Consider for a while *your* woodsman, / Your sacred woodsman, / Who freely, at his own will, in *your* woods / Makes merry without a care, / For with the sound of his voice / He makes *your* trees bend.]

The first two lines refer deictically to 'our forests,' allowing for a historically determined owner. However the woods are subsequently referred to only as Diana's, 'tes bois,' words that appear in all six refrains and that also conclude the whole poem. Historic ownership is surrendered and transferred to the ahistorical domain of poetry itself, and the poet becomes Diana's forester. The forests themselves have nothing that distinguishes them from the forests of Ovid and Sannazaro (the borrowings from both are heavy), except for the reappearance, in the last stanza, of the poet's ash trees, the *fréneaus*, on which he is carving Diana's praises: '[...] à ton seul nom je fais / Sur ces fréneaus fendasser les portraits / De tes clartés' [to your name alone I hew / On these ash trees the portraits / Of your renown] (12). These lines are followed by a close imitation of Thyrsis's desire, in Virgil's Seventh Eclogue, for recognition from the shepherds of Arcadia, and protection from failure as a poet. Virgil writes: 'Shepherds of Arcady, crown with ivy your rising bard [...] or, should he praise me unduly, wreathe my brow with foxglove.'[51] And Vauquelin: 'Cein donc le front de bacche / A ton poète, à fin qu'injurieux / De ses brocards ne nuise l'envieux' [Encircle therefore your poet's brow / With foliage, so that the jealous one with ill intent / Do no harm with his attacks] (13). This anxious moment of defence against a proleptically imagined detractor reveals the fragility of the forest as the guarantor of any kind of reputation.

The first poem thus ends on an intertextual note of doubt that is continued in the following poem. Vauquelin starts the second *Foresterie* with anaphoric moments of rejection by his readers, a reversal of the usual lyric invitation to poetic complicity between writer and reader. The poem imagines readers who are *not* participating in his project of mutual glorification:

> Qui vivre apres sa mort dedans mes vers *refuse*
> Et qui *n'aime* mes bois, et qui *n'aime* ma muse,
> Et qui *dédaigne* voir nos abrisseaus couvers
> De mille petits vers:
> Vraiment, outre son gré, l'honneur qu'il ne mérite
> Il *n'aura pas* de moi.   (14, my emphasis)

> [Whoever refuses to live after death in my poetry, / Whoever does not love my forest and my muse, / Whoever disdains my bushes covered / With thousands of little poems: / Truly, whatever he wants, he won't get from me / The honour that he does not deserve.]

It is a strangely anxious start to a poem, brimming with negations of the renown he imagines for himself and his woods. Indeed, the whole collection, while self-consciously making poetic history, is nevertheless haunted by anticipated failure. But Vauquelin is also excluding bad readers from his poetry, and creating the kind of reader he does want. The ideal reader of his pastoral will be allowed into the domain of his woods and will be rewarded for it: 'Mais celui qui voudra écouter en nos bois / Mille petites voix [...] / Lors il oiroit son nom' [He who wants to listen in our woods / To a thousand little voices ... He would hear his name] (7–14). Both the geography and the readership of Vauquelin's pastoral are selective. The woods of Fresnaye are circumscribed; only well-behaved readers may enter, and that on invitation only. The exclusivity of his pastoral aims to preserve a certain aristocratic and literary ethos from threats from the outside – bad readers, the lower classes, social disorder.[52]

But the bower does not remain protected for long. Vauquelin cannot maintain the absolute purity of the poetic world: the first world is always there, *et in Arcadia*. The first hint of the inextricability of ideal and real is centred on the key figure of Vauquelin's father, the bequeather of the forest and the ghostly presence we see hunting in the woods in the

Satyres. Here, he is named both as biographical father and as the god of pastoral, Pan himself:

> Mais quoi, mes Forestiers, au bords de noz rivages
> Vous augmentez encor les moiteus marécages
> De vos pleurs, regretants votre Pan conducteur,
> De ce lieu le pasteur:
> Votre Pan et mon père.   (30–4)

[But oh, my woodsmen, on our river banks / You make the damp marshes even wetter / With your tears, mourning Pan your leader, / The shepherd of this place: / Your Pan, and my father.][53]

The scene is based on an episode in the fifth chapter of Sannazaro's *Arcadia*, the mourning at the tomb of the wise pastor Androgeo, whom Vauquelin replaces with his father.[54] The arrival of his father means that history has intruded upon his French Arcadia. The father raises the question of debt and ownership; the father is the source of the woods but also of the worries associated with them. The specificity of Vauquelin's financial situation sits uneasily in this sylvan locale:

> Votre Pan et mon père, à qui fut ordonée
> Et pour vous et pour moi ce lieu, cete FRESNEE,
> Dont les bois et les eaus qui furent son souci,
> Le soient du fils aussi.   (34–7)

[Your Pan and my father, to whom was granted, / For your sake and mine, this place, this Fresnaye, / Whose woods and waters which were his care / Have become the son's.]

The 'souci,' in the rhyme position, undoes the cohesion of the Arcadian idyll, as the context of work and care associated with the woods inflects the reader's experience of the entire locale. Biography intersects with poetry; the father and son, and their woods, the source of future French pastoral, are challenged at the outset by financial, real-world concerns. Rather than a *memento mori*, Vauquelin gives us a *memento debitionis*.

After the introduction of the father and of debts, the woods are described encomiastically as a monument to the entire lineage and memory of Vauquelin's family. The model is still Sannazaro, but the imitation is henceforth complicated by the implicit comparison between Androgeo and Vauquelin's father, between Arcadia and Fresnaye. The father replacing Androgeo is the source of financial trouble, and the woods replacing Arcadia are thence contaminated.

> Plustost se cueilleront les olives l'été
> Qu'au bois [mon père] ne soit chanté.
> Car c'est lui, Forestiers, qui joignit à noblesse,
> Maugré le Dieu guerrier, des bois la gentillesse,
> Et lequel est chanté sous l'ombre de vos pins
> L'honneur des VAUQUELINS.
> Et moi son fils seulet à toute heure je porte
> Des lauriers sur sa tumbe, affin qu'il en resorte
> Un laurier verdissant, dont se couronneront
> Ceux qui pasteurs seront.[55]   (40–9)

[Rather will olives be picked in summer / Than will my father's name not be sung in the woods. / For it is he, Woodsmen, who joined nobility / To the sweetness of the woods, despite his soldiering. / And for him is sung, in the shade of your pines, / The honour of the Vauquelins. / And I his son, all alone I constantly bring / Laurels to his tomb, so that from there might spring / A green laurel tree, with which / Future pastors will crown themselves.]

Lines 40–1 and 46–7 are again direct imitations of Sannazaro's fifth chapter.[56] The 'honneur des Vauquelins' in line 45 (almost the exact middle of the poem), is thus framed by two moments of commemoration of someone else, Androgeo. There is another comparison implied by the intertext that is to the detriment of Vauquelin's family: in the *Arcadia*, it is Apollo himself who carries the wreaths to Androgeo's tomb, whereas in Vauquelin's imitation, it is the poet himself. This poet places a laurel wreath on his father's tomb whence will grow a laurel tree whose branches will crown future pastoral poets: the very source of future French bucolic is thus tainted from the beginning by Vauquelin's biography.[57]

The last *Foresterie* of all, 'Le Boquet de Philereme,' is in *prosimetrum*, an alternation of prose and verse (the same form as Sannazaro's *Arcadia*). Here, the poet recounts a stroll around the woods that he took with his fellow poet Charles Toutain, in which they walked from tree to tree and read Philereme's poems engraved on their barks. The geography, a closed-off space dedicated to the writing and reading of pastoral poetry, is an odd confluence of fictional and actual:

[N]ous nous mismes à visiter en nos bois la Nynferie de Diane, et les lieus que les Satyreaus perce-forests pourroient le mieus aimer: […] un ruisseau murmure entre lieus pierreus: ce ruisseau borne de ce côte notre Fresnée au-Sauvage. Et ce lieu est le Bôquet où solitairement le pouvre Philereme a gravé quelque partie de ses vers aux écorces […] (5–15)

[In our woods, we visited Diane's nymphery, and the places where forest-dwelling Satyres like most to visit … a stream murmers between the rocks: on this side the stream borders on our Fresnaye-au-Sauvage. And this place is the thicket where poor lonely Philereme engraved some of his poetry on the bark …]

The forest here is so over-invested with clichés that the insistence on local chorography, on the stream bordering the territory of Fresnaye, falls flat. And the switching back and forth from classical topothesia to local topography is all the more inconsistent because most of the poetry that the two poets find in the woods is derivative of Italian and Latin sources. This inability truly to differentiate his own forest and poetry from that of so many others is seen in a particularly revealing intertextual moment that follows a poem written in praise of the 'frêne,' the tree associated with his family name and renown. The poets have just discovered an encomiastic poem engraved on the bark of a large ash tree, a poem that hails the ash (that is, Vauquelin) as 'l'arbre premier de tant d'arbres divers' [the first among so many different trees] (192). But what comes right after this poem undoes this bid for fame almost entirely:

trouvants à toute rencontre des vers nous ne savions quelquefois ausquelz commancer pour lire, non plus que le fagoteur ou le bucheron arrivants en l'epaise Forest d'Ide, ne sait par où il doit commencer son œuvre. (205–11)

[finding poetry everywhere we looked, we often didn't know where to start, like the man gathering or chopping wood in the thick forest of Ida who does not know where to start his work.]

The poets, having just read the ode to the ash tree, suddenly find themselves overwhelmed by a surplus of poetry; there are so many poems that they do not know where to turn. The image used to describe the poets' uncertainty, the image of the logger who sees so many trees that he does not know where to begin felling, is taken from Theocritus.[58]

Another, more contemporary source is Ronsard, who uses the Theocritan forester-poet in his *Hymne du treschrestien Roy de France*, addressed to Henri II, who also has so many virtues that the poet does not know where to begin.[59] Ronsard expands Theocritus's metaphor somewhat, and gives a list of the types of trees that the forester might have to fell. One of them is, of course, a *frêne* (line 40). Vauquelin's choice of the image of the woodsman is thus a revealing one. The figure of a logger is already an unfortunate choice of image for a poet who is trying to assert the strength and prestige of a particular tree. And the intertextual reference to Ronsard and Theocritus makes the image even more fraught, adding the presence in his woods of better-known and more successful models. The encomium to the *frêne* is an anxious response to Ronsard's logger, who threatens to fell it with the other trees. There is a radical uncertainty in these few lines about the likelihood of his poetry ever being recognized at all: it may be felled at any moment by Ronsardian and Theocritan loggers, the symbolic threat of the presence of exemplar poets. It is hard to imagine a clearer instantiation of Bloom's anxiety of influence.[60]

The fragility of the forest-as-poetry dramatizes Vauquelin's uncertainty about his individual poetic fame. Trying to define a French poetic landscape, to wake up French forests so that they speak again, puts him in the position of imitating Italian and classical models. The woods at Fresnaye potentially offer a way in which Vauquelin can distinguish himself from other poets: no one else wrote about, much less owned, these particular named woods. But the blurring of the boundary in the *Foresteries* between literary and social spheres witnesses to Vauquelin's sense of his uncomfortable dependence on social and economic ties. Sixteenth-century writers were in the paradoxical position of belonging to an increasingly autonomous profession, while also being forced to recognize dependence on, and connections with, other fields of activity.[61] David Quint has posited a relationship between the rise of a mercantile economy and the humanist process of reading and imitation.[62] Quint suggests that humanist readers, displaying borrowings from the classics as their own, show an essentially bourgeois acquisitive behaviour. That is, through the new insistence on individualist accrual of capital, whether financial or literary, the process of social mobility is similar for a financially successful capitalist and for the new 'dynamic and critical' Renaissance reader advocated by Poliziano and Montaigne.[63] Vauquelin's simultaneous quest for literary and social capital through his forest bears out a variant of Quint's notion, with Vauquelin seeking to garner an individual reputation as a writer through the symbolic credit of his status as a landowner. In order to acquire any kind of credence for his forest as his contribution to French poetry, Vauquelin has to rely on a very different value system for his forest – the socio-economic value of the forest as owned property. However, in drawing literary credit from his social credit, he endangers the autonomy of the world of his poetry.

Vauquelin's bid for fame through his land is unlike any other. Unlike Ronsard, he does not put regional landscape in the service of a self-aggrandizing rhetoric, nor does he, like Du Bellay, play it off against a national-scale territory. Rather, Vauquelin dismantles attempts to claim poetic territory even as he writes them, in an oddly self-effacing landscape fraught with psychological and social drama. The forest's status is dual: it appears both as a poetic locale and as actual, owned territory. In both senses, its autonomy is threatened. While the forest is a space of pure poetic production, the guarantor in some respect of his own reputation, it is also a space in which the poet has to confront his French and foreign exemplars. And while Vauquelin presents it as a closed-off territory, a space closely associated with his social standing and public identity, he also undermines its integrity as owned land by references to the economic worries of the family that almost led to its sale. Thus, autobiographical fact and social anxiety contaminate the poetic landscape that he is trying to construct as his own. The result is a fascinating self-portrait, through the anxious and multivalenced representation of the forest identified with his name, of a minor poet and petty noble prey to certain uncomfortable social realities of sixteenth-century France.

'Si loin des maus, desquelz tu es si pres': The Precarity of Refuge in Jacques Peletier's *La Savoye*

Jacques Peletier du Mans (1517–82) was a polymath, expert in mathematics, medicine, astronomy, and Greek, and a chief proponent of French orthographic reform.[64] He knew Ronsard and the other Pléiade poets well; like them, he studied but disliked the law, alternated his time between Paris and the provinces (Maine, in his case), and depended on patrons in the high nobility. He published a volume of *Œuvres poétiques* in 1547, which included poems on the four seasons, an ode inviting Ronsard to join him in the peaceful countryside, and a *débat* on the relative virtues of country versus court life. While Peletier's writing odes in French in 1547 was certainly innovative, these early descriptions of landscape are quite generic. The four seasons, and the ode 'Au seigneur Pierre de Ronsard l'invitant aux champs' [To Sir Pierre de Ronsard inviting him to the countryside], present a series of common poetic tropes on the cycles of nature, many imitated from Virgil's *Georgics* (a translation of the first book of which is included in the *Œuvres*).[65] The 'Louanges de la court, contre la vie de repos,' an exchange between a courtesan and a rurally based gentleman, reprises, again in non-specific terms, the Europe-wide tradition of literary debates pitting court life against the pleasures of (still aristocratic) rusticity.[66]

Like Remy Belleau, Peletier had a significant reputation in the sixteenth century as a poet of nature, largely because he became increasingly interested not just in idealized descriptions of nature, but in exploring nature's structure and workings through poetry. Indeed, his *Amours des amours* (1555) inaugurated the era of high scientific poetry.[67] Like other scientific poets, Peletier believed that one could perceive divine order through natural order, particularly through understanding the higher principles of mathematics manifest in nature.[68] In his 'Louange de la science' published in 1581, he extolled the genius of the divine creator as made visible through the natural world (the poem directly follows a 'Louange du fourmi' [Praise of the Ant], which holds up the ant as a perfect physical creation which also teaches mankind a moral lesson, through its capacity for hard work).[69] Moreover, Peletier proposed that natural phenomena were an appropriate subject for poetry, and that the poet, through correct imitation of natural harmony in the order of poetry, could start to express the underlying structures and secrets of nature.[70] Unlike Tyard, whose scepticism about any real correspondance between word and thing we have seen in his *Douze fables*, Peletier believes in 'l'expression vive des choses par les mots' [the strong expression of things through words].[71] Peletier's interest in nature and natural philosophy has been substantially addressed by several scholars recently, most comprehensively by Sophie Arnaud.[72] As I argued in the case of Remy Belleau, the turn to scientific poetry offers the poet a way out of the dilemmas of landscape representation. The disjuncture between ideal and reality, increasingly unavoidable when describing the places of a politically and socially turbulent France, can be transcended if the focus is on cosmic and natural processes.

Peletier does not tend to describe named landscapes in his poetry. Unlike Ronsard's Vendômois, Du Bellay's Anjou, or Vauquelin's Normandy, the places evoked in his 1547 *Œuvres* are not specifically identifed as French regions.[73] The notable exception to an otherwise unspecific poetic geography is Peletier's *La Savoye*. This long poem, published in Annecy in 1572, was dedicated to Marguerite de France, the daughter of François I and Duchess of Savoy and Berry. It is, in part, the 'souvenir of a delightful place.'[74] Peletier had lived rather an itinerant life – Le Mans, Paris, Poitiers, Bordeaux, Lyon (where he be-friended the Lyonnais poets and claimed to have fallen for Louise Labé),[75] and Rome. In 1570, on his way to Switzerland, he travelled through Savoy, which he liked so much that he stayed in Annecy for two years before returning to Paris as the principal of the Collège du Mans. But the local landscape description is far from idealized: Savoy emerges as a nuanced and complex place, its land both fertile and hos-tile, the mountains both terrifying and awe-inspiring, the inhabitants courageous and foolhardy. And the text is an unusual alliance of *de-scriptio* with scientific poetry. It draws on various literary and geo-graphic sources, including Polybius, Livy, Münster's *Cosmographia*, and a 1562 map of Savoy from Antoine Lafrery's *Geographia*, attributed to Forlani but almost certainly the same one as that executed by Gilles Boileau de Bouillon in 1556.[76] Descriptions of the area had themselves become something of a genre: Guillaume Paradin's 1552 *Cronique de Savoye*, and the description of neighbouring Franche-Comté by Erasmus's secretary Gilbert Cousin, *Descriptio superioris Burgundiae* (1553), certainly were known to Peletier.[77] The result is an eclectic mix of observations of local customs, history, and geography, including speculations on the causes of natural phenomena such as echoes, earthquakes, the formation of metals, glaciers, and avalanches.

The movement of bodies of water is a particularly favoured theme; indeed, it frames the work, presenting a landscape of correspondences, with rivers flowing into each other, lakes, and the ocean, and connecting with each other under the earth's surface. Peletier starts the poem with lengthy explanations of the 'rondeur eternelle' (74)[78] of tides and the sources of water. He then jumps to a strange vision of an acqueous underworld, a subterranean view of the 'palais moites et cavernous' [damp, cavernous rooms] and 'chemins des humides spelonques' (75) [pathways of the damp caves] shown by the nymph Cyrene to her son Aristeus, father of Acteon and, in Virgil's Fourth Georgic, the lover of Eurydice.[79] In Virgil's text, Cyrene shows her son a cavern beneath the surface of a mountain, where Proteus hides. Peletier has this watery journey take place under France, where Cyrene shows her son the Seine, Rhône, Garonne, and Loire, detailing a fluvial cartography of France which gives the confluences, sources, and courses of each. Each river's journey is intellectual and literary as much as it is topographic.

The Rhône, for example, swallows the Sorgue 'à sa Laure parlant' [talking to its Laura]. And the Loire flows

Aupres d'Angers, là ou le Droit s'aprand.
Au mesme lieu les trois Fleuves il prand,
Meine, et le Loir, et nostre Sarte ensemble
Et les trois noms des Poetes assemble.   (79)

[Near Angers, where the law is learned. / Here, it picks up three more rivers, / The Maine, Loir, and our Sarthe together, / And thus brings together our three poets.][80]

We are reminded of Du Bellay's fluvial poetic map of France in *L'Olive*. Savoy, Peletier argues, also deserves to be put on the map because of its rivers – but not because of any of them evoke the name of a poet. Rather, the· region's waterways contain gold: they can compete with any in Europe 'Pour ses Ruisseaux, qui d'or ont pris le nom' [because of its streams, which are named after gold] (86).[81]

Sophie Arnaud emphasizes the importance of water in *La Savoye*, seeing in its order and interconnectedness the key to Peletier's scientific philosophy. For Arnaud, the landscapes of the entire poem are of interest not as descriptions of a particular region but as a study of nature: 'Peletier is not a poet of landscapes but of theories, and we should consider *La Savoye* as a philosophical space.'[82] This space is one of equilibrium, intentional and useful design, and rational causologies: 'Ainsi les faitz de Nature precedent, / Et l'un à l'autre evidemment succedent [...] donnant à l'homme exercise à propos / D'utilité, de peine et de repos' [Thus are the workings of Nature, / And one thing logically follows the other / ... / Providing man with / Useful things, cares, and respite] (82). And, 'Ce qu'en un lieu la Nature defait, / De mesme suite ailleurs elle refait' [What Nature undoes in one way, / She makes up for in another] (90). While the magnificent spectacle of Savoyard nature – mountains, rivers, lakes – certainly is a pretext for philosophical speculations about the sublime and divine order of creation, the specificity of Savoy is above all inextricably linked to the social and historical context. For example, Peletier pays sustained attention to the specific human uses of Savoyard landscape, the 'utile menage' [useful management] of Savoy's 'eureus jardinage' [abundant produce] (107), providing interesting insight into the local products and resources of the region: honey, cedar sap, *sérac* cheese, saffron, artichokes, *guigne* cherries, salt, the animals to hunt, the thermal spas. Book 2 of the work is particularly replete with detailed observations of Savoyard customs and personalities, and the particular relation between man and nature engendered by the mountainous topography.[83]

But the main social interest of Savoy is in its liminal position with respect to France and French civil war. Peletier's Savoy has the potential to be the haven from civil war that other poets have sought to write into their landscapes. Savoy is at the frontier of France, not quite part of the kingdom, but French enough to be imagined by a French poet as its ever-vanishing space of hope. Renaissance Savoy was an independent duchy where French influence had long waxed and waned: in 1536, François I seized it from Charles III, but the treaty of Cateau-Cambrésis in 1559 restored most of the territories to Charles's son, Duke Emmanuel Philibert, who in 1562 moved the capital to Turin in Italy.[84] Situated on the mountainous border between France and Italy, it is both within and outside these national histories. In Peletier's poem, Savoy's almost-French, almost-pastoral landscape openly articulates the tensions between history and ideal, and the position of the poet and poetry caught between them.

In the first few lines, Peletier performs a *translatio studii* that confidently and specifically names Savoy, not the whole French kingdom, as the new locus of inspiration. The Greek Muse is told that she is now 'Savoisienne' (73), and that Peletier has come 'sur le lieu' [on-site] to seek her out. Later, he describes the singing of the Savoyard *bergères* as a kind of transposition of Parisian French, a more pure version of French pastoral:

> Ce sont chansons pleines et pastorals,
> Ce sont des vois fortes et pectorals:
> Motz tous exquis, et de Parisien,
> Tout fraiz tournez en bon Savoisien.   (123)

[They are impressive, pastoral songs / Sung with strong, full-throated voices: / Exquisite Parisian words / Freshly transformed into good Savoy dialect.]

This lusty pastoral relocates poetic and moral purity into this region, contrasted specifically with Paris, which is synonymous with courtly corruption and religious tensions (1572, the year of publication of *La Savoye*, was of course that of the infamous St Bartholomew massacre).

Peletier had witnessed the increasing religious tensions in France, and may himself have been suspected – like Belleau – of early sympathy towards Reformed ideas. (In a 1580 *Apologia* to a rival mathematician, he defends himself from suspicion of heresy, swearing that he has always followed Roman rites and never set foot in Calvin's Geneva while he was in Savoy).[85] Savoy must have appeared as something of a safe haven, and Peletier wonders: 'Tu es en paix, Savoye, et as des homes: / A quoi tient-il qu'eureuse ne te nommes?' [Savoy, you are at peace, and have men / What stops you from being happy?] (118). At times, Savoy seems protected from the troubles:

> Si parmi vous ancor' n'est la macule
> Du sang Civil, duquel je me recule
> Ayant refuge aus asiles sacres,
> Fuiant les lieux poluz et massacrez …

> [You are not yet affected by the stain / Of civil blood, from which I turn, / Finding refuge in sacred hideouts, / Fleeing polluted and murderous places …]

He invites any reader, 'quelqu'un qui fuye / Cet air François' [anyone who would flee / This French place] to come 'en ce lieu que j'ay voulu portrere' [to this place I have described] (125). This status as refuge has much to do with Savoy's geographic marginality and topography, its 'assiette et force naturelle' [natural position and strength] (124). Nature has erected its mountains with good reason, 'pour separations / De ciel, de meurs, de langue, aus nations' [as barriers that separate nations' views, skies, and languages] (99). But Peletier also evokes Savoy's political independence, attributing the relative peace to the governance of the Duke, Emmanuel Philibert: 'Eureuse ell'est du Prince qui la tient / Et en seurté paisible l'entretient' [She is happy because of the Prince who rules her / And keeps her in peaceful security] (124). Her liminality with respect to France leads to a specific comparison of the two, where Savoy is not only far from civil strife, but a model of simplicity and moral rectitude:

> Doncques, Province, ornee de simplesse,
> Sans envier la pompeuse noblesse
> De tes voisins, qui es, par don expres,
> Si loin des maus, desquelz tu es si pres.   (124)

[Therefore, Province, dressed so simply, / Unenvious of the pompous nobility / Of your neighbours, you who are, by special gift (of Nature) / So far from the troubles, to which you are so close.]

If it remains possible to imagine a peaceful, productive landscape, Peletier suggests in the last line above, it is in a liminal zone that is not quite France but close to it (and the same with respect to Italy).[86] In Ronsard's poetry, regionalism is the answer to the corruption of the kingdom as a whole, but regionalism, for Peletier, is not enough in itself. The space of hope must be on the hinterlands of nations.

In 1593, René de Lucinge, an influential political thinker and the Savoyard ambassador at the French court, wrote (but did not publish, due to the political risk) a *Dialogue du François et du Savoisien*, presenting an anthropomorphized Savoy as exempt from, and ignorant of, the wars, but eminently sympathetic to France. Lucinge's contrast of Savoyard innocence with courtly corruption certainly draws on Peletier's troping of the region, but – unsurprisingly for someone with overt political engagements – is more propagandistic.[87] Peletier's presentation of Savoy's exemption from historical troubles is nuanced and provisional. He shows that Savoy's proximity to, and historical ties with, France, which make it possible for the poet to imagine it as a viable alternate French space, is also the cause of worry. The natural barrier of the mountains is being breached, in a repetition of Hannibal's transgressive penetration (which Peletier also discusses, drawing on Livy and Polybius), by the creeping violence of civil war:

Quand le venin des proches regions,
A penetré par ses contagions
Les Mons epais, rompant par sa malice
Bournes, rempars, Nature et sa police.   (101)

[The poison of nearby regions / Has penetrated, with its contagion, / The thick mountains, breaking limits, / Barriers, the very order of Nature, with its evil.]

Like Belleau, who reveals in his *Bergerie* the fictionality of pastoral idealizations, Peletier shows the extent to which his irenic representation of Savoy, despite the region's being 'eureuse par elle' [happy in its own right], is based on poetic troping. There is no escape from history, and poets are implicated in it despite themselves. They may express a yearning, as Peletier himself does, to become 'le laboureur qui cultive le val / Du froid Bessan' [the labourer who cultivates / The valley of cold Bessans] (100). But aristocratic poets are no more willing to become – or capable of becoming – real labourers than kings are to become real shepherds. It is 'fole fantaisie' to imagine that he would be anything other than a world-weary poet, who carries his cares with him everywhere: 'Pourquoi fuiz-tu? Si tes rong'ans travaus / Tu as en croupe et par mons et par vaus?' [Why do you flee, if you carry your troubles / With you through hill and dale?]. His relationship with the landscape would still be that of a pastoral poet, interpolating nature as 'temoins de mes ecriz' [witnesses to my writing] (101). Peletier shows us that there is no unmediated landscape. Indeed, he specifically states, in an anticipation of the theorizations of modern cultural geography, that landscapes are cultural and social, defined by humankind, and pleasing to us inasmuch as they reflect our notions of the good:

C'est l'homme seul, qui rend le lieu spectacle:
Non pas le lieu, qui rend l'homme acceptable:
Et la vertu, jointe a l'humanité
Donne auz païs toute leur dignité.   (118)

[It is man alone who turns space into spectacle, / Not space that makes a man agreeable. / And virtue joined with humanity / Give places all their dignity.]

Any observer will bring his own social position and intellectual framework to his experience and representation thereof, and the filter of a sixteenth-century French poet is affected by his social status, his intellectual heritage, and – especially by the 1570s – the grim reality of civil war.

Spaces of Hope

My concern throughout this study has been the role of poetry in creating spaces of hope, self-conscious places of refuge from social change in sixteenth-century France. This particular chapter has addressed historical shifts in the role of the aristocracy (in particular of the poet-landowner), the identification of the aristocrat with a certain kind of poetry, and the problem of France's internal coherence during civil war. Vauquelin confronts the former two in his *Foresteries*, willing away the reality of financial worry and his work as a lawyer in a sylvan second world populated by an idealized alter ego immune to such concerns. Jacques Peletier seeks a place of refuge from war in the independent territory of Savoy. His *La Savoye* is a fitting work with which to conclude, as it represents one of the last attempts in sixteenth-century lyric to imagine French landscape with hope and idealism, and this is only possible because of Savoy's liminal historical and geographic position with respect to France. The lyric space of hope has been chased to the frontiers, where it ekes out a fragile existence until history catches up with it there, too, sounding its death knell. *Et in Sabaudia.*

Like Vauquelin's forest, and all of the landscapes I have described, Peletier's Savoy contains within itself an awareness of its status as artifice, of the vulnerability of any 'second world' to the violence of history. It is history that wins out, as poets in the last quarter of the century abandon the attempt to imagine any part of France irenically. A Baroque aesthetic of fragmentation comes to dominate court poetry. Poetic transcendence, if it is sought at all, is located no longer in France but in the cosmic spaces of scientific poetry already glimpsed in Belleau's *Bergerie* and Peletier's *La Savoye*. But this turning away from landscape further accentuates the singularity of the poetic moment I have traced here, when poetry reimagines a tumultuous nation as Arcadia, however fragile. It is surely no accident that the poetic spaces we remember and cite today are spaces of hope.

Conclusion

As the trees of Ronsard's Gâtine forest fall down, as Baïf's polluted water-nymph cries out for help, as Peletier flees to Savoy, and Belleau turns away from landscape altogether, they sound the death knell of Du Bellay's 'France mère des arts,' and of poetry's capacity to represent France as an ordered, moral, and beautiful kingdom. The mid-century spaces of hope dissolve; the gossamer that had protected them from the violence of historical change rips. Victim of a disintegration already perceived by the Pléiade poets, French landscape by 1616 is more easily imagined as a bloody, mutilated body than as a tranquil haven: 'les païs ruinez sont membres retranchez / Dont le corps séchera' [the devastated territories are severed limbs / Whose body will dry up].[1] An entire type of pastorally ordered lyric poetry falls with Ronsard's trees, to give way to ... what?

One answer lies in the reinvestment of pastoral with an urgent moral dimension. From the 1570s onward, the gesture of retreat from the court, and the literary descriptions of such retreat, took on a particular ethical significance, attested to by the success and multiple re-editions of *Les plaisirs de la vie rustique* by the jurist Guy Du Faur de Pibrac.[2] The text appeared originally in 1574, one year after the death of Chancellor Michel de L'Hospital, who was considered a champion of the 'Politique' party's interest in tolerance and reasonable reform of religious and juridical institutions; his death was symbolic for many of the end of an era of hope.[3] Pibrac's landscape, like those I have presented here, is torn between an idyllic past and a present spoiled by war and courtly corruption. He describes the return to the pleasures of the 'champ maternel' [maternal field] (4) in a highly moral way: the figurative shepherds and peasants who work the land (153–202) are emblematic not so much of real social types but of a morally purged aristocracy, removed from the intrigues of court, who will bring about a new era of peace. A 'tour de France' follows (575–92), in which the natural resources of various regions are described, with an exhortation to use the land well and provide for all.

But something happens during this long poem, which is emblematic of the general drift in poetic landscapes in the last quarter of the century, a turn away from the specificity of place to more metaphysical concerns. Pibrac describes the diversity of French regions ultimately not as a source of richness but as proof of God's punishment: 'Dieu condamna la Terre et fit la différence / Des lieux et des païs' [God condemned the world and created difference / In places and regions] (678–9). Hope and salvation, then, are not to be found so much in the particular places of France, but in the contemplation of the 'haut firmament' [lofty firmament] (113). The movement is away from specific places to a greater understanding of universal, unifying ideas, and the end of the poem urges transcending local knowledge for a humble understanding of 'les causes' (734), that is, the first principles of things.

Poetry has now left chorography, and geography, and situated places, for the vast spaces of scientific poetry. This metaphysical turn is also seen, as I have argued, at the end of Belleau's *Bergerie*, and in Ronsard's reference to Lucretius at the end of his elegy to the Gâtine. 'La matière demeure, et la forme se perd' [Matter remains, and form is lost], writes Ronsard, as he bids farewell to his forest. A particular form of landscape poetry may be lost, but the substance and stuff of which poetry is made, the imagination and the will to create, remain. When the intrusion upon French poetic landscape by real events becomes impossible to ignore, poets start to seek neater ways of ordering the world, ways that will not fatally invoke the processes of history. Poetry that describes the movement of the planets can imagine itself liberated from the thorny problems of one particular human society; scientific poetry is a search for a new transcendence. It is as if there has been a collective moment of realization, like Belleau's, that writing about France as idealized space does not make poetry do anything beyond imagining. A woodcutter is not stopped by an elegy to a tree; a sonnet to one's homeland does not overwrite the worries of land ownership; and no amount of Golden Age troping will prevent Protestants and Catholics from spilling each other's blood on French soil. Poetry is now placed under a new imperative: to find real relations between language and truth, between places described and places experienced.

'In the sixteenth century, describing the beauties of the universe is only of interest if one can perceive the divine through the natural,' writes Jean-Charles Monferran in a recent critical edition of Peletier's *L'Amour des amours*.[4] The created universe becomes the setting; although the poets differ in the degree to which they make explicit their theology, the ambition is nevertheless to gain knowledge of God through knowledge of Creation. Mere landscape description has little place in this perspective. Scientific poetry abandons the specificity of national or regional space and engages the cosmic. In a sense, it reverses the first sonnet of Du Bellay's *Regrets*, in which the poet rejects metaphysical poetry for the 'accidens divers' of 'ce lieu'; named places are now too violent, too contested, for poetry to engage with unless the very form of poetry itself becomes distorted, as it does in D'Aubigné's *Les Tragiques*, its landscapes describable only by images of rent body parts, blood, and death. Poetry cannot bear too much reality, to paraphrase T.S. Eliot, and so it turns away, or refounds that reality as *scientia*.

However, the brief attempt to 'write France' in poetic landscapes around the mid-century, even if it does mean including in those landscapes the messy facts of historical France, bears witness to a moment when the poetry of place carried the hope of the emerging nation. Its spaces of hope are anything but naïve and escapist. They contain within themselves an acute awareness of their contingent relationship to the history they are trying to rewrite. Renaissance poets maintain, like David Harvey, that we must always imagine alternative worlds with an 'optimism of the intellect' even in the face of the worst depredation.[5] And they have something to tell us about our own modernity. Their understanding of landscapes as socially and ideologically complex can, I believe, be salutary for our current environmental dilemma. It has become common to deplore a perceived increasing alienation from a 'nature' assumed to be pure and pre-cultural. This is not necessarily helpful. Perhaps by accepting just how strong are the links between nature and culture, we can finally realize, as Simon Schama suggests, 'just how much we stand to lose.'[6]

Finally, perceptions of landscape are all, to an extent, libidinal, revealing our 'desiring agenda.'[7] If we continue to draw on the affective appeal of these poetic places today, this surely belies a certain conservative nostalgia (and most nostalgia is conservative), an aristocratic, exclusive, gendered, and agonistic relation to place. To understand the underlying ideologies of landscapes we love is to understand ourselves. Bruno Latour has potently argued that we have 'never been modern.' In France at least, and perhaps beyond, one might more specifically say that one only has to read the landscape to see that we are still Early Modern.

Notes

Introduction

1 Online tourist brochure at http://www.tourmagazine.fr/Vallee-du-Loir-allez-compter-fleurette-le-temps-d-un-week-end_a3295.html. Consulted 16 October 2008. For all primary texts, and if it seems necessary to work with the original French, I will provide both French original and English translation. For secondary texts in French, I will provide only English translation (mine unless indicated otherwise), but reference the page number of the original French.

2 I will use 'sixteenth century' and 'Renaissance' more or less interchangeably with respect to France. When referring to the first three quarters of sixteenth-century France I slightly prefer 'Renaissance' to 'Early Modern' because, to paraphrase Andrew Escobedo, 'Renaissance' at least has the merit of being their fantasy, not ours (*Nationalism and Historical Loss in Renaissance England* [Ithaca: Cornell University Press, 2004], 3). Poets, theologians, historians, philosophers, all subscribed, particularly in the period from 1500 to the 1550s, to the idea that they were part of a glorious rebirth of culture emerging from what Rabelais famously called the 'calamité des Gothz.' This is particularly true of mid-sixteenth-century poets, who did more than any other generation of writers to secure their place as the agents of this rebirth while disdaining the significance of even their immediate predecessors, in particular Marot. I use 'early modern' to refer implicitly to a longer chronological span, or to the general area of study as understood today.

3 Cardinal Poupard was prefacing the proceedings of an international conference on Du Bellay held in Angers: 'À Liré: Message du Cardinal Paul Poupard, Président du Conseil Pontifical de la Culture, originaire de Bouzillé, près de Liré,' in *Du Bellay: Actes du colloque internationale d'Angers* (Angers:

Presses de l'Université d'Angers, 1990), 2:637–9. Note the insistence in the title on his regional credentials: the precise locality of his place of origin, near Du Bellay's own.

4 Michel le Mené, *Les campagnes angevines à la fin du Moyen Âge* (Nantes: Éditions Cid, 1982), 52.

5 17 March 2006, on *Le Franc-parler*, broadcast on France Inter, 19:30–20:15. This poem was part of Bayrou's rhetorical arsenal since before he became 'présidentiable:' at the closing ceremony of the Conseil national de l'UDF (21 April 2001), he referenced it as part of a vision of national greatness. 'Et nous voudrions qu'en Europe, comme autrefois dans le monde, la France redevienne ce qu'elle n'aurait jamais dû cesser d'être et qui depuis du Bellay chante à notre mémoire France mère des arts, des armes et des lois.' Transcript online at http://discours.vie-publique.fr/notices/013001310 .html.

6 Yi-Fu Tuan, *Topophilia: A Study of Environmental Perception, Attitudes, and Values* (Englewood Cliffs, NJ: Prentice Hall, 1974), 4. Gaston Bachelard had already used the term 'topophilie' in French, in *La poétique de l'espace* (Paris: PUF, 1957), his study of 'the human value of spaces' (17).

7 The importance of Renaissance poetic landscapes to modern-day senses of place has been noted in passing by Tom Conley in his invitation to put French studies 'on the map' with historicized studies of the literary production of space, but has not yet been actively studied in ways Conley suggests. 'Putting French Studies on the Map,' *Diacritics* 28 (1998): 23–39, 27.

8 Aristotle argues in the *Poetics*, 48a, that the root of the word 'drama' is the verb *dran*, 'to do, act.' Any discourse, for Aristotle, is necessarily dramatic if it imitates 'agents and people doing things.' Aristotle, *Poetics*, ed. and trans. Malcolm Heath (London: Penguin, 1996), 6.

9 I take the term from David Harvey, *Spaces of Hope* (Berkeley: University of California Press, 2000). For Harvey, the persuasiveness of certain utopian visions depends on the blurring between real and imagined spaces. Harvey's mapping of hope into imagined spaces is helpful for understanding Renaissance landscapes, and I will make the idea of spaces of hope do a considerable amount of work in this study.

10 While there was certainly a perception of aristocratic identity crisis, the reality seems to have been more nuanced. J. Russell Major insists that feudalism in fact remains important throughout the sixteenth century, and is supplemented rather than replaced by patron–client relations, in 'The Crown and the Aristocracy in Renaissance France,' *The American Historical Review* 69 (1964): 631–45. More discussion of class history follows in chap. 5 of this book.

11   The classic study of shifting aristocratic roles is Norbert Elias's 1969 *The Court Society*, trans. Edmund Jephcott (New York: Pantheon, 1983). See also Jonathan Dewald's *Aristocratic Experience and the Origins of Modern Culture* (Berkeley: University of California Press, 1993). For a sustained application of these histories to an understanding of literary form, see Timothy Hampton, *Literature and Nation in the Sixteenth Century: Inventing Renaissance France* (Ithaca: Cornell University Press, 2001).

12   Sonnet 18 of *Les Regrets*. Here and throughout, I use the edition by J. Jolliffe and M. Screech: Joachim Du Bellay, *Les Regrets et autres œuvres poëtiques, suivis des Antiquitez de Rome. Plus un Songe ou Vision sur le mesme subject* (Geneva: Droz, 1979).

13   The busiest period of annexation was the reign of Louis XI, from 1423 to 1483, during which Burgundy, Franche-Comté, Picardy, Maine, Anjou, and Provence were annexed to the crown. Brittany was annexed in 1532, during François I's reign. See C.F. Black, Mark Greengrass, David Howarth et al., *Cultural Atlas of the Renaissance* (New York: Prentice Hall, 1993), 165, for a map of royal domain expansion from 1453 to 1559. I discuss regionalism and provide further references in chap. 1.

14   Harry Berger, 'The Ecology of the Mind: The Concept of Period Imagination – An Outline Sketch,' in *Second World and Green World: Studies in Renaissance Fiction Making* (Berkeley: University of California Press, 1988), 43. Berger identifies a constant and fluid dialogue between history and fiction, rather than a one-directional movement. Berger's dialectic is similar, although couched in phenomenological rather than social/Marxist terms, to Harvey's 'space of hope.'

15   Paul Alpers, *What is Pastoral?* (Chicago: University of Chicago Press, 1997). Nancy Lindheim similarly argues that pastoral is 'not a poetry of place, but of ethos,' in *The Virgilian Pastoral Tradition from the Renaissance to the Modern Era* (Pittsburgh: Duquesne University Press, 2005), 4. Schiller's 1795 essay *On Naïve and Sentimental Poetry* bequeathed to post-Romantic scholars the notion that landscapes in pastoral were about ideal place: Alpers has provided particularly sustained and insightful analyses of Schiller's poetics and the subsequent impact of his version of pastoral on scholars who have privileged the Golden Age and landscape description in their analyses. See, for example, his 'Schiller's *Naïve and Sentimental Poetry* and the Modern Idea of Pastoral,' in *Cabinet of the Muses: Essays on Classical and Comparative Literature in Honor of Thomas G. Rosenmeyer*, ed. Mark Griffith and Donald Mastronarde (Atlanta: Scholars Press, 1990), 319–31.

16   David Quint's reading of Sannazzaro's *Arcadia* has framed my discussion of the pastoral relation to history: 'If history relegates pastoral to the status

of wishful thinking and dream, from the pastoral vantage point history is a nightmare' (*Origin and Originality in Renaissance Literature: Versions of the Source* [Yale University Press. New Haven and London, 1983], 63). Also useful is William Empson's notion of pastoral putting 'the complex into the simple,' in *Some Versions of Pastoral* (New York: New Directions, 1960), 23. Leo Marx also uses the categories of complex and sentimental pastoral in his *The Machine in the Garden: Technology and the Pastoral Ideal in America* (New York: Oxford University Press, 1964). See also Terry Gifford's discussion of anti- and post-pastoral as critiques of the perceived limits of pastoral, in *Pastoral* (London: Routledge, 1999).

17 Luigi Monga, *Le genre pastoral au XVIe siècle: Sannazar et Belleau* (Paris: Éditions Universitaires, 1974), 60.

18 Chris Fitter, *Poetry, Space, Landscape: Toward a New Theory* (Cambridge: Cambridge University Press, 1995), 8. The 'large picture' approach of Fitter's book, which he defends (13–14), is both a strength and a weakness: I propose here a kind of slowing-down of Fitter's approach, a study limited to one short period and one representational mode.

19 '[L]es jardins et les paysages témoignent des pouvoirs de la poésie [...] la production textuelle et les processus naturels partagent la même essence.' Danièle Duport, *Les jardins qui sentent le sauvage: Ronsard et la poétique du paysage* (Geneva: Droz, 2001), 19. Duport takes landscape as an aggregate of metaphors for the poet's creativity, an effort to imitate but also discipline the copious variety of nature. Duport's subsequent book, *Le jardin et la nature: Ordre et variété dans la littérature de la Renaissance* (Geneva: Droz, 2002), opens up to different authors, genres, and contexts (e.g., horticultural treatises, royal entries), but still mainly considers 'le paysage en tant que modèle et qu'exercice d'écriture' (285). Most of the contributions to Yves Giraud's edited volume, *Le paysage à la Renaissance* (Fribourg: Éditions Universitaires, 1988), consider the referential world of represented landscapes (not particular to poetry) as primarily textual and philosophical; the papers in Dominique de Courcelles's edited conference proceedings, *Nature et paysages: L'émergence d'une nouvelle subjectivité à la Renaissance* (Paris: École des Chartes, 2006), identify landscape as a locus for early modern 'subjectivities.' Françoise Joukovksy's *Paysages de la Renaissance* (Paris: PUF, 1974), one of the first and few book-length studies of the subject, does suggest that literary landscapes actively engage external realities, but does not provide in-depth analysis of any particular articulations.

20 *Renaissance Literature and Its Formal Engagements*, ed. Mark Rasmussen (New York: Palgrave, 2002). See also Steven Cohen's essay in this book, which argues that the richest potential of New Historicism is in a 'truly

historico-political formalism' (18).

21 Timothy Hampton, *Literature and Nation*, xi.

22 Neil Smith and Cindi Katz, 'Grounding Metaphor: Towards a Spatialized Politics,' in *Place and the Politics of Identity*, ed. Michael Keith and Steve Pile (London: Routledge, 1993), 75.

23 Stephen Daniels, 'Landscape and Art,' in *A Companion to Cultural Geography*, ed. James Duncan, Nuala Johnson, and Richard Schein (Oxford: Blackwell, 2004), 435.

24 For a study of Ronsard's roses as referencing the notion of 'flowers of rhetoric,' see Cathy Yandell, 'Les roses de Ronsard: Humanisme et subjectivité,' in *Nature et Paysages*, ed. de Courcelles, 29–38.

25 For the complexity of the specifically rhetorical senses of *locus*, see Áron Kibédi-Varga, 'Les lieux de la rhétorique classique,' in *La naissance du roman en France; Papers on French Seventeenth Century Literature*, ed. Nicole Boursier and David Trott (Paris: Papers on French Seventeenth Century Literature, 1990), 101–12. The spatial play is apparent in his guiding metaphor for *lieu* as a 'terrain d'entente' (102).

26 Frances Yates, *The Art of Memory* (Chicago: University of Chicago Press, 1966).

27 See Áron Kibédi-Varga, 'L'histoire de la rhétorique et la rhétorique des genres,' *Rhetorica* 3 (1985): 201–21. He suggests, however, that the history of rhetoric has suffered a slight 'distortion' (203) because of its elaboration by literary scholars who tend to elide the specificity of oratory genres: the point is well taken. For a study of Renaissance poetry that shows nicely how literal place is always overdetermined as figural, even didactic *topoi*, see Cathy Yandell, 'La poétique du lieu: Espace et pédagogie dans les *Solitaires* de Tyard,' in *Pontus de Tyard: Errances et enracinement*, ed. François Rouget (Paris: Champion, 2008), 97–106.

28 See the now-classic study by George Lakoff and Mark Johnson, *Metaphors We Live By* (Chicago: University of Chicago Press, 1980).

29 Dana Phillips, *The Truth of Ecology: Nature, Culture, and Literature in America* (Oxford: Oxford University Press, 2003), 162. See William Cronon, *Uncommon Ground: Rethinking the Human Place in Nature* (New York: Norton, 1996), for a study of how the 'apparently transhistorical ideal of wilderness only acquired connotations of the sublime and sacred in the nineteenth century' (507). See also Max Oelschlaeger, *The Idea of Wilderness from Prehistory to the Age of Ecology* (New Haven: Yale University Press, 1991). Françoise Joukovsky makes the point in *Paysages*, 38, that the nature appreciated by Renaissance writers is already modified by humans, unlike our modern preference for uninhabited spaces. I do not consider urban landscapes here: for an excellent study of urban spaces and subjectivities in Renaissance France, see Elisabeth Hodges, *Urban Poetics in the French Renaissance*

(Burlington, VT: Ashgate, 2008).

30 Colette Beaune, *Naissance de la nation France* (Paris: Gallimard, 1985). Beaune's analysis is that of a medievalist historian: this study picks up chronologically where she leaves off, and focuses on the specific contribution of literature and spatiality to the idea(l) of France. More discussion of the term *nation* and its cognates, and of Beaune's study, follows in chap. 1.

31 Nancy Vickers, 'Diana Described: Scattered Woman and Scattered Rhyme,' *Critical Inquiry* 8 (1981): 265–79.

32 See Timothy Hampton's chapter entitled 'The Garden of Letters,' in his *Literature and Nation in the Sixteenth Century: Inventing Renaissance France* (Ithaca: Cornell University Press, 2001), 1–34.

33 Danièle Duport, *Les jardins*. See n. 19, above. The collection edited by Monique Mosser and Philippe Nys, *Le jardin, art et lieu de mémoire* (Besançon: Éditions de l'Imprimeur, 1995), considers the Renaissance garden as spatialized, static, and solid incarnations of various verbal *mementi*: 'comme une écriture qui vient au secours de la parole qui s'envole' (25). A notable exception is Clément Marot's poetic orchard of Cahors, which is deeply politicized: Timothy Hampton suggests that it reveals an emerging sense of conflict between kingdom and province, in *Literature and Nation*, 14–20. Gardens also took on a particularly theological significance for Protestant writers, for example Bernard Palissy or Salomon De Caus.

34 For example, Du Bellay's 'Patriae desiderium' (in *'The Regrets' with 'The Antiquities of Rome,' Three Latin Elegies, and 'The Defense and Enrichment of the French Language,'* ed. and trans. Richard Helgerson [Philadelphia: University of Pennsylvania Press, 2007], 311–14); or the ode by Jean Dorat 'Ad fontem Arculi' (in Jean Dorat, *Les Odes Latines*, ed. Geneviève Demerson [Clermont-Ferrand: Faculté des lettres et sciences humaines, 1979], no. 3). For the complicated publication history of Dorat's ode, see Demerson, ibid., 8–12. For poetry about Arcueil, see Antoine Desguine, *Arcueil et les poètes du XVIe siècle: La vigne, le vin et la tradition bacchique à Arcueil-Cachan* (Paris: Champion, c. 1950). For an overview of landscape in Latin poetry, see Jean-Yves Boriaud, 'Le paysage et la poésie latine de la Renaissance,' in *Le paysage, 13e colloque d'Albi: Langages et signification*, ed. Georges Maurand (L'Union: CALS, 1993), 107–16.

35 For neo-Latin poetry, see in particular Marc Bizer, *La Poésie au miroir: Imitation et conscience de soi dans la poésie latine de la Pléiade* (Paris: Champion, 1995); also Grahame Castor and Terence Cave, eds., *Neo-Latin and the Vernacular in Renaissance France* (Oxford: Clarendon, 1984); and the first half of Dorothy Coleman's *The Gallo-Roman Muse: Aspects of Roman Literary Tradition in Sixteenth-Century French Literature* (Cambridge: Cambridge

University Press, 1979). For dialectical variations of French itself, see François Rouget, 'La langue française: Obstacle ou atout de l' "État-nation"?' *Renaissance and Reformation / Renaissance et Réforme* 29 (2005): 7–23; and Paul Cohen, 'Illustration du français et persistance des langues régionales: La pluralité linguistique dans la constitution des idéologies sociales en France à l'époque moderne' in Gérard Defaux, ed., *Lyon et l'illustration de la langue française à la Renaissance* (Lyons: ENS, 2003), 147–67.

36 For debates about norms and usage in the sixteenth century, see R. Anthony Lodge, *French: From Dialect to Standard* (London: Routledge, 1993), 165–71. Grammars and treatises published in the mid-sixteenth century include Jean Pillot's *Gallicae linguae institutio* (1550), Henri Estienne's *La Précellence du langage françois* (1579), and the French grammars of Louis Meigret (1550) and Robert Estienne (1557).

37 Yi-Fu Tuan claims that landscape – as a horizontal, three-dimensional perception of land – is not to be found in medieval literature or art, which he argues manifest a vertical world view, looking up from the earth to the heavens (*Topophilia*, 128). It is true that medieval literary landscapes tend to be unnamed, fantastic, or engaging with the philosophical concept of *natura* (see, for example, Michel Zink, *Nature et poésie au Moyen Âge* [Paris: Fayard, 2006]), but there are also numerous examples in medieval literature of a horizontal gaze over land and a sense of belonging to and inhabiting space in the world, not just in the hereafter.

38 In Charles d'Orléans's *Ballade* 75, he writes: 'En regardant vers le païs de France, / Un jour m'avint, a Dovre sur la mer, / Qu'il me souvint de la doulce plaisance / Que souloye oudit pays trouver [...] Mais non pourtant mon cueur ne se lassoit / De voir France que mon cueur amer doit' [While looking towards the country of France one day in Dover overlooking the sea, I happened to remember the sweet pleasure I used to find in that country ... But my heart never did tire of seeing France, which it is bound to love]. In Charles d'Orléans, *Poésies*, ed. Pierre Champion (Paris: Champion, 1956). With respect to epic, I am summarizing key terms of an article by G.A. Knott, '"Une question lancinante": Further Thoughts on Space in the "Chansons de Geste,"' *Modern Language Review* 94 (1999): 22–34. See Joukovsky, *Paysages*, 39–47, for a general overview of pre-Pléiade poetic landscapes, which she argues are mostly generic and mythological.

39 Tom Conley, *The Graphic Unconscious in Early Modern French Writing* (Cambridge: Cambridge University Press, 1992).

40 Anthony Grafton, *Defenders of the Text: The Traditions of Scholarship in an Age of Science* (Cambridge, MA: Harvard University Press, 1991), 180. For a helpful discussion of Renaissance notions of intellectual disciplines, see Anthony Grafton and Lisa Jardine, *From Humanism to the Humanities:*

Education and the Liberal Arts in Fifteenth- and Sixteenth-Century Europe (London: Duckworth, 1986). For some good reflections on comtemporary relations between the disciplines, see Marjorie Garber, *Academic Instincts* (Princeton: Princeton University Press, 2000).

1. Place and Poetry: An Overview

1 See François Rigolot's excellent and authoritative study, *Poésie et Renaissance* (Paris: Seuil, 2002), which illustrates just how rich and diverse Renaissance poetry was, ranging far beyond the Pléiade and Clément Marot. His first chapter provides an important overview of how poetry was seen to relate to other disciplines, including music and mathematics.
2 Joachim Du Bellay, *La Deffence et illustration de la langue françoyse*, ed. Jean-Charles Monferran (Geneva: Droz, 2007), 133. But Du Bellay's detractor, Barthélemy Aneau, argues that lyric poetry is of popular origin – 'lyrique ou laïque, c'est-à-dire populaire' – and that Du Bellay and his friends would not know how to recognize, let alone play, a lyre. See *Traités de poétique et de rhétorique de la Renaissance*, ed. Francis Goyet (Paris: Livre de Poche, 1990), 198, 203. For a study of lyric broadly defined by its epideictic function, see Nathalie Dauvois, *Le sujet lyrique à la Renaissance* (Paris: PUF, 2000). The second half of the book is dedicated to close readings, including considerations of aspects of lyric often neglected by modern critics, such as linguistics and metrics.
3 *La Deffence*, 131–8.
4 The classical ode was particularly favoured by the Pléiade: Ronsard was the first to publish a volume entitled *Odes* (1552). The ode was distinguished from the French vernacular *chant royal* by the freedom of its form and the lofty subject matter, which Du Bellay insisted be 'far from vulgar.' Thomas Sébillet defines the ode as a 'chant lyrique,' giving no other rule, other than that 'you should choose the model of Pindar for Greek and Horace for Latin poetry' (*Art poétique français*, in Goyet, ed., *Traités*, 121). Aneau, ever committed to claiming that the French had got there first, argues that the ode is nothing but the old French *chant* (*Traités*, 197).
5 A sustained attempt at the unification of music and poetry by the Pléiade was not undertaken until later. Royal permission was granted in 1570 for an *Académie de poésie et de musique*, the brainchild of Antoine de Baïf. While some of the discussions involved poets such as Ronsard, Jamyn, and Desportes, the Academy lasted only fifteen years. The Pléiade's rejection of earlier French vernacular poetry undoubtedly contributed to this delay and to the eventual collapse of the endeavour. Medieval poetry could have

offered many models of poetry as musical performance; indeed many of
the genres ridiculed by Du Bellay were written to be sung. As it was, the
theoreticians of the Pléiade were trying to excavate a presumed classical
musical poetics about which they knew very little.

6 Almost half of Alice Hulubei's exhaustive study of the eclogue in France is
dedicated to the genesis of the tradition before the poets of the Pléiade,
showing just how rich the vernacular pastoral was even before its supposed 'reinvention' by the Pléiade: see *L'églogue en France au XVIe siècle* (Paris:
Droz, 1938), chaps. 1–8.

7 Alice Hulubei, *L'églogue*, xii. An important recent study of the specifically
textual tradition of pan-European pastoral is Thomas K. Hubbard, *The
Pipes of Pan: Intertextuality and Literary Filiation from Theocritus to Milton*
(Ann Arbor: University of Michigan Press, 1998), which includes a discussion of Marot's role in the transmission of pastoral genealogy through
Spenser (305–15). Hubbard reads pastoral as a mode that stages Bloom's
anxiety of influence. Du Bellay also, in his *Deffence*, appears to think of
pastoral more as a textual tradition than as a strict form.

8 Raymond Williams, *The Country and the City* (Oxford: Oxford University
Press, 1973).

9 Don Wayne, *Penshurst: The Semiotics of Place and the Poetics of History* (Madison: University of Wisconsin Press, 1984), 152. Wayne suggests that Williams's binary between aristocratic representation and real land (including
labour) is somewhat drastic as it negates the possibility of imagining a co-
existence between capitalism and tradition. James Turner, in *The Politics of
Landscape: Rural Scenery and Society in English Poetry, 1630–1660* (Oxford:
Blackwell, 1979), deeply influenced by Williams, analyses literary rusticity
as 'an instrument to think with.' In the French tradition of *géographie humaine*, there has been a tendency to idealize agriculture and peasants, ex-
emplified by Gaston Roupnel's 1932 *Histoire de la campagne française* (repr.
Paris: Plon, 1974), which discusses agricultural labour as 'poetry,' and
which has an entire chapter on 'The Soul of the Peasant,' who becomes an
essentialized and timeless moral national symbol. Emmanuel Le Roy Ladurie's afterword to the 1974 edition recognizes the political ambiguity of
Roupnel's poeticizing of agriculture, which draws on Pétainiste doctrine
filtered through the post-war Left (360). Roupnel's work was not well re-
garded by the *Annales* school in general, and compares unfavourably with
Marc Bloch's contemporaneous *Les caractères originaux de l'histoire rurale
française* (Oslo: Aschehoug, 1931).

10 One recent exception is a dissertation by Isabelle Fernbach, *Beyond Pastoral:
Rusticity and the Reframing of Court Culture in 16th-Century French Literature*

(PhD diss., University of California, Berkeley, 2006). While not specifically a study of landscape, it argues that literary rusticity, 'le discours rustique,' which is not quite pastoral and not quite georgic (7), is used by sixteenth-century writers as a form of resistance to royal and ecclesiastical power. The *magnum opus* on the French eclogue is still Alice Hulubei's *L'églogue en France*, a mine of biographical, philological and (inter)textual information.

11 Thomas Sébillet, *L'art poétique françoys*, ed. Félix Gaiffe (Geneva: Droz, 1999), 159. Scaliger, on the other hand, while agreeing that pastoral showed princes a better way to live, believed that it was truly of rustic and primaeval origins: see E. Kegel-Brinkgreve, *The Echoing Woods: Bucolic and Pastoral from Theocritus to Wordsworth* (Amsterdam: J.C. Gieben, 1990), 371–5.

12 To name but a few, in 1542, Étienne Dolet published *Du mespris de la court et la louange de la vie rustique*, a translation of a text by Guevara; 1543 saw Béroalde's *De la félicité humaine*; and Maurice Scève's *La Saulsaye* (Lyon, 1547), was published in the same year as Jacques Peletier's *Œuvres poétiques*, which contained two odes in praise of the *repos* of the countryside. Guy Du Faur de Pibrac's *Les plaisirs de la vie rustique* (1574) is a classic of the genre.

13 Charles Estienne, *L'Agriculture, et maison rustique de M. Charles Estienne, et Jean Liebault, docteurs en medecine* (Paris: Jacques du Puys, 1583), iii. The definition, in a georgic treatise, of bucolic songs as the expression of agriculture's purity, shows that there was a certain fluidity in the Renaissance between pastoral and georgic modes, although the first was understood as being in the humble style, and the second in the familiar. Pastoral was not simply an idyll, nor was georgic simply about labour; there was a great deal of cross-pollination between them.

14 See G.E. Fussell, 'The Classical Tradition in West European Farming: The Sixteenth Century,' *Economic History Review* 22 (1969): 538–51, for a discussion of this tradition in Europe, and its application (or not) to farming practice. Chantal Liaroutzos considers the *Agriculture* with Estienne's *Guide* and Corrozet's *Antiquitez*, in *Le pays et la mémoire: Pratiques et représentation de l'espace chez Gilles Corrozet et Charles Estienne* (Paris: Champion, 1998).

15 Guy Du Faur de Pibrac's *Les plaisirs de la vie rustique* (1574), for example, presents pastoral life as an exteriorization of a necessary internal equilibrium that comes from right knowledge of God, and that will in turn lead to greater social stability. For an analysis of how rusticity took on an increasingly moral aspect as the wars continued, see Loris Petris, 'La philosophie morale aux champs: Ethica, œconomica et politica dans *Les plaisirs de la vie rustique* de Pibrac,' *Revue d'histoire littéraire de la France* 107 (2007): 3–18.

16 Estienne, *L'Agriculture*, 1.

17 *Deffence*, 2, 4 (131–2). Timothy Hampton has suggested, with respect to Du Bellay, that the poet, anxious about the meaning of nobility in a new world of courtly bureaucrats, was inventing a new kind of cultural aristocracy for himself based on 'cultural material only available to an educated élite' (*Literature and Nation*, 160). For the Pléiade's downplaying of the significance of their predecessors' contributions to vernacular poetry, see François Rigolot, *Poésie et Renaissance*, chap. 5, and Gérard Defaux, 'Facing the Marot Generation: Ronsard's "Giovenili Errori"' *MLN* 119 (2004): 299–326. Both critics note the 'arrogance' of Ronsard in particular. Alice Hulubei also inscribes her study of the French eclogue into the narrative of usurpation and presumption on behalf of the Pléiade poets whose 'cris et éclats de trompettes' drowned out the developments of the first half of the century: see *L'églogue en France*, 311. Studies of Renaissance imitation are too numerous to list exhaustively. One of the most authoritative works is Thomas Greene, *The Light in Troy* (New Haven: Yale University Press, 1982). A helpful reference book is *The Transmission of Culture in Early Modern Europe*, ed. Anthony Grafton and Ann Blair (Philadelphia: University of Pennsylvania Press, 1990), with its encyclopedic overview of the transmission history of most major classical texts. The under-explored domain of neo-Latin poetry has recently been given attention by Marc Bizer in *La poésie au miroir*. David Quint addresses questions of text and source in several books, most specifically in *Origin and Originality in Renaissance Literature: Versions of the Source* (New Haven: Yale University Press, 1983). For the related question of exemplarity, see John Lyons, *Exemplum: The Rhetoric of Example in Early Modern France and Italy* (Princeton: Princeton University Press, 1990); and Timothy Hampton, *Writing from History: The Rhetoric of Exemplarity in Renaissance Literature* (Ithaca: Cornell University Press, 1990). Hampton sees a crisis of exemplarity particular to Renaissance literature; Michel Jeanneret, in 'The Vagaries of Exemplarity: Distortion or Dismissal?' *Journal of the History of Ideas* 59 (1998): 565–79, argues that the notion of crisis overstates the normal transformations of examplars by writers. François Rigolot provides a helpful overview of both terms in 'The Renaissance Crisis of Exemplarity,' *Journal of the History of Ideas* 59 (1998): 557–63.

18 Sébillet, *Art poétique*, 2.8 (p. 161). Du Bellay, *Deffence*, 1.8 (p. 94).

19 *Les Amours et nouveaux eschanges des pierres précieuses*, ed. Maurice Verdier (Geneva: Droz, 1973), 5.

20 See Michel Simonin, '"Poésie est un pré" "Poème est une fleur": Métaphore horticole et imaginaire du texte à la Renaissance,' in *La letteratura e i giardini: Atti del Convegno Internazionale di Studi di Verona – Garda, 2–5*

ottobre 1985 (Florence: Olschki, 1985), 45–56. Simonin argues in particular for the importance in Renaissance poetics of the rediscovery of Pindar, who wrote in his sixth Olympiad of the creative process as gardening in the fields of Grace. I distinguish between poetic gardens and pastoral landscapes for the purposes of this study: see Introduction, pp. 10–11.

21 Greene, *The Light in Troy*, 205.

22 Also the subject of Michel Jeanneret's seminal study, *Perpetuum mobile: Métamorphoses des corps et des œuvres de Vinci à Montaigne* (Paris: Macula, 1997).

23 See Carolyn Merchant, *The Death of Nature: Women, Ecology, and the Scientific Revolution* (San Francisco: Harper and Row, 1980). The feminization of nature, or the naturalization of the female, is the essential debating point of ecofeminism. For a recent attempt to go beyond the rhetorical impasse of such equivalencies and the feminist rejection of the historical legacy of Mother Earth, see Stacey Alaimo, *Undomesticated Ground: Recasting Nature as Feminist Space* (Ithaca: Cornell University Press, 2000).

24 Cecelia Tichi, *Embodiment of a Nation: Human Form in American Places* (Cambridge, MA: Harvard University Press, 2001), 12.

25 Cheryll Glotfelty, Introduction to *The Ecocriticism Reader,* ed. Glotfelty and Harold Froom (Athens: University of Georgia Press, 1996), xix. The term 'ecocriticism' is by no means uncontested, and it encompasses a wide range of approaches, subjects, and ideological engagements, including ecofeminism. Since it is not my primary critical engagement here, and for reasons of space, I refer the reader elsewhere for an excellent and concisely exhaustive summary of the development and major players of the field: Ursula Heise, 'The Hitchhiker's Guide to Ecocriticism,' *PMLA* 121 (2006): 503–16.

26 Lawrence Buell, *Writing for an Endangered World: Literature, Culture, and Environment in the U.S. and Beyond* (Cambridge, MA: The Belknap Press of Harvard University Press, 2001), 7.

27 Although an early attempt to put ecocriticism and other critical theories in dialogue is SueEllen Campbell, 'The Land and Language of Desire: Where Deep Ecology and Post-Structuralism Meet,' *Western American Literature* 24 (1989): 199–211.

28 One of the more significant challenges to the field is Dana Phillips, *The Truth of Ecology: Nature, Culture, and Literature in America* (Oxford: Oxford University Press, 2003). I share his suspicion of some of the more triumphalist rhetoric of early ecocriticism, although he gives rather short shrift to the sophistication of the work of leading ecocritics such as Lawrence Buell. Perhaps the most potentially pertinent of his points is regarding ecocritics' claims to interdisciplinarity, noting that 'most of ecocriticism's efforts at

being interdisciplinary have been limited to troping on a vocabulary borrowed from ecology' (ix).

29 Nature writing, and nature worship, in the West, has tended to be the purview of an economic and social elite, and early ecocritical practice certainly reflected that. Nevertheless, ecocriticism is becoming considerably more aware of its blind spots. Patrick Murphy challenged the field to be more inclusive and theoretically reflective in *Farther Afield in the Study of Nature-Oriented Literature* (Charlottesville, VA: University of Virginia Press, 2000). ASLE (Association for the Study of Literature and Environment) now boast members in many countries. Significant articulations between ecocriticism and postcolonialism are emerging; see, for example, Richard Watts, 'Towards an Ecocritical Postcolonialism: Val Plumwood's *Environmental Culture* in Dialogue with Patrick Chamoiseau,' *Journal of Postcolonial Writing* 44 (2008): 251–61. Ecofeminists have challenged the gendering of some of ecocriticism's assumptions. Brian Scott Hicks looks at the issue of race and ecocriticism in 'W.E.B. Du Bois, Booker T. Washington, and Richard Wright: Toward an Ecocriticism of Color,' *Callaloo* 29 (2006): 202–22. The issues of class and environmental justice are also starting to be taken seriously: see, for example, the reader edited by Joni Adamson, Mei Mei Evans, and Rachel Stein, *Environmental Justice Reader: Politics, Poetics, and Pedagogy* (Tucson: University of Arizona Press, 2002). And recently, scholars have applied ecocriticism to readings of Renaissance literature, mainly in the English tradition: see in particular Robert Watson, *Back to Nature: The Green and the Real in the Late Renaissance* (Philadelphia: University of Pennsylvania Press, 2006).

30 'Ardens desires, qui les homes affolent, / D'aler plus haut que les oiseauz ne volent' [Burning desire, which makes men crazy, / To climb higher than birds fly]. Jacques Peletier du Mans, *La Savoye*, ed. C. Pagès and F. Ducloz (Annecy: Moutiers-Tarentaise, 1897), 95.

31 Dana Phillips, *The Truth of Ecology*, 14–16, makes the point that ecocritics have sometimes been guilty of this conflation of pastoral with nature writing.

32 Lawrence Buell, *The Environmental Imagination: Thoreau, Nature Writing, and the Formation of American Culture* (Cambridge, MA: Harvard University Press, 1995), 32. For pastoral as a reiterated social impulse to flee modern civilization, see also Leo Marx, *The Machine in the Garden*.

33 Petrarch's ascent of the Ventoux has been hailed, anachronistically, as the first textual account of someone climbing a mountain for pleasure. For an excellent discussion of this text as a reflection on the cultural mediation of experience, see Albert Ascoli, 'Petrarch's Middle Age: Memory, Imagination, History, and "The Ascent of Mount Ventoux,"' *Stanford Italian Review* 10 (1991): 5–43.

34 Stephen Daniels, 'Landscape and Art,' in *A Companion to Cultural Geography*, ed. James Duncan, Nuala Johnson, and Richard Schein (Oxford: Blackwell, 2004), 430. If literature has taken a spatial turn, then geography has certainly taken a cultural turn, with some geographers 'writing of landscapes as texts' (Denis Cosgrove, Introduction to *The Iconography of Landscape: Essays on the Symbolic Representation, Design, and Use of Past Environments*, ed. Cosgrove and Stephen Daniels [Cambridge: Cambridge University Press, 1988], 8).

35 Henri Lefebvre, *La production de l'espace* (Paris: Anthropos, 1974). Some literary critics use Lefebvre specifically to think about landscape: see, for example, Garrett Sullivan, *The Drama of Landscape: Land, Property and Social Relations on the Early Modern Stage* (Palo Alto, CA: Stanford University Press, 1998), which looks at landscape as a way of negotiating social relationships.

36 Edward Said's 'imagined geographies' (*Orientalism* [New York: Vintage, 1978], 54), have been productive of new ways of looking at textual space. Imagined geographies, Said argues, not only write space (*geo* + *graphein*), but also can contain within themselves, repeat, and reify the problematic authorities, such as colonizing nations, that have historically defined certain spaces. Said's imagined geography is somewhat analogous to what Lefebvre means by 'representational space,' a possible space of resistance to the repressive economies that define most of modern social space. A recent volume of *French Literature Series* engages spaces that represent resistance to constitutive authorities: *Geo/graphies: Mapping the Imagination in French and Francophone Literature and Film* (*French Literature Series* 30), ed. Freeman G. Henry (New York: Rodopi, 2003). Demonstrating that such theoretical frameworks are applicable to periods other than the postcolonial, the volume extends its chronological range well beyond modern *Francophonie*: there are, for example, two notable contributions by *seiziémistes*. In Renaissance literary criticism generally, the turn to geography has been more pronounced among scholars working on English literature, partly due to the abiding influence of Raymond Williams.

37 Christian Jacob, *L'empire des cartes* (Paris: Albin Michel, 1992), 21.

38 Tim Cresswell, *Place: A Short Introduction* (Oxford: Blackwell, 2004), 7. The distinction between place and space is defined by Cresswell thus: 'place, at a basic level, is space invested with meaning in the context of power' (12). One of the most informative scholars working on the production of place in the early modern period was the late Denis Cosgrove: for a good programmatic statement, see his introduction to *Mappings*, ed. Denis Cosgrove (London: Reaktion Books, 1999).

39 Michel De Certeau, *L'invention du quotidien* (Paris: Gallimard, 1990), 476. See Cresswell, *Place*, 38, for a discussion of de Certeau.

40 Tuan, *Topophilia*, 183–4, also promotes the idea of the authentic 'feel of a place.' See Cresswell, *Place*, 43 ff., and Lucy Lippard, *The Lure of the Local* (New York: The New Press, 1997), 5–6, for more hybrid understandings of place.

41 Like all binaries, this one too requires complication. *Pays* and *land* are themselves not neutral, positivist words, but are also frequently invested with affect.

42 Denis Cosgrove, *The Palladian Landscape: Geographical Change and Its Cultural Representations in Sixteenth-Century Italy* (Philadelphia: Pennsylvania State University Press, 1993), xiv.

43 Simon Schama, *Landscape and Memory* (New York: Knopf, 1995), 6–7.

44 Chris Fitter, *Poetry, Space, Landscape: Toward a New Theory* (Cambridge: Cambridge University Press, 1995). John Berger, *Ways of Seeing* (London: Penguin, 1972), and Raymond Williams, *The Country and the City* (New York: Oxford University Press, 1973), posed lasting challenges to (post) Romantic views of landscape such as Ruskin's, which would have us search for comfort, continuity, and moral truth in dehumanized (that is, non-industrialized) landscapes. Both insisted on socio-economic factors in the construction of landscape, and the exclusion of all but idealized aristocratic forms of labour. For a good overview, see Denis Cosgrove's Introduction to Denis Cosgrove and Stephen Daniels, eds., *The Iconography of Landscape*, 1–10.

45 André Siganos, 'Paysages et archétypes: Pour une lecture interdisciplinaire du paysage,' in *Paysage et identité régionale: De pays rhônalpins en paysages. Actes du colloque de Valence*, ed. Chrystèle Burgard, Françoise Chenet (Valence: La passe du vent, 1999), 17–22, 21.

46 Alain Roger, 'Un paysage peut-il être érotique?' in *Le paysage et ses Grilles: Actes du colloque de Cerisy-la-Salle*, ed. Françoise Chenet et Jean-Claude Wieber (Paris and Montreal: Harmattan, 1996), 193–206, 193. The French terms are, of course, *pays* and *paysage*. For influential French theorizations of *paysage*, see also Anna Cauquelin, *L'invention du paysage* (Paris: Plon, 1989); Alain Roger, *Court traité de paysage* (Paris: Gallimard, 1997); and *Cinq propositions pour une théorie du paysage*, dir. Augustin Berque (Paris: Champ Vallon, 1994). *Le paysage à la Renaissance*, ed. Yves Giraud (Fribourg: Éditions Universitaires Fribourg Suisse, 1988), is a collection of essays on mostly literary landscapes; Françoise Joukovsky, *Paysages de la Renaissance* (Paris: PUF, 1974), is a descriptive synthesis of landscape-oriented literature which omits discussion of the plastic arts. Her first chapter, 'Le décor réel,' offers a

concise overview of agrarian practice and land-use history for those not in-
clined to read all of Marc Bloch's definitive *Les caractères originaux de l'histoire
rurale française* (Oslo: Aschehoug, 1931). The subject of the *paysage* has inspired, particularly since the 1980s, many a conference and edited volume in
France: see, for example, the special issues of the *Revue des sciences humaines*
209 (1988), 'Écrire le paysage,' ed. Jean-Marc Besse, and of *Critique* 613
(1998), 'Jardins et paysages,' ed. Michel Baridon. Interest in regional landscapes has also prompted reflection on the ways in which landscapes function to construct identities: see, for example, the essays in *Paysage et identité
régionale: De pays rhônalpins en paysages. Actes du colloque de Valence*, ed.
Chrystèle Burgard and Françoise Chenet (Valence: La passe du vent, 1999),
in particular Anne Sgard, 'Qu'est-ce qu'un paysage identitaire?' 23–34.

47 Pierre Sansot, *Variations paysagères: Invitation au paysage* (Paris: Klincksieck,
1983), 8.

48 Frank Lestringant, 'Chorographie et paysage à la Renaissance,' in *Écrire le
monde à la Renaissance* (Caen: Paradigme, 1993), 49–67, 50. The archaic English *landskip* was also used in a more artistic or technical sense than *landscape*: see Fitter, *Poetry*, 10.

49 Robert Estienne's 1549 *Dictionnaire francoislatin* lists forty-eight sub-entries
under *nature* (p. 400). See Boas and Lovejoy, *Primitivism and Related Ideas in
Antiquity* (1935; New York: Doubleday, 1965), 447–56, for over sixty meanings of 'nature' in philosophical and literary discourse. See also Michel
Jeanneret's important study of movement and metamorphosis in Renaissance writing and painting, *Perpetuum mobile*, and Danièle Duport, *Les jardins*, which considers the philosophical notion that the ordering of nature
is reflected in Ronsard's poetic order.

50 The *magnum opus* on nature and culture through the ages in the west is
Clarence Glacken's *Traces on the Rhodian Shore: Nature and Culture in Western Thought from Ancient Times to the End of the Eighteenth Century* (Berkeley:
University of California Press, 1967). For Renaissance France in particular,
see Jean Céard, *La nature et les prodigues* (Geneva: Droz, 1996). Some of the
best scholars working with the Renaissance have applied wide reading
and erudition to such questions: a small sampling would start with the essays in part 3 of *The Cambridge History of Renaissance Philosophy*, ed. C.B.
Schmidt, Quentin Skinner, Ekhard Kessler, and Jill Kraye (Cambridge:
Cambridge University Press, 1988); and Lorraine Daston and Katharine
Park, *Wonders and the Order of Nature* (New York: Zone Books, 1998). For a
helpful bibliography, see the end of Ian Maclean's essay review of the latter, 'Natural and Preternatural in Renaissance Philosophy and Medicine,'
in *Studies in History and Philosophy of Science* 31 (2000): 331–42. Two excellent

single-author studies are Ann Blair, *The Theater of Nature: Jean Bodin and Renaissance Science* (Princeton: Princeton University Press, 1997); and Anthony Grafton, *Cardano's Cosmos: The Worlds and Work of a Renaissance Astrologer* (Cambridge, MA: Harvard University Press, 1999).

51 This distinction is well discussed by D.R. Wilson in *Ronsard: Poet of Nature* (Manchester: Manchester University Press, 1961), chaps. 1 and 2.

52 *Mythologies* (Paris: Seuil, 1957), 140 ff. Barthes argues that science, like literature, has its enunciative modalities, its *images-repertoires*, and that the only honest science is that which reflects on its status as discourse.

53 A particularly cogent critique of social construction is Ian Hacking, *The Social Construction of What?* (Cambridge, MA: Harvard University Press, 1999). For a more environmentally oriented engagement, see, for example, Donald Worster, 'Seeing Beyond Culture,' *Journal of American History* 76 (1990): 1142–7. These disciplinary differences have been cast rather simplistically as the so-called Science Wars of the 1980s and '90s, whose stakes were made bizarrely apparent in the 1996 Sokal Affair. See Glen Love, *Practical Ecocriticism: Literary, Biology, and the Environment* (Charlottesville, VA: Virginia University Press, 2003), especially chap. 2, for a helpful overview of this 'war' and a plea to humanists to create new relationships with the life sciences in their scholarship.

54 Ernest Renan's lecture 'Qu'est-ce qu'une nation?' was delivered at the Sorbonne in March 1882. It was published in *Discours et conférences* (Paris: Calman-Levy, 1887), 277–310, and has been frequently reprinted and translated. It has been extremely influential in thinking about the nation as a psychological and social process. Many scholars maintain a distinction between *nation* and *state*, the latter being the apparatus of power. See, for example, Hagen Schulze, *States, Nations, and Nationalism: From the Middle Ages to the Present* (Oxford: Blackwell, 1994).

55 '[U]n plébiscite de tous les jours,' Renan, 'Qu'est-ce qu'une nation?' 277; and Benedict Anderson, *Imagined Communities: Reflections on the Origin and Spread of Nationalism* (London: Verso, 1983). Anderson's imagined community has become somewhat overused and overgeneralized in literary studies. While important in creating new fields of analysis in literary studies and beyond, the notion now needs to be interrogated and refined with more specific evidence and more attention to cultural and historical contexts. Also absent from Anderson's model is a focus on the spatial imaginary, and a consideration of the specific relationship between literary form (e.g., poetry, rather than simply 'print culture') and national space.

56 Jacques Revel, 'Knowledge of the Territory,' *Science in Context* 4 (1991): 133–61, 133. Revel is part of the French tradition of *géographie humaine*

going back to Vidal de la Blache at the start of the twentieth century, which emphasizes the extent to which territory is an idea. See also the volume *L'espace français* in the series directed by Revel, *Histoire de la France* (Paris: Seuil, 1989). Xavier de Planhol and Paul Claval show that the geographical space of France, before the twentieth century, was a composite of shifting political and religious fragments, in *Géographie historique de la France* (Paris: Fayard, 1988). See also Alfred Fierro-Domenech, *Le pré carré: Geographie historique de la France* (Paris: Laffont, 1986). I will address *géographie humaine* again in the next chapter.

57 In the address to the reader of his *Theatrum orbis terrarum* (1570). For a wide-ranging analysis of history's relations to landscape, environmental, and regional geographies, see Alan Baker, *Geography and History: Bridging the Divide* (Cambridge: Cambridge University Press, 2003).

58 John Agnew, 'Nationalism,' in Duncan, Johnson, and Schein, eds., *A Companion*, 223–37.

59 One important exception for Renaissance France is Timothy Hampton, *Literature and Nation*. Scholarship on English Renaissance place description and nationhood has been more abundant: see Richard Helgerson's classic *Forms of Nationhood: The Elizabethan Writing of England* (Chicago: University of Chicago Press, 1992); and Claire McEachern, *The Poetics of English Nationhood, 1590–1612* (Cambridge: Cambridge University Press, 1996), which takes literature as one of multiple forms of 'political discourse that inscribe and imagine a nation' (139).

60 For Benedict Anderson, the nation is a fundamentally Enlightenment concept. Ernest Gellner in *Nations and Nationalism* (Ithaca: Cornell University Press, 1983), and Eric Hobsbawm, *Nations and Nationalism since 1780: Programme, Myth, Reality* (Cambridge: Cambridge University Press, 1990), argue that the nation is a modern idea. Liah Greenfeld argues that the idea of a *nation* coalesced with other developments to form *nationalism*, an 'emergent phenomenon' that enabled modernity (*Nationalism: Five Roads to Modernity* [Cambridge, MA: Harvard University Press, 1992], 7). David Bell, while claiming that 'nationalism' makes no sense before the eighteenth century in France, makes the key distinction between nationalism and national sentiment (*The Cult of the Nation in France: Inventing Nationalism, 1680–1800* [Cambridge, MA: Harvard University Press, 2001]); others have avoided semantic pitfalls with similar distinctions: John Breuilly, in *Nationalism and the State* (Manchester: Manchester University Press, 1982), distinguishes between nationalism and national consciousness, as does Cathy Shrank in *Writing the Nation in Reformation England, 1530–1580* (Oxford: Oxford University Press, 2004). John Agnew, 'Nationalism,' 235,

defends the use of nation for pre-modern periods: 'Though nationalism is a modern phenomenon, therefore, there is no need to presume that nations or nationalities are likewise.' Colette Beaune, *Naissance*; Myriam Yardeni, *Enquêtes sur l'identité de la 'nation France': De la Renaissance aux lumières* (Seyssel: Champ Vallon, 2005); and Alain Tallon, *Conscience nationale et sentiment religieux en France au XVIe siècle* (Paris: PUF, 2002), all use the word *nation* to refer to pre-Enlightenment periods, while insisting on how it is a mobile concept tied to ideology and belief.

61 Claire McEachern, *The Poetics of English Nationhood*, 22. See also Helgerson, *Forms*; and Timothy Hampton, *Literature and Nation*, who presents his study as a 'prehistory of the national [...] a history of nationhood' (8).

62 R.J. Knecht sees François I as an anticipation of the absolutist king, in *Francis I* (Cambridge: Cambridge University Press, 1982). For the complex relations between monarchy and the idea of representative government in early modern France, see J. Russell Major's collected essays in *The Monarchy, the Estates, and the Aristocracy in Renaissance France* (London: Variorum, 1988). Major argues that the sixteenth-century monarchy is inherently *de*-centralized, with much provincial power actually increasing until the seventeenth century. The teleology of the 'becoming' of the nation, and its projection back into the Renaissance and beyond, seems particularly strong in French scholarship: see Colette Beaune, *Naissance*; Myriam Yardeni, *Enquêtes*; Marie-Madeleine Martin, *Histoire de l'unité française* (Paris: PUF, 1949); Jean Lestocquoy, *Histoire du patriotisme français des origines à nos jours* (Paris: Albin Michel, 1968). For a helpful literature review of scholarship on the early modern French nation, see Paul Cohen, 'Poets into Frenchmen: Timothy Hampton on Literature and National Sentiment in Renaissance France,' *Shakespeare Studies* 33 (2005): 173–204. For a rigorous study of the complexity of the power structures of the early modern state, including a helpful glossary of terms, see James Collins, *The State in Early Modern France* (Cambridge: Cambridge University Press, 1995). Emmanuel Le Roy Ladurie provides an ambitious history of the French region in *Histoire de France des régions: La périphérie francaise des origines à nos jours* (Paris: Seuil, 2001).

63 Marc Augé, *Non-lieux: Introduction à une anthropologie de la surmodernité* (Paris: Seuil, 1992), 48; Lucy Lippard, *The Lure of the Local* (New York: The New Press, 1997). Projection backwards in time of the nation–region opposition is to be done with care. The vocabulary that does this work for us was more fluid in the sixteenth century. Robert Estienne's 1549 French-Latin dictionary, for example, translates 'pais ou pays' as the Latin 'Orbis, Regio, Tractus, Natio, Patria, Terra' (*Dictionnaire francoislatin* [Paris, 1549],

428). Despite terminological differences, however, the region as an ideological function has a great deal of agency in the sixteenth century, with
the outside threat being that of the kingdom rather than the modern nation
state or a global economy.

64 Eugen Weber, *Peasants into Frenchmen: The Modernization of Rural France,
1870–1914* (Palo Alto, CA: Stanford University Press, 1976). For a programmatic complication of the nation–region binary, see Brett Bowles, 'La République régionale: Stade occulté de la "synthèse républicaine,"' *The
French Review* 69 (1995): 103–17; also Celia Applegate, 'A Europe of Regions: Reflections on the Historiography of Sub-National Places in Modern
Times,' *The American Historical Review* 104 (1999): 1157–82. For an excellent
summary by a literary scholar of the challenges and limits of regionalism
conceived as opposite to (and oppressed by) nationalism, see Roberto Dainotto, *Place in Literature: Regions, Cultures, Communities* (Ithaca: Cornell
University Press, 2000), 1–33. With respect to early modern Europe, William Kennedy has identified, not an opposition, but a 'tensile drift of local
or regional identities toward a larger corporate whole' which he is careful
to distinguish from modern national identities: see *The Site of Petrarchism:
Early Modern National Sentiment in Italy, France, and England* (Baltimore:
Johns Hopkins University Press, 2003), 4.

65 Benedict Anderson, *Imagined Communities*; Richard Helgerson, *Forms of
Nationhood*.

66 In his Introduction to *Mappings*, ed. Denis Cosgrove (London: Reaktion
Books, 1999), 3.

67 Bruno Latour, *Nous n'avons jamais été modernes* (Paris: Éditions La Decou-
verte & Syros, 1997). Jeffrey Peters uses Latour's critique of the idea of modernity to subtend his study of seventeenth-century allegorical
cartography, *Mapping Discord: Allegorical Cartography in Early Modern
French Writing* (Newark: University of Delaware Press, 2004), 20 and passim, showing how literary cartographies evidence the continuation of hybrid forms of knowledge even in a period usually presented as the
beginning of modern scientific epistemologies. See also Christian Jacob,
L'empire des cartes (Paris: Albin Michel, 1992).

68 This is a paraphrase of Matthew Edney's important essay, 'Cartography
with "Progress": Reinterpreting the Nature and Historical Development of
Mapmaking,' *Cartographica* 30 (1993): 54–68. Gerald Crone's frequently reprinted *Maps and Their Makers: An Introduction to the History of Cartography*
(London: Hutchinson's University Library, 1953) is usually held up as representative of the teleology of increasing accuracy.

69 J. Brian Harley, 'Maps, Knowledge, and Power,' in *The Iconography of Land-scape: Essays on the Symbolic Representation, Design, and Use of Past Environ-ments*, ed. Denis Cosgrove and Stephen Daniels (Cambridge: Cambridge University Press, 1988), 277–312, 7. Mark Monmonier's *How to Lie with Maps* (Chicago: University of Chicago Press, 1991) is a good example of Harleian theorizing about maps as ideological artefacts. The collection of Harley's essays by Paul Laxton, *The New Nature of Maps: Essays in the His-tory of Cartography* (Baltimore: Johns Hopkins University Press, 2001), has a useful introduction and preface. For engagements with Harley's work and legacy, see especially Matthew Edney, 'Cartography,' and idem, 'Brian Harley's Career and Intellectual Legacy,' *Cartographica* 40 (2005): 1–17. See also Barbara Belyea, 'Images of Power: Derrida/Foucault/Harley,' *Carto-graphica* 29 (1992): 1–9; and James Corner, 'The Agency of Mapping,' in Cosgrove, *Mappings*, 213–52. For explicit position papers on cartographic theory, see the selected proceedings of a panel on 'theoretical aspects of the history of cartography' at the 16th International Conference on the History of Cartography, published in *Imago Mundi* 48 (1996): 185–205. Especially pertinent is the contribution by Delano-Smith, 'Why Theory in the History of Cartography?' (198–203), who considers cartographic and literary theory together.

70 A WorldCat search on 4 February 2010, for book-length studies using the combined keyword search terms 'cartography and literature,' yielded 754 results for all dates; 575 (76 per cent) of these titles were published after 1980. It should be noted that the categorization of books not in English re-sults in some important titles not being included: the results given for French titles, for example, do not include any work by Frank Lestringant, one of the leading scholars to ally literary and cartographic criticism.

71 Roland Barthes, 'De l'œuvre au texte,' in *Œuvres complètes*, vol. 2, ed. Eric Marty (Paris: Seuil, 1994), 1211–17.

72 Alba Newmann, *'Language is not a vague province': Mapping and Twentieth-Century American Poetry* (PhD diss., University of Texas, Austin, 2006), 1. An example of the kind of scholarship she means might be Sylviane Coyault, *L'histoire et la géographie dans le récit poétique* (Clermont-Ferrand: Centre de Recherches sur les Littératures Modernes et Contemporaines, 1997).

73 Michael Schoenfeldt, 'Recent Studies in the English Renaissance,' *Studies in English Literature, 1500–1900* 44 (2004): 189–228, 189.

74 Cited terms are from Stephen Daniels, 'Landscape and Art,' in *A Compan-ion to Cultural Geography*, ed. James Duncan, Nuala Johnson, and Richard Schein (Oxford: Blackwell, 2004), 430–46, 434.

75 Tom Conley, 'Putting French Studies on the Map,' *Diacritics* 28 (1998): 23–
    39, 27. Conley's 'graphic unconscious' (*The Graphic Unconscious in Early
    Modern French Writing* [Cambridge: Cambridge University Press, 1992]),
    and his later 'cartographic writing' (*The Self-Made Map: Cartographic Writ-
    ing in Early Modern France* [Minneapolis: University of Minnesota Press,
    1996]) have become mandatory references for anyone working on space
    and place in Renaissance France. Frank Lestringant's studies of geographic
    literature in sixteenth-century France (Rabelais, Thevet, Léry, Postel) go be-
    yond metaphoric notions of 'mapping' to show the many congruences be-
    tween verbal and cartographic epistemologies. See in particular his
    collections of essays, *Écrire le monde: Quinze études sur Rabelais, Postel, Bodin
    et la littérature géographique* (Caen: Paradigme, 1993), and *L'atelier du cos-
    mographe: ou, L'image du monde à la Renaissance* (Paris: A. Michel, 1991). In
    Le Livre des îles: Atlas et récits insulaires de la Genèse à Jules Verne (Geneva:
    Droz, 2002), he shows that the cartographic genre of the *insulaire*, and car-
    tographic images of the New World, are espoused overtly by and for frag-
    mented and open-ended literary narratives (2002). Jeffrey Peters's *Mapping
    Discord* treats seventeenth-century France. For Spain, see Ricardo Padrón,
    The Spacious Word: Cartography, Literature, and Empire in Early Modern Spain
    (Chicago: University of Chicago Press, 2004); and among the numerous
    cartographically oriented studies of Renaissance English literature, see
    Richard Helgerson, *Forms of Nationhood*; John Gillies, *Shakespeare and the
    Geography of Difference* (Cambridge: Cambridge University Press, 1994);
    Garrett Sullivan, *The Drama of Landscape: Land, Property, and Social Relations
    on the Early Modern Stage* (Palo Alto, CA: Stanford University Press, 1998);
    Rhonda Sanford, *Maps and Memory in Early Modern England: A Sense of
    Place* (New York: Palgrave, 2002).

76 The discipline of *poésie* was added in the second edition. Harvard Univer-
    sity has a copy of the 1587 edition; the Bibliothèque Nationale has the sec-
    ond edition published in Paris in 1619, which I consulted. The printer of
    the second edition, Jean Libert, writes in his dedication that the book was
    so popular that a new edition was required. The full title and subtitle of
    this edition are: *Tableaux accomplis de tous les arts liberaux contenans brieve-
    ment et clerement par singuliere methode de doctrine, une generale et sommaire
    partition desdicts arts, amassez et reduicts en ordre pour le soulagement et profit
    de la jeunesse. Encyclopedie, ou la suite et liaison de tous les Arts et Sciences.* The
    pairing of *arts* and *sciences* does not indicate the same kind of division as it
    does today in the Anglophone academy: *art* was closely linked to artisan-
    ship and the idea of technique, whereas *science* has a more encyclopedic
    sense that included the *litterae humaniores*, closer to the Latin root *scio*.

77 The term 'knowledge space' is from David Turnbull, 'Cartography and Science in Early Modern Europe: Mapping the Construction of Knowledge Spaces,' *Imago Mundi* 48 (1996): 5–24. His article argues that knowledge of space is produced locally, then assembled into a larger conceptual unit such as the nation.

2. The Poet and the Mapmaker: Lyric and Cartographic Images of France

1 A superb resource on the wars of religion is *Histoire et dictionnaire des guerres de religion* by Arlette Jouanna et al. (Paris: R. Laffont, 1998). See also J.H.M. Salmon's classic *Society in Crisis: France in the Sixteenth Century* (London: Methuen, 1975).

2 Mireille Pastoureau's definition of the atlas is 'any book in which the maps – or plans or views, as long as they are geographic – take up more space than the text': see 'Les Atlas imprimés en France avant 1700,' *Imago Mundi* 32 (1980): 45–72, 46. Bouguereau's text, and the genre of the *Theatrum* in general, do not fit this definition: rather, the *Theatrum* can be considered an intermediary stage between the Renaissance *Cosmographia* and the atlas as defined by Pastoureau, and, implicitly, by James Akerman, 'The Structuring of Political Territory in Early Printed Atlases,' *Imago Mundi* 47 (1995): 138–54. For the decline of the cosmographic genre, see Frank Lestringant, 'Le déclin d'un savoir: La crise de la cosmographie à la fin de la Renaissance,' in *Écrire le monde à la Renaissance* (Caen: Paradigme, 1993), 319–30. The circumstances of the compilation, printing, and publication of Bouguereau's *Théâtre* have been studied by François de Dainville, 'Le premier atlas de France: *Le Théâtre françoys* de M. Bouguereau, 1594,' in *Comité des travaux historiques et scientifiques: Actes du 85e congrès national des sociétés savantes, Chambéry-Annecy, 1960* (Paris: Bibliothèque nationale, 1961), 1–50. The very first French atlas to be published anywhere was Mercator's *Gallia*, published (with a *Germania*) in Duisberg in 1585. This little-studied work has recently been granted its due place in the history of French cartography by Mireille Pastoureau's excellent essay 'Entre Gaule et France, la "Gallia,"' in *Gérard Mercator cosmographe: Le temps et l'espace*, ed. M. Watelet (Anvers: Fonds Mercator Paribas, 1994), 317–33.

3 Tom Conley, *The Self-Made Map: Cartographic Writing in Early Modern France* (Minneapolis and London: University of Minnesota Press, 1996), 202–47, 203.

4 James Akerman says that Bouguereau simply compiled whatever maps were available at the time ('Early Atlases,' 149). Akerman sees the atlas coming into its own in the seventeenth and eighteenth centuries as a structural icon for the territorial and then the nation state, whereas a

sixteenth-century atlas 'in the interest of a particular European state tended to be a scattered, informal, and highly personal enterprise depending
on the sometimes fleeting good will, power, and map-consciousness of the
sovereign and the individuals at court' (146). Tom Conley, *Self-Made Map*,
208, and Frank Lestringant, 'La littérature géographique sous le règne de
Henri IV,' in *Écrire le monde*, 314–68, 342, further suggest that he did this to
be timely with Henri IV's claiming of Paris in March 1594.

5 Ibid., 238.

6 Tom Conley suggests that this word play actually disrupts the king's *renommé* (ibid., 219). His reading of the spatial verbal play in the sonnet is
extremely insightful; particularly pertinent is his pointing out the cartographic grid effect of the vertical acrostic letters with the horizontal naming of Bourbon in the last line of the sonnet (218–19).

7 For all citations from French primary texts, whether prose or poetry, I will
provide, throughout the book, the original French (with occasionally stan-
dardized orthography) with an English translation. Translations are mine
unless otherwise specified. For citations of secondary and critical works in
French, I will provide only my English translation, with references to the
page numbers of the original French. For primary texts in Latin or Italian,
I provide English translations in the main text, with original text footnoted
at my discretion.

8 The plural 'Seigneurs de Langey' seems to refer to the four brothers,
Guillaume, René, Martin, and Jean, who were the poet Joachim's cousins.

9 It should be noted that there are many different kinds of map in the Renaissance, as well summarized by Chandra Mukerji, 'Printing, Cartography, and Conceptions of Place in Renaissance Europe,' *Media, Culture, &
Society* 28 (2006): 651–69. See also the collection of essays by W.G.L. Randles, *Geography, Cartography, and Nautical Science in the Renaissance* (Burlington, VT: Ashgate, 2000). Portolan and marine charts used by sailors had
their own techniques and traditions, as did very local topographies such as
cadastral maps, on which see Roger Kain and Elizabeth Baigent, *The Cadastral Map in the Service of the State: A History of Property Mapping* (Chicago:
University of Chicago Press, 1992). Of interest here are chorographic-
geographic maps, which are mostly high-status objects, dedicated to powerful patrons and circulating in printed books or as separate *objets de luxe*.

10 For discussion of terminology, in particular the limits and pertinence of the
term *nation* to sixteenth-century France, see the preceding chapter.

11 This goes back to the 'géographie humaine' of Paul Vidal de la Blache in
Tableau de la géographie de la France (Paris: Tallandier, 1979, repr. from 1903),

which advances the idea of France as a symbiotic relation between humans and the 'unité toute faite' of its land (3). Anne Buttimer provides a good review of this tradition in French thought in *Society and Milieu in the French Geographic Tradition* (Chicago: Rand McNally, 1971). For studies of the specifically spatial ways in which France was produced as an idea as well as a political entity, see Daniel Nordman, *Frontières de France: De l'espace au territoire, XVIe–XIXe siècle* (Paris: Gallimard, 1998); and Peter Sahlins, *Boundaries: The Making of France and Spain in the Pyrenees* (Berkeley: University of California Press, 1989). Adding the sacred as a vital constitutive category, Jason Nice provides a good summary of recent scholarship on geography and nation in Renaissance England and France: '"The Peculiar Place of God": Early Modern Representations of England and France,' *The English Historical Review* 121 (2006): 1002–18.

12 See C.F. Black, Mark Greengrass, David Howarth et al., *Cultural Atlas of the Renaissance* (New York: Prentice Hall, 1993), 165, for maps of French expansion from 1453 to 1559.

13 Mireille Pastoureau, 'Entre Gaule,' 325. See also Paul Cohen, 'Poets into Frenchmen: Timothy Hampton on Literature and National Sentiment in Renaissance France,' *Shakespeare Studies* 33 (2005): 173–204, for a consideration of how French nationhood was complicated by regionalisms. For a general history of regional France, see Emmanuel Le Roy Ladurie, *Histoire de France des régions: La périphérie francaise des origines à nos jours* (Paris: Seuil, 2001).

14 Cosmography is not treated in the *Geographia*, but it is in the *Almagest*. For the Renaissance variations in meaning of the terms cosmography, geography, chorography, and topography, see Francesca Fiorani, *The Marvel of Maps: Art, Cartography, and Politics in Renaissance Italy* (New Haven: Yale University Press, 2005), 98–100. The cartographic changes of the early modern period have been well studied in both European and national contexts. Good overviews are found in François de Dainville, *La géographie des humanistes* (Geneva: Slatkine reprints, 1969; repr. from 1940); Numa Broc, *La géographie de la Renaissance (1420–1620)* (Paris: Bibliothèque nationale, 1980); Tony Campbell, *The Earliest Printed Maps, 1472–1500* (London: The British Library, 1987); Jean-Marc Besse, *Les grandeurs de la Terre: Aspects du savoir géographique à la Renaissance* (Paris: ENS Éditions, 2003); and Rodney Shirley, *The Mapping of the World: Early Printed World Maps, 1472–1700* (London: Holland Press, 1983). Robert Karrow, Jr, provides an invaluable version of Leo Bagrow's 1928–30 edition of Ortelius's catalogue, *Mapmakers of the Sixteenth Century and Their Maps* (Chicago: Speculum Orbis, 1993). For France, see the numerous

articles by François de Dainville and by Mireille Pastoureau, in particular the latter's 'Les Atlas imprimés en France avant 1700,' *Imago Mundi* 32 (1980): 45–72, which provides a list of all maps in French atlases through the end of the seventeenth century; Monique Pelletier, ed., *Géographie du monde au Moyen Âge et à la Renaissance* (Paris: Éditions du CTHS, 1989); Monique Pelletier and Henriette Ozanne, *Portraits de la France: Les cartes, témoins de l'histoire* (Paris: Hachette, 1995); Jacques Revel, ed., *Histoire de la France*, vol. 1, *L'espace français* (Paris: Seuil, 1989). The first scholarly studies of French Renaissance cartography, although very positivist in their approach to the map, are still valuable, e.g., Ludovic Drapeyron, 'L'image de la France sous les derniers Valois (1525–1589) et sous les premiers Bourbons (1589–1682),' *Revue de Géographie* 24 (1889): 1–15.

15 Matthew Edney, 'Cartography.' The practical distinctions, Edney tells us, operate between charting, chorography, and topography, the latter two of which merged during the sixteenth century to become geodesy.

16 This is suggested by Lucia Nuti's essay on the artistic aspects of chorography, 'Mapping Places: Chorography and Vision in the Renaissance,' in *Mappings*, ed. Denis Cosgrove (London: Reaktion Books, 1999), 90–108.

17 Frank Lestringant, 'Chorographie et paysage à la Renaissance,' in *Écrire le monde*, 50. Lestringant also provides a summary of Apian's definitions of chorography and geography, and a reproduction of his illustrations of their differences (52–4).

18 See Pelletier, ed., *Géographie du monde*, and Pelletier and Ozanne, *Portraits de la France*; also Pelletier, 'Des cartes pour partager: Divisions administratives, frontières, plans terriers,' in *La cartografía francesa* (Barcelona: Institut Cartogràfic de Catalunya, 1996), 17–32. Richard Helgerson, *Forms of Nationhood*, 131–9, makes a similar case for chorography disrupting royalist teleologies of nationhood in Renaissance England.

19 Ludovic Drapeyron, 'L'image,' 8–9, provides a long list.

20 See David Buisseret, 'Monarchs, Ministers, and Maps in France before the Accession of Louis XIV,' in *Monarchs, Ministers, and Maps: The Emergence of Cartography as a Tool of Government in Early Modern Europe*, ed. David Buisseret (Chicago: Chicago University Press, 1992), 99–123. The history of Renaissance cartography is usually seen as tied in with the beginnings of the modern nation-state. The 2007 volume of Woodward's *History of Cartography* dedicated to the European Renaissance, for example, takes a national approach, which is defended in Woodward's first chapter: *Cartography in the European Renaissance*, vol. 3 of *The History of Cartography* (Chicago: University of Chicago Press, 2007).

21 The 1525 map has been lost; the Bibliothèque nationale in Paris has reproductions of prints from 1538 and 1553.

22 The mural was made around 1565, and is discussed by François de Dainville, who identifies Stefano Francese as Étienne Du Pérac, a French architect and painter working at the Papal court, in 'Jean Jolivet's "Description des Gaules,"' in *Imago Mundi* 18 (1964): 45–52, 50. Jolivet's original 1560 *Vraye description des Gaules* is lost, but the Bibliothèque nationale in Paris has a 1570 version published in Paris by Marc du Chesne, as well as a Latin print also from 1570, the *Galliae regni potentiss. nova descriptio*.

23 Nicolay finished 'descriptions' of several provinces before his death: Berry (1567), Bourbonnais (1569), and Lyonnais (1573). Nicolas de Nicolay, Seigneur d'Arfeuille, engineer and secret agent, was first 'géographe ordinaire,' then 'cosmographe du Roi.' For details of his career, see Robert Barroux, 'Nicolaï d'Arfeuille, agent secret, géographe et dessinateur (1517–83),' *Revue d'histoire diplomatique* 51 (1937): 88–109; Roger Hervé, 'L'œuvre cartographique de Nicolas de Nicolay et d'Antoine de Laval,' *Bulletin de la Section de géographie* 68 (1955): 223–63; and Frank Lestringant, *L'atelier*, 257–74. His nephew, Antoine de Laval, a man of letters and a poet, collected his maps at the château du Moulins, where Henri III enjoyed visiting and poring over them. The text of Charles IX's *lettre patente* ratifying the commission is printed in appendix to the 1881 edition of Nicolay's *Description* of the Lyonnais.

24 Of course, this also plays out between France and Italy: the disputed frontier and territories of northern Italy furnished the impulse for many early maps. Jacques Signot's 1515 *Carte d'Italie* was a tool in Charles VIII's military campaigns, and his 1539 *La division du monde*, containing prose descriptions of Europe, Asia, and Africa, contained a separate section on the ten passages from France to Italy with clearly strategic intent. Signot's text was reprinted several times until the 1560s, but never mentioned the Americas, showing the delay in the transmission of new cartographic knowledge.

25 The Greek manuscript of the *Geography* was brought in 1406 from Constantinople to Florence, where it was translated into Latin and first became known to Renaissance Europe. Many other translations followed, Latin and vernacular. See Broc, *La géographie*, and Besse, *Grandeurs*, who insists on the paradigmatic as well as the technical shifts inaugurated by Ptolemy's text in the Renaissance; see also Samuel Edgerton, Jr, 'From Mental Matrix to *Mappamundi* to Christian Empire: The Heritage of Ptolemaic Cartography in the Renaissance,' in *Art and Cartography: Six Historical Essays*, ed. David Woodward (Chicago and London: University of Chicago Press,

1987), 10–50, for a provocative argument that the Ptolemaic grid came to symbolize the expansionist ideology of European Renaissance Christian powers.

26 Besse, *Grandeurs*, 19. For the ongoing redrawing of the Ptolemaic maps, see Anthony Grafton, *New Worlds, Ancient Texts: The Power of Tradition and the Shock of Discovery* (Cambridge: Harvard University Press, 1992), 48–58.

27 Pastoureau, 'Entre Gaule,' 326.

28 See the previous chapter, n. 17, for a bibliography on imitation.

29 Joachim Du Bellay, *La Deffence et illustration de la langue françoyse, et L'Olive*, ed. Jean-Charles Monferran and Ernesta Caldarini (Geneva: Droz, 2007), 173. This and subsequent references to the *Deffence* give page numbers to this edition in the text. All translations from the *Deffence* are taken from Richard Helgerson's excellent translation, *'The Regrets' with 'The Antiquities of Rome,' Three Latin Elegies, and 'The Defense and Enrichment of the French Language'* (Philadelphia: University of Pennsylvania Press, 2007).

30 *Georgics*, 2.136–76. The praise of Italy comes in the context of the book's discussion of the types of soil propitious for particular trees. The Virgilian passage includes the conjunction, perhaps odd to the modern reader, of rustic landscapes with cities (Du Bellay, however, adds the munitions).

31 Bibliothèque nationale, Paris, département des Cartes et Plans, Ge F carte 6752.

32 Viros genuit qui gloria rerum gestarum opum abundantia et doctrinarum monumentis clarissimi semper extitere. Solum habet ita foecundum ut nulla in re cedat florentissimae italiae.

33 Bibliothèque nationale, Paris, département des Cartes et Plans, Res. Ge D 7642.

34 Candido lectori s.d. 'Gallia tota iam olim non ob opes solum, et virtutem bellicam, quibus semper prestitit, verum etiam ob continentia et disciplinam, quaesummum apud illos locum habuit celebris fuit. Nam et artium illustrium, et Graecae etiam linguae peritia excelluit, matre ut arbitror Massilia Graeca urbe, in maritima ora provinciae sita, ad quam quondam disciplarum gratia vel ex ipsa urbe Roma missi sunt qui docerentur.' My translation is based on that given by Marcel van den Broecke and Deborah van den Broecke-Günzburger in their online project 'Cartographica Neerlandica,' at http://www.orteliusmaps.com/topnames/ort34.html.

35 Anderson, *Imagined Communities*, 44–6.

36 Bibliothèque nationale, Paris, département des Cartes et Plans, Res. Ge D 7668. The full title is *Vraye et entiere description du royaume de france, et ses confins, avec l' addresse des chemins et distances aux Villes inscriptes es Provinces d'iceluy*. In the frame is 'Totius galliae exactissima descriptio.'

37 François Rigolot, 'Interpréter Rabelais aujourd'hui: Anachronies et catachronies,' *Poétique* 103 (1995): 269–83, argues convincingly that while
   'anachronie' is irresponsible scholarship, so too is 'catachronie,' which is
   denying that our enquiries and research are always determined by our
   own intellectual context. What is required, then, is a combination of erudition and honest assessment of our own positionality. I have found Rigolot's article helpful in imagining an approach to Renaissance culture that
   takes seriously the problem of anachronism while also avoiding the conceit that the past is graspable independently of the present.

38 'The Mapping Impulse in Dutch Art,' in Woodward, ed., *Art and Cartography*, 51–96, 69.

39 Mukerji, 'Printing,' 651, 664. She argues, contrary to Elizabeth Eisenstein,
   that map printing was 'designed to serve markets, not intellectual
   progress' (651).

40 Alpers, 'The Mapping Impulse,' 60.

41 In Goyet, *Traités*, 293.

42 Edmond Huguet summarizes Renaissance meanings of the word *géographie* in *L'évolution du sens des mots depuis le XVIe siècle* (Paris: Droz, 1934),
   51–2. The Renaissance 'cosmography,' although it subsumed both geography and astronomy, was often used interchangeably with 'geography,' as
   witnessed by the fact that Ptolemy's text went by either title. For the confusion between the two terms in the early sixteenth century, see Dainville,
   'Jean Jolivet.' For the sixteenth-century genre of the *cosmographie* in France,
   and the work of the royal cosmographer André Thevet in particular, see
   Lestringant, *L'atelier*. Readers of Rabelais will recall that Gargantua urges
   his son to study cosmography in order better to understand history (*Pantagruel*, chap. 8): the pairing of history with geography-cosmography is frequent in the Renaissance. Ortelius famously described geography as the
   eye of history (historiae oculus) in his 1570 *Theatrum*.

43 'Prendendo ad raccontar chose al presente / Con tutto lo habitato inrima
   en verso / Da far maravigliar ciaschuna gente: / Pero chel canto mio non
   sia diverso / Da te fulgente Apollo ma conforme / Manifestando tutto lu-
   niverso / Quale ignorare e chosa troppo enorme.' Francesco Berlinghieri
   and Claudius Ptolemy, *Geographia di Francesco Berlinghieri Fiorentino in terza
   rima et lingva Toscana distincta con le sve tavole in varii siti et provincie secondo
   la geographia et distinctione dele tauole di Ptolomeo* (Florence: Laurentii, 1482),
   fol a:i r. Thanks to Susan Gaylard for help with the translation.

44 Jean Jolivet's 1560 and 1570 maps of France are addressed 'au lecteur' and
   'candido lectori' respectively.

45 The translation from the Latin is from Ludovic Drapeyron, 'L'image,' 9. For details of Fayen's life, see idem, 'Jean Fayen et la première carte du Limousin (1594),' *Bulletin de la Société archéologique et historique du Limousin* 42 (1894): 61–105.

46 See, for example, the sonnet 'Lassare il velo' in Petrarch's *Rime*, or Ronsard's 'Lorsque le Ciel te fist' in the *Second Livre des sonnets pour Hélène*.

47 Pierre de Ronsard, *Œuvres complètes*, ed. Jean Céard, Daniel Ménager, and Michel Simonin (Paris: Gallimard, 1994), 2:1127.

48 The full contents of Belleau's library are listed in Philippe Hamon and Jean Jacquart, *Archives de la France*, vol. 3: *XVI siècle* (Paris: Fayard, 1997), 315–23.

49 The modern edition by Marie-Christine Gomez-Géraud and Stéphane Yérasimos, *Dans l'empire de Soliman le magnifique* (Paris: Presses du CNRS, 1989), is based on the second edition of Nicolay's text, *Les Navigations, pérégrinations et voyages faicts en la Turquie par Nicolas de Nicolay seigneur d'Arfeuille* ... (Antwerp, 1576), in the Paris Bibliothèque nationale. In the end, it was none other than Pierre de Ronsard himself who penned the dedicatory elegy. See Marcus Keller, 'Nicolas de Nicolay's *Navigations* and the Domestic Politics of Travel Writing,' *L'esprit créateur* 48 (2008): 18–31, for a good recent study of the *Navigations*.

50 Nicolay, *Navigations*, fol a:3 v–a:4.

51 *Générale Description de l'antique et célèbre cité de Lyon du pais de Lyonnois et du Beaujollois selon l'assiette limites et confins d'iceux pais* (1573), in the manuscript department of the Bibliothèque nationale, Paris. The text was also published by the Société de topographie historique de Lyon as *Description générale de la ville de Lyon et des anciennes provinces du Lyonnais et du Beaujolais, 1573*, ed. Victor Advielle (Lyon: Imprimerie Mougin-Rusand, 1881).

52 Ibid., 3–4. It was clearly difficult for the geographer to perform his task in the midst of civil war: Nicolay mentions in his preface to this work 'the instability of the time' and 'the pausing and complication of some necessary research' (11).

53 Nicolay presents most of his maps this way. Charles IX himself, in the *lettre patente* giving Nicolay his commission, uses the same formula. I plan to publish in a separate article a more detailed study of the question of how Renaissance cartographers presented their work rhetorically to prospective and actual patrons.

54 David Buisseret, 'Monarchs,' focuses more on the seventeenth century, but does include some useful pages on sixteenth-century cartography as it anticipates the full-scale royal co-opting of cartography as a military and government tool (99–107).

55 A certain M.F. Du Boys, for example, in a liminal poem addressed to Nicolay in his 1569 *Bourbonnais*, praises Nicolay for providing to the monarch information and examples which will help him understand and govern his subjects.

56 Margaret McGowan, *Ideal Forms in the Age of Ronsard* (Berkeley: University of California Press, 1985), 38.

57 Joachim Blanchon (1540?–1597?) was a native of Limoges, like Jean Dorat with whom he exchanged encomiastic poems. Very little is known of his life. He is mentioned in La Croix du Maine's *Bibliothèque françoyse* (François Grudé La Croix du Maine et Antoine Du Verdier, *Les Bibliothèques françoyses* [Paris: Saillant et Nyon, 1772–3], 2:3), and L'Abbé Gouget dedicated nine pages to him (*Bibliothèque françoyse* [1741–7; Geneva: Slatkine Reprints, 1966], 13:164–3). He published a *Sommaire discours de la guerre civile* […] (Paris: Denis du Pré, 1569), and his *Premières œuvres poétiques* in 1583 (Paris: Thomas Perier).

58 For a detailed description and history of the map, see Antoine Vacher, 'La carte du Berry par Jean Jolivet (1545),' *Bulletin de géographie historique et déscriptive* 22 (1907): 258–67.

59 The *pays d'élection* were provinces taxed by the king's representatives, as opposed to the *pays d'état*, which were taxed locally. See Salmon, *Society in Crisis*, 74–5.

60 Among Thiboust's manuscripts are a *liber amicorum*, an interesting insight into the community of intellectuals he assembled around him in Berry, as well as documents relating to the management of his estate – rare testimonials to how a sixteenth-century man of letters conceived of his relation to his territory. For details, see Françoise Michaud-Fréjaville, 'Tradition et innovation horticole en Berry: Jean Rogier et Jacques Thiboust dans leur jardin de Quantilly (1503–26),' in *Flore et jardins: Usages, savoirs et représentations du monde végétal au Moyen Âge*, ed. Pierre-Gilles Girault (Paris: Le Léopard d'or, 1997), 51–70. See Hippolyte Boyer, *Un ménage littéraire en Berry au XVIe siècle: Jacques Thiboust et Jeanne de la Font* (Bourges: Jollet-Souchois, 1859), for biography; and for his literary relations, S. Le Clech-Charton, 'Jacques Thiboust, notaire et secrétaire du roi et familier de Marguerite de Navarre: Amitiés littéraires dans le Berry du "beau seizième siècle,"' *Cahiers d'archéologie et d'histoire du Berry* 96 (1989): 17–27.

61 See G. Marcel, 'Le comte d'Alsinoys géographe,' *Revue de géographie* 35 (1894): 193–9.

62 For a discussion of this controversy, see Michel Simonin, 'La disgrâce d'Amadis,' *Studi Francesi* 82 (1984): 1–35.

63 Henri Mettrier, 'Les cartes de Savoie au XVIe siècle. La carte de B. de Bouíllon, 1556,' *Bulletin de la section de géographie* 32 (1917): 16–129, 34.

64 Reproduced in Georges Reverdy, *Atlas historique des routes de France* (Paris: Presses de l'école nationale des ponts et chaussées, 1986), 4–5. Boileau also made maps of the Franche Comté in 1556 and Belgium in 1557. More than anything else, the map of Savoy attests to the acute political tension surrounding the duchy, which had been seized from the duke Emmanuel Phillibert by François I in 1536. In 1556, when Boileau made the map, the Duke – who was supported by Philip II of Spain and his uncle the Emperor Charles V – had won important victories against the French, and would regain Savoy in the treatise of Cateau-Cambrésis three years later. Boileau sought the favour of Emmanuel Phillibert, and drew at the top of his map a golden fleece (the Duke's emblem) and the arms of Savoy. The supposed boundary between Savoy and the French king's territories is sketched in a faint dotted line. The poet Jacques Peletier will later dedicate his long poem *La Savoie* (1572), a written and laudatory description of much of the duchy which I discuss in chap. 6, to Marguerite de France, daughter of François I and duchess of Savoy and Berry.

65 Conley, 'Putting French Studies on the Map,' 23.

66 Newmann, *Language*, 1.

3. The Poet, the Nation, and the Region: Constructing Anjou and France

1 Jean Dorat was the preceptor of the Pléiade poets at the Collège de Coqueret. The sonnet is in Greek, illustrating not only the importance of classical learning at the college, but more importantly the paradoxes of Du Bellay's linguistic project, which proposed imitation of and borrowing from Greek, Latin, and Italian in order to render French illustrious. I use the French translation by Jean-Charles Monferran in his edition of the *Deffence* published with Ernesta Caldarina's edition of *L'Olive*: Monferran and Caldarini, eds., *La Deffence et illustration de la langue françoyse, et L'Olive* (Geneva: Droz, 2007), 71n. 13.

2 Du Bellay borrows particularly heavily from the Italian humanist Sperone Speroni's 1542 *Dialogo delle lingue*, sometimes, as in the famous opening passage, translating him almost word for word. Since the revelation of this Italian source by Pierre Villey, in *Les sources italiennes de la 'Deffense et illustration de la langue françoise' de Joachim du Bellay* (Paris: Champion, 1908), many critics have seen it as diminishing the originality and power of the *Deffence*. More recently, this view has been complicated. One of the best articles on the Du Bellay–Speroni relationship is Ignacio Navarrete, 'Strategies of

Appropriation in Speroni and Du Bellay,' *Comparative Literature* 41 (1989): 141–54. Navarrete shows that Du Bellay's use of Speroni is very intelligent and intentional, illustrating the very principle of cultural assimilation for which his text argues. As for Du Bellay's original Latin poetry, the best-known volume is *Joachimi Bellaii Andini poematum libri quatuor* (Paris, 1558). The *Poemata* are edited in Joachim Du Bellay, *Œuvres poétiques*, vol. 7, *Œuvres latines: Poemata*, ed. and trans. Geneviève Demerson, preface by Alain Michel (Paris: Nizet, 1984). Demerson has authored several articles on Du Bellay's neo-Latin verse, listed in her edition, and an authoritative book which discusses the relation between the poet's French and Latin work, *Joachim Du Bellay et la belle romaine* (Orléans: Paradigme, 1996). See also the chapter on Du Bellay in Marc Bizer, *La poésie au miroir: Imitation et conscience de soi dans la poésie latine de la Pléiade* (Paris: Champion, 1995), which discusses the contradictions in Du Bellay's espousal of Latin. Some of the contributions to the edited volume by Terence Cave and Grahame Castor, *Neo-Latin and the Vernacular in Renaissance France* (Oxford: Clarendon, 1984), show that even the great poets of the French vernacular were often more at home writing in Latin. The book was a tribute to Ian McFarlane, whose contributions to studies of neo-Latin poetry in France were foundational.

3 See, on the many linguistic variations within France, Paul Cohen, 'Illustration du français et persistance des langues régionales: La pluralité linguistique dans la constitution des idéologies sociales en France à l'époque moderne,' in *Lyon et l'illustration de la langue française à la Renaissance*, ed. Gérard Defaux (Lyons: ENS, 2003), 147–67; and 'L'imaginaire d'une langue nationale: L'État, les langues, et l'invention du mythe de l'Ordonnance de Villers-Cotterêts à l'époque moderne,' *Histoire epistémologie langage* 25 (2003): 19–69.

4 From his polemic response to Du Bellay, the *Quintil Horacien*, published in *Traités de poétique et de rhétorique de la Renaissance*, ed. Francis Goyet (Paris: Livre de Poche, 1990), 175–218, 179. Margaret Ferguson, *Trials of Desire: Renaissance Defenses of Poetry* (New Haven: Yale University Press, 1983), provides an influential and insightful (psycho)analysis of Du Bellay's defensive rhetoric. For a good summary of criticism on the posture of defence, see Hassan Melehy, 'Du Bellay and the Space of Early Modern Culture,' *Neophilologus* 84 (2000): 501–15, 501–2.

5 Marc Bizer, '"Qui a pais n'a que faire de patrie": Joachim Du Bellay's resistance to a French identity,' *Romanic Review* 91 (2000): 375–95, 375. See also David Hartley, 'Du Bellay et la patrie: Échos littéraires,' in *Du Bellay: Actes du colloque international d'Angers du 26 ou 29 mai 1989*, ed. Georges Cesbron, 2 vols. (Angers: Presses de l'Université d'Angers, 1990), 2:653–62, which makes the key distinction between local and national patriotism.

6 Tim Cresswell, *Place: A Short Introduction* (Oxford: Blackwell, 2004), 43.
  Michel Deguy reduces the distance between Rome and France to a struc-
  turalist question, in his aptly styled 'méditation,' *Tombeau de Du Bellay*
  (Paris: Gallimard, 1973).

7 Tom Conley, 'Putting French Studies on the Map,' *Diacritics* 28 (1998):
  23–39, 23.

8 Fernand Hallyn, 'Le paysage anthropomorphe,' in *Le paysage à la Renaissance*, ed. Yves Giraud (Fribourg: Éditions Universitaires Fribourg Suisse,
  1988), 43–54, 43.

9 The fraught relationship between Du Bellay and his classical and Italian
  models, which are simultaneously to be emulated and surpassed, has been
  well studied by Margaret Ferguson, *Trials of Desire*, who frames it as a
  Bloomian anxiety of influence.

10 For the importance of the Giolito anthology to Du Bellay, see especially
   JoAnn DellaNeva, 'Variations in a Minor Key: Du Bellay's Imitations of the
   Giolito Anthology Poets.' *French Forum* 14 (1989): 133–46.

11 Petrarch is the *sine quo non* of French lyric poetry in the sixteenth century,
   largely because of the influence of his *Rime*. For an idea of the extent of
   Petrarch's influence (as opposed to Petrarch*ism*) on Renaissance French
   poetry, see the collection of essays published on the 700th anniversity of
   Petrarch's birth, edited by Jean Balsamo, *Les poètes français de la Renaissance
   et Pétrarche* (Geneva: Droz, 2004); for Du Bellay and Petrarch in particular,
   see the contribution of Olivier Millet, 'Du Bellay et Pétrarche autour de
   L'Olive,' 253–66. For a Europe-wide study of the influence and diffusion
   of Petrarch via his commentators, see William J. Kennedy's *Authorizing
   Petrarch* (Ithaca: Cornell University Press, 1994); and *The Site of Petrarchism:
   Early Modern National Sentiment in Italy, France, and England* (Baltimore:
   Johns Hopkins University Press, 2003). Cécile Alduy has shown that a collection of 'Amours,' in the style of the *Rime*, became the sixteenth-century
   French poet's rite of passage that one had to perform in order to show off
   one's talent as a poet: *Politique des 'Amours': Poétique et genèse d'un genre
   français nouveau (1544–1560)* (Geneva: Droz, 2007). Petrarch and Laura became objects not only of literary imitation and adulation but also cultural
   cult figures – Maurice Scève caused a sensation when he claimed to have
   discovered Laura's tomb in Lyons. See Sarah Sturm-Maddox, 'The French
   Petrarch,' *Annali d'Italianistica* 22 (2004): 171–88. For consideration of the
   many other Italian vernacular influences on French Renaissance poetry,
   see the work of JoAnn DellaNeva, in particular 'Teaching Du Bellay a Lesson: Ronsard's Rewriting of Ariosto's Sonnets,' in *French Forum* 24 (1999):

285–301; and 'An Exploding Canon: Petrarch and the Petrarchists in Renaissance France' in *Annali d'Italianistica* 22 (2004): 189–206.

12 William Kennedy, *The Site of Petrarchism*, 1. See chaps. 4–7 for his discussion of Du Bellay.

13 Kennedy's attention to the communitary aspect of French poetry is particularly welcome, as it has been neglected by many critics trained in the 'sa vie, son œuvre' approach to single authors; no doubt I myself do not give it the weight it deserves.

14 Kennedy, *The Site of Petrarchism*, 4.

15 JoAnn DellaNeva, 'Illustrating the *Deffence*: Imitation and Poetic Perfection in Du Bellay's *Olive*,' *French Review* 61 (1987): 39–49, 48. My reading of *L'Olive* has been greatly influenced by both DellaNeva and Kennedy.

16 Lucy Lippard, *The Lure of the Local* (New York: The New Press, 1997).

17 Yvonne Bellenger points out that Du Bellay's idealization of French land is necessarily predicated upon his distance from it through a process of mythologizing, in *Du Bellay: Ses 'Regrets' qu'il fit dans Rome* (Paris: Nizet, 1975), 201–11.

18 Philip Schwyzer, 'The Beauties of the Land: Bale's Books, Aske's Abbeys, and the Aesthetics of Nationhood,' *Renaissance Quarterly* 57 (2004): 99–125, 125.

19 David Harvey, *Spaces of Hope* (Berkeley: University of California Press, 2000).

20 Conley, 'Putting French Studies on the Map.'

21 Joachim Du Bellay, *La Deffence et illustration de la langue françoyse, et L'Olive*, ed. Jean-Charles Monferran and Ernesta Caldarini (Geneva: Droz, 2007), 241. As indicated in n. 1, above, all citations from *L'Olive* and *La Deffence* are from this edition. Translations of *L'Olive* are my own. Translations from *La Deffence* and *Les Regrets* are from Richard Helgerson's excellent dual-language edition, *'The Regrets' with 'The Antiquities of Rome,' Three Latin Elegies, and 'The Defense and Enrichment of the French Language'* (Philadelphia: University of Pennsylvania Press, 2007). Henceforth I will provide the sonnet numbers for references to *L'Olive* and *Les Regrets*, and page numbers to Monferran and Caldarini's edition for references to the *Deffence*.

22 François Rigolot, 'Du Bellay et la poésie du refus,' *Bibliothèque d'humanisme et Renaissance* 36 (1974): 489–502, 492. For a consideration of the poetic *recusatio* in all its intertextual complexity, and with specific respect to landscape, see Hugo Tucker, '"Ce tenebreux voyle" de *L'Olive* (1549; 1550): Formes et significations du recueil augmenté de 1550 (par rapport au recueil de 1549) vers une lecture textuelle, métatextuelle et intertextuelle,' in *'L'Olive' de Joachim Du Bellay: Actes des Seminaires d'analyse textuelle Pasquali*

(Lucelle 1er–4 Dec. 2005), ed. Ruggero Campagnoli, Eric Lysøe, and Anna Soncini Fratta (Bologna: CLUEB, 2007), 47–102.

23 For the theme of poetic glory, see Françoise Joukovsky, *La gloire dans la poésie française et néolatine du XVIe siècle: Des rhétoriqueurs à Agrippa d'Aubigné* (Geneva: Droz, 1969).

24 One of many examples is in *Canzoniere* 30: 'I shall follow the shadow of that sweet laurel … Love leads to the foot of the harsh laurel / That has branches of diamond and golden locks.' Petrarch, *Petrarch's Lyric Poems: The 'Rime sparse' and Other Lyrics*, ed. and trans. Robert Durling (Cambridge, MA: Harvard University Press, 1976), 86. For the laurel-Laura question, see Sara Sturm-Maddox, *Petrarch's Laurels* (Philadelphia: Pennsylvania State University Press, 1992). A classic article-length study is John Freccero's 'The Fig Tree and the Laurel: Petrarch's Poetics,' *Diacritics* 5 (1975): 34–40.

25 JoAnn DellaNeva, 'Illustrating the *Deffence*, 40.

26 The particular relationship between the *Deffence* and *L'Olive* is well exposed by, e.g., Floyd Gray, *La poétique de Du Bellay* (Paris: Nizet, 1978). Chap. 2 of Gray's book discusses Du Bellay's uses of the sonnet form. On the French sonnet, see also François Rigolot, 'Qu'est-ce qu'un sonnet? Perspectives sur les origines d'une forme poétique,' *Revue d'histoire littéraire de la France* 84 (1984): 3–18. The *Deffence* itself goes to some lengths to convince its reader of the interest of using the sonnet, that 'invention italienne.'

27 Olive may have been inspired by the poet's cousin, Olive de Sévigné. Christophe Gagneux, in *Liré, avant-hier et hier* (Maulevrier: Hérault-Éditions, 1982), 36, is sure of it, following A. Bourdeaut's 1910 *Joachim du Bellay et Olive de Sévigné* (Angers: Grassin, 1910). But even if this were the case, the rich allusiveness of the name, in particular its anagram *vôile*, renders biographical fact, if indeed there is any, secondary. As Michel Deguy insists, Olive is above all a name (*Tombeau*, 55–7). For a detailed discussion of the poetic significance, the anagrams, and wordplay, suggested by the name (similar to that of Laura – lauro – l'aura for Petrarch), see Tucker, 'Ce tenebreux voyle.' For the importance of onomastics to Renaissance poetry, even far beyond the Rhétoriqueurs, see François Rigolot, *Poétique et onomastique: L'exemple de la Renaissance* (Geneva: Droz, 1977).

28 *Odes*, 1.7. In Horace, *Odes and Epodes*, ed. and trans. Niall Rudd (Cambridge, MA: Harvard University Press, 2004), 36–9. The Biblical symbolism of the olive branch as a sign of peace plays at best a secondary role to classical symbols of glory in Du Bellay's collection. For the olive branch as symbol of fame, see Françoise Joukovsky, *La gloire*, 382–3. For the allusiveness of the olive tree, see Tucker, 'Ce tenebreux voyle,' 63–75.

29 Praise of rivers will become a lyric tradition in its own right in France in the following decades. See, for example, Pierre Le Loyer's first Idyll, 'Le Loir Angevin,' published in his *Œuvres et mélanges* (Paris, 1579), in which the poet adds his praise of the Loir to that of Pierre de Ronsard before him, making it a mutual glorification project. In 1549, however, Du Bellay's fluvial encomium is rather novel.

30 Although the Loire – the longest river in France – was indeed an important artery in sixteenth-century France (commercial traffic quadrupled during the sixteenth century), and also the site of many new aristocratic building projects, the position of the address in a love sonnet indicates that this is not quite what Du Bellay means. For details of the history of the Loire, see Christine Bonneton, ed., *Anjou* (Condé-sur-Noireau: Corlet, 1985).

31 For a discussion of the sixteenth-century notion of poetic source in which water imagery is shown to be inextricably linked to concerns about the origin and creation of poetry, see David Quint, *Origin and Originality in Renaissance Literature: Versions of the Source* (New Haven: Yale University Press, 1983), especially the introduction and pp. 43–80.

32 Schwyzer, 'The Beauties of the Land,' 100, 114.

33 Nancy Vickers, 'Diana Described: Scattered Woman and Scattered Rhyme,' *Critical Inquiry* 8 (1981): 265–79, has shown how the body of the female is divided and scattered in Petrarchan lyric by the poet's insistence on the particular over the whole: specific body parts are chosen for inclusion and elaboration in different poems, in a series of synecdoches which never allows the reader to see the whole woman. In sixteenth-century France, these corporeal descriptives are so common as to become cliché: the woman's teeth are like pearls, her eyes like stars, her skin like marble or ivory, her hair like gold.

34 Lawrence Kritzman, *The Rhetoric of Sexuality and the Literature of the French Renaissance* (Cambridge: Cambridge University Press, 1991), 97. The tradition of the 'blasons,' while indebted, as Kritzman shows, to native French traditions as well as to Petrarchism, takes fragmentation to the extreme: entire poems are written in praise of one body part, sometimes even parodically, as with the poem addressed to one old wrinkled nipple. For an overview of the fortunes of the genre, see Alison Saunders, *The Sixteenth-Century 'Blason poétique'* (Bern: Peter Lang, 1981).

35 *Rime sparse*, 129, translation from Durling, *Petrarch's Lyric Poems*, 266. A good book-length study of metamorphosis in Petrarch is Sara Sturm-Maddox, *Petrarch's Metamorphoses: Text and Subtext in the 'Rime sparse'* (Columbia: University of Missouri Press, 1985). For a consideration of Ovidian metamorphosis in Petrarch as a figure of loss, see Philip Hardie, 'Ovid into

Laura: Absent Presences in the *Metamorphoses* and Petrarch's *Rime sparse*,' in *Ovidian Transformations: Essays on Ovid's 'Metamorphoses' and Its Reception*, ed. Philip Hardie, Alessando Barchiesi, and Stephen Hinds (Cambridge: Cambridge Philological Society, 1999), 254–70. Ann Moss shows the importance to Pléiade poetic fables of the *Metamorphoses*, and also the medieval allegorizations of Ovid, in *Ovid in Renaissance France* (London: The Warburg Institute, 1982), 23–59.

36 See Michel Jeanneret's important study, *Perpetuum mobile: Métamorphoses des corps et des œuvres de Vinci à Montaigne* (Paris: Macula, 1997), which proposes that this sense of fundamental flux bottoms all creative activity of the Renaissance. For an art historian's perspective on this Renaissance idea with respect to the variation and circulation of wealth in various forms of gold artwork, see Rebecca Zorach, *Blood, Milk, Ink, Gold: Abundance and Excess in the French Renaissance* (Chicago: University of Chicago Press, 2005), 196–203.

37 For mythology in Renaissance poetry, Guy Demerson's study is still informative, in particular the chapter on Renaissance theories of the role of myth in poetry, *La mythologie classique dans l'œuvre lyrique de la Pléiade* (Geneva: Droz, 1972). See also Françoise Joukovsky, *Poésie et mythologie au XVIe siècle: Quelques mythes de l'inspiration chez les poètes de la Renaissance* (Paris: Nizet, 1969).

38 We find the same rhyme in sonnet 61, directly following this one. See Kennedy, *The Site of Petrarchism*, 138–9, for an analysis of the Du Bellay–Ronsard relationship in this sonnet.

39 'I find a weight that is not for my arms, a work not to be polished with my file […] Many times have I begun to write verses, but my pen and my hand and my intellect have been vanquished in the first assault.' Durling, ed., *Petrarch's Lyric Poems*, 54.

40 In the 1550 edition, this sonnet is number 59. Criticism has almost exclusively focused on this augmented edition. For a study of the specificity of the 1549 edition, see Michel Magnien, 'La première *Olive*,' in Campagnoli et al., eds., *'L'Olive' de Joachim Du Bellay*, 7–45.

41 Perhaps in rivalry with the confluence of the Rhône and the Saône in Scève's Lyon. Jerry Nash, in 'Mont côtoyant le Fleuve et la Cité: Scève, Lyons, and Love,' *French Review* 69 (1996): 943–54, has shown the extent to which the referential world of Scève's *Délie* is 'inextricably connected with Lyons, with its local landscape of two rivers and a mountain' (943). Nash also makes note of Du Bellay's association between Petrarch and the Arno, and Scève and the Rhône/Saône. For the importance of this confluence in Scève, and his sense of place more generally, see also Hodges, *Urban Poetics*, 77–102.

42 Tom Conley, *The Graphic Unconscious in Early Modern French Writing* (Cambridge: Cambridge University Press, 1992).

43 See Henri Weber, *La création poétique au XVIe siècle en France* (Paris: Nizet, 1955), 265–8.

44 Durling, ed., *Petrarch's Lyric Poems*, 264.

45 Op. cit., 266.

46 But see G. Hugo Tucker, *'Homo Viator': Itineraries of Exile, Displacement, and Writing in Renaissance Europe* (Geneva: Droz, 2003), for the important qualification that Petrarch's exiliary posture is finally liberating rather than punishing, in that it becomes the very vehicle of his poetic identity.

47 *Canzoniere* 248, in Durling, ed., *Petrarch's Lyric Poems*, 410–11. For a detailed reading of Du Bellay's sonnet in relation to Petrarch's, see DellaNeva, 'Illustrating the *Deffence*.'

48 Florence – Petrarch; Mantova – Virgil; Smyrna – Homer; Thebes – Pindar; Calabria – Horace; Touvre – Saint-Gelais; Seine – Héroet; Saone – Scève.

49 Ronsard, who had just published his *Odes*.

50 Athens – Demosthenes; Arpinum – Cicero; Mantua – Virgil; Smyrna – Homer; the two lyres – Greek and Latin lyric.

51 Durling, ed., 408. My emphasis.

52 See DellaNeva, 'Illustrating the *Deffence*,' 41, for an insightful discussion of the significance of the phrase 'digne objet' in Du Bellay's lyric project.

53 Charles Estienne, *La guide des chemins de France* (Paris, 1552), 4.

54 Cynthia Skenazi, 'Une pratique de la circulation: *La guide des chemins de France* de Charles Estienne,' *Romanic Review* 94 (2003): 153–66, pp. 154, 153, 162.

55 Estienne, *La guide*, pp. 112, 51–2.

56 Conley, *The Self-Made Map*, 237–43. (Carto)graphic descriptions of France's rivers took a lot longer to appear than verbal ones: the first fluvial map of France was not until 1643, the *Carte des rivières de la France* by Nicolas Sanson.

57 Symphorien Champier, *Petit traitté des fleuves et fontaines admirables desdites Gaules jadis composé par Messire Symphorien Champier, Chevallier, nouvellement traduit* […], translated by Claude Champier. The text was published in Lyon in 1556 with Gilles Corrozet's *Le bastiment des antiques erections des principales villes et citez* (Lyon, 1556). Conley misattributes this quote from Champier to Charles Estienne's *Guide* (*The Self-Made Map*, 336n. 24). For Corrozet's text and the enthusiasm for 'antiquités' as part of a national historiography, see Magali Vene, 'Les *Anticques erections des Gaules* de Corrozet,' *Journal de la Renaissance* 2 (2004): 101–6.

58 See W.H. Herendeen, 'Castara's Smiles ... Sabrin's Tears: Nature and Setting in Renaissance River Poems,' *Comparative Literature* 39 (1987): 289–305, for a comparative study of river poetry (which she identifies as a distinct poetic type in the Renaissance) from England, Italy, and France.

59 I do not consider Scève specifically as intertext here: for a reading of Scève as intertext in the *Olive*, see JoAnn DellaNeva, 'Du Bellay: Reader of Scève, Reader of Petrarch,' *Romanic Review* 79 (1988): 401–11; and Kennedy, *The Site of Petrarchism*, chap. 6.

60 For the images of flight in Du Bellay, in particular the failed flight of Icarus, emblem of Du Bellay's claimed modesty, compared with the glorious flight of the swan associated with Scève and Ronsard, see Peter Sharratt, 'Du Bellay and the Icarus Complex,' in *Myth and Legend in French Literature*, ed. Keith Aspley, David Bellos, and Peter Sharratt (London: Modern Humanities Research Association, 1982), 73–92.

61 *Deffence*, book 2, chap. 4. Richard Helgerson, *The Regrets* 375–7, trans. 374–6.

62 Lestringant, 'Chorographie et paysage à la Renaissance,' in *Écrire le monde à la Renaissance* (Caen: Paradigne, 1993), 50.

63 The relevant page from Apian is reproduced in Lestringant, 'Chorographie et paysage,' 65.

64 Ibid., 50.

65 See Hugo Tucker, 'Homo viator,' 239–67, for a cogent discussion of Du Bellay's pose of exile as a 'liminary space for writing and for the creation of an autonomous poetic identity' (241).

66 Gray, *La poétique de Du Bellay*, 165.

67 Marc Bizer proposes that the 'new poetics' of *Les Regrets* is due to Du Bellay's use of 'epistolary and secretarial traditions,' in 'Letters from Home: The Epistolary Aspects of Joachim Du Bellay's *Les Regrets*,' *Renaissance Quarterly* 52 (1999): 140–79, 141. Du Bellay's own definition of the epigram and the epistle in the *Deffence* as 'plaisans,' 'choses familieres et domestiques,' better describes the content of *Les Regrets* than his description of the ode or sonnet, which are included in the definition of lyric poetry: that recited or sung 'au son de la lyre grecque et romaine.' The ode, in particular, is considered a particularly weighty genre, 'éloigné du vulgaire.'

68 Note the semantic richness of the word 'accidents,' which a direct translation would not capture. The word in the sixteenth century had a philosophical connotation which is largely lost today; it was understood in opposition to the concept of 'universal,' and thus meant anything particular, specific, local. It also has a sense which is preserved in the modern French 'accidenté' referring to terrain and meaning rough, bumpy.

69 Although see Gilbert Gadoffre, *Du Bellay et le sacré* (Paris: Gallimard, 1978), which argues for the pervasiveness in all of Du Bellay's work of religious and theological concerns, whether humanist neo-Platonism, or politically engaged Gallicanism.

70 Tim Cresswell, *Place: An Introduction* (Oxford: Blackwell, 2004), 10.

71 On the complex contributions of pro- and anti-Italian sentiment to French cultural identity, see Jean Balsamo, *Les rencontres des Muses: Italianisme et anti-italianisme dans les lettres françaises de la fin du XVIe siècle* (Geneva: Slatkine, 1992). See Henry Heller, *Anti-Italianism in Sixteenth-Century France* (Toronto: University of Toronto Press, 2003), for a historical insight into how Italians in France were marginalized, and the collected essays in Lionello Sozzi, *Rome n'est plus Rome: La polémique anti-italienne et autres essais sur la Renaissance suivis de 'La dignité de l'homme'* (Paris: Champion, 2002).

72 See Eric MacPhail, *The Voyage to Rome in French Renaissance Literature* (Saratoga, CA: ANMA Libri, 1990), for a sustained discussion on Rome as a formative experience for the French aristocracy; see chap. 2 for Du Bellay's Roman experience and how disillusion shaped his poetic voice.

73 Marc Augé, *Non-lieux: Introduction à une anthropologie de la surmodernité* (Paris: Seuil, 1992).

74 For a sustained discussion on how space works to construct the poet's relationship with his country in this sonnet, see Hampton, *Literature and Nation in the Sixteenth Century: Inventing Renaissance France* (Ithaca: Cornell University Press, 2001), 171–7.

75 Timothy Hampton proposes that Du Bellay in the sonnet 'France mère des arts,' by citing Petrarch's description of Italy in his poem 'Ad Italiam,' sets himself up as the 'anti-Petrarch, as the figure who cannot return home' (*Literature and Nation*, 172). This particular intertextual point is well taken. However, I would propose that the attempt to present himself as the anti-Petrarch of 'Ad Italiam' (which certainly does subtend *Les Regrets*) ironically and necessarily turns him into the Petrarch of the *Canzoniere*.

76 The estate was on his mother's side. The family settled there in 1506, when Du Bellay's father married Renée Chabot, daughter of Christophe Chabot, the seigneur of Liré. The estate was a source of worry to the family: Du Bellay's older brother René had married Madeleine de Malestroict, from Oudon. When Madeleine's brothers were both condemned to death for murder, Oudon was confiscated. In 1532, René sold two parcels of family land in order to buy Oudon back on the urging of his wife. This acquisition gained him the hostility of the entire Malestroict family, leading to endless trials which exhausted the Du Bellay family's finances. Details from Gagneux, *Liré*, 33–4.

77 This sonnet, and the allusion to Ulysses and Jason in particular, has received much attention: for a summary, see G.H. Tucker, 'Ulysses and Jason: A Problem of Allusion in Sonnet XXXI of *Les Regrets*,' in *French Studies* 36 (1982): 385–96. Tucker offers possibly the fullest consideration to date of the dual allusion and the contradictions inherent therein, through close intertextual readings. He proposes that what is at stake in the dual allusion is the classical ironic literary attitude to voyage. Frank Lestringant has shown the range of writers who styled themselves as Ulysses and their homelands as smoking chimneys, in 'De *L'Olive* à la *Cosmographie*: Joachim Du Bellay et André Thevet,' in *Du Bellay: Actes du colloque internationale d'Angers*, 2 vols. (Angers: Presses de l'Université d'Angers, 1990), 1:103–18. Lestringant points out the rewriting of Du Bellay's 'Heureux qui comme Ulysse' by Thevet in the liminary sonnets to Thevet's *Cosmographie*, and also explores the limits and contradictions of this *rapprochement* of New World cosmographers and lyric poets.

78 Tucker, 'Ulysses and Jason,' provides ample intertextual evidence to prove that Du Bellay's 'beau voyage' was intended to be read as anything but. The happy return to the family is also to be read ironically. While Tucker provides detailed readings of classical intertexts to support his argument, he does not consider what actually happened on Du Bellay's return, which is my main concern here. For a reading of this sonnet which shows how classical and Italian references work here and in 'France mère des arts' to defamiliarize the French and make it foreign, see Richard Helgerson, 'Remembering, Forgetting, and the Founding of a National Literature: The Example of Joachim Du Bellay,' in *The Yearbook of Research in English and American Literature* 21 (2005): *Literature, Literary History, and Cultural Memory*, ed. Herbert Graves (Tübingen: Gunter Narr Verlag, 2005), 19–44.

79 *Odyssey*, 1.57–9.

80 *Aeneid*, 3.206.

81 My reading here is strongly influenced by Yvonne Bellenger's *Du Bellay: Ses 'Regrets.'*

82 Bellenger, *Du Bellay: Ses 'Regrets,'* 90 ff.; W.J.A Bots, *Joachim Du Bellay entre l'histoire littéraire et la stylistique* (Groningue: Van Denderen, 1970), 93 ff.

83 Louis Terreaux, '*Du Bellay et la douceur …*' [*sic*], in *Du Bellay: Actes du colloque internationale d'Angers*, 2 vols. (Angers: Presses de l'Université d'Angers, 1990), 2:641–51.

84 Kennedy, *The Site of Petrarchism*, chap. 6.

85 Parentheses added to Helgerson's translation to emphasize more specifically the sense of the French *metairies*. The sense of these last lines is more

figurative than literal: it is the draining of the *fortunes* of French estates towards Italy that Du Bellay is observing, rather than the houses themselves.

86 See Marc Bloch's *Les caractères originaux de l'histoire rurale française* (Oslo:
Aschehoug, 1931), chaps. 4–5, for the shifts in agricultural practice from
the late Middle Ages to the Revolution, which he characterizes as an
evolving revenue crisis for the *seigneurie*, due to the elimination or radical
restructuring of serfdom, and decline in the lord's judicial power. For
Bloch, sharecropping constitutes the single most dramatic event in French
social history, leading to stagnation of rural economies. Philip Hoffman argues that Bloch's view of sharecropping is too drastic, in 'The Economic
Theory of Sharecropping in Early Modern France,' *The Journal of Economic
History* 44 (1984): 309–19.

87 Marguerite de France (1523–74), Duchesse de Berry, who married the Duc
de Savoie in 1559. Not to be confused with the two other sixteenth-century
princesses named Marguerite: François I's sister Marguerite d'Angoulême
(or Navarre) (1492–1549), famous in literary history as the author of the
Héptaméron; and Marguerite de Valois (1553–1615), daughter of Henri II,
known popularly as the 'Reine Margot.' The Marguerite to whom Du Bellay addresses his praise was known as one of Ronsard's first promoters at
the royal court, and seems to have been as interested in the world of letters
as her more famous aunt, with whom she was close. Little has been published on her compared to her more famous homonyms, but see Roger
Peyre, *Une princesse de la Renaissance: Marguerite de France, duchesse de Berry,
duchesse de Savoie* (Paris: E. Paul, 1902).

88 See Marc Carnel, *Le sang embaumé des roses* (Geneva: Droz, 2004), 445.

89 Michael Screech, in rather a wishful conditional tense, suggests that they
were not written as part of *Les Regrets* (Joachim Du Bellay, *Les Regrets et autres œuvres poétiques*, ed. M. Screech and J. Jolliffe [Geneva: Droz, 1974]), 29:
'Nous placerions volontiers la fin des *Regrets* proprement dits au sonnet
130. Quelle belle fin ce serait!' Philippe Desan proposes that Du Bellay is
consciously highlighting some of the more cynical aspects of praise poetry
in 'De la poésie de circonstance à la satire: Du Bellay et l'engagement poétique,' in *Du Bellay: Actes du colloque internationale d'Angers*, 2:421–39.

90 The *princesse* of this sonnet is Catherine de' Medici, who was from
Florence.

91 The Dream of Scipio at the end of Cicero's *De republica*, for example. For a
study of the history of this cosmographic perspective in geographic texts,
in which it is argued that Renaissance geographers, too, considered this
Apollonian position as the one of greatest wisdom, see Denis Cosgrove,

Apollo's Eye: A Cartographic Genealogy of the Earth in the Western Imagination
(Baltimore: Johns Hopkins University Press, 2001).

92 Melin de Saint-Gelais, Jean Dorat, Étienne Jodelle, Pierre de Ronsard,
Gournay, Jean de Morel, Jacques Bouju, Forget, Philibert Duval, Buchanan, Pierre de Pascal, Peletier Du Mans.

93 It is worth recalling here Kennedy's insistence on the lateral relations between poets in *The Site of Petrarchism*. Du Bellay's flock of poets is an instantiation of the 'collective poetics' anticipated in the *Deffence* (Margaret
Ferguson, *Trials of Desire*, 18).

94 In Du Bellay, *Les Regrets*, ed. Screech and Jolliffe, 267.

95 This recalls David Harvey's insistence on the role of the imagination in
creating alternatives to the spaces we inhabit, an 'optimism of the intellect' which responds to what he sees as the agonistic impasse of Lefebvre's relational space (*Spaces of Hope* [Berkeley: University of California
Press, 2000], 7).

96 Marguerite de France was represented as Pallas/Minerva in a Limoges
enamel from 1555: see Suzanne Higgot and Isabelle Biron, 'Marguerite de
France as Minerva: A Sixteenth-Century Limoges Painted Enamel by Jean
de Court in the Wallace Collection,' *Apollo* 504 (2004): 21–30.

97 See Terence Cave's classic analysis of this opposition between the promise of plenty and the fear of its impossibility in *The Cornucopian Text: Problems of Writing in the French Renaissance* (Oxford: Oxford University Press,
1979).

98 Hassan Melehy, 'Du Bellay and the Space of Early Modern Culture,'
Neophilologus 84 (2000): 501–15, 501.

99 Margaret Ferguson, 'The Exile's Defense: Du Bellay's *La Deffence et illustration de la langue françoyse*,' *PMLA* 93 (1978): 275–89, 283.

100 The idea goes back to classical rhetoric, where the architectural metaphor
for writing and oratory is fully developed by Cicero, Quintilian, and the
anonymous *Rhetorica ad Herennium*. For detailed analyses of the architectural metaphors in classical rhetoric, with the emphasis on the use of
structural visualization techniques to improve the orator's memory, see
Frances Yates's *The Art of Memory* (Chicago: University of Chicago Press,
1966).

101 Although Ferguson argues that 'the architectural metaphor is most fully
developed in a negative context,' *Trials of Desire*, 45.

102 As pointed out in the last chapter, this passage in Du Bellay is an imitation of Virgil's praise of Italy in the *Georgics*.

103 The reference to the 'Gallogrecz' is an allusion to the Gallic invasion of
Greece in 279 B.C. The Gauls, chased from Delphi, fled north and some

ended up in Asia Minor, where they settled and bred, producing the Galatian nation.

104 Simon Schama, *Landscape and Memory* (New York: Knopf, 1995), 7.

4. The Poet and the Painter: Problems of Representation

1 For example, Savigny's 1587 *Tableaux accomplis de tous les arts*, a chart of the different fields of knowledge and their relationships (discussed in chap. 1), maintains this distinction.

2 For the biography of Denisot, also known by his anagram 'Le conte d'Alsinois,' see Roland Jousselin, *Nicolas Denisot: Poète de la Pléiade* (Paris: Christian, 2007). I will further discuss Clouet below.

3 See François Lecercle, *La chimère de Zeuxis: Portrait poétique et portrait peint en France et en Italie à la Renaissance* (Tübingen: Narr, 1987), which shows how the *paragone* affected Petrarchan poetry. For some useful distinctions and parallels between the painter's and the writer's vocabulary and conceptions of their work, see Francis Ames-Lewis, *The Intellectual Life of the Early Renaissance Artist* (New Haven: Yale University Press, 2000).

4 See Rensselaer Lee, *Ut pictura poesis: The Humanistic Theory of Painting* (New York: Norton, 1967), for an overview of this Renaissance trope; also Wesley Trimpi, 'The Meaning of Horace's *ut pictura poesis*,' *Journal of the Warburg and Courtauld Institutes* 36 (1973): 1–34, for discussion of the ways in which Horace's meaning has been misunderstood through time. For French Renaissance poetry, see Roberto Campo, 'Pictorial Concerns in the Ronsardian *Exegi monumentum*,' *Sixteenth-Century Journal* 24 (1993): 671–83, and his book *Ronsard's Contentious Sisters: The Paragone between Poetry and Painting in the Works of Pierre de Ronsard* (Chapel Hill: University of North Carolina Press, 1998); Campo argues that Ronsard did not accept the notion of parity, proposing, not without reservations, a tenuous superiority for the representational possibilities of poetry. See his chap. 1 for a good historical overview of the *paragone*; also Margaret McGowan, *Ideal Forms in the Age of Ronsard* (Berkeley: University of California Press, 1985), chap. 2.

5 In Francis Goyet, ed., *Traités de poétique et de rhétorique de la Renaissance* (Paris: Livre de Poche, 1990), 230–1, 131.

6 Pierre de Ronsard, *Abrégé de l'art poétique françois*, in *Œuvres complètes*, Bibliothèque de la Pléiade, 2 vols. (Paris: Gallimard, 1994), 2:1179–80, my emphasis. Subsequent references to Ronsard's works will provide page numbers from this edition in the text, and line numbers from long poems. See my chap. 2 for a discussion on the graphic and visual connotations of the word *description* in the sixteenth century.

7 The *Métamorphose figurée* was printed by Jean de Tournes in Lyon. The woodcuts are attributed to Bernard Salomon, a highly influential figure in book illustration. For Salomon, see Peter Sharratt, *Bernard Salomon: Illustrateur lyonnais* (Geneva: Droz, 2005). The authoritative study of Ovid in Renaissance France is Ann Moss, *Ovid in Renaissance France* (London: The Warburg Institute, 1982). A wonderful electronic resource for Renaissance editions of Ovid, including the 1557 *figurée*, can be found at the University of Virginia's E-Text Center; all resources are described and linked by Daniel Kinney and Elizabeth Styron at http://etext.lib.virginia.edu/latin/ovid/about.html: 'Ovid Illustrated: The Renaissance Reception of Ovid in Image and Text.'

8 Marcel Raymond, ed., *La poésie française et le maniérisme 1546–1610 (?)* (Geneva: Droz, 1971), 23.

9 *Ekphrasis* is usually defined as the poetic description of a work of art. Murray Krieger's 1967 article is often cited as seminal: 'The Ekphrastic Principle and the Still Movement of Poetry,' in *The Play and Place of Criticism* (Baltimore: Johns Hopkins University Press, 1967); see also his more recent book, *Ekphrasis: The Illusion of the Natural Sign* (Baltimore: Johns Hopkins University Press, 1992). But see Janice Hewlett Koelb, *The Poetics of Description* (New York: Palgrave, 2006), for an attempt to show that this exclusive definition is a twentieth-century error, and that 'the continuity of classical ecphrasis was assured not so much by art descriptions as by descriptions of significant places' (5).

10 For a good interdisciplinary study of the gallery (both art-historical and architectural), see Pierre Joukovsky and Françoise Joukovsky, *À travers la Galerie François I* (Paris: Champion, 1992).

11 The 'second wave' under Henri IV has significantly fewer foreign artists. The authoritative reference book on Fontainebleau Mannerism is Sylvie Beguin, *L'école de Fontainebleau: Le maniérisme à la cour de France* (Paris: Gonthier-Seghers, 1960).

12 Among critics who accept the term, Mannerist art is usually understood as that between Renaissance and Baroque, but ultimately, as John Shearman suggests, the term is only useful if each critic defines it anew: *Mannerism* (Baltimore: Penguin Books, 1967). Ernst Curtius sees it as a portable aesthetic category that reoccurs at the end of great eras, a principle of dissolution and self-conscious failure. Heinrich Wölfflin's dialectically constructed categories of Renaissance (order, calm, beauty) and Baroque (disorder, restlessness) have been instrumental in foregrounding a commitment to understanding a style by putting it 'within its general historical context,' *Renaissance and Baroque*, trans. Kathrin Simon (Ithaca: Cornell University

Press, 1964), 79. Some of what Wölfflin characterizes as Baroque is applied to Mannerism by others, but Wylie Sypher insists that the two are distinct, arguing that the tensions of Mannerism are resolved by the 'plenitude' of Baroque, in *Four Stages of Renaissance Style* (New York: Doubleday, 1955), 181. See Ernst Gombrich, 'Mannerism: The Historiographic Background,' in his *Norm and Form* (London: Phaidon, 1966), 99–106, for a reflection on the usefulness of the term as mediating between Renaissance and Baroque.

13 James Mirollo, *Mannerism and Renaissance Poetry: Concept, Mode, Inner Design* (New Haven: Yale University Press, 1984), 68. While he treats Italian and English texts, his approach is pertinent to French (Fontainebleau) Mannerism both because of its inherent flexibility, and because the style was so international, as Patricia Falguières shows in *Le maniérisme: Une avant-garde au XVIe siècle* (Paris: Gallimard, 2004). For a consideration of the adaptability of Mannerism to literary works from the French Renaissance, see Marcel Raymond's Introduction to his *La poésie française*.

14 John Shearman, *Mannerism* (Baltimore: Penguin, 1967), 35.

15 Shearman, *Mannerism*, 76; Sypher, *Four Stages*, 33.

16 Charles Sterling, *Le triomphe du maniérisme européen: De Michel-Ange au Greco*, Catalogue of exhibition 1 July–16 October 1955 (Amsterdam: Rijksmuseum, 1955), 27.

17 Raymond, *La poésie française*, 6, 20–1. Michel Jeanneret's major study of the theme of instability in Renaissance art and literature, *Perpetuum mobile: Métamorphoses des corps et des œuvres de Vinci à Montaigne* (Paris: Macula, 1997), passes over Mannerism rather summarily (p. 8). One concept developed by Raymond, which could have informed Jeanneret's project in particular, is that of the perpetual movement of the Mannerist subject (Raymond, *La poésie française*, 19–21).

18 Janet was the nickname for both the French Mannerist painter François Clouet (c. 1510–72) and his father Jean (1480–1541). For a study of both in historical context, see Jean Adhémar, *Les Clouet et la cour des rois de France* (Paris: Bibliothèque nationale, 1970). In an early article, 'Les arts et les artistes de la Renaissance française jugés par les écrivains du temps,' *Revue d'histoire littéraire de la France* 21 (1914): 481–502, Henri Plattard suggests that Ronsard's poem not only does not refer to any actual painting executed by François Clouet, but that its *descriptio* did not even correspond to Clouet's general style. Richard Sayce challenges Plattard's denial of a connection between Ronsard's elegy and Clouet's style, comparing specific traits of Ronsard's mistress with the Diana in the painting *Le bain de Diane* (1558–9) attributed to Clouet. Sayce stops short of claiming that Clouet's Diana is Ronsard's source, but insists that Ronsard shows 'affinities …

with Mannerist painting in general,' in 'Ronsard and Mannerism: The *Elégie a Janet,*' *Esprit Créateur* 6 (1966), 234–47, 247. Roberto Campo's *Ronsard's Contentious Sisters,* a meticulous study of Ronsard and the poetry–painting comparison (which he recasts more as a rivalry) contains a long section on the *Elégie* (169–98) and argues, convincingly, that it enacts Ronsard's uneasy preference for the variety of perspectives offered by poetry over painting.

19 Henri Zerner, *L'art de la Renaissance en France: L'invention du classicisme* (Paris: Flammarion, 1996), 124. On the other hand, Lucile M. Golson, in one of the very few studies of sixteenth-century French landscape art, sees the flourishing of landscape *gravures* as a bone fide 'contribution to the new European art of landscape in its very period of inception,' in 'Landscape Prints and Landscapists of the School of Fontainebleau, c. 1543–c. 1570,' *Gazette des beaux-arts* 73 (1969): 95–110, 95. I do not define or theorize landscape art here: for a view of landscape as a body of signs or a text to be read, see *Reading Landscape: Country–City–Capital,* ed. Simon Pugh (Manchester: Manchester University Press, 1990). A more politically oriented collection of essays on the transformation of nature into ideology is *Landscape and Power,* ed. W.J.T. Mitchell (Chicago: University of Chicago Press, 1994). One of the classic studies on Renaissance landscape is Ernst Gombrich's 1953 essay 'The Renaissance Theory of Art and the Rise of Landscape,' in *Norm and Form: Studies in the Art of the Renaissance* (London: Phaidon, 1966), 107–21. Kenneth Clarke popularizes Gombrich's school of thought in *Landscape into Art* (London: Beacon, 1956).

20 Robert Estienne, *Dictionaire francoislatin, autrement dict Les mots Francois avec les manieres duser diceulx, tournez en Latin* (Paris, 1549), 428. The documentary evidence for landscape decoration in various castles is summarized in Golson, 'Landscape Prints,' 101–3.

21 See Golson, 'Landscape Prints.'

22 M. Vasselin makes this point in 'L'antique et l'école de Fontainebleau,' in *Le paysage à la Renaissance,* ed. Yves Giraud (Fribourg: Éditions Universitaires Fribourg Suisse, 1988), 281–96, 282. Even the rustically themed etchings of Étienne Delaune, e.g., his *Allégorie des douze mois* (1568), which show peasants at work, do not name the landscape as French. One of the rare works to identify its landscape as French is the anonymous oil painting, the *Nymphe de Fontainebleau,* from the second half of the sixteenth century (in the New York Metropolitan Museum of Art). The imagery depicts the legendary origin of the name Fontainebleau: the forest of Bliaud, the name of the hound who discovered the spring, personified by a nymph. Benvenuto Cellini executed a bronze *Nymphe de Fontainebleau* (1542–3)

based on a now-lost fresco by Rosso; Cellini's work decorated the entrance to the château d'Anet. See Zerner, *L'art de la Renaissance*, chap. 4, for a discussion of Fontainebleau art in general and the nymph in particular; for Cellini's *Nymph*, see Katherine Marsengill, 'Identity Politics in Renaissance France: Cellini's *Nymph of Fontainebleau*,' *Athanor* 19 (2001): 35–41.

23 In a 1554 letter, published in *Les œuvres d'Étienne Pasquier*, 2 vols. (Amsterdam, 1723), 1:7. Further biographical details can be found in part 1 of Eva Kushner's comprehensive study, *Pontus de Tyard et son œuvre poétique* (Paris: Champion, 2001). His work has enjoyed a fairly sustained interest among *seiziémistes*, and we now have two good recent critical editions of his poetic works: *Œuvres complètes*, vol. 1, *Œuvres poétiques*, ed. Eva Kushner, Sylviane Bokdam, Gisèle Mathieu-Castellani et al. (Paris: Champion, 2004); also *Œuvres poétiques complètes*, ed. John C. Lapp (Paris: Dider, 1966).

24 See Heidi Marek, *Le mythe antique dans l'œuvre de Pontus de Tyard* (Paris: Champion, 2006), for a study that brings together the many fields of knowledge from which Tyard's poetry draws. Pages 257–308 deal with the *Douze fables*.

25 Page numbers for the *Fables* refer to the edition by Kushner, Mathieu-Castellani et al. English translations are my own.

26 Valérie Auclair, 'De l'invention à l'œuvre: Les *Douze fables de fleuves ou fontaines* de Pontus de Tyard,' *Bibliothèque d'humanisme et Renaissance* 68 (2006): 63–85. Pierre Roussel in the nineteenth century stated that the paintings did exist and that they were in the Salon des Glaces, to be replaced in the seventeenth century by mirrors (*Histoire et description du château d'Anet* [Paris: Jouaust, 1875], 58); Frances Yates thinks they ended up being tapestries, based on the mention in Tyard's will of some tapestries (*The French Academies of the Sixteenth Century* [London: Warburg Institute, 1947], 135–9); Eva Kushner thinks there is not sufficient evidence that the paintings were done (*Pontus de Tyard*, 315–16).

27 Kushner, *Pontus de Tyard*, 316.

28 Roberto Campo, 'Tyard's Graphic Metamorphoses: Figuring the Semiosic Drift in the *Douze fables de fleuves ou fontaines*,' *Renaissance Quarterly* 54 (2001): 776–800.

29 For the role of poets in particular around Anet, see Jean Balsamo, 'Les poètes d'Anet,' in *Henri II et les arts: Actes du colloque international, École du Louvre et Musée national de la Renaissance – Écouen, 25, 26, 27 septembre 1997*, ed. Hervé Oursel and Julia Fritsch (Paris: École du Louvre, 2003), 417–25. More generally, on the collaborations between poets and other artists, see Margaret McGowan, *Ideal Forms*; and on the many artistic media that came together for royal entry ceremonies, see the essays in *French Ceremonial*

Entries in the Sixteenth Century: Event, Image, Text, ed. Nicolas Russell and Hélène Visentin (Toronto: Centre for Reformation and Renaissance Studies, 2007).

30 The barking dogs of the twelfth fable, against which the *Lavatoire d'Isis* is said to protect, may refer to the automatic barking dogs at the entrance to the castle, themselves part of the iconography of Diana the huntress (Auclair, 'De l'invention à l'œuvre,' 77). On the iconography of Diane de Poitiers, see Françoise Bardon, *Diane de Poitiers et le mythe de Diane* (Paris: PUF, 1963).

31 The technical perspectival vocabulary, according to Auclair, is from a 1505 treatise by Jean Pélerin, *De artificiali perspectiva* (Auclair, 'De l'invention,' 81–5).

32 Marek, *Le mythe antique*, 261–8, details some of the Mannerist iconographic tradition behind Tyard's descriptions. Roberto Campo, 'Tyard's Graphic Metamorphoses,' argues that the Mannerist aesthetic of flux and instability in Tyard's descriptions witness to a philosophical anxiety about the difficulty of fixing meaning. Campo uses the term 'Mannerist' in a way that 'reconciles the aesthetic with the psychological' (798). For a semiotic definition of Mannerism applied to Renaissance poetry, see James Sacré, *Pour une définition sémiotique du maniérisme et du baroque: Des 'Sonnets pour Hélène' de Ronsard à 'La maison d'Astrée' de Tristan l'Hermite* (Besançon: Groupe de recherches sémio-linguistiques, École des hautes études en sciences sociales, Centre national de la recherche scientifique, 1979).

33 Campo, 'Tyard's Graphic Metamorphoses,' 784. For the idea of the fable as fiction, see Teresa Chevrolet, *L'idée de fable: Théories de la fiction poétique à la Renaissance* (Geneva: Droz, 2007).

34 *Metamorphoses*, 15.308–9. The passage, lines 307–34, lists examples of water changing form and virtue.

35 Classical sources include the pseudo-Plutarch's *De fluviorum montium nominibus*; Plutarch's *Lives*; Ovid's *Metamorphoses*; and Pausanias's *Description of Greece*.

36 Campo, 'Tyard's Graphic Metamorphoses,' 787.

37 The Champion series of Tyard's complete works, under the direction of Eva Kushner, has recently published this text for the first time since its original publication in 1603: *Œuvres complètes*, vol. 7, *La droite imposition des noms (De recta nominum impositione)*, ed. Jean Céard and Jean-Claude Margolin (Paris: Champion, 2007). For a study of this text as a contribution to the Cratylist debate, see Jean-Claude Margolin, 'À propos de l' "imposition" des noms propres chez Pontus de Tyard, extraits de l'histoire ou de la géographie: Cratylisme ou non-cratylisme?' in *Pontus de Tyard, poète*,

philosophe, théologien: Colloque international de l'Université Créteil-Val-de-Marne, 19–20 novembre 1998, ed. Sylviane Bokdam and Jean Céard (Paris: Champion, 2003), 357–69.

38 Pontus de Tyard, *Œuvres poétiques*, ed. Kushner et al., 615n. 34. The *Oxford Classical Dictionary* (3rd ed.) renders the name as 'beautifully flowing.' Lapp gives it as 'le beau ruisseau' [beautiful stream] (264n. 1). From the Greek *kallos* (beautiful) + the noun *rhoé* (flow, flux). Thanks to Douglas Machle for referring me to the *OCD* entry and for confirming the Greek.

39 The same conflation of Fontainebleau and Anet is marked at the latter's entrance, where Cellini's *Nymphe de Fontainebleau* was displayed.

40 Auclair, 'De l'invention à l'œuvre,' 73–4.

41 The fountain, attributed to Jean Goujon, is now in the Louvre.

42 Jan Miernowski, 'La Poésie et la peinture: Les *Douze fables de fleuves ou fontaines* de Pontus de Tyard,' *Réforme, Humanisme, Renaissance* 18 (1984): 12–22, suggests that Tyard's text provides a kind of supplement to the visual. Marek, *Le mythe antique*, 269–308, shows that Tyard may be referring, as well as to classical texts and Mannerist paintings, to Ficinian Neoplatonism, Dionysianism, and occult traditions of numerology and alchemy.

43 See J.T.D. Hall, 'Was Ronsard's *Bergerie* performed at Fontainebleau in 1564?' *Bibliothèque d'humanisme et Renaissance* 51 (1989): 301–9. According to Alice Hulubei, it was commissioned in 1565 by Catherine de' Medici on the occasion of her reconciliation with Elizabeth I of England (*L'églogue en France*, 489). Paul Laumonier thinks it was written in 1564 during the royal visit to Fontainebleau, where Ronsard himself was at that time, specifically for performance at a *fête royale*. In his edition of Ronsard, *Œuvres complètes* (Paris: Hachette, 1924), 13:75, Paul Laumonier has identified the characters as: Henri d'Orléans (the future Henri III); François d'Anjou, his youngest brother; Henri de Navarre (the future Henri IV); his wife Marguerite de Navarre; and Henri de Guise, who conspired against Henri III.

44 All references to Ronsard give the page number of the *Bibliothèque de la Pléiade* edition, followed by line numbers: Pierre de Ronsard, *Œuvres complètes*, ed. Jean Céard, Daniel Ménager, and Michel Simonin, 2 vols. (Paris: Gallimard, 1994).

45 The pastor and the sheep are of course also Christian images, which work with the pastoral images to reinforce the idea of France as the jewel of Christendom.

46 Luigi Monga, *Le genre pastoral au XVIe siècle: Sannazar et Belleau* (Paris: Éditions universitaires, 1974), 52. Monga's study provides a helpful history of the development of the pastoral in the French Renaissance; see also Alice Hulubei's monumental *L'églogue en France au XVIe siècle* (Geneva: Droz,

1938). Guy Demerson's introduction to his edition of the 1565 *Bergerie* provides a good overview (xii–xxi).

47 See my discussion of the pastoral mode in the Introduction and chap. 1, in which I follow theorizations by, e.g., Paul Alpers, which reveal pastoral's social complexity and its problematizing of the very gesture of idealized distance.

48 Harry Berger, *Second World and Green World: Studies in Renaissance Fiction Making* (Berkeley: University of California Press, 1988), 12, 43. This is similar, although couched in phenomenological rather than social/Marxist terms, to Harvey's 'space of hope,' discussed in the Introduction.

49 See Roberto Campo, 'Du miroir à la mémoire: Sur les jeux ecphrastiques dans *La Bergerie* de Remy Belleau,' *Nouvelle revue du seizième siècle* 20 (2002): 5–23, for a consideration of the tension between verbal and pictorial in Belleau's *ekphrases*. Campo proposes that Belleau illustrates the power of the former over the weakness of the latter. Similar arguments for the superiority of verbal representation over visual in Belleau can be found in Paul J. Smith, 'Remy Belleau et la peinture: Aspects du métadiscours poétique de la Pléiade,' in *Word and Image* 4 (1988): 331–7; and to a lesser extent, Josiane Rieu, '*La Bergerie* de Remy Belleau: Une 'fête' poétique à la gloire des Guises,' in *Le mécénat et l'influence des Guises: Actes du colloque organisé par le Centre de recherche sur la littérature de la Renaissance de l'Université de Reims et tenu à Joinville du 31 mai au 4 juin 1994*, ed. Yvonne Bellenger (Paris: Champion, 1997), 251–77. Aspects of the *paragone* debate certainly subtend Belleau's works of art, but I am proposing that verbal representation itself is problematized, in particular the traditional descriptive modes of pastoral.

50 Marie Madeleine Fontaine, 'Postface,' in Remy Belleau, *Œuvres Poétiques*, vol. 2, ed. Guy Demerson and Marie Madeleine Fontaine (Paris: Champion, 2001), 201.

51 See Sandor Eckhardt, *Remy Belleau, sa vie, sa Bergerie* (Geneva: Slatkine Reprints, 1969; reprint of Budapest 1917 edition), 54–61. Guy Demerson, in his recent edition of Belleau's works, argues that Belleau did not openly condemn the Reformation until the late 1560s: Remy Belleau, *Œuvres poétiques*, vol. 1, *Petites inventions–Odes d'Anacréon–Œuvres diverses* (1554–1561), ed. K. Cameron, G. Demerson, F. Joukovsky et al. (Paris: Champion, 1995), 17. Françoise Joukovsky mentions also that Belleau went against the opinion of the Guises in his 1559 praise of the treaty of Cateau-Cambrésis, in her introduction to Belleau's *Pièces diverses* contained in the same volume (203).

52 Remy Belleau, *Œuvres Poétiques*, vol. 2, *La Bergerie* (1565), ed. Guy Demerson and Marie Madeleine Fontaine (Paris: Champion, 1995), 3. All subsequent

references to the 1565 *Bergerie* will give page numbers for this edition. Translations are my own. Demerson's team has now edited the entire Belleau corpus in six volumes, all published by Champion, between 1995 and 2003. The 1572 *Bergerie* is contained in vol. 4 (2001): any references to the 1572 version will be to page numbers from this edition.

53 The 1560 *conspiration d'Amboise* was a Huguenot plot to dispose of François II and capture François de Guise and his brother. It was brutally punished when discovered. François de Guise, whose military exploits are celebrated by Belleau, was instrumental in seizing northern towns from the Huguenots. He was killed in the fight for Orléans in 1563.

54 Jean Braybrook, 'Space and Time in Remy Belleau's *Bergerie,' Bibliothèque d'humanisme et Renaissance* 57 (1995): 369–80. Braybrook argues that the *Bergerie* was composed as a kind of poetic therapy.

55 Belleau claims in his preface that it is a 'nouvelle façon d'escrire' (4) that has not yet been used in France: if he is merely referring to the *prosimetrum*, he is discounting the vernacular contributions of Jean Lemaire and Vauquelin de la Fresnaye. It may be that the novelty he identifies has more to do with the structural importance of *ekphrasis*. For an overview of the *prosimetrum* from antiquity through the Renaissance, see Nathalie Dauvois, *De la 'Satura' à la 'Bergerie': Le prosimètre pastoral en France et à la Renaissance et ses modèles* (Paris: Champion, 1998). See pp. 198–227 for discussion of Belleau's *Bergerie*. Jean Braybrook compares and contrasts the *Arcadia* and the *Bergerie* in 'Jacopo Sannazaro's *Arcadia* and Remy Belleau's *Bergerie,'* in *Reinventing the Past: Essays in Honour of Ann Moss* (Durham: University of Durham, 2003), 177–94.

56 See Françoise Joukovsky, 'La composition de la *Bergerie* de Remy Belleau,' in *La pastorale française de Remy Belleau à Victor Hugo*, ed. Alain Niderst (Paris: Centre d'étude et de recherche d'histoire des idées de la sensibilité, 1991), 15. Joukovsky, while she does acknowledge the fiction of the poetic Joinville, posits that this fiction is built as a testimony to 'l'existence paisible qu'il a connue à Joinville.' Jean Braybrook reads the *Bergerie* as an affectionate encomium to the family in 'Joinville, les Guises, et l'œuvre de Belleau,' in Bellenger, ed., *Le mécénat*, 233–49. In an important contribution to our understanding of the *Bergerie*, Josiane Rieu argues that it represents a poetic *fête*, a veritable genre to which all kinds of artists contribute, which celebrates the glory of powerful families, in 'La *Bergerie* de Remy Belleau.' There are indeed many praise poems in the *Bergerie* celebrating events and exploits by the Guise family, but I think that the idea of the Guises as 'princes modèles' (ibid., 267), is subtly questioned by what Belleau is doing with the pastoral mode. Rieu herself notes this 'interrogation

sur la valeur de la parole par rapport au prince' (271); I am here putting
more pressure on this move.

57 Doris Delacourcelle, *Le sentiment de l'art dans la 'Bergerie' de Remy Belleau*
(Oxford: Blackwell, 1945), 27–37. Joinville was destroyed during the
French Revolution, and there are few works that reconstitute it. Émile
Humblot's *Notre vieux Joinville: Son chateau d'autrefois* (Dijon: Éditions du
Raisin, 1928), is a valuable resource but it is hard to find; luckily Delacour-
celle provides a summary of it.

58 To take but one example, Primaticcio, the Italian painter who arrived at
Fontainebleau in 1532, best known for his *Galerie d'Ulysse* in the castle, was
also employed regularly by the Guise family, Belleau's patrons. Notably,
Primaticcio was commissioned by his wife Antoinette de Bourbon to draw
the plans for the Duke's *tombeau* in 1550, which Belleau describes in his
Bergerie. Many critics remark on the remarkable technical precision of Belleau's painterly vocabulary. See, e.g., Maurice Verdier's introduction to the
5-volume edition of Belleau's *Œuvres poétiques*, ed. Guy Demerson et al.
(Paris: Champion, 1995), vol. 1. See also Eckhardt, *Remy Belleau*, 191–206.

59 This neo-scepticism, so typical of Montaigne, perhaps witnesses to what
Jonathan Dewald identifies, in his important study of aristocracy, as 'an individualistic, skeptical, and in many ways anxious culture emerg[ing]
within a "society of orders."' *Aristocratic Experience and the Origins of Modern Culture* (Berkeley: University of California Press, 1993), 3.

60 Jean Braybrook, 'Space and Time,' argues that the *prosimetrum* structure allowed Belleau to cobble together pre-existing poems with the loose thread
of the prose tying them together. Counteracting the 'tendency to shapeless-
ness' of these fragments, however, she sees a 'framework that locates them
in a particular place and moment in time' (371). Belleau insists on the ordering of space and time as a palliative to the troubles of the civil war.

61 For a reproduction of the *Jugement*, see Zerner, *L'art de la Renaissance*, plate
243, p. 216. For the *Massacres*, see Sylvie Béguin, *L'école de Fontainebleau: Le
maniérisme à la cour de France* (Paris: Gonthier-Seghers, 1960), 89. Marcel
Raymond describes the Mannerist body thus: 'dont les attitudes, les gestes,
les formes allongées ou tordues […] varieront jusqu'à l'impossible,' *La
poésie française*, 19.

62 Notably in Michel Jeanneret, 'Les œuvres d'art dans la *Bergerie* de Belleau,'
Revue d'histoire littéraire de la France 70 (1970): 1–14. On the other hand,
Doris Delacourcelle, in the introduction to her edition, writes that she has
chosen the first *journée* because of its 'spontanéité charmante' (*Bergerie*, 17).
Françoise Joukovsky, 'La composition de la *Bergerie* de Belleau,' in *La Pas-
torale française de Remy Belleau à Victor Hugo*, ed. Alain Niderst (Paris:

Centre d'étude et de recherche d'histoire des idées de la sensibilité, 1991), argues that the 1565 *Bergerie* and the first *journée* of 1572 are organized by a Boccaccian structure. Josiane Rieu provides an elaborate ordering of the pieces of the first *journée* of 1572 along spatial, chronological, and thematic lines, particularly the theme of glory, in '*La Bergerie* de Remy Belleau.'

63 Raymond, *La poésie française*, 19, 25. In the ninth *Prosa* of the *Arcadia*, we find 'bright daylight was come, the rays of the sun appearing on the tops of the lofty mountains' (Jacopo Sannazaro, *Arcadia and Piscatorial Eclogues*, trans. Ralph Nash [Detroit: Wayne State University Press, 1966], 90). In Ovid, *Metamorphoses*, 4.81–2, 'The next morning had put out the starry beacons of the night, and the sun's rays had dried the frosty grass,' *Metamorphoses*, trans. Frank Justus Miller (Cambridge: Harvard University Press, 1966), 185.

64 Guy Demerson points out that Belleau's narrator here goes through the three stages of *ek-stasis* or 'ravissement' (*Œuvres*, 131).

65 Enamelling was a new technique in France. Bernard Palissy had seen Florentine enamel when in Italy, and had recreated the technique by himself around 1550.

66 Jacques Amyot anonymously published his translation of the Greek into French in 1559. Although not as immediately successful as his translation of Plutarch, published the same year, the long-term success and influence of this pastoral was considerable. See the series of three lectures by Giles Barber on the transmission of the tale from the Middle Ages through to the early twentieth century, *Daphnis and Chloe: The Markets and Metamorphoses of an Unknown Bestseller*, The Panizzi Lectures, 1988 (London: British Library, 1989), in particular the first essay, 'From Primavera to Fête champêtre.' For Belleau's borrowings from Longus, see Frank Lestringant, 'Les amours pastorales de Daphnis et Chloé: fortunes d'une traduction de J. Amyot,' in *Fortunes de Jacques Amyot: Actes du colloque international*, ed. M. Balard (Paris: Nizet, 1986), 237–57.

67 Longus's narrator makes explicit the preference for painted over natural beauty: 'No doubt the woods were beautiful, with many trees, flowers and streams [...] but the painting was even more precious, offering both a prodigious artistry and a love story,' Longus, *Pastorales*, trans. Jean-René Vieillefond (Paris: Belles Lettres, 1987), 1.

68 This was brought to my attention by Barber, *Daphnis and Chloe*, 10–11. The sketches are attributed to Dubois by Sylvie Béguin in *L'école de Fontainebleau*, ed. Béguin, Bertrand Jestaz, and Jacques Thirion (Paris: Éditions des Musées Nationaux, 1972). See also the reproduction of 'Daphnis et Chloé épiés par Lycénion' in this volume, plate 89.

69 For a reproduction of this painting, see *L'école de Fontainebleau*, ed. Sylvie Béguin et al., plate 61.

70 The idea of a representation so closely resembling a naturally created landscape as to cause confusion can be found, among others, in Bernard Palissy's blueprint for a garden in his *Recepte veritable*, ed. Keith Cameron (Geneva: Droz, 1988). Michel de Montaigne appreciates this aesthetic in his travels to Italy. This is of course prior to the age of the classical French garden, whose guiding aesthetic, in service of a symbolism of royal power, was the display of a high degree of human control over nature. Sixteenth-century France had adopted Italy's taste for gardens that appear almost disconcertingly wild, and that serve less as a reassuring reminder of royal power than as reminders – through ruins, grottos, and rebuses – of human finitude. See Jean Lauxerois, 'Le jardin de la mélancolie,' in Philippe Nys and Monique Mosser, eds., *Le jardin: Art et lieu de mémoire* (Besançon: Éditions de l'imprimeur, 1995), 87–104, for a discussion of the Renaissance garden as a rhetorical site which reminds us, through allegory, of mortality and of our inscription in time. For a consideration of 'naïveté' as a writing style, see Giselle Mathieu-Castellani, '"Simplement" ou "Naivement Écrire": La question du style au XVIe siècle en France,' *Rivista di letterature moderne e comparate* 52 (1999): 213–27.

71 The tree-carvings that grow in size as the trees do is found in Virgil's Tenth Eclogue, line 54. For a fuller discussion of tree-carvings in pastoral, see Rensselaer W. Lee, *Names on Trees: Ariosto into Art* (Princeton: Princeton University Press, 1977), which contains a brief history of the topos before his discussion of the pictorial transmission of Ariosto's nineteenth canto.

72 Belleau's Arcadian Charles IX does appear to be an echo of Ronsard's in his *Bergerie*. Belleau will later include actual verses from his friend's *Bergerie* in his own.

73 However, the wind that carries things away is reminiscent of medieval lyrics, notably of François Villon's 'Ballade en vieil langage françoys,' often read as a lament on the decline of language and thus of poetry, and whose refrain is 'Autant en emporte ly vens.' See also Rutebeuf's *La complainte Rutebeuf*, where the poet's friends are 'amis que vent emporte,' and *La grièche d'hiver*, where the wind is associated with the poet's Villonesque impoverishment, 'Le vent me vient, le vent m'évente.' Toinet's words evoke a certain type of lyric melancholia, an *ubi sunt* lamentation, through this medieval trope.

74 Delacourcelle cites an extract from the Duke's Testament, reproduced in René de Bouillé, *Histoire des ducs de Guise* (Paris: Amyot, 1849–50), 2:582: 'quant aux trophées des victoires qu'il a eues et faicts d'armes par luy

exploictez pour les justes querelles des Roys ses seigneurs et princes naturels, il désire qu'elles soient peinctes ou engravées en la grande salle
dudict Joinville' (*Le sentiment*, 31).

75 Michel Jeanneret, 'Les œuvres d'art dans la *Bergerie* de Belleau,' *Revue
d'histoire littéraire de la France* 70 (1970): 1–14, 5. The transposition from narrative to plastic and back again is, for Jeanneret, the key to the whole
work: the objects described only take on meaning in relationship to the
text as a whole.

76 The 1565 edition gives a few lines from the *Chant pastoral de la paix*, which
the narrator cuts off, saying that 'le berger ne les retint en son cerveau ou
qu'il n'eut le loisir de les achever' [the shepherd didn't remember them, or
wasn't able to finish]. In the 1572 edition, the *Chant pastoral de la paix* as we
have seen is reproduced elsewhere in its entirety, and the poems given
here are rather longer, *Avril* and *May*, with no apology for them being unfinished. The 1572 edition thus seems to fill in at least some of the holes
left in 1565, as suggested by Josiane Rieu, 'La *Bergerie* de Remy Belleau.'

77 This, too, is presented in the 1565 edition as being unfinished: 'croy qu'il
doit avoir quelque autre suitte mais elle n'est pas là' [I think there must be
something else, but it is missing]. In 1572, the 'suitte' is there in the form of a
much-expanded version of the poem, which again pushes the boundaries of
what we can believe about what can be woven into the edges of a tapestry.
Again, the second edition finishes what the first quite self-consciously left
incomplete.

78 Belleau's poem is distinctly reminiscent, again, of *Daphnis et Chloé* (1.23.1).
Like most of Belleau's imitations from classical sources, this has a distinctly visual feel.

79 The shepherd-girls probably represent the young girls of the family, most
of whom were raised by Antoinette, along with some young women who
were sent to Joinville to perfect their education under the tutelage of Antoinette, who had the reputation of great wisdom and virtue.

80 For reproductions of Primaticcio's drawings, as well as the remaining fragments of the tomb carved by Domenico Barbiere, see Béguin et al., *L'école
de Fontainebleau*, plates 515–17.

81 Delacourcelle, *Le sentiment*, 64.

82 Jean Braybrook, 'Space and Time,' pays particular attention to the function
of time in the *Bergerie*: she proposes that it functions as an *ars memoriae* to
the Guise. For a broad thesis on the development of temporality in literature from the Middle Ages through the Renaissance, which proposes that
notions of time in the Renaissance become increasingly secularized and
detached from Christian teleologies, see Miha Pintarič, *Le sentiment du*

temps dans la littérature française: XIIe s.–fin du XVIe s. (Paris: Champion, 2002).

83 In the 1572 edition, the voice of Ronsard is distanced somewhat; he is speaking not as himself but as an allegorical 'Pierrot' ventriloquized by Belleau's narrator, and he is not reciting his own *Bergerie*. Despite this change, Belleau is still careful to keep the fact that it is Ronsard who is cut off by the clock.

84 The question of perspective, termed a 'machine à regarder le paysage' by Anna Cauquelin in *L'invention du paysage* (Paris: Plon, 1989), 67, is of course a crucial development in visual landscape representation. It had become a standard mode of representing space in Renaissance painting, rediscovered by Brunelleschi and Donatello, and theorized by Alberti in *Della pittura* (1435). Alberti's was a system based on the notion of visual pyramids, borrowing from geometry. For the geometric basis of perspective, see J.V. Field, *The Invention of Infinity: Mathematics and Art in the Renaissance* (Oxford: Oxford University Press, 1997). For a summary of different kinds of perspective, see Wylie Sypher, *Four Stages*, 28–9.

85 Delacourcelle does not mention this episode, and even if there were a source painting for this description, the point is not, as Jeanneret reminds us, simply to locate the source. Jeanneret concludes: 'La recherche des sources plastiques ne résout pas grand-chose et l'explication réaliste néglige l'essentiel' (*Les œuvres d'art*, 13). For this particular painting, there is no direct source as far as we know. However the detail of the painting makes it sound most like the chorographic sketch 'Plan de Ville de Joinville' in Belleforest's 1575 *Cosmographie universelle* (reproduced in Delacourcelle, *Le sentiment*, plate 3). Published after Belleau's *Bergerie*, it is unlikely to have been a direct source, but is important in establishing the existence of a type of pictorial representation of castles and their grounds. The pursuit of Chastity through the woods reminds one perhaps of Diana espied, a favoured theme of Fontainebleau painters, e.g., François Clouet's *Le bain de Diane* (see Zerner, *L'art de la Renaissance*, 204, for a reproduction).

86 One thinks in particular of the portraits and nudes of François Clouet, e.g., *La dame au bain* (c. 1570), in which the female body is represented with no muscle tone or visible bone structure. See Henri Zerner, *L'art*, chap. 2.

87 For discussion of Ronsard's *Elégie*, see p. 90 and n. 18, above. The Anacreontic sources are the odes XVI and XVII, 'To a Maid' and 'To Bathyllus' (*The Odes of Anacreaon*, trans. Erastus Richardson [New Haven: Yale University Press, 1928], 18–21).

88 See Campo, 'Du miroir,' who argues that the length of the description, and the fact that the mirror as described is virtually impossible to imagine

visually, pleads in favour of the rhetorical power of words. Guy Demerson, in the Preface to Remy Belleau, *Œuvres*, ed. Demerson, 4:xxxi–xxxv, argues, following Paul J. Smith, that the mirror is the centrepiece of the whole *Bergerie*, as it encapsulates in precious style the themes of poetry: love, death, nature, and war.

89 The river Huisne, in Belleau's natal region of Perche. Note that the marketplace allows for the inclusion of characters from outside the vicinity of the Joinville castle, an anticipation of a national economy that transcends the exclusivity of the local.

90 See Braybrook, 'Space and Time,' 371–2, for discussion of this object. She proposes that its ability to measure space and time is central to the work, as it counters the chaos of history with neat images of order. This is similar to Guy Démerson's more general argument that the ornamental in Belleau substitutes 'un monde harmonieux à l'immonde chaos des apparences,' 'Remy Belleau et la naissance du monde,' in *La naissance du monde et l'invention du poème: Mélanges de poétique et d'histoire littéraire du XVIe siècle offerts à Yvonne Bellenger*, ed. Jean-Claude Ternaux (Paris: Champion, 1998), 193–215, 201.

91 Ronsard had described originary poetry as a 'théologie allégoricque' in his *Abrégé de l'art poétique* of 1565. (*Œuvres complètes*, 2:1175). Although there are differences between the poets, the teleology of most scientific poetry can generally said to be Christian-eschatological, epitomized by Du Bartas's invocation at the start of *La sepmaine*: 'O grand Dieu, donne-moy que j'estale en mes vers / Les plus rares beautez de ce grand univers. / Donne-moy qu'en son front ta puissance je lise / Et qu'enseignant autruy, moy-mesme je m'instruise' (9–12). For the genre of scientific poetry, see the classic study of Albert-Marie Schmidt, *La poésie scientifique en France au seizième siècle* (Paris: Albin Michel, 1938); and Isabelle Pantin, *La poésie du ciel en France dans la seconde moitié du seizième siècle* (Geneva: Droz, 1995).

92 Dudley Wilson, *French Renaissance Scientific Poetry* (London: Athlone, 1974). Even Albert-Marie Schmidt, author of the only book-length study of the genre before 1995, *La poésie scientifique en France au seizième siècle* (1938), does not give a definition.

93 Wilson, *French Renaissance Scientific Poetry*, 151n. 3. Among the works generally considered as scientific poetry are Jacques Peletier du Mans's *L'Amour des amours* (1555), Ronsard's *Hymnes* (1555–6), Maurice Scève's *Microcosme* (1562), Baïf's *Premier des météores* (1567), Guy Lefebvre de la Boderie's *L'Enciclie des secrets de l'éternité* (1571), Remy Belleau's *Amours et nouveaux eschanges des pierres précieuses* (1576), Guillaume du Bartas's *Premiere* and *Seconde sepmaine* (1578, 1585).

94 For a good introduction to Belleau's exegetical purpose in his *Pierres*, see Jean Braybrook, 'Science and Myth in the Poetry of Remy Belleau,' *Renaissance Studies* 5 (1991): 277–87.

95 Lorraine Daston and Katharine Park have shown that wonder and scientific enquiry significantly overlapped and shaped each other in early modern epistemologies, in their authoritative interdisciplinary study *Wonders and Order of Nature: 1150–1750* (New York: Zone Books, 1998). See also Brian Vickers's introduction to *Occult and Scientific Mentalities in the Renaissance* (Cambridge: Cambridge University Press, 1984), where he argues that Renaissance scientists were able to operate within traditions that later became incompatible.

96 For this theme in Renaissance writing, see Michel Jeanneret, *Perpetuum mobile*. Jeanneret does not consider Belleau in this study, but his book is a useful compendium of the themes of change, form, and matter, a testimony to a period 'plus sensible a l'émergence de la force qu'à la rigeur de la forme' (5). Of particular note here is his reminder that 'la sensibilité métaphorique prêtée au baroque est déjà largement répandue de 1480 à 1600' (10), although he specifically rejects discussion of Mannerism, which would seem to be the most useful category for pre-baroque sensibilities.

97 Maurice Verdier, Introduction to Remy Belleau, *Pierres précieuses*, ed. Verdier, 42.

98 Françoise Joukovsky, 'La composition de la *Bergerie* de Remy Belleau,' in *La Pastorale française de Remy Belleau à Victor Hugo*, ed. Alain Niderst (Paris: Centre d'étude et de recherche d'histoire des idées de la sensibilité, 1991), 9–22, 19.

99 Michel Jeanneret, 'Les œuvres d'art,' 9.

100 Monga, *Le genre pastoral*, 24.

101 Campo, 'Tyard's Graphic Metamorphoses,' 796.

102 Josiane Rieu, 'La temporalisation de l'espace dans la peinture française du XVIe siècle,' in Giraud, ed., *Le paysage*, 297.

5. The Poet and the Environment: Naturalizing Conservative Nostalgia

1 Arcueil, now in the commune of Cachan, derives its name from the Latin for arches, *arculi*. For historical details about Arcueil and the Bièvre, see the *Dictionnaire géographique et administratif de la France et de ses colonies*, dir. Adolphe Joanne (Paris: Hachette, 1890–1905), 1:446–7.

2 Charles Estienne, *La guide des chemins de France* (Paris, 1553), 226.

3 For a history of the Gobelin family, see J. Guiffrey, 'Les Gobelin, teinturiers en écarlate,' in *Mémoires de la Société de l'histoire de Paris* 31 (1904): 1–92.

Guiffrey includes the *arrêt* as a *pièce justificative* in an appendix. It was not until the seventeenth century that the Manufacture des Gobelins became associated with tapestry: in 1662, Colbert grouped all the royal artisans together in one place, including silversmiths and furniture makers, and by the end of the century the Manufacture was specializing in tapestry.

4 For details of sixteenth-century French poets' representations of Arcueil, and a French translation of Dorat's ode to the fountain, 'Ad fontem Arculli sive Herculei,' see Antoine Desguine, *Arcueil et les poètes du XVIe siècle: La vigne, le vin et la tradition bachique à Arcueil-Cachan* (Paris: Champion, c. 1950).

5 The full title was 'Les Bacchanales ou le folastrissime voyage d'Hercueil pres Paris, dedié à la joyeuse trouppe de ses compaignons. Fait en l'an 1549.' It appeared first in the *Cinquième livre des odes* and then was included in the *Second livre des poèmes* (1560) under the title 'Le voyage d'Hercueil.' The poets mentioned are Ronsard, Baïf, Du Bellay, Dorat, Denisot, and a minor figure, Bertrand Berger, whose fortuitously pastoral name Ronsard particularly appreciated. See V.-L. Saulnier, 'Des vers inconnus de Bertrand Berger et les relations du poète avec Dorat et Du Bellay,' *Bibliothèque d'humanisme et Renaissance* 19 (1957): 245–51.

6 See Desguine, *Arcueil*, 31, 60. A certain Jean Macer also published a pamphlet *Phillippique de Jean Macer contre les poetastres et rimailleurs francois de nostre temps* (Paris, 1557). Ronsard defended himself against Grévin and Macer in his 1563 *Responses aux injures*. On the *Phillippique*, see Marcel Raymond, 'Deux pamphlets inconnus contre Ronsard et la Pléiade,' *Revue du seizième siècle* 13 (1926): 234–64. For the Pléiade's pagan practices and poetics, see Guy Demerson, *La mythologie classique dans l'œuvre lyrique de la Pléiade* (Geneva: Droz, 1972), chap. 1; for the question of the *Pompe du bouc* in particular, see Jean-Antoine de Baïf, *Œuvres en rime, première partie: Neuf livres des poemes*, ed. Jean Vignes, Guy Demerson et al. (Paris: Champion, 2002), 776–81. Vignes's edition, the first volume of a projected complete works, is the most recent and authoritative of Baïf's *Neuf livres*. I will refer to this edition subsequently as *Œuvres*.

7 Ronsard's 'Dithyrambes à la pompe du bouc de Jodelle' first appeared in his 1553 *Livret de folastries*. Baïf's poem of the same title was published in 1573 but probably written before Ronsard's. For a summary of the debate about who imitated whom, see the notes to *Œuvres*, 777. The text of Baïf's 'Dithyrambes' starts on p. 294 of this edition.

8 See Isidore Silver, *Ronsard and the Hellenic Renaissance in France* (St Louis: Washington University, 1961); Kenneth Lloyd-Jones, 'The Humanist *Apologia* for Hellenism in the French Renaissance,' *Romance Languages Annual* 3 (1992): 72–7.

9 French historiographers and royal iconographers alike made much of the figure of Hercules, with whom François I in particular was associated. See Marc Jung, *Hercule dans la littérature française du seizième siècle* (Geneva: Droz, 1966).

10 Yvonne Roberts convincingly makes this argument in *Jean-Antoine de Baïf and the Valois Court* (Oxford: Lang, 2000). See also Vignes, ed., *Œuvres*, 25–6.

11 The nine books of *Poemes* constituted the first volume of Baïf's *Œuvres en rime*. They are contained in Vignes, ed., *Œuvres*. Elizabeth Vinestock has reckoned the date of composition to be between 1569 and 1572, in 'Myth and Environmentalism in a Renaissance Poem: Jean-Antoine de Baïf's *La ninfe Bievre*,' *New Comparison* 27–28 (1999): 22–33, 23n3.

12 Vinestock, 'Myth and Environmentalism,' 24. Jean Gobelin, it seems, had been accused of making a pact with the devil, a legend to which his name and the scarlet colour of the dye lent themselves (Guiffrey, *Les Gobelin*, 7–8).

13 *Œuvres*, 501, line 2. From here on, I will give line numbers directly after the citation. For Brulart, see Nicola Mary Sutherland, *The French Secretaries of State in the Age of Catherine de Medici* (Chicago: University of Chicago Press, 1962), 172–4. Baïf wrote a second polemical poem to Brulart in his *Poemes*. For analyses of both, see Elizabeth Vinestock, *Poétique et pratique dans les 'Poemes' de Jean-Antoine de Baïf* (Paris: Champion, 2006); and idem, '"J'ose attaquer les plus mutins": Baïf's Poetical and Rhetorical Means of Engaging in Conflict,' in *Writers in Conflict in Sixteenth-Century France: Essays in Honour of Malcolm Quainton*, ed. Elizabeth Vinestock and David Foster (Durham: Durham Modern Language Series, 2006), 103–25.

14 Around Glacière, the Bièvre divided into the *Rivière de Bièvre* and the *Rigole des Gobelins*, which united again at the rue Mouffetard.

15 Vinestock, 'Myth and Environmentalism,' 25.

16 See my discussion in chap. 4 of Cratylism – the notion that there is an essential relation between signifier and signified – in Pontus de Tyard, who is more cynical about it than Baïf is here.

17 From Auden's 'In Memory of W.B. Yeats': 'For poetry makes nothing happen: it survives.' See my discussion of the end of Du Bellay's *Regrets* in chap. 3.

18 Gaston Bachelard, *La poétique de l'espace* (Paris: PUF, 1957), 172. Gaston Roupnel consecrates an entire chapter to the forest, which like his other rural spaces is heavily invested with topophilia: *Histoire de la campagne française* (1932 ; Paris: Plon, 1974), chap. 3.

19 The odes *À sa lyre*, 'Lyre dorée, ou Phoebus seulement,' in Pierre de Ronsard, *Œuvres complètes* (Paris: Gallimard, 1993), 1:676–8; *O terre fortunée*, 'Des-Autels, qui redore,' 1:699–700; *À la forest de Gastine*, 'Couché sous tes

ombrages vers,' 1:703–4; ode to Gaspar d'Auvergne, 'Gaspard, qui loing de Peguse' (a transposition of Horace 1.31), 1:782–3; *À son lut*, 'Si autre-fois sous l'ombre de Gastine,' 1:962–5; the sonnets 'Ciel, air et vents,' 1:7–8; 'Je te hay peuple,' 1:87–8; 'Saincte Gastine, o douce secretaire,' 1:111; 'Que Gastine ait tout le chef jaunissant,' 1:491; and the 'Voyage de Tours,' 1:204–11. For references to shorter poems, I give incipits or titles, as well as the page numbers for the Pléiade edition, rather than the number of a particular poem or even, in certain cases, the name of the collection in which it appears. Ronsard regularly reorganized his entire corpus, shifting poems from one collection to another, cutting them entirely from new editions, reorganizing the order within a collection, or adding new material. This makes the task of editing Ronsard an unenviable one. It also renders virtually redundant many designations of poems – especially the earlier works – by number and collection. For the sustained discussion of the twenty-fourth elegy, however, I will use the title *Élégie XXIIII*.

20 At least, in the ordering of the 1584 *Œuvres* which we are following here. I follow the editors of the Pléiade volumes, who give the ordering of the 1584 *Œuvres* since it was the last edition supervised by Ronsard himself.

21 For an extensive study of the image of the lyre in Ronsard, see Isidore Silver, *Ronsard and the Grecian Lyre* (Geneva: Droz, 1981). For the theme of glory in French Renaissance poetry, see Françoise Joukovsky, *La gloire dans la poésie française et néolatine du XVIe siècle: Des rhétoriqueurs à Agrippa d'Aubigné* (Geneva: Droz, 1969); with respect to Ronsard, see in particular pp. 204–14, and for the theme of glory inscribed in landscape, pp. 323–64.

22 For exact borrowings, see the notes to the Pléiade *Œuvres*, 1515.

23 'O golden lyre, that art owned alike by Apollo and by the violet-tressed Muses! thou lyre, which the footstep heareth, as it beginneth the gladsome dance; lyre, whose notes the singers obey, whenever, with thy quivering strings, thou preparest to strike up the prelude of the choir-leading overture!' Pindar, *Odes*, trans. J.E. Sandys (Cambridge, MA: Harvard University Press, 1915), 1.

24 H.M. Richmond compares Ronsard's affirmation of local identity with Clément Marot's abandoning of his, in *Renaissance Landscapes: English Lyrics in a European Tradition* (The Hague: Mouton, 1973), chap. 2.

25 See chap. 2 for this distinction in the Renaissance, and chap. 3 for its poetic implications in Du Bellay.

26 *Odes*, 4.3.10–12. In Horace, *Odes and Epodes*, ed. and trans. Niall Rudd (Cambridge, MA: Harvard University Press, 2004), 226–7. The ode contrasts sporting achievement with the superior glory of being known as a poet. Interestingly, it comes right after a long encomiastic ode to Pindar,

the 'sports poet' of the Greeks. The lines Ronsard imitates are: 'But the waters that flow past fertile Tiber, and the thick foliage of the woods, will shape him for fame in Aeolian song' [Sed quae Tibur aquae fertile praefluunt, / Et spissae nemorum comae / Fingent Aeolio carmine nobilem] (10–13). Translations from Horace are Rudd's.

27 Ibid., lines 21–4. [Totum muneris hoc tui est, / Quod monstror digito praetereuntium / Romanae fidicen lyrae: / Quod spiro et placeo, si placeo, tuum est.] This itself seems to be a transformation of the image of the lyric poet being pointed out and laughed at in public places for his unrequited love for a woman. There is some interesting work to be done on such moments of public recognition in lyric.

28 It appeared in the first edition of the *Quatre premiers livres des Odes* (1550). The original text was substantially different from Ronsard's rewrite, which appeared in all editions after 1555. However, the contrast I discuss is operative in both versions of this particular ode, suggesting that it was structurally and thematically important enough for Ronsard to have kept it despite other significant changes.

29 Erymanthus: a mountain in Arcadia, a supposed haunt of Diana.

30 Horace, *Odes*, 1.21.

31 'Praise, you girls, her who delights in rivers and the leafy groves that stand out boldly on cold Algidus or in the dark woods of Erymanthus or verdant Cragus / […] / He (Apollo) will drive away mournful warfare, he will drive away wretched famine and plague from our people and Caesar, our leader.' [Vos laetam fluviis et nemorum coma / Quaecumque aut gelido prominet Algido, / Nigris aut Erymanthi / Silvis aut viridis Cragi. / … / Hic bellum lacrimosum, hic miseram famen / Pestemque a populo et principe Caesare.] Ibid., lines 5–14.

32 Roberto M. Dainotto, *Place in Literature: Regions, Cultures, Communities* (Ithaca and London: Cornell University Press, 2000), 173, 11. Dainotto's introduction offers a comprehensive survey of the nationalist/regionalist debate, including ways in which these terms have been used, or not, by Marxist and postcolonial critics. He understands the region as contiguous to Derridean *différance*: 'because the region *is* not, it always defers itself to a hypothetical future that is the coming back of an original past – the realization, in other words, of what was always supposed to be' (11). I put more interpretive weight on the category of the region as an interpretive key in my article, '"Ce ne sont pas des bois": Poetry, Regionalism, and Loss in Ronsard's Gâtine Forest,' *Journal of Medieval and Early Modern Studies* 32 (2002): 343–74.

33 The last lines of 'A son retour de Gascongne voiant de loin Paris,' published in the 1550 *Bocage*. Like his classical and Italian lyric models, Ronsard usually made this promise of eternal fame to women, as in the sonnet
'A fin qu'à tout jamais,' where he tells Hélène 'You will live, believe me,
equal to Laura in reputation / For as long as there are pens and books'
(*Second livre des sonnets pour Hélène*, II). There is a particular fluidity, in
Ronsard, between women and landscape. For a reading of the ways in
which Ronsard transfers traditional epithets of lyric praise for a woman's
body onto landscape, see Thomas Greene, *The Light in Troy* (New Haven:
Yale University Press, 1982), 201–13.

34 This sonnet first appeared in the *Bocage* of 1554; in 1584, it concludes the
Second livre des Amours de Marie.

35 Françoise Joukovsky has linked the constantly shifting landscapes to the
construction of the poet's interior 'moi esthétique'; they exist primarily to
glorify the poet's own power of invention, constituting a Mallarmean 'autonomous whole' which is about nothing more and nothing less than itself:
'this reduced nature ... is in fact an autonomous whole that creates its own
space ... The landscape thus displays the self-sufficiency of the work of
art, a world turned in on itself.' 'Qu'est-ce qu'un paysage?' in Yves Giraud,
ed., *Le paysage à la Renaissance* (Fribourg: Éditions Universitaires Fribourg
Suisse, 1988), 66.

36 Edmond Rocher, *Pierre de Ronsard, prince des poètes* (Paris: PUF, 1924), 29.

37 I have chosen to avoid using 'capitalism' or even 'proto-capitalism': however, Philippe Desan and others have identified an 'élan du capitalisme à
la Renaissance' and a 'mentalité capitaliste' focused on profit, which were
supported by changing economic and trade structures. See Philippe Desan,
L'imaginaire économique à la Renaissance (Mont-de-Marsan: Éditions Inter-
Universitaires, 1993), 26. See Desan's first chapter for a general overview
of Renaissance France's economy. For a study of the material aspects of
Renaissance economies, see Fernand Braudel, *Civilisation matérielle, économie et capitalisme: Xve-XVIe siècle*, 3 vols. (Paris: Armand Colin, 1979).

38 The idea of a redemptive design in the natural order has been discussed
with reference to Sidney and Shakespeare by Eric LaGuardia in *Nature Redeemed* (The Hague: Mouton, 1966).

39 The forest was sold in small parcels, and the sale took a long time. The details of the sale can be found in R. Caisso's article, 'La vente de la forêt de
Gâtine au temps de Ronsard,' *Humanisme et Renaissance* 4 (1937): 274–85.

40 This is, for example, Caisso's reading, which was not really challenged
until Ian McFarlane's article 'Neo-Latin Verse, Some New Discoveries: A

Possible Source of Ronsard's *Elégie XXIV*,' in *Modern Language Review* 54 (1959): 24–8.

41 In the Découvertes Gallimard volume, *Des hommes et des forêts* (Raphaël Larrère and Olivier Nougarède, 1993), for example, this very extract is given in bold type at the beginning of a chapter, enlisting the poet's words rhetorically as a protest.

42 Ute Margarete Saine, 'Dreaming the Forest of Gâtine: Ecology and Antiquity in Ronsard,' *Cincinnati Romance Review* 9 (1990): 1–12.

43 For an interesting study of how Greeks managed forest resources, in particular sanctuaries and shrines, see Matthew Dillon, 'The Ecology of the Greek Sanctuary,' *Zeitschrift für Papyrologie und Epigraphik* 118 (1997): 113–27. A good summary of some ancient Roman and Greek deplorations of environmental damage caused by felling trees, is J. Donald Hughes, 'How the Ancients Viewed Deforestation,' *Journal of Field Archeology* 10 (1983): 435–45.

44 'Ille et nefasto te posuit die, / quicumque primum, et sacrilega manu / produxit, arbos, in nepotum / perniciem opprobiumque pagi,' *Odes*, pp. 120–1.

45 Richard Seaford, 'Money Makes the (Greek) World Go Round: What the Ancient Greek Anxiety about Money Has to Tell Us about Our Own Economic Predicaments,' *Times Literary Supplement*, 19 June 2009. In *Money and the Early Greek Mind: Homer, Philosophy, Tragedy* (Cambridge: Cambridge University Press, 2004), Seaford had argued that the rise of a Greek money economy in the sixth century B.C. is essential to understanding Presocratic metaphysics and the myths of tragedy. The book does not discuss the Erysichthon myth (which arose later than the period Seaford considers), but the *TLS* article makes a direct connection between Erysichton and our current environmental predicament, which Seaford argues stems from 'pathological insatiability, the unlimited need for a source of income that sacrifices the future.'

46 Ovid, *Metamorphoses*, 8.741–878.

47 Philippe Desan identifies a new type of 'Renaissance entrepreneur' who 'thinks mainly in terms of profit, who redefines his morality and religion with respect to his business,' *L'imaginaire économique*, 26.

48 For an ecocritical argument that the Erysichthon myth is of particular pertinence to contemporary relations between man and the natural world, see Jill Da Silva, 'Ecocriticism and Myth: The Case of Erysichthon,' *Interdisciplinary Studies in Literature and Environment* 15 (2008): 103–16.

49 Raymond Rogers, *Nature and the Crisis of Modernity* (New York and Montreal: Black Rose Books, 1994).

50 Elizabeth Armstrong, in *Ronsard and the Age of Gold* (Cambridge: Cambridge University Press, 1968), has traced Ronsard's use of the Golden Age trope exhaustively. She shows that some writers believed in it as more than a trope; they earnestly believed that a modern-day age of gold would be possible. Whereas Armstrong discusses Ronsard's landscapes as part of the repertoire of Golden Age clichés, I ask what it is about certain landscapes – the forest in particular – which allows the past–present confrontation to be staged, and what the stakes are.

51 *Metamorphoses*, 8.762 [haud aliter fluxit discusso cortice sanguis] and 771 [nympha sub hoc ego sum Cereri gratissima ligno].

52 Ian McFarlane, 'Neo-Latin Verse,' 28.

53 The reception of Palissy among the greater literary community in Renaissance France has not been researched. Attention has focused on Palissy as a forerunner of certain scientific/agricultural techniques and discourses, or on his role as a Protestant activist. Isabelle Fernbach, in *Beyond Pastoral: Rusticity and the Reframing of Court Culture in 16th-Century French Literature* (PhD diss., University of California, Berkeley, 2006), chap. 7, effectively combines both tendencies in her argument about the centrality of rusticity to Palissy's vision of reform.

54 Ronsard opposed Protestantism both theologically and politically; he developed his polemical stance in a series of 'plaquettes' written in the 1560s. In 1562, Ronsard published his *Discours des misères de ce temps*; a year later, the *Remontrance au peuple de France* and the *Reponse aux injures ...* which entrenched his solidly royalist and Catholic position.

55 There is a good modern critical edition, Bernard Palissy, *Recepte véritable*, ed. Keith Cameron (Geneva: Droz, 1988); the title, which is actually over ten lines long in its full version, is abbreviated. For a discussion of Palissy as part of a shifting Christian humanist relationship to nature that justified new land management techniques, see Chandra Mukerji, 'Material Practices of Domination: Christian Humanism, the Built Environment, and Techniques of Western Power,' *Theory and Society* 31 (2002): 1–34, esp. 16–19.

56 Ronsard's treatment of economic themes is highly ironic; he sees gold, for example, as a fitting reward for his poetry, as a cornucopian source of abundance, and also as the source of greed and corruption. See Jean-Claude Margolin, '"L'Hymne de l'Or" et son ambiguïté,' *Bibliothèque d'humanisme et Renaissance* 28 (1966): 271–93. For gold in the Renaissance imaginary more generally, see Véronique Marcou, *L'ambivalence de l'or à la Renaissance* (Paris: L'Harmattan, 1998).

57 The image of the trees as houses for birds is in Virgil, *Georgics*, 2.209. For a consideration of Ronsard's sensibility to the animal world in his poetry,

see Hélène Naïs, *Les animaux dans la poésie française de la Renaissance: Science, symbolique, poésie* (Paris: Dider, 1961).

58 Virgil, *Eclogues*, 1.1–2.
59 Ibid, 5.5.
60 Ovid, *Metamorphoses*, 1.101–2.
61 Saine, 'Dreaming the Forest,' 4–5. The *Elégie XXIIII* appeared for the first time in the *Œuvres* of 1584. It was not the last but the penultimate poem of the cycle. And the elegy cycle itself was far from being the last in the 1584 edition: it was followed by the hymns, the 'Livres des poèmes,' the epitaphs, and the 'Discours des misères de ce temps.'
62 'What youths! See how much courage they display / Their temples adorned with the civic oak!' [Qui iuvenes! quantas ostentant, aspice, viris, / atque umbrata gerunt civili tempora quercu!], *Aeneid*, 6.771–2.
63 The right to use the forest – wood, game, and land – for subsistence needs had been guaranteed to the people in most regions of France by local custom, although there were of course many conflicting interests and particularly royal restrictions imposed on common use. In the sixteenth century, however, many more of these local customs start to be eroded by the crown than in the Middle Ages: scores of royal edicts were aimed at centralizing forest management and at excluding all but the crown and landed nobility from the right to hunt. See, for an exhaustive history of the forest in Renaissance France, Michel Devèze, *La vie de la forêt française au XVIe siècle*, 2 vols. (Paris: SEVPEN, 1961).
64 McFarlane, 'Neo-Latin Verse,' 28.
65 Michel Jeanneret, *Perpetuum mobile: Métamorphoses des corps et des œuvres de Vinci à Montaigne* (Paris: Macula, 1997). In his discussion of this one line, he puts Ronsard's sensibility to the inconstancy of form in the greater context of an Aristotelean displacement of the Platonic primacy of Form (31–3).
66 This is also the thrust of Susan Silver's reading of the poem, in '"Adieu vielle forest …": Myth, Melancholia, and Ronsard's Family Trees,' *Neophilologus* 86 (2002): 33–43. She argues that in the elegy and in Ronsard's 'Le Pin,' the figure of Chronos confronts the poet with the mortality of matter, but that this 'death and dearth in the natural world bring about new life in poetry' (36).
67 Lucretius, *De rerum naturae*, 5.260.
68 Ibid., 2.1173–4.
69 Ovid, *Metamorphoses*, 15.236 ff.
70 Henri Lefebvre, *La production de l'espace* (Paris: Anthropos, 1974).
71 Harvey, *Spaces of Hope* (Berkeley: University of California Press, 2000), 183.

72 Harvey's challenge to the Lefevrian impasse of agonistic desire is at the
    heart of his concept of 'dialectic utopianism' (182–96). Franco Moretti also
    reminds us that literary geography tells us both 'what could be […] and
    what is,' in *Atlas of the European Novel* (London and New York: Verso,
    1998), 1. Gaston Bachelard, in his phenomenological study of the experi-
    ence of 'espaces heureux,' considers the imagination as a 'puissance ma-
    jeure de la nature humaine': *La poétique de l'espace* (Paris: PUF, 1957), 16.

6. The Poet and the Bower: Escaping History

1 David Posner, *The Performance of Nobility in Early Modern European Literature* (Cambridge: Cambridge University Press, 1999).
2 For the Pléiade's borrowings from Vauquelin, see Marc Bensimon, 'Les Foresteries de Jean Vauquelin de la Fresnaye et les productions pastorales de la
   Pléiade,' *Modern Language Notes* 73 (1958): 25–33. Vauquelin's *œuvre*
   consists of: *Les deus premiers livres des Foresteries* (Poitiers, 1555); *Pour la
   monarchie de ce royaume contre la division* (Paris, 1563); *Oraison de ne croire
   legerement à la calomnie* (Caen, 1587); *Oraison funèbre sur le trepas de sieur de
   Bretheville Rouxel* (Caen, 1586); and *Les diverses poésies du sieur de la Fresnaie*
   (Caen, 1605), which contains the *Art poétique, Satyres, Idillies,* and assorted
   sonnets and epigrams, many started in Vauquelin's youth but not previously published. All of these are extremely rare. Only one edition of each
   of his works was published in his lifetime, followed by two and a half centuries of obscurity. The *Art poétique* attracted the attention of Romantic
   publishers in Paris (Poulet Malassis in 1862 and Garnier in 1885). Sainte-
   Beuve owned a 1605 *Diverses poésies,* and wrote with reserved admiration
   of Vauquelin. The only modern edition of the *Diverses poésies* is that edited
   by Julien Travers in Vauquelin's native Normandy (Caen, 1869–70, 2 vols.);
   Marc Bensimon edited *Les Foresteries* in 1956 (Geneva: Droz).
3 Alice Hulubei has shown in some detail Vauquelin's contribution to the
   development of the eclogue in her still-authoritative study *L'églogue en
   France au XVIe siècle: Époque des Valois (1515–1589)* (Paris: Droz, 1938), 349,
   359–63; see also Marc Bensimon, 'Les Foresteries de Jean Vauquelin.' More
   recently, Jean Balsamo has made a case for the reconsideration of Vauquelin's contributions to vernacular lyric: 'Jean Vauquelin de la Fresnaye et "la
   nature en chemise": Quelques remarques sur les origines de l'idylle,' in *La
   naissance du monde et l'invention du poème: Mélanges de poétique et d'histoire
   littéraire du xvie siècle offerts à Yvonne Bellenger,* ed. Jean-Claude Ternaux
   (Paris: Champion, 1998), 175–91.

4 On the lack of sixteenth-century interest in Vauquelin's poetry, see A.-P. Lemercier, *Étude littéraire et morale sur les poésies de Jean Vauquelin de la Fresnaye* (Nancy, 1887; repr. Geneva: Slatkine, 1970), 266–7. Vauquelin's *Art poétique*, while heavily derivative of Horace and Aristotle, does have some strikingly original passages. Of particular interest is his reversal of the usual French paranoia concerning their imitation of Italian poetry. It is true that French poetry of his time was based mostly on Italian models, he writes, but Petrarch himself imitated French troubadours. Italians have stolen French poetry from the French, made it theirs, and 'sold it back dearly' to the French. *Art poétique* (Paris, 1885; repr. Geneva: Slatkine, 1970), 1.555–66.

5 For the concept of noble identity and social hierarchy in the sixteenth century, see, e.g., Arlette Jouanna, *Ordre social: Mythes et réalités dans la France du XVIe siècle* (1977). The idea of social and economic decline gathered momentum in the first half of the twentieth century, culminating in Davis Bitton's *The French Nobility in Crisis, 1560–1640* (Stanford: Stanford University Press, 1969), and has since been refuted by most historians: see, for example, the work of J.B. Wood, succinctly summed up in 'The Decline of the Nobility in Sixteenth- and Early Seventeenth-Century France: Myth or Reality?' *The Journal of Modern History* 48 (1976): 1–29. R.J. Knecht, *The Rise and Fall of Renaissance France*, 2nd ed. (Oxford: Blackwell, 2001), 266–74, has a good summary of this debate.

6 R.J. Knecht, *The Rise and Fall*, 267. See J. Russell Major, 'The Crown and the Aristocracy in Renaissance France,' *American Historical Review* 69 (1964): 631–45, for a study of continuities and changes in the structure of the landed nobility.

7 Liah Greenfeld, *Nationalism: Five Roads to Modernity* (Cambridge, MA: Harvard University Press, 1992), 135.

8 In all references to the *Satyres*, I give the page numbers of the Travers edition of Vauquelin's *Diverses poésies*. Vauquelin's *Satyres* are one of the first collections of Lucilian satire in French. See J.H.M. Salmon, 'French Satire in the Late Sixteenth Century,' *Sixteenth-Century Journal* 6 (1975): 57–88, for an overview of the variants and fortunes of the genre during Vauquelin's lifetime, although Salmon considers Vauquelin to be 'palid and innocuous' as a satirist (88).

9 In particular by Lemercier, *Étude littéraire*, the only book-length study of Vauquelin's life and work, and still used as a reference.

10 *Personae* (or masks, in Latin) have become a key interpretive approach to classical satire. See, for example, Susanna Morton Braund, *The Roman Satirists and Their Masks* (Bristol: Bristol Classical Press, 1996).

11 Ovid's *Tristia* begin thus: 'Little book, you will go to the city without me, and I don't envy you. Woe is me, since I am not permitted to go to your lord.' Du Bellay, in a liminary sonnet entitled 'À son livre,' paraphrases Ovid: 'My book (and I do not begrudge your good fortune) you will go without me to see my prince's court. Ah, miserable as I am.' *'The Regrets' with 'The Antiquities of Rome,' Three Latin Elegies, and 'The Defense and Enrichment of the French Language,'* ed. and trans. Richard Helgerson (Philadelphia: University of Pennsylvania Press, 2007), 51.

12 For the idea of social order reflecting the order of nature, see, e.g., Arlette Jouanna, *Ordre social*, part 2, and Jonathan Dewald, *Aristocratic Experience and the Origins of Modern Culture* (Berkeley: University of California Press, 1993).

13 From Parfouru d'Eclin, in Lower Normandy.

14 'Ceres [...] / De ses pas sacrez toucha / Cete terre, et se coucha / Lasse sur ton verd rivage,' *Vers lyriques*, in *Poésies françaises et latines de Joachim Du Bellay*, ed. E. Courbet (Paris: Garnier, 1919), 107. The ode is entitled 'Les louanges d'Anjou: Au fleuve de Loyre.'

15 Or, as Timothy Hampton puts it, the new nobility was characterized, at least in the literary imaginary, by 'diplomats and bureaucrats, instead of romance heroes' (*Literature and Nation in the Sixteenth Century: Inventing Renaissance France* [Ithaca: Cornell University Press, 2001], 124). Nobert Elias's *The Court Society* (trans. Edmund Jephcott, New York: Pantheon, 1983), a book that has influenced most subsequent historians of class in early modern Europe, shows the problems posed to Renaissance Europe's aristocrats by the necessity of engaging in a money economy that had traditionally been defined as that with which the nobility do *not* occupy themselves. J.H.M. Salmon's discussion on the liminal position of the court poets is helpful, caught as they were between a traditional aristocratic hierarchy in which their own family names figured low, and a merit-based sytem of advancement at court that led them to study other careers, mostly law, in order to compete with the *noblesse de robe* (*Society in Crisis: France in the Sixteenth Century* [London: Methuen, 1979], especially chap. 5). See also Jonathan Dewald's *Aristocratic Experience*, which traces 'how an individualistic, skeptical, and in many ways anxious culture emerged within a "society of orders"' (2). While noting the centrality of 'anxiety,' Dewald sees the aristocracy as more innovative and adaptive than the notion of crisis would give them credit for. Liah Greenfeld, *Nationalism*, 133–88, discusses the changes in the French nobility as they relate to the emergence of modern nationalism.

16 Claude de Seyssel, *La Monarchie de France*, 1.14, ed. Jacques Poujol (Paris: Argences, 1961), 121. Feigned indifference to money was key to the

performance of early modern nobility, despite actual participation in monetary economies. Montaigne famously defines the nobility as *oisive*, 'qui ne vit, comme on dict, que de ses rentes; car ailleurs, la vie est questuaire' (*Essais*, 2.8). For the tension between the ideal of autarchy and the reality of economic activity, see George Huppert, *Les bourgeois gentilshommes: An Essay on the Definition of Elites in Renaissance France* (Chicago: University of Chicago Press, 1977); and Dewald, *Aristocratic Experience*, chap. 5.

17 Lemercier, *Étude littéraire*, 12.

18 Salmon, *Society in Crisis*, 92. Dewald also reminds us that many nobles never went to war: bearing arms was more part of the myth of nobility than of its reality (*Aristocratic Experience*, 45). For a study of the remarkably humdrum day-to-day life of a Norman *gentilhomme campagnard* of Vauquelin's generation, see Madeleine Foisil, *Le sire de Gouberville: Un gentilhomme normand au XVIe siècle* (Paris: Aubier Montaigne, 1981).

19 See Jouanna, *Ordre social*, 139–59.

20 Posner, *The Performance*, 15.

21 Timothy Hampton suggests that the Pléiade poets respond to this by creating the idea of a nobility of the spirit, to carve out for themselves a space of symbolic capital (*Literature and Nation*, 160–1).

22 Little is known about these two gentleman-poets. Both were, like Vauquelin, Norman. Toutain is the author of *La Tragédie d'Agamenmon, avec deux lives de chants de philosophie et d'amour*, published in Paris in 1557. Grimoult is supposed to have written some *Observations sur la France*, according to Julien Travers in his edition of *Les Diverses poésies*.

23 For the circle of poets in Poitiers during this period, see Hulubei, *L'églogue*, 357–85.

24 The classic literary example of the itinerant scholar is of course Rabelais's Pantagruel, whose grand tour of French universities starts in fact in Poitiers, one of the most flourishing universities of the time. For a variety of essays on the *peregrinatio academica* with a particular focus on France, see *Les échanges entre les universités européennes à la Renaissance: Colloque international organisé par la Société française d'étude du XVIe siècle et l'Association Renaissance-Humanisme-Réforme. Valence, 15–18 mai 2002*, ed. Michel Bideaux and Marie-Madeleine Fragonard (Geneva: Droz, 2003); and for an overview of the often dynamic cultural roles played by European universities, see Paul F. Grendler, 'The Universities of the Renaissance and Reformation,' *Renaissance Quarterly* 57 (2004):1–42.

25 See, for example, Vauquelin's description of Du Bellay's influence on him when in Paris: Du Bellay's poetry is said quite literally to have inscribed itself in Vauquelin's body: 'je portoy toute vive / Telle qu'en ses Sonnets,

au coeur sa rude Olive' (*Satyres*, 188). This image of one poet's creation colonizing the body of another is an interesting testimony to what must have been a widespread anxiety underlying the rhetoric of fraternal collaboration and admiration. Marc Bizer addresses the question of imitation and anxiety amongst the Pléiade in 'Ronsard the Poet, Belleau the Translator: The Difficulties of Writing in the Laureate's Shadow,' in *Translation and the Transmission of Culture between 1300 and 1600*, ed. Jeanette Beer and Kenneth Lloyd-Jones (Kalamazoo: Medieval Institute Publications, Western Michigan University, 1995), 175–226.

26 All tributaries of the Loire River. The Loir joins the Sarthe just above Angers, and the Sarthe after this confluence changes its name to Maine, which in turn flows into the Loire.

27 Note the French rhyming of *lois* (laws) and *bois* (woods), not rendered in the English translation. This rhyme, which I shall discuss below, resumes a central opposition in Vauquelin's work between the professions and poetry.

28 Charles de Bourgueville (1534–93) climbed the ladder of the king's judiciary in Caen, and became *lieutenant-général* in 1558. It was through him that Vauquelin obtained this position in 1572.

29 Jacques Lacan, 'Le stade du miroir comme formateur de la fonction du Je telle qu'elle nous est révélée dans l'expérience psychanalytique,' in *Écrits* (Paris: Seuil, 1966), 93–100. Lacan continues to intrigue scholars of early modern literature, mostly in English. For Renaissance France, Nancy Frelick has convincingly applied Lacanian models to readings of Scève in *Délie as Other: Toward a Poetics of Desire in Scève's Délie* (Lexington, KY: French Forum, 1994). One of the most influential position papers on the general applicability of psychoanalytic approaches to Renaissance texts is Stephen Greenblatt, 'Psychoanalysis and Renaissance Culture,' in *Renaissance Theory / Literary Texts*, ed. Patricia Parker and David Quint (Baltimore: Johns Hopkins University Press, 1986), 210–24, which has often been read as setting up the modern analysable subject as a straw man for early modern critics. Greenblatt has a more nuanced view of psychoanalysis than the reception of this essay suggests, and himself uses Lacan to great effect in a reading of Othello in *Renaissance Self-Fashioning from More to Shakespeare* (Chicago: Chicago University Press, 1980), 232–54. My suggestion of Lacanian models here is not intended as an intervention in such debates, or in Lacanian criticism itself, but simply because in the case of an anxious writer such as Vauquelin, they are useful less as 'a theory than a practice of interpretation that lends an ear to what is not said' (Juliana Schiesari, 'The Gendering of Melancholia: Torquato Tasso and Isabella di

Morra,' in *Refiguring Women: Perspectives on Gender and the Italian Renaissance*, ed. Marilyn Migiel and Juliana Schiesari [Cornell: Cornell University Press, 1991], 233–62, 253). Schiesari's essay of course addresses the problematic question of gender within psychoanalytic theory, which I do not consider here at all.

30 The Lacanian *nom du père* suggests itself here, as a function attributed to the father-in-law rather than the actual father ('Function and Field of Speech and Language,' in Jacques Lacan, *Écrits: A Selection*, trans. Alan Sheridan (London: Tavistock Publications, 1977), 67.

31 Jean Imbert, author of the four-volume *Institutiones forenses* (first edition in Latin in 1541), a civil and criminal legal treatise which was long authoritative in Ancien Régime France. For a description of Imbert's procedures, see John Langbein, *Prosecuting Crime in the Renaissance* (Clark, NJ: The Lawbook Exchange, 2005), 224–43.

32 Symbols of pastoral and georgic poetry respectively.

33 In the Lacanian schema, this would be in the domain of the imaginary, of unconscious desires, and identification with the parent.

34 Matt Cartmill, *A View to a Death in the Morning: Hunting and Nature through History* (Cambridge, MA: Harvard University Press, 1996), chaps. 4 and 5, shows the increasing association between noble identity and hunting through the Middle Ages and the sixteenth century, although the Renaissance saw a few high-profile protests against hunting, such as those of Erasmus, More, and Montaigne.

35 The strong association between his mother and the woods may have been suggested to him by her maiden name, Blanche Boislichausse. The poetic possibilities of association offered by this name do not appear in his poetry, however, so one cannot push this too far.

36 The definition of 'garde-noble' is 'Droit qu'avait le survivant de deux époux nobles de jouir des biens des enfants, venant de la succession du prédécédé, jusqu'à ce qu'ils eurent atteint un certain âge, à la charge de les nourrir, de les entretenir et de payer toutes les dettes, sans être tenu de rendre aucun compte.' *Dictionnaire de l'Académie française*, 6me édition, 1835. The 'Dictionnaires d'autrefois' search engine is part of the University of Chicago's ARTFL project, online at http://artfl-project.uchicago.edu/node/17.

37 Hulubei, *L'églogue*, 9, 21, 360. Statius's *Silvae* were discovered by the Italian humanist Bracciolini in the early 1400s in Saint Gallen. Poliziano's *Silvae*, written in the 1480s as part of the university courses he taught in Florence, were instrumental in starting a Europe-wide vogue for the genre. The French humanist Nicolas Petit published a volume of *Silvae* in Paris in 1522, which shows significant influence from both Poliziano and Statius.

38 Marc Bensimon, *Les Foresteries*, xiv; Lemercier, *Étude*, 26.

39 The *Idillies* were published in the *Poésies* of 1605, though written in the late 1550s when the poet was still smarting from the failure of the *Foresteries*.

40 *Eclogues*, 6.1–2: 'Prima Syracosio dignata est ludere versu / nostra nec erubuit silvas habitare Thalia.' Text and translations of Virgil are from the Loeb edition, trans. H. Rushton Fairclough, 2 vols. (Cambridge: Harvard University Press, 1934–5). Vauquelin is not the first to write an eclogue in French: Du Bellay and Sebillet had both called for French poets to write more eclogues, and Salel, Marot, Scève, and Ronsard had written individual ones.

41 Land ownership has been more studied in relation to literature in early modern English studies. Raymond Williams's hugely influential *The Country and the City* (New York: Oxford University Press, 1973), has given rise to some historically oriented studies of the 'country house poem' in Renaissance England. See, e.g., Don Wayne, *Penshurst: The Semiotics of Place and the Poetics of History* (Madison: University of Wisconsin Press, 1984); and Hugh Jenkins, *Feigned Commonwealths: The Country-House Poem and the Fashioning of Ideal Community* (Pittsburgh: Duquesne University Press, 1998).

42 The seven-fluted pipe or pan pipes, formed when the nymph Syrinx, pursued by the god Pan, was transformed into hollow reeds (Ovid, *Metamorphoses*, 1.689 ff.). It is also (under the name of *sampogna*) the instrument of choice of Sannazaro's Arcadian shepherds. In the tenth *Prosa* of the *Arcadia*, it is described as being made of seven reeds (the transformed nymph Syrinx) by a lovesick Pan. Theocritus then acquired it and first made the trees listen to his songs; Virgil's shepherds then played it, and hung it up in Arcadia when Virgil started the *Aeneid*, where Sannazaro's shepherds find it.

43 I give page numbers from Marc Bensimon's 1956 edition of the *Foresteries*.

44 In Virgil's Tenth Eclogue, Gallus carves his love on the young trees which, as they grow, bestow upon his verse a measure of immortality. Ovid takes up the same conceit in his fifth *Heroides*, and there too, as the trees grow, so does the name of Oenone carved by Paris. Sannazaro briefly uses the motif in the fifth *capitolo* of the *Arcadia*. For a brief history of the motif up to and including the sixteenth century, see Rensselaer W. Lee, *Names on Trees: Ariosto into Art* (Princeton: Princeton University Press, 1977), chap. 2.

45 Lee, *Names*, 19, 30. This is in contrast with the use of the motif by Ariosto's Latin and Italian predecessors, where tree-carving is always elegiac in nature.

46 Sannazaro was well known in France, thanks not only to Jean Martin's translation, but also to the extensive circulation of manuscripts and books between French and Italian scholars and printers. Sannazaro himself had

travelled in France (1501) while following king Frederick of Aragon in his exile. For a study of the exchanges between French and Italian intellectuals, printers, etc., as well as of Sannazaro's encounters and exchanges while in France, see Carlo Vecce's *Iacopo Sannazaro in Francia: Scoperte di codici all'inizio del XVI secolo* (Padua: Antenore, 1988).

47 The detailed description of the fictional gardens, monuments, statues, etc., in the *Hypnerotomachia Poliphili* (1499) was imitated in actual gardens throughout France and Italy for over a century afterwards. For the reception in France of the *Polyphilus*, see Gilles Polizzi's introduction to his edition of Martin's translation, *Le songe de Poliphile* (Paris: Imprimerie nationale, 1994). For the importance of the Italian garden style in France – and the mass importing by French royalty of Italian landscape gardeners – see Terry Comito, *The Idea of the Garden in the Renaissance* (New Brunswick: Rutgers University Press, 1978), chap. 1, and chap. 3, for Italian and French gardening practices and literary gardens. There are many studies by landscape architects of the Renaissance garden, in particular the Italian model: a good overview of gardens in early modern Europe as a whole is Torsten Olaf Enge's *Garden Architecture in Europe, 1450–1800: From the Villa Garden of the Italian Renaissance to the English Landscape Garden* (Koln: Taschen, 1990).

48 Jacopo Sannazaro, *Arcadia and Piscatorial Eclogues*, trans. R. Nash (Detroit: Wayne State University Press, 1966), 153.

49 The tenth chapter of Sannazaro's *Arcadia*, in imitation of Virgil, also describes the era of talking pines as the prelapsarian era of pastoral poetry, before vice took root in the world.

50 For an excellent study on the topos of the source in Renaissance literature, see David Quint's *Origin and Originality in Renaissance Literature: Versions of the Source* (New Haven: Yale University Press, 1983). My reading of Vauquelin owes a lot to Quint's chap. 2 on Sannazaro.

51 *Eclogues*, 7.25–8. 'Pastores, hedera nascentem ornate poetam, / Arcades ...' / ... baccare frontem / cingite, ne vati noceat mala lingua futuro.' Foxglove was seen as a protection against the jealousy of the gods, therefore against bad luck and bad reputation.

52 For French pastoral as retreat into a courtly ethos that excludes class struggle, see Carole Deering Paul's reading of *L'Astrée* in 'Images of Retreat: Geography in the Pastoral Novel,' *Cincinnati Romance Review* 1 (1982): 65–71.

53 In the fifth *Prosa* and eclogue, Ergasto's elegy to Androgeo recalls the pastor as one whose piping 'made the whole wood happy with pleasant harmony.'

54 Sannazaro, *Arcadia*, 59.

55 Pasteurs = poets.

56 Ergasto sings to the dead Androgeo, 'sooner shall we gather black olives in the summer, than ever your fame will grow silent in these regions,' and 'look how the shepherd god Apollo all festive is coming to your sepulchre to give you ornament with his sweet floral crowns.' *Arcadia*, 60.

57 Indeed, towards the end of his life, in his *Art poétique*, Vauquelin revisits this anxiety about himself as a source; he has, he says, been too occupied by public duties to write poetry. Once again, the world of 'affaires' intrudes on and taints the world of poetry: 'Je suis toujours troublé, les affaires me tuent; / Je suis comme un grand lac où beaucoup vont a l'eau / Qui tarissent ma source et troublent mon ruisseau' (lines 1164–6).

58 Theocritus begins his *Idyll* 17, the 'Praise of Ptolemy,' with the classic *embarras de choix*: the king's merits are so great, he writes, that he is like the woodsman who 'sees green Ida rise / Pine above pine, and ponders which to fell / First of those myriads' (*Idyll* 17.9–11). Theocritus, *Theocritus Translated into English Verse*, trans. Charles Calverley (London: Bell, 1869).

59 Vauquelin had frequented Ronsard and the Pléiade in Paris, so he most likely read the *Hymnes* at least in manuscript form before he left (the 'privilège' is from 1553), before publishing his own *Foresteries*.

60 Harold Bloom, *The Anxiety of Influence: A Theory of Poetry* (New York: Oxford University Press, 1973).

61 Pierre Bourdieu shows in *Les règles de l'art: Genèse et structure du champ littéraire* (Paris: Seuil, 1992), that the emergence of an autonomous field of literary production is a fiction in that it depends on the development and activity of many other not strictly literary fields – publishing, the creation of and marketing to a readership, etc.

62 David Quint, Introduction to *Literary Theory / Renaissance Texts*, ed. Parker and Quint (Baltimore and London: Johns Hopkins University Press, 1986), 3. The situating of textual production within the context of economic macro- and micro-structures has of course been crucial to the study of the ides of author and authorship. Authorship studies have focalized – not always uncritically – around Michel Foucault's seminal essay, 'Qu'est-ce qu'un auteur?' in *Dits et Écrits, 1954–1988*, ed. Daniel Defert, François Ewald, and Jacques Lagrange (Paris: Gallimard, 1994), 789–821, which posited the idea of an author-function. Roger Chartier, *Culture écrite et société: L'ordre des livres, XIVe–XVIIIe siècle* (Paris: Albin Michel, 1996), is one of the best sociologically based studies of print culture, authorships, and readerships for the early modern period. See also Séan Burke's anthology *Authorship: From Plato to the Postmodern: A Reader* (Edinburgh: Edinburgh University Press, 1995).

63 For Montaigne's use of economic imagery, see Philippe Desan, *Les commerces de Montaigne: Le discours économique des 'Essais'* (Paris: Nizet, 1992). Desan argues that Montaigne's economic language conveys a tension between bourgeois and noble values within Montaigne's own family. For the notion of symbolic credit with respect to linguistic performance, see Pierre Bourdieu, *Ce que parler veut dire: L'économie des échanges linquistiques* (Paris: Fayard, 1982).

64 Peletier's 1552 *Arithmétique* went through many reprints. For Peletier's contribution to mathematics, see Jean-Claude Margolin, 'L'enseignement des mathématiques en France (1540–1570): Charles de Bovelles, Finé, Peletier, Ramus,' *French Renaissance Studies (1540–1570): Humanism and the Encyclopedia*, ed. Peter Sharratt (Edinburgh: Edinburgh University Press, 1976), 110–55. For Peletier and orthography, see, e.g., Jean-Charles Monferran, 'Le *Dialogue de l'ortografe et prononciation françoese* de Peletier,' *Bibliothèque d'humanisme et Renaissance* 60 (1998): 405–12; for a general overview of orthographic reform, see Marie-Luce Demonet, *Les voix du signe: Nature du langage à la Renaissance* (Paris: Champion, 1992), 408–14; and Mireille Huchon, *Le français de la Renaissance* (Paris: PUF, 1988), 35–47.

65 Albert-Marie Schmidt, in *La poésie scientifique en France au seizième siècle* (Paris: Albin Michel, 1938), 15, credits Peletier's translation for the surge in scientific poetry in the mid-sixteenth century, since Peletier often naturalized Virgil's mythological references.

66 Peletier, like many aristocrats, divided his time between town and country, enjoying a particularly leisured four years from 1540 to 1544 in Maine as the nominal secretary of René Du Bellay, but his evocation of the city–country distinction is much more a rehashing of a literary tradition than autobiography.

67 For an in-depth consideration of the *Amours* as scientific poetry, see Isabelle Pantin, *La poésie du ciel en France dans la seconde moitié du seizième siècle* (Geneva: Droz, 1995), 197–224.

68 For the importance of mathematics to Peletier's world view, see Sophie Arnaud, *La voix de la nature dans l'œuvre de Jacques Peletier du Mans (1517–82)* (Paris: Champion, 2005), 16 and passim.

69 For a discussion of the 'Louange de la science,' see Isabelle Pantin, *La poésie du ciel*, 163–6. At the time of writing, the *Louanges* are the only part of Peletier's corpus to have been published in the modern serial edition of his complete works directed by Isabelle Pantin.

70 'Les faits de la Nature se peuvent aussi traiter en Poésie, bien que […] l'entreprise est rare pour le Poète,' Jacques Peletier, *Art poétique*, in *Traités de poétique et de rhétorique de la Renaissance*, ed. Francis Goyet (Paris: Poche,

1990), 231. For Peletier, the equivalent harmony of nature and poem has a lot to do with the musical sonority of words which reflects the music of the cosmos. See Jean-Charles Monferran, 'La poésie sonore de Jacques Peletier du Mans,' in *À haute voix: Diction et prononciation au XVIe et XVIIe s. Actes du colloque de Rennes, 17–18 juin 1996*, ed. Olivia Rosenthal (Paris: Klincksieck, 1998), 35–54.

71 Peletier, *Art poétique*, in Goyet, ed., *Traités*, 255. For Renaissance theories of the origins of language, see Marie-Luce Demonet, *Les voix du signe*.

72 Arnaud, *La voix de la nature*.

73 One exception is the last poem in the collection, a *dizain* by Du Bellay in praise of Le Mans as Peletier's birthplace.

74 Louis Terreaux, 'Jacques Peletier et *La Savoie*,' in *Le paysage à la Renaissance*, ed. Yves Giraud (Fribourg: Éditions Universitaires Fribourg Suisse, 1988), 215–27, 216.

75 Whose existence has of course been called into question by Mireille Huchon in *Louise Labé: Une créature de papier* (Geneva: Droz, 2006). Huchon posits that Peletier was – along with Scève, Magny, Claude de Taillemont, Des Autels, and others – an active part of the literary hoax that fabricated Louise.

76 See chap. 1 for discussion of Boileau. For the attribution of Forlani's map to Boileau, see Henri Mettrier, 'Les cartes des Savoie au XVIe siecle. La carte de B. de Bouillon 1556,' *Bulletin de la section de géographie* 32 (1917): 16–129. Louis Terreaux, 'Jacques Peletier,' provides a good summary of the content of the poem, including a list of the places Peletier describes. Peletier is by no means exhaustive in his descriptions – he does not mention the Mont Blanc, for example (nor does Forlani, or even Mercator later on). This is also a stylistic choice: at the beginning of book 2 of *La Savoye*, Peletier explicitly states that exhaustive description is not pleasing.

77 Paradin had a particularly close connection with the Lyonnais printer Jean de Tournes from the 1550s, and was familiar with the circle of Lyonnais poets that Peletier was associated with at that time.

78 I give page numbers for an 1897 edition of *La Savoye*, the most recent available at the time of writing: Jacques Peletier du Mans, *La Savoye*, ed. C. Pagès and F. Ducloz (Annecy: Moutiers-Tarentaise, 1897).

79 In Pindar's ninth Pythian Ode, Cyrene, a huntress and maiden, caught Apollo's attention while hunting; Aristeus was the result of their union. Virgil has Aristeus involuntarily causing Euridyce's death by pursuing her; Proteus advises him to sacrifice four bulls and heiffers, and a swarm of bees comes out of the thigh of one of the dead bulls. Aristeus is also credited with teaching men the arts of tending troops and beekeeping.

80 Du Bellay, Ronsard, and Peletier, respectively.
81 Perhaps a reference to Doran, the name of several rivers in Savoie. The rivers and streams of Savoy had apparently been described in some detail by an Aymar Du Rival in his *Histoire des Allobroges* (c. 1536). See M.-A. de Lavis-Trafford, 'L'évolution de la cartographie de la région du Mont-Cenis et de ses abords aux XVe et XVIe siècles' (Chambéry: Lavis-Trafford, 1949).
82 Arnaud, *La voix de la nature*, 148–9.
83 Peletier has a mixed reaction to Savoyard hardiness. On the one hand, he sees in their adaptation of their natural environment a proud will to dominate: 'Les Montagnes n'echapent / L'effort cruel des homes qui les sapent' (91). On the other, he admires the courage that has 'osé mettre le pic es lieus, / Qui de ça bas donnent horreur aus yeus: / D'avoir rendu la hauteur accessible' (96). For the shifting aesthetic values that culture has assigned to mountains, see Walther Kirchner, 'Mind, Mountain, and History,' *Journal of the History of Ideas* 11 (1950): 412–47.
84 For historical maps of the shifting territories of the duchy, see *Atlas historique français: Le territoire de la France et de quelques pays voisins: Savoie*, ed. Jean-Yves Mariotte et André Perret (Paris: CNRS, 1979).
85 See Isabelle Pantin's Introduction to Jacques Peletier, *Œuvres complètes*, vol. 10, ed. Sophie Arnaud, Stephen Bamforth, and Jan Miernowski, dir. Isabelle Pantin (Paris: Champion, 2005), 7–18, for a summary of this and other intellectual controversies involving Peletier, mostly concerning points of logic and mathematics.
86 Towards the end of the second book, he will also contrast Savoy with Italy, in an analogous exploration of relative distance. Turin, the capital of Savoy, is of course presented as a centre of learning and refinement, but as Peletier leads us further into Italy, the idealized gives way to the corrupt – political conflict, the courtesans of Venice, the double-dealing of the Vatican – further emphasizing Savoy's detached and privileged position on the frontier.
87 Lucinge, a known critic of Machiavelli, disapproved of Emmanual-Philibert's pro-Italian policy, lobbying instead for a closer alliance between France and Savoy. See Olivier Zegna Rata, *René de Lucinge entre l'écriture et l'histoire* (Geneva: Droz, 1993).

Conclusion

1 Agrippa d'Aubigné, *Les Tragiques*, 'Misères,' line 607.
2 Guy Du Faur de Pibrac, *Les quatrains, Les plaisirs de la vie rustique, et autres poésies*, ed. Loris Petris (Geneva: Droz, 2004). This edition provides the much longer version of the *Plaisirs* published in Paris in 1584.

3 The dead Chancellor appears in the *Plaisirs* as the shepherd Michau, who urges France to rid herself of foreign corrupting influences.

4 Jacques Peletier du Mans, *L'Amour des amours*, ed. Jean-Charles Monferran (Paris: Société des textes français modernes, 1996), lxiii.

5 David Harvey, *Spaces of Hope* (Berkeley: University of California Press, 2000), 7.

6 Simon Schama, *Landscape and Memory* (New York: Knopf, 1995), 14. With more explicit critique of economic valuations of nature, Raymond Rogers also argues for the need to embrace the 'social basis for the relationship between human society and the natural world,' in *Nature and the Crisis of Modernity: A Critique of Contemporary Discourse on Managing the Earth* (New York: Black Rose Books, 1994), 2.

7 Chris Fitter, *Poetry, Space, Landscape*, 11.

Bibliography

Adams, William. *The French Garden, 1500–1800*. New York: Braziller, 1979.

Adamson, Joni, Mei Mei Evans, and Rachel Stein, eds. *Environmental Justice Reader: Politics, Poetics, and Pedagogy*. Tucson: University of Arizona Press, 2002.

Adhémar, Jean. 'Ronsard et l'école de Fontainebleau.' *Bibliothèque d'humanisme et Renaissance* 20 (1958): 344–8.

– *Les Clouet et la cour des rois de France*. Paris: Bibliothèque nationale, 1970.

Agnew, John. 'Nationalism.' In *A Companion to Cultural Geography*, ed. James Duncan, Nuala Johnson, and Richard Schein, 223–37. Oxford: Blackwell, 2004.

Agnew, John, and James Duncan. *The Power of Place: Bringing Together Geographical and Sociological Imaginations*. Boston: Unwin Hyman, 1989.

Ahmed, Ehsan. 'Pierre de Ronsard's *Odes* and the Law of Poetic Space.' *Renaissance Quarterly* 44 (1991): 757–75.

Akerman, James. 'The Structuring of Political Territory in Early Printed Atlases.' *Imago Mundi* 47 (1995): 138–54.

Alaimo, Stacy. *Undomesticated Ground: Recasting Nature as Feminist Space*. Ithaca: Cornell University Press, 2000.

Alduy, Cécile. *Politique des 'amours': Poétique et genèse d'un genre français nouveau (1544–1560)*. Geneva: Droz, 2007.

Alpers, Paul. *The Singer of the Eclogues*. Berkeley: University of California Press, 1979.

– 'Schiller's *Naïve and Sentimental Poetry* and the Modern Idea of Pastoral.' In *Cabinet of the Muses: Essays on Classical and Comparative Literature in Honor of Thomas G. Rosenmeyer*, ed. Mark Griffith and Donald Mastronarde, 319–31. Atlanta: Scholars Press, 1990.

– *What Is Pastoral?* Chicago: University of Chicago Press, 1996.

Alpers, Svetlana. 'The Mapping Impulse in Dutch Art.' In *Art and Cartography: Six Historical Essays*, ed. David Woodward, 51–96. Chicago: University of Chicago Press, 1987.

Amat, Robert. 'Quelques remarques cursives sur les rapports de l'écriture poétique au paysage.' In *Paysage et identité régionale*, dir. Burgard and Chenet, 319–24. Valence: La passe du vent, 1999.

Ames-Lewis, Francis. *The Intellectual Life of the Early Renaissance Artist*. New Haven: Yale University Press, 2000.

Anacreaon. *The Odes of Anacreaon*. Trans. Erastus Richardson. New Haven: Yale University Press, 1928.

Anderson, Benedict. *Imagined Communities: Reflections on the Origin and Spread of Nationalism*. London: Verso, 1983.

Applegate, Celia. 'A Europe of Regions: Reflections on the Historiography of Sub-National Places in Modern Times.' *American Historical Review* 104 (1999): 1157–82.

Aristotle. *Poetics*. Ed. and trans. Malcolm Heath. London: Penguin, 1996.

Armbruster, Karla, and Kathleen Wallace, eds. *Beyond Nature Writing: Expanding the Boundaries of Ecocriticism*. Charlottesville, VA: University of Virginia Press, 2001.

Armstrong, Elizabeth. *Ronsard and the Age of Gold*. Cambridge: Cambridge University Press, 1968.

Arnaud, Sophie. *La voix de la nature dans l'œuvre de Jacques Peletier du Mans (1517–1582)*. Paris: Champion, 2005.

Ascoli, Albert. 'Petrarch's Middle Age: Memory, Imagination, History, and "The Ascent of Mount Ventoux."' *Stanford Italian Review* 10 (1991): 5–43.

Atkins, Peter. *People, Land, and Time: An Historical Introduction to the Relations between Landscape, Culture, and Environment*. London: Arnold, 1998.

Atkinson, James. 'Naiveté and Modernity: The French Renaissance Battle for a Literary Vernacular.' *Journal of the History of Ideas* 35 (1974): 179–96.

Aubigné, Agrippa d'. *Les Tragiques*. Ed. Frank Lestringant. Paris: Gallimard, 1995.

Auclair, Valérie. 'De l'invention à l'œuvre. Les *Douze fables de fleuves ou fontaines* de Pontus de Tyard.' *Bibliothèque d'humanisme et Renaissance* 68 (2006): 63–85.

Augé, Marc. *Non-lieux: Introduction à une anthropologie de la surmodernité*. Paris: Seuil, 1992.

Bachelard, Gaston. *La poétique de l'espace*. Paris: PUF, 1957.

Baïf, Jean-Antoine de. *Œuvres en rime, première partie: Neuf livres des poemes*. Ed. Jean Vignes, Guy Demerson et al. Paris: Champion, 2002.

Baker, Alan. *Geography and History: Bridging the Divide*. Cambridge: Cambridge University Press, 2003.

Balsamo, Jean. *Les rencontres des Muses: Italianisme et anti-italianisme dans les lettres françaises de la fin du XVIe siècle*. Geneva: Slatkine, 1992.

– 'Jean Vauquelin de la Fresnaye et "la nature en chemise": Quelques remarques sur les origines de l'idylle.' In *La naissance du monde et l'invention du poème: Mélanges de poétique et d'histoire littéraire du xvie siècle offerts à Yvonne Bellenger*, ed. Jean-Claude Ternaux, 175–91. Paris: Champion, 1998.

– 'Les poètes d'Anet,' in *Henri II et les arts: Actes du colloque international, École du Louvre et Musée national de la Renaissance – Écouen, 25, 26, 27 septembre 1997*, ed. Hervé Oursel and Julia Fritsch, 417–25. Paris: École du Louvre, 2003.

Balsamo, Jean, ed. *Les poètes français de la Renaissance et Pétrarche*. Geneva: Droz, 2004.

Bamforth, Stephen. 'Peletier du Mans and "Scientific Eloquence."' *Renaissance Studies* 3 (1989): 202–11.

Barber, Giles. *Daphnis and Chloe: The Markets and Metamorphoses of an Unknown Bestseller*. The Panizzi Lectures, 1988. London: British Library, 1989.

Bardon, Françoise. *Diane de Poitiers et le mythe de Diane*. Paris: PUF, 1963.

Baridon, Michel. 'Jardins et paysages.' *Critique* 613 (1998).

Barroux, R. 'Nicolas d'Arfeuille, agent secret, géographe et dessinateur (1517–83).' *Revue d'histoire diplomatique* 51 (1937): 88–109.

Barthes, Roland. *Mythologies*. Paris: Seuil, 1957.

– 'De l'œuvre au texte.' In *Œuvres complètes*, vol. 2., ed. Eric Marty, 1211–17. Paris: Seuil, 1994.

Baxandall, Michael. *Painting and Experience in Fifteenth-Century Italy: A Primer in the Social History of Pictorial Style*. Oxford: Clarendon Press, 1972.

Beaune, Colette. *Naissance de la nation France*. Paris: Gallimard, 1985.

Béguin, Sylvie. *L'école de Fontainebleau: Le maniérisme à la cour de France*. Paris: Gonthier-Seghers, 1960.

Béguin, Sylvie, Bertrand Jestaz, and Jacques Thirion, eds. *L'école de Fontainebleau*. Paris: Éditions des Musées Nationaux, 1972.

Bell, David. *The Cult of the Nation in France: Inventing Nationalism, 1680–1800*. Cambridge, MA: Harvard University Press, 2001.

Belleau, Remy. *La Bergerie*. Ed. Doris Delacourcelle. Geneva: Droz, 1954.

– *Les Amours et nouveaux eschanges des pierres precieuses*. Ed. Maurice Verdier. Geneva: Droz, 1973.

– *Œuvres poétiques*. Ed. Marty-Laveaux. Paris, 1878.

– *Œuvres poétiques*. Vol. 1, *Petites inventions–Odes d'Anacréon–Œuvres diverses (1554–1561)*. Ed. K. Cameron, G. Demerson, F. Joukovsky et al. Paris: Champion, 1995.

– *Œuvres poétiques*. Vol. 2, *La Bergerie (1565)*, ed. Guy Demerson and Marie Madeleine Fontaine. Paris: Champion, 1995.

– *Œuvres poétiques*. Vol. 4, *La Bergerie (1572)*, ed. Guy Demerson. Paris: Champion, 2001.

Bellenger, Yvonne. *Du Bellay: Ses 'Regrets' qu'il fit dans Rome*. Paris: Nizet, 1975.

– 'Les paysages de montagne: L'évolution des descriptions du début à la fin du XVI siècle.' In *Le paysage à la Renaissance*, ed. Giraud, 121–33. Fribourg: Éditions Universitaires Fribourg Suisse, 1988.

Bellenger, Yvonne, ed. *Le mécénat et l'influence des Guises: Actes du colloque organisé par le Centre de recherche sur la littérature de la Renaissance de l'Université de Reims et tenu à Joinville du 31 mai au 4 juin 1994*. Paris: Champion, 1997.

Belyea, Barbara. 'Images of Power: Derrida/Foucault/Harley.' *Cartographica* 29 (1992): 1–9.

Bensimon, Marc. '*Les Foresteries* de Jean Vauquelin de la Fresnaye et les productions pastorales de la Pléiade.' *Modern Language Notes* 73 (1958): 25–33.

Berger, Harry. *Second World and Green World: Studies in Renaissance Fiction-Making*. Berkeley: University of California Press, 1988.

Berger, John. *Ways of Seeing*. London: Penguin, 1972.

Berque, Augustin, dir. *Cinq propositions pour une théorie du paysage*. Paris: Champ Vallon, 1994.

Bertho-Lavenir, Catherine. 'La fragmentation de l'espace national en paysages régionaux, 1800–1900.' In *Le paysage et ses grilles: Colloque de Cerisy-la-Salle*, ed. Françoise Chenet and Jean-Claude Wieber, 29–40. Paris: Harmattan, 1996.

Besse, Jean-Marc. *Les grandeurs de la Terre: Aspects du savoir géographique à la Renaissance*. Paris: ENS Éditions, 2003.

Besse, Jean-Marc, ed. 'Écrire le paysage.' *Revue des sciences humaines* 209 (1988).

Bideaux, Michel, and Marie-Madeleine Fragonard, eds. *Les échanges entre les universités européennes à la Renaissance: Colloque international organisé par la Société française d'étude du XVIe siècle et l'Association Renaissance-Humanisme-Réforme. Valence, 15–18 mai 2002*. Geneva: Droz, 2003.

Bitton, Davis. *The French Nobility in Crisis, 1560–1640*. Stanford: Stanford University Press, 1969.

Bizer, Marc. *La poésie au miroir: Imitation et conscience de soi dans la poésie latine de la Pléiade*. Paris: Champion, 1995.

– 'Ronsard the Poet, Belleau the Translator: The Difficulties of Writing in the Laureate's Shadow.' In *Translation and the Transmission of Culture between 1300 and 1600*, ed. Janette Beer and Kenneth Lloyd-Jones, 175–226. Kalamazoo: Medieval Institute Publications, Western Michigan University, 1995.

– 'Letters from Home: The Epistolary Aspects of Joachim Du Bellay's *Les Regrets*.' *Renaissance Quarterly* 52 (1999): 140–79.

– '"Qui a pais n'a que faire de patrie": Joachim Du Bellay's Resistance to a French Identity.' *Romanic Review* 91 (2000): 375–95.

Black, C.F., Mark Greengrass, David Howarth et al. *Cultural Atlas of the Renaissance*. New York: Prentice Hall, 1993.

Blair, Ann. *The Theater of Nature: Jean Bodin and Renaissance Science*. Princeton: Princeton University Press, 1997.

Bloch, Marc. *Les caractères originaux de l'histoire rurale française*. Oslo: Aschehoug, 1931.

Bloom, Harold. *The Anxiety of Influence: A Theory of Poetry*. New York: Oxford University Press, 1973.

Blunt, Anthony. *French Art and Music since 1500*. London: Methuen, 1972.

– *Art and Architecture in France, 1500–1700*. New Haven: Yale University Press, 1999.

Boas, George, and Arthur Lovejoy. *Primitivism and Related Ideas in Antiquity*. New York: Octagon, 1935.

Bonneton, Christine, ed. *Anjou*. Condé-sur-Noireau: Corlet, 1985.

Bonnot, Jacques. *Humanisme et Pléiade: Histoire, la doctrine, les œuvres*. Paris: Hachette, 1959.

Bono, James. *The Word of God and the Languages of Man: Interpreting Nature in Early Modern Science and Medicine*. Madison: University of Wisconsin Press, 1995.

Boriaud, Jean-Yves. 'Le paysage et la poésie latine de la Renaissance.' In *Le paysage*, ed. Maurand, 107–16. L'Union: CALS, 1993.

Bots, W.J.A. *Joachim Du Bellay entre l'histoire littéraire et la stylistique*. Groningue: Van Denderen, 1970.

Bouguereau, Maurice. *Le théatre françoys*, ed. François de Dainville. Amsterdam: Theatrum Orbis Terrarum, 1966.

Bourdeaut, A. *Joachim du Bellay et Olive de Sévigné*. Angers: Grassin, 1910.

Bourdieu, Pierre. *Ce que parler veut dire: L'économie des échanges linquistiques*. Paris: Fayard, 1982.

– *Les règles de l'art: Genèse et structure du champ littéraire*. Paris: Seuil, 1992.

Bowles, Brett. 'La république régionale: Stade occulté de la "synthèse républicaine."' *French Review* 69 (1995): 103–17.

Boyer, Hippolyte. *Un ménage littéraire en Berry au XVIe siècle: Jacques Thiboust et Jeanne de la Font*. Bourges: Jollet-Souchois, 1859.

Braudel, Fernand. *Civilisation materielle, économie et capitalisme: XVe–XVIIIe siècle*. 3 vols. Paris: A. Colin, 1979.

– *The Identity of France*. Trans. Siân Reynolds. New York: Harper and Row, 1988.

Braund, Susanna Morton. *The Roman Satirists and Their Masks*. Bristol: Bristol Classical Press, 1996.

Braybrook, Jean. 'Remy Belleau and the Figure of the Artist.' *French Studies* 37 (1983): 1–16.

- 'Science and Myth in the Poetry of Remy Belleau.' *Renaissance Studies* 5 (1991): 277–87.
- 'Space and Time in Remy Belleau's *Bergerie.' Bibliothèque d'humanisme et Renaissance* 57 (1995): 369–80.
- (1997). 'Joinville, les Guises, et l'œuvre de Belleau.' In *Le mécénat et l'influence des Guises*, ed. Bellenger, 233–49. Paris: Champion, 1997.
- 'Jacopo Sannazaro's *Arcadia* and Remy Belleau's *Bergerie.'* In *Reinventing the Past: Essays in Honour of Ann Moss*, ed. Gary Ferguson and Catherine Hampton, 177–94. Durham: University of Durham, 2003.
- Breuilly, John. *Nationalism and the State*. Manchester: Manchester University Press, 1982.
- Broc, Numa. *La géographie de la Renaissance (1420–1620)*. Paris: Bibliothèque nationale, 1980.
- Broton, Jerry. *Trading Territories: Mapping the Early Modern World*. London: Reaktion Books, 1997.
- Buell, Lawrence. *The Environmental Imagination: Thoreau, Nature Writing, and the Formation of American Culture*. Cambridge, MA: Harvard University Press, 1995.
- 'Toxic Discourse.' *Critical Inquiry* 24 (1998): 639–65.
- *Writing for an Endangered World: Literature, Culture, and Environment in the U.S. and Beyond*. Cambridge, MA: Harvard University Press, 2001.
- Buisseret, David. 'Monarchs, Ministers, and Maps in France before the Accession of Louis XIV.' In *Monarchs, Ministers, and Maps: The Emergence of Cartography as a Tool of Government in Early Modern Europe*, ed. Buisseret, 99–123. Chicago: Chicago University Press, 1992.
- Burgard, Chrystèle, and Françoise Chenet, eds. *Paysage et identité régionale: De pays rhônalpins en paysages. Actes du colloque de Valence*. Valence: La passe du vent, 1999.
- Burke, Séan, ed. *Authorship: From Plato to the Postmodern: A Reader*. Edinburgh: Edinburgh University Press, 1995.
- Buttimer, Anne. *Society and Milieu in the French Geographic Tradition*. Chicago: Rand McNally, 1971.
- Caisso, R. 'La vente de la forêt de Gâtine au temps de Ronsard.' *Humanisme et Renaissance* 4 (1937): 274–85.
- Campagnoli, Ruggero. 'L'occhio di Jean-Antoine de Baïf.' In *La percezione del paesaggio nel rinascimento*, ed. Ruggero Campagnoli, Fulvio Pezzarossa and Anna Soncini Fratta. Bologna: CLUEB, 2004. 69–80.
- Campagnoli, Ruggero, Eric Lysøe, and Anna Soncini Fratta, eds. *'L'Olive' de Joachim Du Bellay: Actes des seminaires d'analyse textuelle Pasquali (Lucelle, 1er–4 Dec. 2005)*. Bologna: CLUEB, 2007.

Campbell, SueEllen. 'The Land and Language of Desire: Where Deep Ecology and Post-Structuralism Meet.' *Western American Literature* 24 (1989): 199–211.

Campbell, Tony. *The Earliest Printed Maps, 1472–1500*. London: British Library, 1987.

Campo, Roberto. 'Pictorial Concerns in the Ronsardian *Exegi Monumentum*.' *Sixteenth-Century Journal* 24 (1993): 671–83.

– *Ronsard's Contentious Sisters: The Paragone between Poetry and Painting in the Works of Pierre de Ronsard*. Chapel Hill: University of North Carolina Press, 1998.

– 'Tyard's Graphic Metamorphoses: Figuring the Semiosic Drift in the *Douze fables de fleuves ou fontaines*.' *Renaissance Quarterly* 54 (2001): 776–800.

– 'Du miroir à la mémoire: Sur les jeux ecphrastiques dans *La Bergerie* de Remy Belleau.' *Nouvelle revue du seizième siècle* 20 (2002): 5–23.

Carnel, Marc. *Le sang embaumé des roses*. Geneva: Droz, 2004.

Cartmill, Matt. *A View to a Death in the Morning: Hunting and Nature through History*. Cambridge, MA: Harvard University Press, 1993.

Castor, Grahame. *Pléiade Poetics: A Study in Sixteenth-Century Thought and Terminology*. Cambridge: Cambridge University Press, 1964.

Castor, Grahame, and Terence Cave, eds. *Neo-Latin and the Vernacular in Renaissance France*. Oxford: Clarendon, 1984.

Catach, Nina. *L'Orthographe française à l'époque de la Renaissance*. Geneva: Droz, 1986.

Cauquelin, Anne. *L'invention du paysage*. Paris: Plon, 1989.

Cave, Terence. *The Cornucopian Text: Problems of Writing in the French Renaissance*. Oxford: Oxford University Press, 1979.

Céard, Jean. *La nature et les prodigues*. Geneva: Droz, 1996.

Certeau, Michel de. *La fable mystique*. Paris: Gallimard, 1982.

– *L'invention du quotidien*. Paris: Gallimard, 1990.

Cesbron, Georges, ed. *Du Bellay: Actes du colloque international d'Angers du 26 ou 29 mai 1989*. 2. vols. Angers: Presses de l'Université d'Angers, 1990.

Chamard, Henri. *Histoire de la Pléiade*. Paris: H. Didier, 1961–3.

Champier, Symphorien. *Petit traitté des fleuves*. Lyon, 1556.

Charles d'Orléans. *Poésies*. Ed. Pierre Champion. Paris: Champion, 1956.

Chartier, Roger. *Culture écrite et société: L'ordre des livres, XIVe–XVIIIe siècle*. Paris: Albin Michel, 1996.

Chevrolet, Teresa. *L'idée de fable: Théories de la fiction poétique à la Renaissance*. Geneva: Droz, 2007.

Clark, Albert. *The Descent of Manuscripts*. Oxford: Clarendon, 1918.

Clarke, Kenneth. *Landscape into Art*. London: Beacon, 1956.

Clement, N.H. 'Nature and the Country in Sixteenth- and Seventeenth-Century French Poetry.' *PMLA* 44 (1929): 1005–47.

Clements, Robert. *Critical Theory and Practice of the Pléiade*. Cambridge, MA: Harvard University Press, 1942.

Cohen, Paul. 'Illustration du français et persistance des langues régionales: La pluralité linguistique dans la constitution des idéologies sociales en France à l'époque moderne.' In *Lyon et l'illustration de la langue française à la Renaissance*, ed. Gérard Defaux, 147–67. Lyon: ENS, 2003.

– 'L'imaginaire d'une langue nationale: L'État, les langues, et l'invention du mythe de l'Ordonnance de Villers-Cotterêts à l'époque moderne.' *Histoire epistémologie langage* 25 (2003): 19–69.

– 'Poets into Frenchmen: Timothy Hampton on Literature and National Sentiment in Renaissance France.' *Shakespeare Studies* 33 (2005): 173–204.

Cohen, Stephen. 'Between Form and Culture: New Historicism and the Promise of a Historial Formalism.' In *Renaissance Literature and Its Formal Engagements*, ed. Rasmussen, 17–41. New York: Palgrave, 2002.

Coleman, Dorothy. *The Gallo-Roman Muse: Aspects of Roman Literary Tradition in Sixteenth-Century French Literature*. Cambridge: Cambridge University Press, 1979.

Colie, Rosalie. *The Resources of Kind: Genre Theory in the Renaissance*. Berkeley: University of California Press, 1973.

Collingwood, R.G. *The Idea of Nature*. Oxford: Oxford University Press, 1945.

Collins, James. *The State in Early Modern France*. Cambridge: Cambridge University Press, 1995.

Colonna, Francesco (?). *Le songe de Poliphile*. Ed. Gilles Polizzi, trans. Henri Martin. Paris: Imprimerie nationale, 1994.

Comito, Terry. *The Idea of the Garden in the Renaissance*. New Brunswick, NJ: Rutgers University Press, 1971.

Conley, Tom. *The Graphic Unconscious in Early Modern French Writing*. Cambridge: Cambridge University Press, 1992.

– *The Self-Made Map: Cartographic Writing in Early Modern France*. Minneapolis: University of Minnesota Press, 1996.

– 'Putting French Studies on the Map.' *Diacritics* 28 (1998): 23–39.

Corner, James. 'The Agency of Mapping.' In *Mappings*, ed. Denis Cosgrove, 213–52. London: Reaktion Books, 1999.

Cosgrove, Denis. 'Prospect, Perspective, and the Evolution of the Landscape Idea.' *Transactions, Institute of British Geographers* 1 (1985): 45–62.

– *The Palladian Landscape: Geographical Change and Its Cultural Representations in Sixteenth-Century Italy*. Philadelphia: Pennsylvania State University Press, 1993.

– *Apollo's Eye: A Cartographic Genealogy of the Earth in the Western Imagination.* Baltimore: Johns Hopkins University Press, 2001.

Cosgrove, Denis, ed. *Mappings.* London: Reaktion Books, 1999.

Cosgrove, Denis, and Stephen Daniels, eds. *The Iconography of Landscape: Essays on the Symbolic Representation, Design, and Use of Past Environment.* Cambridge: Cambridge University Press, 1988.

Coyault, Sylviane. *L'histoire et la géographie dans le récit poétique.* Clermont-Ferrand: Centre de recherches sur les littératures modernes et contemporaines, 1997.

Cresswell, Tim. *Place: A Short Introduction.* Oxford: Blackwell, 2004.

Crone, Gerald. *Maps and Their Makers: An Introduction to the History of Cartography.* London: Hutchinson's University Library, 1953.

Cronon, William. *Uncommon Ground: Rethinking the Human Place in Nature.* New York: Norton, 1996.

Dainotto, Roberto. *Place in Literature: Regions, Cultures, Communities.* Ithaca and London: Cornell University Press, 2000.

Dainville, François de. *Cartes anciennes de l'église de France: Historique, répertoire, guide d'usage.* Paris: Vrin, 1956.

– 'Le premier atlas de France: *Le Théâtre françoys* de M. Bouguereau, 1594.' In *Comité des travaux historiques et scientifiques: Actes du 85e Congrès national des Sociétés savantes, Chambéry-Annecy, 1960,* 1–50. Paris: Bibliothèque nationale, 1961.

– 'Jean Jolivet's "Description des Gaules."' *Imago Mundi* 18 (1964): 45–52.

– *Le langage des géographes.* Paris: Picard, 1964.

– *La géographie des humanistes.* Geneva: Slatkine Reprints, 1969. (Orig. pub. 1940.)

Daniels, Stephen. 'Landscape and Art.' In *A Companion to Cultural Geography,* ed. James Duncan, Nuala Johnson, and Richard Schein, 430–46. Oxford: Blackwell, 2004.

Da Silva, Jill. 'Ecocriticism and Myth: The Case of Erysichthon.' *Interdisciplinary Studies in Literature and Environment* 15 (2008): 103–16.

Daston, Lorraine, and Katharine Park. *Wonders and Order of Nature: 1150–1750.* New York: Zone Books, 1998.

Dauvois, Nathalie. *De la 'Satura' à la 'Bergerie': Le prosimètre pastoral en France à la Renaissance et ses modèles.* Paris: Champion, 1998.

– *Le sujet lyrique à la Renaissance.* Paris: PUF, 2000.

Debus, Allen. *Man and Nature in the Renaissance.* Cambridge: Cambridge University Press, 1978.

de Courcelles, Dominique, ed. *Nature et Paysages: L'émergence d'une nouvelle subjectivité à la Renaissance.* Paris: École des Chartes, 2006.

Defaux, Gérard. 'Facing the Marot Generation: Ronsard's "giovenili errori."'
  Modern Language Notes (MLN) 119 (2004): 299–326.
Deguy, Michel. *Tombeau de Du Bellay.* Paris: Gallimard, 1973.
Delacourcelle, Doris. *Le sentiment de l'art dans la 'Bergerie' de Remy Belleau.*
  Oxford: Blackwell, 1945.
Delano-Smith, Catherine. 'Why Theory in the History of Cartography?' *Imago
  Mundi* 48 (1996): 198–203.
DellaNeva, JoAnn. *Song and Counter-Song: Scève's 'Délie' and Petrarch's 'Rime.'*
  Lexington, KY: French Forum, 1983.
– 'Illustrating the *Deffence*: Imitation and Poetic Perfection in Du Bellay's
  Olive.' French Review 61 (1987): 39–49.
– 'Du Bellay: Reader of Scève, Reader of Petrarch.' *Romanic Review* 79 (1988):
  401–11.
– 'Variations in a Minor Key: Du Bellay's Imitations of the Giolito Anthology
  Poets.' *French Forum* 14 (1989): 133–46.
– 'Teaching Du Bellay a Lesson: Ronsard's Rewriting of Ariosto's Sonnets.'
  French Forum 24 (1999): 285–301.
– 'An Exploding Canon: Petrarch and the Petrarchists in Renaissance France.'
  Annali d'italianistica 22 (2004): 189–206.
Demaizière, Colette. 'De la muse à l'écriture: Le choix linguistique comme
  support de l'invention.' In *La naissance du monde et l'invention du poème.
  Mélanges de poétique et d'histoire littéraire du xvie siècle offerts à Yvonne
  Bellenger,* ed. Jean-Claude Ternaux, 22–36. Paris: Champion, 1998.
Demerson, Geneviève. *Joachim Du Bellay et la belle romaine.* Orléans:
  Paradigme, 1996.
Demerson, Guy. *La mythologie classique dans l'œuvre lyrique de la Pléiade.*
  Geneva: Droz, 1972.
– *La notion de genre à la Renaissance.* Geneva: Slatkine Reprints, 1984.
– 'Remy Belleau et la naissance du monde.' In *La naissance du monde et
  l'invention du poème: Mélanges de poétique et d'histoire littéraire du XVIe siècle
  offerts à Yvonne Bellenger,* ed. Jean-Claude Ternaux, 93–215. Paris: Champion,
  1998.
Demonet, Marie-Luce. *Les voix du signe: Nature du langage à la Renaissance.*
  Paris: Champion, 1992.
De Planhol, Xavier, and Paul Claval. *Géographie historique de la France.* Paris:
  Fayard, 1988.
Desan, Philippe. 'De la poésie de circonstance à la satire: Du Bellay et
  l'engagement poétique,' in *Du Bellay: Actes du colloque internationale
  d'Angers,* ed. Cesbron, 2:421–39. Angers: Presses de l'Université d'Angers,
  1990.

– *Les commerces de Montaigne: Le discours économique des 'Essais.'* Paris: Nizet, 1992.
– *L'imaginaire économique de la Renaissance.* Mont-de-Marsan: Éditions InterUniversitaires, 1993.
– *Penser l'histoire à la Renaissance.* Caen: Paradigme, 1993.
Desguine, Antoine. *Arcueil et les poètes du XVIe siècle: La vigne, le vin et la tradition bachique à Arcueil-Cachan.* Paris: Champion, c. 1950.
Devèze, Michel. *La vie de la forêt française au XVIe siècle.* Paris: SEVPEN, 1961.
Dewald, Jonathan. *Aristocratic Experience and the Origins of Modern Culture.* Berkeley: University of California Press, 1993.
Dillon, Matthew. 'The Ecology of the Greek Sanctuary.' *Zeitschrift für Papyrologie und Epigraphik* 118 (1997): 113–27.
Dorat, Jean. *Les odes latines.* Ed. Geneviève Demerson. Clermont-Ferrand: Faculté des lettres et sciences humaines, 1979.
Downs, Roger, and David Stea. *Maps in Minds: Reflections on Cognitive Mapping.* New York: Harper and Row, 1977.
Drapeyron, Ludovic. 'L'image de la France sous les derniers Valois (1525–1589) et sous les premiers Bourbons (1589–1682).' *Revue de Géographie* 24 (1889): 1–15.
– 'Jean Fayen et la première carte du Limousin (1594).' *Bulletin de la Société archéologique et historique du Limousin* 42 (1894): 61–105.
Du Bartas, Guillaume. *La sepmaine.* Ed. Yvonne Bellenger. Paris: Nizet, 1981.
Du Bellay, Joachim. *Poésies françaises et latines de Joachim Du Bellay.* Ed. E. Courbet. Paris: Garnier, 1919.
– *La Deffence et illustration de la langue francoyse.* Ed. Henri Chamard. Paris: M. Didier, 1948.
– *Les Regrets et autres œuvres poétiques.* Ed. M. Screech and J. Jolliffe. Geneva: Droz, 1974.
– *Œuvres poétiques.* Vol. 7, *Œuvres latines: Poemata.* Ed. and trans. Geneviève Demerson, preface by Alain Michel. Paris: Nizet, 1984.
– *La Deffence et illustration de la langue françoyse, et L'Olive.* Ed. Jean-Charles Monferran and Ernesta Caldarini. Geneva: Droz, 2007.
– 'The Regrets' with 'The Antiquities of Rome,' Three Latin Elegies, and 'The Defense and Enrichment of the French Language.' Ed. and trans. Richard Helgerson. Philadelphia: University of Pennsylvania Press, 2007.
Dubois, Claude. *L'imaginaire de la Renaissance.* Paris: PUF, 1985.
Du Faur de Pibrac, Guy. 'Les quatrains,' 'Les plaisirs de la vie rustique,' et autres poésies.* Ed. Loris Petris. Geneva: Droz, 2004.
Duncan, James, Nuala Johnson, and Richard Schein, eds. *A Companion to Cultural Geography.* Oxford: Blackwell, 2004.

Dunn, Kevin. *Pretexts of Authority*. Stanford: Stanford University Press, 1994.

Duport, Danièle. *Les jardins qui sentent le sauvage: Ronsard et la poétique du paysage*. Geneva: Droz, 2001.

– *Le jardin et la nature: Ordre et variété dans la littérature de la Renaissance*. Geneva: Droz, 2002.

Eckhardt, Sandor. *Remy Belleau, sa vie, sa Bergerie*. Geneva: Slatkine Reprints, 1969. (Orig. pub. 1917.)

Edgerton, Samuel Y., Jr. 'From Mental Matrix to *Mappamundi* to Christian Empire: The Heritage of Ptolemaic Cartography in the Renaissance.' In *Art and Cartography: Six Historical Essays*, ed. David Woodward, 10–50. Chicago: University of Chicago Press, 1987.

Edney, Matthew. 'Cartography with "Progress": Reinterpreting the Nature and Historical Development of Mapmaking.' *Cartographica* 30 (1993): 54–68.

– 'Brian Harley's Career and Intellectual Legacy.' *Cartographica* 40 (2005): 1–17.

Elias, Norbert. *The Court Society*. Trans. Edmund Jephcott. New York: Pantheon, 1983.

Empson, William. *Some Versions of Pastoral*. Norfolk: New Directions, 1950.

Enge, Torsten. *Garden Architecture in Europe, 1450–1800: From the Villa Garden of the Italian Renaissance to the English Landscape Garden*. Koln: Taschen, 1990.

Escobedo, Andrew. *Nationalism and Historical Loss in Renaissance England*. New York: Cornell University Press, 2004.

Estienne, Charles. *La guide des chemins de France de 1553*. Ed. J. Bonnerot. Geneva: Slatkine Reprints, 1978.

– *L'Agriculture, et maison rustique de M. Charles Estienne, et Jean Liebault, docteurs en medecine*. Paris: Jacques du Puys, 1583.

Estienne, Robert. *Dictionaire francoislatin, autrement dict Les mots Francois avec les manieres duser diceulx, tournez en Latin*. Paris, 1549.

Evernden, Neil. *The Social Creation of Nature*. Baltimore: Johns Hopkins University Press, 1992.

Falguières, Patricia. *Le maniérisme: Une avant-garde au XVIe siècle*. Paris: Gallimard, 2004.

Ferguson, Margaret. 'The Exile's Defense: Du Bellay's *La Deffence et illustration de la langue françoyse*.' *PMLA* 93 (1978): 275–89.

– *Trials of Desire: Renaissance Defenses of Poetry*. New Haven: Yale University Press, 1983.

Fernbach, Isabelle. *Beyond Pastoral: Rusticity and the Reframing of Court Culture in 16th-Century French Literature*. PhD diss., University of California, Berkeley, 2006.

Ferry, Luc. *Le nouvel ordre écologique: L'arbre, l'animal et l'homme*. Paris: Grasset, 1993.

Field, J.V. *The Invention of Infinity: Mathematics and Art in the Renaissance.* Oxford: Oxford University Press, 1997.

Fierro-Domenech, Alfred. *Le pré carré: Géographie historique de la France.* Paris: Laffont, 1986.

Fiorani, Francesca. *The Marvel of Maps: Art, Cartography, and Politics in Renaissance Italy.* New Haven: Yale University Press, 2005.

Fitter, Chris. *Poetry, Space, Landscape: Toward a New Theory.* Cambridge: Cambridge University Press, 1995.

Foisil, Madeleine. *Le sire de Gouberville: Un gentilhomme normand au XVIe siècle.* Paris: Aubier Montaigne, 1981.

Foucault, Michel. *Les mots et les choses.* Paris: Gallimard, 1966.

– 'Qu'est-ce qu'un auteur?' In *Dits et écrits, 1954–1988*, ed. Daniel Defert, François Ewald, and Jacques Lagrange, 789–821. Paris: Gallimard, 1994.

Freccero, John. 'The Fig Tree and the Laurel: Petrarch's Poetics.' *Diacritics* 5 (1975): 34–40.

Freedman, Luba. *The Classical Pastoral in the Visual Arts.* New York: Peter Lang, 1989.

Frelick, Nancy. *Délie as Other: Toward a Poetics of Desire in Scève's 'Délie.'* Lexington, KY: French Forum, 1994.

Frémont, Armand. *La région espace vécu.* Paris: PUF, 1976.

Fussell, George. 'The Classical Tradition in West European Farming: The Sixteenth Century.' *Economic History Review* 22 (1969): 538–51.

Gadoffre, Gilbert. *Du Bellay et le sacré.* Paris: Gallimard, 1978.

Gagneux, Christophe. *Liré, avant-hier et hier.* Maulevrier: Hérault-Editions, 1982.

Gambino Longo, Susanna. *Savoir de la nature et poésie des choses.* Paris: Champion, 2004.

Garane, Jeanne. 'Introduction.' In *Geo/graphies: Mapping the Imagination in French and Francophone Literature and Film* (French Literature Series 30), ed. G. Henry Freeman, 9–13. New York: Rodopi, 2003.

Garber, Marjorie. *Academic Instincts.* Princeton: Princeton University Press, 2000.

Garrard, Greg. *Ecocriticism.* New York: Routledge, 2004.

Gellner, Ernest. *Nations and Nationalism.* Ithaca: Cornell University Press, 1983.

Giamatti, A. Bartlett. *The Earthly Paradise and the Renaissance Epic.* Princeton: Princeton University Press, 1966.

Giesey, Ralph. 'Rules of Inheritance and Strategies of Mobility.' *American Historical Review* 82 (1977): 271–89.

– *Rulership in France, 15th–17th Centuries.* Burlington, VT: Ashgate, 2004.

Gifford, Terry. *Pastoral.* London: Routledge, 1999.

Gillies, John. *Shakespeare and the Geography of Difference*. Cambridge: Cambridge University Press, 1994.

Giraud, Yves, ed. *Le paysage à la Renaissance*. Fribourg: Éditions Universitaires, 1988.

Glacken, Clarence. *Traces on the Rhodian Shore: Nature and Culture in Western Thought from Ancient Times to the End of the Eighteenth Century*. Berkeley: University of California Press, 1967.

Glotfelty, Cheryll, and Harold Fromm, eds. *The Ecocriticism Reader*. Athens: University of Georgia Press, 1996.

Golson, Lucile M. 'Landscape Prints and Landscapists of the School of Fontainebleau, c. 1543–c. 1570.' *Gazette des beaux-arts* 73 (1969): 95–110.

Gombrich, Ernst. 'Mannerism: The Historiographic Background.' In Gombrich, *Norm and Form: Studies in the Art of the Renaissance*, 99–106. London: Phaidon, 1966.

– 'The Renaissance Theory of Art and the Rise of Landscape.' In Gombrich, *Norm and Form*, 107–21. London: Phaidon, 1966.

Gorris Camos, Rosanna. '"Ses montz trez haultz haulsent notre desir": Marguerite de Navarre, Peletier du Mans: Poètes de la montagne.' In *Les montagnes de l'esprit: Imaginaire et histoire de la montagne*, ed. Rosanna Gorris Camos, 51–77. Aoste: Musumeci, 2005.

Goujet, Claude-Pierre (Abbé). *Bibliothèque françoyse*. 1741–7. Geneva : Slatkine Reprints, 1966.

Goyet, Francis, ed. *Traités de poétique et de rhétorique de la Renaissance*. Paris: Livre de Poche, 1990.

– 'Qu'est-ce que l'Idée d'un texte? (Littérature vs. rhétorique).' In *What Is Literature? France 1100–1600*, ed. François Cornilliat, Ullrich Langer, and Douglas Kelly, 33–52. Lexington, KY: French Forum, 1993.

Grafton, Anthony. *Defenders of the Text: The Traditions of Scholarship in an Age of Science*. Cambridge, MA: Harvard University Press, 1991.

– *New Worlds, Ancient Texts: The Power of Tradition and the Shock of Discovery*. Cambridge, MA: Harvard University Press, 1992.

– *Commerce with the Classics: Ancient Books and Renaissance Readers*. Ann Arbor: University of Michigan Press, 1997.

– *Cardano's Cosmos: The Worlds and Work of a Renaissance Astrologer*. Cambridge, MA: Harvard University Press, 1999.

Grafton, Anthony, and Lisa Jardine. *From Humanism to the Humanities: Education and the Liberal Arts in Fifteenth- and Sixteenth-Century Europe*. London: Duckworth, 1986.

Grafton, Anthony, and Ann Blair, eds. *The Transmission of Culture in Early Modern Europe*. Philadelphia: University of Pennsylvania Press, 1990.

Gray, Floyd. *La poétique de Du Bellay*. Paris: Nizet, 1978.

Greenblatt, Stephen. *Renaissance Self-Fashioning from More to Shakespeare*. Chicago: Chicago University Press, 1980.

– 'Psychoanalysis and Renaissance Culture.' In *Renaissance Theory / Literary Texts*, ed. Patricia Parker and David Quint, 210–24. Baltimore: Johns Hopkins University Press, 1986.

Greene, Thomas. *The Light in Troy*. New Haven: Yale University Press, 1982.

Greenfeld, Liah. *Nationalism: Five Roads to Modernity*. Cambridge, MA: Harvard University Press, 1992.

Grendler, Paul F. 'The Universities of the Renaissance and Reformation.' *Renaissance Quarterly* 57 (2004): 1–42.

Grove, Richard. *Green Imperialism*. Cambridge: Cambridge University Press, 1995.

Grudé La Croix du Maine, François, and Antoine Du Verdier. *Les Bibliothèques françoyses*. Paris: Saillant et Nyon, 1772–3.

Guiffrey, J. 'Les Gobelin, teinturiers en écarlate.' *Memoires de la Société de l'histoire de Paris* 31 (1904): 1–92.

Guillement, Dominique, and Jacques Peret, eds. *Les cahiers du Gerhico: Pour une histoire des pays. Tables rondes, Poitiers – 1999/2000*. Poitiers: Université de Poitiers, 2003.

Hacking, Ian. *The Social Construction of What?* Cambridge, MA: Harvard University Press, 1999.

Hall, J.T.D. 'Was Ronsard's *Bergerie* Performed at Fontainebleau in 1564?' *Bibliothèque d'humanisme et Renaissance* 51 (1989): 301–9.

Hallyn, Fernand. 'Le paysage anthropomorphe.' In *Le paysage à la Renaissance*, ed. Yves Giraud, 43–54. Fribourg: Éditions Universitaires Fribourg Suisse, 1988.

Hamon, Philippe, and Jean Jacquart, eds. *Archives de la France*. Vol. 3, *XVI siècle*. Paris: Fayard, 1997.

Hampton, Timothy. *Writing from History: The Rhetoric of Exemplarity in Renaissance Literature*. Ithaca: Cornell University Press, 1990.

– *Literature and Nation in the Sixteenth Century: Inventing Renaissance France*. Ithaca: Cornell University Press, 2001.

Hardie, Philip. 'Ovid into Laura: Absent Presences in the *Metamorphoses* and Petrarch's *Rime sparse*.' In *Ovidian Transformations: Essays on Ovid's 'Metamorphoses' and Its Reception*, ed. Hardie, Alessando Barchiesi, and Stephen Hinds, 254–70. Cambridge: Cambridge Philological Society: 1999.

Harley, J.B. 'The Iconology of Early Maps.' *Imago et mensura mundi: Atti del IX Congresso internazionale di storia della cartografia* 1 (1985): 29–38.

– 'Maps, Knowledge, and Power.' In *The Iconography of Landscape: Essays on the Symbolic Representation, Design, and Use of Past Environments*, ed. Denis

Cosgrove and Stephen Daniels, 277–312. Cambridge: Cambridge University Press, 1988.

- 'Silences and Secrecy: The Hidden Agenda of Cartography in Early Modern Europe.' *Imago Mundi* 40 (1988): 57–76.
- 'Deconstructing the Map.' *Cartographica* 26 (1989): 1–20.
- *The New Nature of Maps: Essays in the History of Cartography*, ed. Paul Laxton. Baltimore: Johns Hopkins University Press, 2001.

Harley, J.B., and David Woodward, eds. *History of Cartography: Cartography in Prehistoric, Ancient, and Medieval Europe and the Mediterranean*. Chicago: University of Chicago Press, 1987.

Hartley, David. 'Du Bellay et la patrie: Échos littéraires.' In *Du Bellay: Actes du colloque international d'Angers*, ed. Cesbron, 2:653–62. Angers: Presses de l'Université d'Angers, 1990.

- *Patriotism in the Work of Joachim Du Bellay: A Study of the Relationship between the Poet and France*. Lewiston, NY: Edwin Mellen, 1993.

Harvey, David. *Spaces of Hope*. Berkeley: University of California Press, 2000.

Heise, Ursula. 'The Hitchhiker's Guide to Ecocriticism.' *PMLA* 121 (2006): 503–16.

Helgerson, Richard. *Forms of Nationhood: The Elizabethan Writing of England*. Chicago: University of Chicago Press, 1992.

- 'Remembering, Forgetting, and the Founding of a National Literature: The Example of Joachim Du Bellay.' In *The Yearbook of Research in English and American Literature* 21 (2005): *Literature, Literary History, and Cultural Memory*, ed. Herbert Graves, 19–44. Tübingen: Gunter Narr Verlag, 2005.

Helgerson, Richard, and Joann Grenfell, eds. *Literature and Geography*. Early Modern Literary Studies 4, 1998.

Heller, Henry. *Anti-Italianism in Sixteenth-Century France*. Toronto: University of Toronto Press, 2003.

Hellwig, Fritz. 'La carte de Lorraine.' In *Gerard Mercator cosmographe: Le temps et l'espace*, ed. Marcel Watelet, 297–315. Antwerp: Fonds Mercator, 1994.

Henry, Freeman, ed. *Geo/graphies: Mapping the Imagination in French and Francophone Literature and Film*. New York: Rodopi, 2003.

Herendeen, W.H. 'Castara's smiles ... Sabrin's tears: Nature and Setting in Renaissance River Poems.' *Comparative Literature* 39 (1987): 289–305.

Hervé, Roger. 'L'œuvre cartographique de Nicolas de Nicolay et d'Antoine de Laval.' *Bulletin de la Section de géographie* 68 (1955): 223–63.

Hicks, Brian Scott. 'W.E.B. Du Bois, Booker T. Washington, and Richard Wright: Toward an Ecocriticism of Color.' *Callaloo* 29 (2006): 202–22.

Higgot, Suzanne, and Isabelle Biron. 'Marguerite de France as Minerva: A Sixteenth-Century Limoges Painted Enamel by Jean de Court in the Wallace Collection.' *Apollo* 504 (2004): 21–30.

Hobsbawm, Eric. *Nations and Nationalism Since 1780: Programme, Myth, Reality*. Cambridge: Cambridge University Press, 1990.

Hodges, Elisabeth. *Urban Poetics in the French Renaissance*. Burlington, VT: Ashgate, 2008.

Hoffman, Philip. 'The Economic Theory of Sharecropping in Early Modern France.' *Journal of Economic History* 44 (1984): 309–19.

Hooson, David, ed. *Geography and National Identity*. Oxford: Blackwell, 1994.

Horace. *Odes and Epodes*. Ed. and trans. Niall Rudd. Cambridge, MA: Harvard University Press, 2004.

Hubbard, Thomas. *The Pipes of Pan: Intertextuality and Literary Filiation from Theocritus to Milton*. Ann Arbor: University of Michigan Press, 1998.

Huchon, Mireille. *Le français de la Renaissance*. Paris: PUF, 1988.

– *Louise Labé: Une créature de papier*. Geneva: Droz, 2006.

Hughes, J. Donald. 'How the Ancients Viewed Deforestation.' *Journal of Field Archeology* 10 (1983): 435–45.

Huguet, Edmond. *L'évolution du sens des mots depuis le XVIe siècle*. Paris: Droz, 1934.

Hulubei, Alice. *L'églogue en France au XVIe siècle: Époque des Valois (1515–1589)*. Paris: Droz, 1938.

Humblot, Émile. *Notre vieux Joinville: Son château d'autrefois*. Dijon: Éditions du Raisin, 1928.

Hunt, J.D., ed. *The Pastoral Landscape*. Hanover and London: University Press of New England, 1992.

Huppert, George. *Les bourgeois gentilshommes: An Essay on the Definition of Elites in Renaissance France*. Chicago: University of Chicago Press, 1977.

Jacob, Christian. *L'empire des cartes*. Paris: Albin Michel, 1992.

– 'Toward a Cultural History of Cartography.' *Imago Mundi* 48 (1996): 191–8.

Jeanneret, Michel. 'Les œuvres d'art dans la *Bergerie* de Belleau.' *Revue d'histoire littéraire de la France* 70 (1970): 1–14.

– 'The Vagaries of Exemplarity: Distortion or Dismissal?' *Journal of the History of Ideas* 59 (1998): 565–79.

– *Perpetuum mobile: Métamorphoses des corps et des œuvres de Vinci à Montaigne*. Paris: Macula, 1997.

Jenkins, Hugh. *Feigned Commonwealths: The Country-House Poem and the Fashioning of Ideal Community*. Pittsburgh: Duquesne University Press, 1998.

Joanne, Adolphe, dir. *Dictionnaire géographique et administratif de la France et de ses colonies*. Paris: Hachette, 1890–1905.

Jouanna, Arlette. *Ordre social: Mythes et réalités dans la France du XVIe siècle*. Paris: Hachette, 1977.

Jouanna, Arlette, Jacqueline Boucher, Dominique Biloghi, and Guy Thiec, eds. *Histoire et dictionnaire des guerres de religion*. Paris: Laffont, 1998.

Joukovsky, Françoise. *La gloire dans la poésie française et néolatine du XVIe siècle: Des rhétoriqueurs à Agrippa d'Aubigné*. Geneva: Droz, 1969.
- *Poésie et mythologie au XVIe siècle: Quelques mythes de l'inspiration chez les poètes de la Renaissance*. Paris: Nizet, 1969
- *Paysages de la Renaissance*. Paris: PUF, 1974.
- 'L'écriture artiste dans quelques proses de la *Bergerie*.' In *Prose et prosateurs de la Renaissance: Mélanges offerts à R. Aulotte*, ed. Robert Aulotte, 259–68. Paris: Sedes, 1988.
- 'Qu'est-ce qu'un paysage? L'exemple des odes ronsardiennes.' In *Le paysage à la Renaissance*, ed. Yves Giraud, 55–66. Fribourg: Éditions Universitaires Fribourg Suisse, 1988.
- *Le bel objet: Les paradis artificiels de la Pléiade*. Paris: Champion, 1991.
- 'La composition de la *Bergerie* de Remy Belleau.' In *La pastorale française de Remy Belleau à Victor Hugo*, ed. Alain Niderst, 9–22. Paris: Centre d'étude et de recherche d'histoire des idées de la sensibilité, 1991.
Joukovsky, Françoise, and Pierre Joukovsky. *À travers la Galerie François I*. Paris: Champion, 1992.
Jousselin, Roland. *Nicolas Denisot: Poète de la Pléiade*. Paris: Christian, 2007.
Jung, Marc. *Hercule dans la littérature française du seizième siècle*. Geneva: Droz, 1966.
Kain, R.J.P., and Elizabeth Baigent. *The Cadastral Map in the Service of the State: A History of Property Mapping*. Chicago: University of Chicago Press, 1992.
Karrow, Robert W., Jr. *Mapmakers of the Sixteenth Century and Their Maps*. Chicago: Speculum Orbis, 1993.
Kaufmann, Thomas. *The Mastery of Nature: Aspects of Art, Science, and Humanism in the Renaissance*. Princeton: Princeton University Press, 1993.
Keating, L. Clark. *Studies on the Literary Salon in France, 1550–1615*. Cambridge, MA: Harvard University Press, 1941.
Kedourie, Elie. *Nationalism*. New York: Praeger, 1960.
Kegel-Brinkgreve, E. *The Echoing Woods: Bucolic and Pastoral from Theocritus to Wordsworth*. Amsterdam: Gieben, 1990.
Keller, Marcus. 'Nicolas de Nicolay's *Navigations* and the Domestic Politics of Travel Writing.' *L'esprit créateur* 48 (2008): 18–31.
Kennedy, William. *Jacopo Sannazaro and the Uses of Pastoral*. Hanover and London: University Press of New England, 1983
- *Authorizing Petrarch*. Ithaca: Cornell University Press, 1994.
- *The Site of Petrarchism: Early Modern National Sentiment in Italy, France, and England*. Baltimore: Johns Hopkins University Press, 2003.
Ketcham, Herbert. *Nature in Old and Middle French Poetry and in the First Poet of the Renaissance*. PhD diss., University of Pennsylvania, 1950.
Kibédi-Varga, Áron. 'L'histoire de la rhétorique et la rhétorique des genres.' *Rhetorica* 3 (1985): 201–21.

– 'Les lieux de la rhétorique classique.' In *La naissance du roman en France*, ed. Nicole Boursier and David Trott, 101–12. Paris: Papers on French Seventeeth-Century Literature, 1990.

Kinney, Daniel, and Elizabeth Styron. 'Ovid Illustrated: The Renaissance Reception of Ovid in Image and Text.' http://etext.lib.virginia.edu/latin/ovid/about.html.

Kirchner, Walther. 'Mind, Mountain, and History.' *Journal of the History of Ideas* 11 (1950): 412–47.

Knecht, R.J. *Francis I*. Cambridge: Cambridge University Press, 1982.

– *The Rise and Fall of Renaissance France*. 2nd ed. Oxford: Blackwell, 2001.

Knott, G.A. '"Une question lancinante": Further Thoughts on Space in the Chansons de Geste.' *Modern Language Review* 94 (1999): 22–34.

Koelb, Janice Hewlett. *The Poetics of Description*. New York: Palgrave, 2006.

Krieger, Murray. *The Play and Place of Criticism*. Baltimore: Johns Hopkins University Press, 1967.

– *Ekphrasis: The Illusion of the Natural Sign*. Baltimore: Johns Hopkins University Press, 1992.

Kristeller, Paul. *Renaissance Thought and Its Sources*. New York: Columbia University Press, 1979.

Kritzman, Lawrence. *The Rhetoric of Sexuality and the Literature of the French Renaissance*. Cambridge: Cambridge University Press, 1991.

Kroeber, Karl. *Ecological Literary Criticism: Romantic Imagining and the Biology of Mind*. New York: Columbia University Press, 1994.

Kushner, Eva. 'Le rôle de la temporalité dans la pensée de Pontus de Tyard.' In *Le temps et la durée dans la littérature au Moyen Âge et à la Renaissance*, ed. Yvonne Bellenger, 211–30. Paris: Nizet, 1986.

– *Pontus de Tyard et son œuvre poétique*. Paris: Champion, 2001.

– *Le dialogue à la Renaissance: Histoire et poétique*. Geneva: Droz, 2004.

Lacan, Jacques. *Écrits: A Selection*. Trans. Alan Sheridan. London: Tavistock, 1977.

Ladurie, Emmanuel Le Roy. *Histoire de France des régions: La périphérie française des origines à nos jours*. Paris: Seuil, 2001.

– *Histoire des paysans français: De la peste noire à la Révolution*. Paris: PUF, 2002.

La Fresnaye, Vauquelin de. *L'art poétique de Vauquelin de La Fresnaye*. Ed. Georges Pellissier. Geneva: Slatkine Reprints, 1970. (Orig. pub. Paris: Garnier, 1885.)

– *Les Diverses poésies*. Ed. Julien Travers. 2 vols. Caen, 1869–70.

– *Les Foresteries*. Ed. Marc Bensimon. Geneva: Droz, 1956.

LaGuardia, Eric. *Nature Redeemed: The Imitation of Order in Three Renaissance Poems*. London: Mouton, 1966.

Lakoff, George, and Mark Johnson. *Metaphors We Live By*. Chicago: University of Chicago Press, 1980.

Langbein, John. *Prosecuting Crime in the Renaissance*. Clark, NJ: The Lawbook Exchange, 2005.

Langer, Ullrich. *Divine and Poetic Freedom in the Renaissance*. Princeton: Princeton University Press, 1990.

Larrère, Raphaël, and Olivier Nougarède, eds. *Des hommes et des forêts*. Découvertes Gallimard. Paris: Gallimard, 1993.

Larsen, Svend. '"To see things for the first time": Before and After Ecocriticism.' *Journal of Literary Studies* 23 (2007): 341–73.

Latour, Bruno. *Nous n'avons jamais été modernes*. Paris: La Découverte & Syros: 1997.

Lauxerois, Jean. 'Le jardin de la mélancolie.' In *Le jardin: Art et lieu de mémoire*, ed. Philippe Nys and Monique Mosser, 87–104. Besançon: Éditions de l'imprimeur, 1995.

Lavis-Trafford, M.-A. de. *L'évolution de la cartographie de la région du Mont-Cenis et de ses abords aux XVe et XVIe siècles: Étude critique des méthodes de travail des grands cartographes du XVIe siècle*. Chambéry: Lavis-Trafford, 1949.

Lebègue, Raymond. *La Pléiade et les beaux-arts*. Florence: Valmartina, 1955.

Lecercle, François. *La chimère de Zeuxis: Portrait poétique et portrait peint en France et en Italie à la Renaissance*. Tübingen: Narr, 1987.

Le Clech-Charton, S. 'Jacques Thiboust, notaire et secrétaire du roi et familier de Marguerite de Navarre: Amitiés littéraires dans le Berry du "beau seizième siècle."' *Cahiers d'archéologie et d'histoire du Berry* 96 (1989): 17–27.

Leclerc, M. *Cartes anciennes de l'Anjou: Essai de cartographie*. Angers: Sauvegarde de l'Anjou, 1974.

le Dantec, Jean-Pierre. 'Traités et non-traités.' In *Le jardin, art et lieu de mémoire*, ed. Philippe Nys and Monique Mosser. Besançon: Éditions de l'imprimeur, 1995.

Lee, Rensselaer. *Ut pictura poesis: The Humanistic Theory of Painting*. New York: Norton, 1967.

– *Names on Trees: Ariosto into Art*. Princeton: Princeton University Press, 1977.

Lefebvre, Henri. *La production de l'espace*. Paris: Anthropos, 1974.

Lefebvre, Raymond, and Louis Bougenot. *Les eaux et forêts du 12e au 20e siècle*. 2 vols. Histoire de l'administration française. Paris: CNRS, 1987.

Legrand, Marie-Dominique. 'La référence picturale dans l'œuvre de Joachim Du Bellay.' In *Du Bellay: Actes du colloque internationale d'Angers*, ed. Cesbron, 1:325–36. Angers: Presses de l'Université d'Angers, 1990.

Lekan, Thomas. *Imagining the Nation in Nature: Landscape Preservation and German Identity, 1885–1945*. Cambridge, MA: Harvard University Press, 2004.

Le Loyer, Pierre. *Œuvres et mélanges*. Paris: 1579.

le Mené, Michel. *Les campagnes angevines à la fin du Moyen Âge*. Nantes: Éditions Cid, 1982.

Lemercier, A.-P. *Étude littéraire et morale sur les poésies de Jean Vauquelin de la Fresnaye*. Geneva: Slatkine Reprints, 1970. (Orig. pub. Nancy: Paul Sordoillet, 1887.)

Lestocquoy, Jean. *Histoire du patriotisme français des origines à nos jours*. Paris: Albin Michel, 1968.

Lestringant, Frank. 'Les amours pastorales de Daphnis et Chloé: Fortunes d'une traduction de J. Amyot.' In *Fortunes de Jacques Amyot: Actes du colloque international*, ed. M. Balard, 237–57. Paris: Nizet, 1986.

– 'De *L'Olive* à la *Cosmographie*: Joachim Du Bellay et André Thevet.' In *Du Bellay: Actes du colloque internationale d'Angers*, ed. Cesbron, 1:102–18. Angers: Presses de l'Université d'Angers, 1990.

– *L'atelier du cosmographe: ou, L'image de monde à la Renaissance*. Paris: A. Michel, 1991.

– 'Chorographie et paysage à la Renaissance.' In *Écrire le monde à la Renaissance: Quinze études sur Rabelais, Postel, Bodin et la littérature géographique*, ed. Lestringant, 49–67. Caen: Paradigme, 1993.

– 'Le déclin d'un savoir: La crise de la cosmographie à la fin de la Renaissance.' In *Écrire le monde à la Renaissance*, ed. Lestringant, 319–30. Caen: Paradigme, 1993.

– *Le livre des îles: Atlas et récits insulaires de la Genèse à Jules Verne*. Geneva: Droz, 2002.

Lewis, M. *Green Delusions: A Environmentalist Critique of Radical Environmentalism*. Durham: Duke University Press, 1992.

Liaroutzos, Chantal. 'L'appréhension du paysage dans *La guide des chemins de France*.' In *Le paysage à la Renaissance*, ed. Yves Giraud, 27–33. Fribourg: Éditions Universitaires Fribourg Suisse, 1988.

– *Le pays et la mémoire: Pratiques et représentation de l'espace chez Gilles Corrozet et Charles Estienne*. Paris: Champion, 1998.

Lindheim, Nancy. *The Virgilian Pastoral Tradition from the Renaissance to the Modern Era*. Pittsburgh: Duquesne University Press, 2005.

Lippard, Lucy. *The Lure of the Local*. New York: New Press, 1997.

Lloyd-Jones, Kenneth. 'The Humanist *Apologia* for Hellenism in the French Renaissance.' *Romance Languages Annual* 3 (1992): 72–7.

Lodge, R. Anthony. *French: From Dialect to Standard*. London: Routledge, 1993.

Longus. *Pastorales*. Trans. Jean-René Vieillefond. Paris: Belles lettres, 1987.

Love, Glen. *Practical Ecocriticism: Literature, Biology, and the Environment*. Charlottesville: University of Virginia Press, 2003.

Lucretius. *De rerum natura*. Trans. W. Rouse. Cambridge, MA: Harvard University Press, 1959.

Lyons, John. *Exemplum: The Rhetoric of Example in Early Modern France and Italy*. Princeton: Princeton University Press, 1990.

Mackenzie, Louisa. '"Ce ne sont pas des bois": Poetry, Regionalism, and Loss in Ronsard's Gâtine Forest.' *Journal of Medieval and Early Modern Studies* 32 (2002): 343–74.

Maclean, Ian. 'Foucault's Renaissance Episteme Reassessed: An Aristotelean Counterblast.' *Journal of the History of Ideas* 59 (1988): 149–69.

– 'Natural and Preternatural in Renaissance Philosophy and Medicine.' *Studies in History and Philosophy of Science* 31 (2000): 331–42.

MacPhail, Eric. *The Voyage to Rome in French Renaissance Literature*. Saratoga, CA: ANMA Libri, 1990.

Magnien, Michel. 'La première *Olive*.' In *'L'Olive' de Joachim Du Bellay*, ed. Campagnoli et al., 7–45. Bologna: CLUEB, 2007.

Major, J. Russell. 'The Crown and the Aristocracy in Renaissance France.' *American Historical Review* 69 (1964): 631–45.

– *The Monarchy, The Estates, and the Aristocracy in Renaissance France*. London: Variorum, 1988.

Marcel, Gabriel. 'Le conte d'Alsinoys géographe.' *Revue de géographie* (1894): 193–9.

Marcou, Véronique. *L'ambivalence de l'or à la Renaissance*. Paris: L'Harmattan, 1998.

Marek, Heidi. *Le mythe antique dans l'œuvre de Pontus de Tyard*. Paris: Champion, 2006.

Margolin, Jean-Claude. '"L'Hymne de l'Or" et son ambiguïté.' *Bibliothèque d'humanisme et Renaissance* 28 (1966): 271–93.

– 'L'enseignement des mathématiques en France (1540–1570): Charles de Bovelles, Finé, Peletier, Ramus.' In *French Renaissance Studies (1540–1570): Humanism and the Encyclopedia*, ed. Peter Sharratt, 110–55. Edinburgh: Edinburgh University Press, 1976.

– 'À propos de l' "imposition" des noms propres chez Pontus de Tyard, extraits de l'histoire ou de la géographie: Cratylisme ou non-cratylizsme?' In *Pontus de Tyard: Poète, philosophe, théologien. Colloque international de l'Université Créteil-Val-de-Marne, 19–20 novembre 1998*, ed. Sylviane Bokdam and Jean Céard, 357–69. Paris: Champion, 2003.

Marin, Louis. *Utopiques: Jeux d'espaces*. Paris: Minuit, 1973.

Mariotte, Jean-Yves, and André Perret. *Atlas historique français: Le territoire de la France et de quelques pays voisins: Savoie*. Paris: CNRS, 1979.

Marsengill, Katherine. 'Identity Politics in Renaissance France: Cellini's *Nymph of Fontainebleau.' Athanor* 19 (2001): 35–41.

Martignon, L. 'Les différentes éditions de la carte du Limousin de Jean Fayan 1594.' *Bulletin de la Société archéologique et historique du Limousin* 84 (1952): 128–30.

Martin, Marie-Madeleine. *Histoire de l'unité française.* Paris: PUF, 1949.

Marx, Leo. *The Machine in the Garden: Technology and the Pastoral Ideal in America.* New York: Oxford University Press, 1964.

Mathieu-Castellani, Giselle. '"Simplement" ou "naïvement écrire": La question du style au XVIe siècle en France.' *Rivista di letterature moderne e comparate* 52 (1999): 213–27.

Maurand, Georges, ed. (1993). *Le paysage: Actes du 13e colloque d'Albi: Langages et signification.* L'Union: CALS, 1993.

McEachern, Claire. *The Poetics of English Nationhood, 1590–1612.* Cambridge: Cambridge University Press, 1996.

McFarlane, Ian. 'Neo-Latin Verse, Some New Discoveries: A Possible Source of Ronsard's *Elegie XXIV.' Modern Language Review* 54 (1959): 24–8.

McGowan, Margaret. *Ideal Forms in the Age of Ronsard.* Berkeley: University of California Press, 1985.

McIntosh, Robert. *The Background of Ecology: Concept and Theory.* Cambridge: Cambridge University Press, 1985.

Meerhoff, Kees. *Rhétorique et poétique au XVIe siècle en France: Du Bellay, Ramus et les autres.* Leiden: Brill, 1986.

Melehy, Hassan. 'Du Bellay and the Space of Early Modern Culture.' *Neophilologus* 84 (2000): 501–15.

Ménager, Daniel. *Ronsard: Le roi, le poète et les hommes.* Geneva: Droz, 1971.

Merchant, Carolyn. *The Death of Nature: Women, Ecology, and the Scientific Revolution.* San Francisco: Harper and Row, 1980.

Mettrier, Henri. 'Les cartes de Savoie au XVIe siècle: La carte de B. de Bouillon, 1556.' *Bulletin de la Section de géographie* 32 (1917): 16–129.

Michaud-Fréjaville, Françoise. 'Tradition et innovation horticole en Berry: Jean Rogier et Jacques Thiboust dans leur jardin de Quantilly (1503–1526).' In *Flore et jardins: Usages, saviors et représentations du monde végétal au Moyen Âge,* ed. Pierre-Gilles Girault, 51–70. Paris: Léopard d'or, 1997.

Miernowski, Jan. 'La Poésie et la peinture: Les *Douze fables de fleuves ou fontaines* de Pontus de Tyard.' *Réforme, Humanisme, Renaissance* 18 (1984): 12–22.

– 'La poésie scientifique française à la Renaissance: Littérature, savoir, altérité.' In *What is Literature? France, 1100–1600,* ed. François Cornilliat,

Ullrich Langer, and Douglas Kelly, 85–99. Lexington, KY: French Forum, 1993.

Miller, Naomi. *Mapping the City: The Language and Culture of Cartography in the Renaissance.* London and New York: Continuum, 2003.

Millet, Olivier. 'Du Bellay et Pétrarche autour de *L'Olive*.' In *Les poètes français de la Renaissance et Pétrarche*, ed. Jean Balsamo, 253–66. Geneva: Droz, 2004.

Mirollo, James. *Mannerism and Renaissance Poetry: Concept, Mode, Inner Design.* New Haven: Yale University Press, 1984.

Mitchell, W.J., ed. *Landscape and Power.* Chicago and London: University of Chicago Press, 1994.

Monferran, Jean-Charles. 'La poésie sonore de Jacques Peletier du Mans.' In *À haute voix: Diction et prononciation au XVIe et XVIIe s.: Actes du colloque de Rennes, 17–18 juin 1996*, ed. Olivia Rosenthal, 35–54. Paris: Klincksieck, 1998.

– 'Le *Dialogue de l'ortografe et prononciation françoese* de Peletier.' *Bibliothèque d'humanisme et Renaissance* 60 (1998): 405–12.

Monga, Luigi. *Le genre pastoral au XVIe siècle: Sannazar et Belleau.* Paris: Éditions Universitaires, 1974.

Monmonier, Mark. *How to Lie with Maps.* Chicago: University of Chicago Press, 1991.

Montrose, Louis. 'The Work of Gender in the Discourse of Discovery.' *Representations* 33 (1991): 1–41.

Moore, Charles, William J. Mitchell, and William Turnbull, eds. *The Poetics of Gardens.* Cambridge, MA: MIT Press, 1988.

Moretti, Franco. *Atlas of the European Novel.* London and New York: Verso, 1998.

Moss, Ann. *Ovid in Renaissance France.* London: The Warburg Institute, 1982.

Mosser, Monique, and Philippe Nys, eds. *Le jardin, art et lieu de mémoire.* Besançon: Éditions de l'imprimeur, 1995.

Mukerji, Chandra. *Territorial Ambitions and the Gardens of Versailles.* Cambridge: Cambridge University Press, 1997.

– 'Material Practices of Domination: Christian Humanism, the Built Environment, and Techniques of Western Power.' *Theory and Society* 31 (2002): 1–34.

– 'Printing, Cartography, and Conceptions of Place in Renaissance Europe.' *Media, Culture, & Society* 28 (2006): 651–69.

Murphy, Patrick D. *Farther Afield in the Study of Nature-Oriented Literature.* Charlottesville, VA: University of Virginia Press, 2000.

Naïs, Hélène. *Les animaux dans la poésie française de la Renaissance: Science, symbolique, poésie.* Paris: Didier, 1961.

Nash, Jerry. '"Mont côtoyant le Fleuve et la Cité": Scève, Lyons, and Love.' *French Review* 69 (1996): 943–54.

– 'Le voyage comme motif poétique à la Renaissance.' *Romanic Review* 94 (2003): 207–25.

Navarrete, Ignacio. 'Strategies of Appropriation in Speroni and Du Bellay.' *Comparative Literature* 41 (1989): 141–54.

Nell, Sharon. 'A Bee in Pindar's Bonnet: Humanistic Imitation in Ronsard, La Fontaine and Rococo Style.' In *Recapturing the Renaissance: New Perspectives on Humanism, Dialogue, and Texts*, ed. D. Wood and P. Miller, 181–220. Knoxville, TN: New Paradigm, 1996.

Newmann, Alba R. *'Language is not a vague province': Mapping and Twentieth-Century American Poetry.* PhD diss., University of Texas, Austin, 2006.

Nice, Jason A. '"The Peculiar Place of God": Early Modern Representations of England and France.' *English Historical Review* 493 (2006): 1002–18.

Nicolay, Nicolas de. *Les navigations, pérégrinations et voyages faicts en la Turquie par Nicolas Nicolay.* Antwerp: Silvius, 1576.

– *Generale description du Bourbonnais.* Ed. A. Vayssière. Moulins: E. Durond, 1889.

– *Description générale du pais et duché de Berry et Diocèse de Bourges.* Ed. Victor Advielle. Paris, 1865.

– *Description générale de la ville de Lyon et des anciennes provinces du Lyonnais et du Beaujolais, 1573.* Ed. Victor Advielle. Lyon: Imprimerie Mougin-Rusand, 1881.

– *Dans l'empire de Soliman le magnifique.* Ed. Marie-Christine Gomez-Géraud and Stéphane Yérasimos. Paris: Presses du CNRS, 1989

Nora, Pierre. *Les lieux de mémoire.* 3 vols. Paris: Gallimard, 1997.

Nordman, Daniel. *Frontières de France: De l'espace au territoire, XVIe–XIXe siècle.* Paris: Gallimard, 1998.

Nuti, Lucia. (1999). 'Mapping Places: Chorography and Vision in the Renaissance.' In *Mappings*, ed. Denis Cosgrove, 90–108. London: Reaktion Books, 1999.

Oelschlaeger, Max. *The Idea of Wilderness from Prehistory to the Age of Ecology.* New Haven: Yale University Press, 1991.

Olwig, Kenneth. *Nature and the Body Politic.* Madison: University of Wisconsin Press, 2002.

Ovid. *Metamorphoses.* Ed. Frank Miller. Cambridge, MA: Harvard University Press, 1996.

– *La Métamorphose d'Ovide figurée.* Lyon: Jean de Tournes, 1557.

Padrón, Ricardo. *The Spacious Word: Cartography, Literature, and Empire in Early Modern Spain.* Chicago: University of Chicago Press, 2004.

Palissy, Bernard. *Recepte véritable.* Ed. Keith Cameron. Geneva: Droz, 1988.

Pantin, Isabelle. *La poésie du ciel en France dans la seconde moitié du seizième siècle.* Geneva: Droz, 1995.

Parker, Patricia. *Literary Fat Ladies: Rhetoric, Property, Gender*. London and New York: Methuen, 1987.

Parker, Patricia, and David Quint, eds. *Literary Theory / Renaissance Texts*. Baltimore and London: Johns Hopkins University Press, 1986.

Pasquier, Étienne. *Les œuvres d'Étienne Pasquier*. 2 vols. Amsterdam, 1723.

Pastoureau, Mireille. 'Les atlas imprimés en France avant 1700.' *Imago Mundi* 32 (1980): 45–72.

– 'Entre la Gaule et France, la "Gallia."' In *Gerard Mercator cosmographe: Le temps et l'espace*, ed. M. Watelet, 317–33. Anvers: Fonds Mercator Paribas, 1994.

Patterson, Annabel. *Pastoral and Ideology: Virgil to Valéry*. Berkeley: University of California Press, 1987.

Paul, Carole Deering. 'Images of Retreat: Geography in the Pastoral Novel.' *Cincinnati Romance Review* 1 (1982): 65–71.

Peletier du Mans, Jacques. *La Savoye*. Ed. C. Pagès and F. Ducloz. Annecy: Moutiers-Tarentaise, 1897.

– *L'Amour des amours*. Ed. Jean-Charles Monferran. Paris: Société des textes français modernes, 1996.

– *Œuvres complètes*. Vol. 10. Ed. Sophie Arnaud, Stephen Bamforth, and Jan Miernowski, dir. Isabelle Pantin. Paris: Champion, 2005.

Pelletier, Monique. 'Des cartes pour partager: Divisions administratives, frontières, plans terriers.' In Pelletier, Philippe Prost, and Gilles Palsky, *La cartografia francesa*, 17–32. Barcelona: Institut Cartogràfic de Catalunya, 1996.

Pelletier, Monique, ed. *Géographie du monde au Moyen Âge et à la Renaissance*. Paris: Éditions du CTHS, 1989.

Pelletier, Monique, and Henriette Ozanne. *Portraits de la France: Les cartes, témoins de l'histoire*. Paris: Hachette, 1995.

Peters, Jeffrey. *Mapping Discord: Allegorical Cartography in Early Modern French Writing*. Newark: University of Delaware Press, 2004.

Petrarch, Francesco. *Petrarch's Lyric Poems: The 'Rime sparse' and Other Lyrics*. Ed. and trans. Robert Durling. Cambridge, MA: Harvard University Press, 1976.

Peyre, Robert. *Une princesse de la Renaissance: Marguerite de France, duchesse de Berry, duchesse de Savoie*. Paris: E. Paul, 1902.

Phillips, Dana. *The Truth of Ecology: Nature, Culture, and Literature in America*. Oxford: Oxford University Press, 2003.

Pindar. *Odes*. Trans. J.E. Sandys. Cambridge, MA: Harvard University Press, 1915.

Pintarič, Miha. *Le sentiment du temps dans la littérature française: XIIe s.–fin du XVIe s.* Paris: Champion, 2002.

Plattard, Henri. 'Les arts et les artistes de la Renaissance française jugés par les écrivains du temps.' *Revue d'histoire littéraire de la France* 21 (1914): 481–502.

Posner, David. *The Performance of Nobility in Early Modern European Literature.* Cambridge: Cambridge University Press, 1999.

Pot, Olivier. *Inspiration et mélancolie: L'épistémologie poétique dans les 'Amours' de Ronsard.* Geneva: Droz, 1990.

Poupard, Paul. 'A Liré: Message du Cardinal Paul Poupard, Président du Conseil Pontifical de la Culture, originaire de Bouzillé, près de Liré.' In *Du Bellay: Actes du colloque internationale d'Angers*, ed. Cesbron, 2:637–9. Angers: Presses de l'Université d'Angers, 1990.

Ptolemy, Claudius, and Francesco Berlinghieri. *Geographia di Francesco Berlinghieri Fiorentino in terza rima.* Florence: Laurentii, 1482.

Pugh, Simon. *Reading Landscape: Country–City–Capital.* Manchester: Manchester University Press, 1990.

Pumfrey, Stephen, ed. *Science, Culture, and Popular Belief in Renaissance Europe.* Manchester: Manchester University Press, 1991.

Py, Albert. *Imitation et Renaissance dans la poésie de Ronsard.* Geneva: Droz, 1984.

Quint, David. *Origin and Originality in Renaissance Literature: Versions of the Source.* New Haven: Yale University Press, 1983.

– *Epic and Empire: Politics and Generic Form from Virgil to Milton.* Princeton: Princeton University Press, 1993.

Quint, David, Margaret W. Ferguson, Wayne A. Rebhorn, G.W. Pigman, eds. *Creative Imitation: New Essays on Renaissance Literature in Honor of Thomas M. Greene.* Binghamton, N.Y.: Medieval and Renaissance Texts and Studies, 1992.

Randles, W.G.L. *Geography, Cartography, and Nautical Science in the Renaissance: The Impact of the Great Discoveries.* Aldershot and Burlington, VT: Ashgate, 2000.

Rasmussen, Mark, ed. *Renaissance Literature and Its Formal Engagements.* New York: Palgrave, 2002.

Raymond, Marcel. 'Deux pamphlets inconnus contre Ronsard et la Pléiade.' *Revue du seizième siècle* 13 (1926): 234–64.

Raymond, Marcel, ed. *La poésie française et le maniérisme, 1546–1610 (?) [sic].* Geneva: Droz, 1971.

Rebhorn, Wayne. *The Emperor of Men's Minds: Literature and the Renaissance Discourse of Rhetoric.* Ithaca and London: Cornell University Press, 1995.

Renan, Ernst. 'Qu'est-ce qu'une nation?' In *Discours et conférences*, 277–310. Paris: Calman-Levy, 1887.

Revel, Jacques. 'Knowledge of the territory.' *Science in Context* 4 (1991): 133–61.

Revel, Jacques, and L. Bergeron, eds. *L'histoire de la France.* Vol. 1, *L'espace français.* Paris: Seuil, 1989.

Reverdy, Georges. *Atlas historique des routes de France*. Paris: Presses de l'École nationale des ponts et chaussées, 1986.

Reynolds, L.D. *Texts and Transmission: A Survey of the Latin Classics*. Oxford: Clarendon, 1983.

Reynolds, L.D., and Nigel Wilson, eds. *Scribes and Scholars: A Guide to the Transmission of Greek and Latin Literature*. Oxford: Clarendon, 1974.

Richmond, H. M. *Renaissance Landscapes: English Lyrics in a European Tradition*. The Hague: Mouton, 1973.

Rieu, Josiane. 'La temporalisation de l'espace dans la peinture française du XVIe siècle.' In *Le paysage à la Renaissance*, ed. Yves Giraud, 297–310. Fribourg: Éditions Universitaires Fribourg Suisse, 1988.

– 'La *Bergerie* de Remy Belleau: Une "fête" poétique à la gloire des Guises.' In *Le mécénat et l'influence des Guises*, ed. Bellenger, 251–77. Paris: Champion, 1997.

Rigolot, François. 'Du Bellay et la poésie du refus.' *Bibliothèque d'humanisme et de Renaissance* 36 (1974): 489–502.

– *Poétique et onomastique: L'exemple de la Renaissance*. Geneva: Droz, 1977.

– *Le texte à la Renaissance: Des Rhétoriqueurs à Montaigne*. Geneva: Droz, 1982.

– 'Qu'est-ce qu'un sonnet? Perspectives sur les origines d'une forme poétique.' *Revue d'histoire littéraire de la France* 84 (1984): 3–18.

– 'Interpréter Rabelais aujourd'hui: Anachronies et catachronies.' *Poétique* 103 (1995): 269–83.

– 'The Renaissance Crisis of Exemplarity.' *Journal of the History of Ideas* 59 (1998): 557–63.

– *Poésie et Renaissance*. Paris: Seuil, 2002.

Roberts, Yvonne. *Jean-Antoine de Baïf and the Valois Court*. Oxford: Lang, 2000.

Rocher, Edmond. *Pierre de Ronsard, prince des poètes, 1524–1585: Étude suivie d'une bibliographie du poète et de ses œuvres*. Paris: PUF, 1924.

Roger, Alain. 'Un paysage peut-il être érotique?' In *Le paysage et ses Grilles: Colloque de Cerisy-la-Salle*, ed. Françoise Chenet et Jean-Claude Wieber, 193–206. Paris: Harmattan, 1996.

– *Court traité de paysage*. Paris: Gallimard, 1997.

Rogers, Raymond. *Nature and the Crisis of Modernity: A Critique of Contemporary Discourse on Managing the Earth*. New York and Montreal: Black Rose Books, 1994.

Ronsard, Pierre de. *Œuvres complètes*. Ed. Paul Laumonier, Isidore Silver, and Raymond Lebègue. 18 vols. Paris: Droz, 1931–.

– *Œuvres complètes*. Ed. Jean Céard, Daniel Ménager, and Michel Simonin. 2 vols. Paris: Gallimard, 1994.

Rothenberg, David. *Hand's End: Technology and the Limits of Nature*. Berkeley: University of California Press, 1993.

Rouget, François. 'Ronsard palimpseste.' *Romance Notes* 39 (1998): 25–33.

– '"Sans plus partir de France": Ronsard et l'écriture du voyage.' *Romanic Review* 94 (2003): 185–205.

– 'La langue française: Obstacle ou atout de l' "État-nation"?' *Renaissance and Reformation / Renaissance et Réforme* 29 (2005): 7–23.

Roupnel, Gaston. *Histoire de la campagne française*. Paris: Plon, 1932.

Roussel, Pierre. *Histoire et description du château d'Anet*. Paris: Jouaust, 1875.

Russell, Nicolas, and Hélène Visentin, eds. *French Ceremonial Entries in the Sixteenth Century: Event, Image, Text*. Toronto: Centre for Reformation and Renaissance Studies, 2007.

Sacré, James. *Pour une définition sémiotique du maniérisme et du baroque: Des 'Sonnets pour Hélène' de Ronsard à 'La Maison d'Astrée' de Tristan l'Hermite*. Besançon: Groupe de recherches sémio-linguistiques, École des hautes études en sciences sociales, Centre national de la recherche scientifique, 1979.

Sahlins, Peter. *Boundaries: The Making of France and Spain in the Pyrenees*. Berkeley: University of California Press, 1989.

Said, Edward. *Orientalism*. New York: Vintage, 1978.

Saine, Ute Margarete. 'Dreaming the Forest of Gâtine: Ecology and Antiquity in Ronsard.' *Cincinnati Romance Review* 9 (1990): 1–12.

Salmon, J.H.M. *Society in Crisis: France in the Sixteenth Century*. London: Methuen, 1975.

– 'French Satire in the Late Sixteenth Century.' *Sixteenth-Century Journal* 6 (1975): 57–88.

Sanford, Rhonda. *Maps and Memory in Early Modern England: A Sense of Place*. New York: Palgrave, 2002.

Sannazaro, Jacopo. *Arcadia and Piscatorial Eclogues*. Trans. R. Nash. Detroit: Wayne State University Press, 1966.

Sansot, Pierre. *Poétique de la ville*. Paris: Klincksieck, 1971.

– *Variations paysagères: Invitation au paysage*. Paris: Klincksieck, 1983.

Saulnier, V.-L. 'Des vers inconnus de Bertrand Berger et les relations du poète avec Dorat et Du Bellay.' *Bibliothèque d'humanisme et Renaissance* 19 (1957): 245–51.

Saunders, Alison. *The Sixteenth-Century Blason Poétique*. Bern: Peter Lang, 1981.

Sauret, Martine. *Les voies cartographiques: À propos des influences des cartographes sur les écrivains français des XVe et XVIe siècles*. Lewiston, NY: Mellen, 2004.

Savigny, Christophe de. *Tableaux accomplis de tous les arts*. Paris, 1619.

Sayce, Richard. 'Ronsard and Mannerism: The *Elégie à Janet*.' *L'esprit créateur* 6 (1966): 234–47.

Schama, Simon. *Landscape and Memory*. New York: Knopf, 1995.

Schiesari, Juliana. 'The Gendering of Melancholia: Torquato Tasso and Isabella di Morra.' In *Refiguring Women: Perspectives on Gender and the Italian Renaissance*, ed. Marilyn Migiel and Juliana Schiesari, 233–62. Cornell: Cornell University Press, 1991.

Schmidt, Albert-Marie. *La poésie scientifique en France au seizième siècle.* Paris: Albin Michel, 1938.

Schmidt, C.B., Quentin Skinner, Ekhard Kessler, and Jill Kraye, eds. *The Cambridge History of Renaissance Philosophy*. Cambridge: Cambridge University Press, 1988.

Schoenfeldt, Michael. 'Recent Studies in the English Renaissance.' *Studies in English Literature, 1500–1900*, 44 (2004): 189–228.

Schulze, Hagen. *States, Nations, and Nationalism: From the Middle Ages to the Present.* Oxford: Blackwell, 1994.

Schwyzer, Philip. 'The Beauties of the Land: Bale's Books, Aske's Abbeys, and the Aesthetics of Nationhood.' *Renaissance Quarterly* 57 (2004): 99–125.

Seaford, Richard. *Money and the Early Greek Mind: Homer, Philosophy, Tragedy.* Cambridge: Cambridge University Press, 2004.

– 'Money Makes the (Greek) World Go Round: What the Ancient Greek Anxiety about Money Has To Tell Us about Our Own Economic Predicaments.' *Times Literary Supplement*, 19 June 2009.

Sébillet, Thomas. *L'art poétique françoys.* Ed. Félix Gaiffe. Geneva: Droz, 1999.

Semler, L.E. *The English Mannerist Poets and the Visual Arts.* Madison, NJ: Fairleigh Dickinson University Press, 1998.

Seton-Watson, Hugh. *Nations and States: An Enquiry into the Origins of Nations and the Politics of Nationalism.* Boulder, CO: Westview, 1977.

Seyssel, Claude de. *La Monarchie de France.* Ed. Jacques Poujol. Paris: Argences, 1961.

Sgard, Anne. 'Qu'est-ce qu'un paysage identitaire?' In *Paysage et identité régionale*, ed. Burgard and Chenet, 23–34. Valence: La passe du vent, 1999.

Sharp, Joanna. 'Feminisms.' In *A Companion to Cultural Geography*, ed. James Duncan, Nuala Johnson, and Richard Schein, 66–78. Oxford: Blackwell, 2004.

Sharratt, Peter. 'Du Bellay and the Icarus Complex.' In *Myth and Legend in French Literature*, ed. K. Aspley, D. Bellos, and P. Sharratt, 73–92. London: MHRA, 1982.

– *Bernard Salomon: Illustrateur lyonnais.* Geneva: Droz, 2005.

Shearman, John. *Mannerism.* Baltimore: Penguin, 1967.

Shirley, Rodney. *The Mapping of the World: Early Printed World Maps, 1472–1700.* London: Holland Press, 1983.

Shrank, Cathy. *Writing the Nation in Reformation England, 1530–1580.* Oxford: Oxford University Press, 2004.

Siganos, André. 'Paysages et archétypes: Pour une lecture interdisciplinaire du paysage.' In *Paysage et identité régionale*, ed. Burgard and Chenet, 17–22. Valence: La passe du vent, 1999.

Silver, Isidore. *Ronsard and the Hellenic Renaissance in France*. St Louis: Washington University, 1961.

– 'Ronsard's Reflections on Cosmogony and Nature.' *PMLA* 79 (1964): 219–33.

– *Ronsard and the Grecian Lyre*. Geneva: Droz, 1981.

Silver, Susan. '"Adieu vieille forest ...": Myth, Melancholia, and Ronsard's Family Trees.' *Neophilologus* 86 (2002): 33–43.

Simonin, Michel. 'La disgrâce d'Amadis.' *Studi Francesi* 28 (1984): 1–35.

– '"Poésie est un pré" "Poème est une fleur": Métaphore horticole et imaginaire du texte à la Renaissance.' In *La letteratura e i giardini: Atti del Convegno internazionale di studi di Verona – Garda, 2–5 Ottobre 1985*, 45–56. Florence: Olschki, 1985.

Skenazi, Cynthia. 'Une pratique de la circulation: *La guide des chemins de France* de Charles Estienne.' *Romanic Review* 94 (2003): 153–66.

Smith, Neil, and Cindi Katz. 'Grounding Metaphor: Towards a Spatialized Politics.' In *Place and the Politics of Identity*, ed. Michael Keith and Steve Pile, 67–83. London: Routledge, 1993.

Smith, Paul J. 'Remy Belleau et la peinture: Aspects du métadiscours poétique de la Pléiade.' *Word and Image* 4 (1988): 331–7.

Sozzi, Lionello. *Rome n'est plus Rome: La polémique anti-italienne et autres essais sur la Renaissance suivis de 'La dignité de l'homme.'* Paris: Champion, 2002.

Spiller, Elizabeth. *Science, Reading, and Renaissance Literature*. Cambridge: Cambridge University Press, 2004.

Starobinski, Jean. 'Poetic Language and Scientific Language.' *Diogenes* (1977): 128–45.

Steadman, John. *The Lamb and the Elephant: Ideal Imitation and the Content of Renaissance Allegory*. San Marino: The Huntington Library, 1974.

– *Nature into Myth*. Pittsburgh: Duquesne University Press, 1979.

Sterling, Charles. *Le triomphe du maniérisme européen: De Michel-Ange au Greco*. Catalogue of exhibition 1 July–16 October 1955. Amsterdam: Rijksmuseum, 1955.

Sturm-Maddox, Sara. *Petrarch's Metamorphoses: Text and Subtext in the 'Rime sparse.'* Columbia: University of Missouri Press, 1985.

– *Petrarch's Laurels*. Philadelphia: Pennsylvania State University Press, 1992.

– 'The French Petrarch.' *Annali d'Italianistica* 22 (2004): 171–88.

Sullivan, Garrett. *The Drama of Landscape: Land, Property, and Social Relations on the Early Modern Stage*. Palo Alto, CA: Stanford University Press, 1998.

Sutherland, Nicola. *The French Secretaries of State in the Age of Catherine de Medici*. Chicago: University of Chicago Press, 1962.

Sypher, Wylie. *Four Stages of Renaissance Style*. New York: Doubleday, 1955.

Takata, Isamu. 'Poétique de l'*Olive* et des *Amours*: L'ombre de Du Bellay chez Ronsard.' In *Du Bellay: Actes du colloque international d'Angers*, ed. Cesbron, 2:509–21. Angers: Presses de l'Université d'Angers, 1990.

Tallon, Alain. *Conscience nationale et sentiment religieux en France au XVIe siècle*. Paris: PUF, 2002.

Tarte, Kendall. 'Seductive Topographies: The Languages of Landscape in *La Puce de Madame des Roches*.' *Romanic Review* 95 (2004): 249–69.

Taylor, Edward. *Nature and Art in Renaissance Literature*. New York: Columbia University Press, 1964.

Terreaux, Louis. 'Jacques Peletier et *La Savoie*.' In *Le paysage à la Renaissance*, ed. Yves Giraud, 215–27. Fribourg: Éditions Universitaires Fribourg Suisse, 1988.

– '*Du Bellay et la douceur ...*' In *Du Bellay: Actes du colloque internationale d'Angers*, ed. Cesbron, 2:641–51. Angers: Presses de l'Université d'Angers, 1990.

Theocritus. *Theocritus Translated into English Verse*. Trans. Charles Stuart Calverley. London: Bell and Daldry, 1869.

– *Idylls*. Trans. Robert Wells. London: Penguin, 1988.

Thomas, Keith. *Man and the Natural World*. New York: Pantheon, 1983.

Tichi, Cecelia. *Embodiment of a Nation: Human Form in American Places*. Cambridge, MA: Harvard University Press, 2001.

Trimpi, Wesley. 'The Meaning of Horace's *ut pictura poesis*.' *Journal of the Warburg and Courtauld Institutes* 36 (1973): 1–34.

Tuan, Yi-Fu. *Topophilia: A Study of Environmental Perception, Attitudes, and Values*. Englewood Cliffs, NJ: Prentice Hall, 1974.

Tucker, G.H. 'Ulysses and Jason: A Problem of Allusion in Sonnet XXXI of *Les Regrets*.' *French Studies* 36 (1982): 385–96.

– 'Joachim Du Bellay, poète français et néo-latin, entre l'exil et la patrie.' *Revue de littérature française et comparée* 3 (1994): 57–63.

– '*Homo Viator*': Itineraries of Exile, Displacement, and Writing in Renaissance Europe. Geneva: Droz, 2003.

– '"Ce tenebreux voyle" de *L'Olive* (1549; 1550): Formes et significations du recueil augmenté de 1550 (par rapport au recueil de 1549) vers une lecture textuelle, métatextuelle et intertextuelle.' In '*L'Olive*' de Joachim Du Bellay, ed. Campagnoli et al., 47–102. Bologna: CLUEB, 2007.

Turnbull, David. 'Cartography and Science in Early Modern Europe: Mapping the Construction of Knowledge Spaces.' *Imago Mundi* 48 (1996): 5–24.

Turner, A. Richard. *The Vision of Landscape in Renaissance Italy.* Princeton: Princeton University Press, 1966.

Turner, James. *The Politics of Landscape: Rural Scenery and Society in English Poetry, 1630–1660.* Oxford: Blackwell, 1979.

Tyard, Pontus de. *Œuvres poétiques complètes.* Ed. John C. Lapp. Paris: Dider, 1966.

– *Œuvres complètes.* Vol. 1, *Œuvres poétiques.* Ed. Eva Kushner, Sylviane Bokdam, Gisèle Mathieu-Castellani et al. Paris: Champion, 2004.

– *Œuvres complètes.* Vol. 7, *La droite imposition des noms (De recta nominem impositione).* Ed. Jean Céard and Jean-Claude Margolin. Paris: Champion, 2007.

Vacher, Antoine. 'La carte du Berry par Jean Jolivet (1545).' *Bulletin de géographie historique et déscriptive* 22 (1907): 258–67.

Vasselin, M. 'L'antique et l'école de Fontainebleau.' In *Le paysage à la Renaissance*, ed. Yves Giraud, 281–96. Fribourg: Éditions Universitaires Fribourg Suisse, 1988.

Vauquelin. *See* La Fresnaye, Vauquelin de.

Vecce, Carlo. *Iacopo Sannazaro in Francia: Scoperte di codici all'inizio del XVI secolo.* Padua: Antenore, 1988.

Vene, Magali. 'Les *Anticques erections des Gaules* de Corrozet.' *Journal de la Renaissance* 2 (2004): 101–6.

Vickers, Brian, ed. *Occult and Scientific Mentalities in the Renaissance.* Cambridge: Cambridge University Press, 1984.

Vickers, Nancy. 'Diana Described: Scattered Woman and Scattered Rhyme.' *Critical Inquiry* 8 (1981): 265–79.

Vidal de la Blache, Paul. *Tableau de la géographie de la France.* Paris: Tallandier, 1979; repr. from 1903.

Villey, Pierre. *Les sources italiennes de la 'Deffense et illustration de la langue francoise.'* Paris: Champion, 1908.

Vinestock, Elizabeth. 'Myth and Environmentalism in a Renaissance Poem: Jean-Antoine de Baïf's *La Ninfe Bievre.'* *New Comparison* 27–8 (1999): 22–33.

– *Poétique et pratique dans les 'Poemes' de Jean-Antoine de Baïf.* Paris: Champion, 2006.

– '"J'ose attaquer les plus mutins": Baïf's Poetical and Rhetorical Means of Engaging in Conflict.' In *Writers in Conflict in Sixteenth-Century France: Essays in Honour of Malcolm Quainton*, ed. Elizabeth Vinestock and David Foster, 103–25. Durham: Durham Modern Language Series, 2006.

Virgil. *Eclogues, Georgics, Aeneid 1–6.* Trans. H. Rushton Fairclough. Cambridge, MA: Harvard University Press, 1996.

Watson, Robert. *Back to Nature: The Green and the Real in the Late Renaissance.* Philadelphia: University of Pennsylvania Press, 2006.

Watts, Richard. 'Towards an Ecocritical Postcolonialism: Val Plumwood's *Environmental Culture* in Dialogue with Patrick Chamoiseau.' *Journal of Postcolonial Writing* 44 (2008): 251–61.

Wayne, Don. *Penshurst: The Semiotics of Place and the Poetics of History.* Madison: University of Wisconsin Press, 1984.

Weber, Eugen. *Peasants into Frenchmen: The Modernization of Rural France, 1870–1914.* Palo Alto, CA: Stanford University Press, 1976.

Weber, Henri. *La création poétique au XVIe siècle en France.* Paris: Nizet, 1955.

Weinberg, Bernard, ed. *Critical Prefaces of the French Renaissance.* Evanston, IL: Northwestern University Press, 1950.

Williams, Raymond. *The Country and the City.* New York: Oxford University Press, 1973.

Wilson, Dudley B. *Ronsard: Poet of Nature.* Manchester: Manchester University Press, 1961.

– *French Renaissance Scientific Poetry.* London: Athlone, 1974.

Wintroub, Michael. *A Savage Mirror: Power, Identity, and Knowledge in Early Modern France.* Stanford: Stanford University Press, 2006.

Wölfflin, Heinrich. *Renaissance and Baroque.* Trans. Kathrin Simon. Ithaca: Cornell University Press, 1964.

Wood, J.B. 'The Decline of the Nobility in Sixteenth- and Early Seventeenth-Century France: Myth or Reality?' *The Journal of Modern History* 48 (1976): 1–29.

Woods, Dennis, and John Fels. *The Power of Maps.* New York: Guilford Press, 1992.

Woodward, David. 'Introduction.' In *Art and Cartography: Six Historical Essays*, ed. Woodward, 1–9. Chicago: University of Chicago Press, 1987.

Woodward, David, ed. *The History of Cartography.* Vol. 3, *Cartography in the European Renaissance.* Chicago: University of Chicago Press, 2007.

Worster, Donald. 'Seeing Beyond Culture.' *Journal of American History* 76 (1990): 1142–7.

Yandell, Cathy. 'La poétique du lieu: Espace et pédagogie dans les *Solitaires* de Tyard.' In *Pontus de Tyard: Errances et enracinement*, ed. François Rouget, 97–106. Paris: Champion, 2008.

Yardeni, Myriam. *Enquêtes sur l'identité de la 'Nation France': De la Renaissance aux Lumières.* Seyssel: Champ Vallon, 2005.

Yates, Francis. *The French Academies of the Sixteenth Century.* London: Warburg Institute, University of London, 1947.

– *The Art of Memory.* Chicago: University of Chicago Press, 1966.

Zegna Rata, Olivier. *René de Lucinge: Entre l'écriture et l'histoire.* Geneva: Droz, 1993.

Zerner, Henri. *L'art de la Renaissance en France: L'invention du classicisme*. Paris: Flammarion, 1996.

Zink, Michel. *Nature et poésie au Moyen Âge*. Paris: Fayard, 2006.

Zorach, Rebecca. *Blood, Milk, Ink, Gold: Abundance and Excess in the French Renaissance*. Chicago: University of Chicago Press, 2005.

Index